The Making of Glo

This book presents a challenge to the discipline of International Relations (IR) to rethink itself, in the light of both its own modern origins and the two centuries of world history that have shaped it. By tracking the development of thinking about IR and the practice of world politics, this book shows how they relate to each other across five time periods from nineteenth-century colonialism, through two world wars, the Cold War and decolonisation, to twenty-first century globalisation. It gives equal weight to the neglected voices and histories of the Global South and the traditionally dominant perspectives of the West, showing how they have moved from nearly complete separation to the beginnings of significant integration. The authors argue that IR needs to continue this globalising movement if it is to cope with the rapidly emerging post-Western world order, with its more diffuse distribution of wealth, power and cultural authority.

Amitav Acharya is Distinguished Professor at the School of International Service, American University, Washington, DC. His recent books include *Constructing Global Order* (Cambridge, 2018) and *The End of American World Order* (2014). His previous book with Barry Buzan is *Non-Western International Relations Theory: Perspectives on and Beyond Asia* (2010). He is the recipient of Distinguished Scholar Awards from the International Studies Association's Global South Caucus (2015) and International Organization Section (2018).

Barry Buzan is Emeritus Professor in the London School of Economics Department of International Relations, Honorary Professor at Copenhagen, Jilin and China Foreign Affairs Universities, and a Fellow of the British Academy. His recent books include *Global International Society*, with Laust Schouenborg (Cambridge, 2018) and *The Global Transformation*, with George Lawson (Cambridge, 2015), which won the Francesco Guicciardini Prize for Best Book in Historical International Relations (2017).

The Making of Global International Relations

Origins and Evolution of IR at its Centenary

Amitav Acharya

American University, Washington, DC

Barry Buzan

London School of Economics and Political Science

CAMBRIDGE
UNIVERSITY PRESS

CAMBRIDGE
UNIVERSITY PRESS

University Printing House, Cambridge CB2 8BS, United Kingdom

One Liberty Plaza, 20th Floor, New York, NY 10006, USA

477 Williamstown Road, Port Melbourne, VIC 3207, Australia

314-321, 3rd Floor, Plot 3, Splendor Forum, Jasola District Centre, New Delhi - 110025, India

79 Anson Road, #06-04/06, Singapore 079906

Cambridge University Press is part of the University of Cambridge.

It furthers the University's mission by disseminating knowledge in the pursuit of education, learning and research at the highest international levels of excellence.

www.cambridge.org
Information on this title: www.cambridge.org/9781108480178
DOI: 10.1017/9781108647670

© Amitav Acharya and Barry Buzan 2019

First published 2019

A catalogue record for this publication is available from the British Library

ISBN 978-1-108-48017-8 Hardback
ISBN 978-1-108-72711-2 Paperback

Contents

Tables

Acknowledgements

This book is a development from our earlier work on 'Non-Western' IR theory (Acharya and Buzan, 2007a, b, 2010).[1] When we wrote a 'ten years on' retrospective on this work (Acharya and Buzan, 2017) the centenary (at least according to its founding myth) of IR in 2019 was on the horizon, and seemed an obvious target for the next stage of our project. Our individual work during the last decade was strikingly parallel in outlook, so we had firm foundations on which to build. We set out the details of all this in Chapter 10.

The project has benefitted from the international conference on 'African Voices in IR Theory' at Rhodes University, South Africa in May 2013 (Bischoff, Aning and Acharya, 2016), and 'Latin America in Global IR' ('América Latina en la Disciplina Global de las Relaciones Internacionales') in Buenos Aires on 2–3 November 2017. We would also like to thank our colleagues in the Political Science department at Copenhagen University for their comments on a sketch of the project and an early draft of Chapter 2 in November 2017.

Thanks also to Peter Wilson, Hitomi Koyama, Randolph Persaud, Qin Yaqing and Arlene Tickner, for their advice on specific aspects of the story. We are very grateful to Allan Layug and Jiajie He for their valuable research assistance and to Sahil Mathur for both research and editorial assistance.

We would also like to thank John Haslam, and Cambridge University Press, not only for taking on this book, but particularly for getting it out in time to launch in early 2019.

---

[1] The label 'Non-Western' is placed in quotes to indicate two, simultaneous conditions: (1) no one comes from a pristine origin anymore, given the impact of globalisation today and colonialism yesterday; nonetheless, (2) Non-Western ways of being and knowing still figure powerfully in the lifeworlds of their cultural heirs. This second condition includes the ontologies and epistemologies of indigenous peoples in what the Europeans called the 'New World'. They are located geographically in the West but their epistemes do not stem from the Eurocentric definition of the 'West'. For the sake of stylistic simplicity, however, the scare quotes are omitted from subsequent uses of the term Non-Western. We are grateful to L. H. M. Ling for these important clarifications.

Abbreviations

ADIZ	Air Defense Identification Zone
AI	Artificial Intelligence
AIIB	Asian Infrastructure Investment Bank
ARC	Asian Relations Conference
ASEAN	Association of Southeast Asian Nations
AU	African Union
BISA	British International Studies Association
BRI	Belt and Road Initiative
BRICS	Brazil, Russia, India, China, South Africa
CCP	Chinese Communist Party
CEE	Central and Eastern Europe
CEEISA	Central and East European International Studies Association
CFR	Council on Foreign Relations
DPT	Democratic Peace Theory
ECOWAS	Economic Community of West African States
EEC	European Economic Community
EISA	European International Studies Association
ES	English School
EU	European Union
EUISS	European Union Institute for Security Studies
G8	Group of 8
G20	Group of 20
G77	Group of 77
GATT	General Agreement on Tariffs and Trade
GDP	gross domestic product
GIS	global international society
GWoT	global war on terrorism
HST	Hegemonic Stability Theory
IAB	Inter-American Bank
IBSA	India, Brazil, South Africa

ICISS	International Commission on Intervention and State Sovereignty
ICWA	Indian Council of World Affairs
IGO	intergovernmental organisation
IIIC	International Institute of Intellectual Cooperation
IMF	International Monetary Fund
INGO	international non-governmental organisation
IPE	International Political Economy
IPR	Institute of Pacific Relations
IPSA	International Political Science Association
IR	International Relations (discipline)
ir	international relations (practice)
ISA	International Studies Association
ISC	International Studies Conference
ISS	International Security Studies
JAIR	Japan Association of International Relations
KMT	Kuomintang
LN	League of Nations
MNE	multinational enterprise
NAM	Non-Aligned Movement
NATO	North Atlantic Treaty Organisation
NEFOS	New Emerging Forces
NIEO	New International Economic Order
NNWS	non-nuclear weapon state
NWS	nuclear weapon state
OAU	Organization of African Unity
OECD	Organisation for Economic Co-operation and Development
OEP	Open Economy Politics
OLDEFOS	Old Established Forces
OPEC	Organization of the Petroleum Exporting Countries
R2P	Responsibility to Protect
SCO	Shanghai Cooperation Organisation
SSA	sub-Saharan Africa
TPP	Trans-Pacific Partnership
TNC	transnational corporation
TRIP	Teaching, Research and International Policy
UDHR	Universal Declaration of Human Rights
UK	United Kingdom
UN	United Nations
UNCTAD	UN Conference on Trade and Development
UNDP	UN Development Programme

UNHCR	UN High Commissioner for Refugees
UNSC	UN Security Council
US	United States
WHO	World Health Organization
WILPF	Women's International League for Peace and Freedom
WISC	World International Studies Committee
WST	World Systems Theory
WTO	World Trade Organization

Introduction

Aims and Approaches

One principal motive for writing this book is to take advantage of what many, though not all, in the field of International Relations (IR) will take to be the centenary of the discipline in 2019. It is the longstanding founding 'myth' of IR, widely taught in introductory courses, that it came into being as a formal field of study in 1919 in response to the catastrophe of the First World War. That 'myth' sets IR up as being a response to the urgent problem of how to understand the whole problem of peace and war in the society of states (we review this 'myth' and the debate around it more fully in Chapter 2). Big anniversaries like this one are good opportunities to pause, take stock, review what has been accomplished, and what not, and think about where to go from here.

Another motive, no less important, is to reflect on the growing debates about the nature and scope of IR coming from those who feel that the field has remained too parochially Eurocentric for too long, and needs to show greater inclusiveness. While such writings have been around for some time, they have intensified during the past decade. Yet there is no single, consolidated study that puts IR thinking outside the West into the larger context of IR's evolution and directions. Ours is such an attempt, though in this book we cannot do much more than sketch in some of the missing or neglected aspects of Non-Western IR thinking that would lend IR a more universal flavour. Compared to that for the United Kingdom or the United States, there is very little literature or information on the origins and evolution of IR outside the West in the English language. Most work on the historiography of IR as a discipline outside the West starts after the Second World War (e.g. Tickner and Wæver, 2009a). Information is especially sketchy on the universities and centres of learning, syllabi and textbooks in IR outside of Europe and the United States. To offer a comprehensive account of the emergence of IR beyond the West is not our goal. What we aim for is to offer a broad-brush overview of some of the key themes and where possible institutional centres of IR in regions outside of Europe and North America.

This book is designed to be part of IR's centennial reflection, and to contribute to the debate in three main ways:

(1) Deepening the existing questioning of the 1919 founding story and providing an alternative, layered framing for the development of IR.
(2) Linking the development of IR to the actual practice of international relations (ir) from the nineteenth century onwards, to show how closely IR has reflected the existing order through time.[1]
(3) Opening up the neglected story of thinking about IR that took place outside the West throughout the period under study.

The book also provides a one-stop introductory text to the history and evolution of IR as a discipline.

Summary of the Argument

Our overall story is that the development of IR actually tracks quite closely the nature and practices of ir. Given that IR has always had strong connections to current events and foreign-policy making, this link is not, in itself, particularly surprising.[2] Its utility for our purposes is that it enables us to develop a nuanced insight into when, how and why IR acquired its notoriously West-centric structure. Although an oversimplification, it remains broadly true that contemporary mainstream IR theory is not much more than an abstraction of Western history interwoven with Western political theory. Realism is an abstraction from eighteenth-century European balance-of-power, behaviour combined with sixteenth- and seventeenth-century, and indeed ancient Greek, political theory. Liberalism is an abstraction from nineteenth- and twentieth-century Western intergovernmental organisations (IGOs) and theories of political economy. Marxism is an abstraction from another branch of nineteenth- and twentieth-century European theories of political economy and historical sociology. The English School (ES) is an abstraction from nineteenth-century European diplomatic behaviour and a long European tradition of legal theory resting on the assumption that all law, including international law, presupposes the existence of a society. Constructivism

---

[1] Our approach thus differs from, but we hope is complementary to, that of Schmidt (1998a, b) and others who explore the origins and roots of the discipline by examining the discourses of those scholars within it.

[2] For detailed argument on how IR theory and World History are co-constitutive, see: Lawson (2012) and Buzan and Lawson (2018). For another work taking a similar approach to relating the practice of ir to the thinking about it, see Knutsen (2016).

is not so obviously abstracted from Western practice, but is drawn from Western philosophy of knowledge. IR has been largely built on the assumption that Western history and Western political theory *are* world history and world political theory.

The fallacy of this assumption is easily exposed by asking what IR theory would look like had the discipline been developed elsewhere than in the West. China, for example, has a radically different history and political theory from that of the West. Whereas Western thinking and practice have been drawn more towards sovereignty, territoriality, international anarchy, war and international society, Chinese theory and practice have been drawn more towards unity, hierarchy, *Tianxia* (all under heaven) and tribute system relations.[3] In the Chinese system, war, diplomacy and trade all embodied quite different practices and understandings from those in the West, and what is now called soft power played a much larger role. China's claim to be the 'Middle Kingdom' was an assertion of cultural as much as material superiority, and Chinese practice and thinking do not fit all that comfortably with Western concepts such as great power, empire and suzerainty. Had IR come out of Islamic history and political theory, it might well have been much more focused on world society rather than on a system of sovereign, territorial states. As the fourteenth-century travels of Ibn Battutah show, an Islamic world society stretched from Spain to China – within which an individual could travel more or less safely, and have his standing and credentials recognised along the way (Mackintosh-Smith, 2002).

Further evidence that Western history and political theory do not adequately represent the rest of the world has arisen during the past few decades, as the study of IR has gained popularity around the world. IR scholarship in Latin America, Africa, the Middle East and Southeast Asia is showing a growing disconnect between the dominant IR concepts developed in the West – including the nation state, power, institutions and norms – and the realities that local scholars perceive and analyse in these different regions.

Given that IR should be the most global of the social sciences, how did this lopsided structure happen? The answer to that question, and a sense of how the discipline of IR might rebalance itself, can both be found in the linkage between ir and IR over the past two centuries.

During the nineteenth century and up to the First World War, the nature and practices of ir were structured by an intensely unequal relationship between a relatively small, but very powerful core, and a large,

---

[3] For an excellent review of how and why the Chinese system behaved and thought as it did, see Pines (2012).

but relatively weak periphery. The core was mainly Western, plus Japan, and its practice was to make a sharp distinction between 'civilised' states, who composed international society, and 'barbaric' or 'savage' societies, mostly dealt with by degrees of colonial subordination and not counted as part of international society. The development of IR during this period was much more substantial than is implied by the 1919 founding myth. Most of the foundations of modern IR were developed before 1914, and this 'IR before IR' mirrored ir in its concerns and definitions, being almost entirely a view from the core. Despite the trauma of the First World War in the core, the highly unequal colonial structure of core–periphery carried over largely unaltered into the interwar period. Indeed, the trauma of the war put the question of great power peace and war at the centre of concern in both ir and IR. From 1919, IR went through its first formal founding and naming, and reflected both the marginalisation of the periphery, and, as its 1919 founding myth suggests, the obsession with great power war. It remained almost entirely focused on the war/peace concerns and divided ideological perspectives of the Western core, with the periphery remaining marginalised inside Western and Japanese empires. Throughout this time of extreme core dominance, views about ir/IR were developing in the periphery. But since many of them were motivated by anti-colonialism, they were largely ignored or marginalised in the West-centric discourses of IR. The colonies were largely excluded from international society in their own right, and they were not much part of IR concerns during this period either.

During the Cold War/decolonisation era up to 1989, this extreme core–periphery construction of both ir and IR began to change. After the Second World War, between the mid-1940s and the mid-1970s, decolonisation brought almost the entire periphery into formal membership of international society as sovereign equals. At the same time, IR underwent what was in effect a second foundation, with massive increases in the size and institutionalisation of the field. The delegitimation of colonialism and human inequality were major transformations in ir, and to some extent this was reflected in IR. The Third World and Development Studies became part of IR's curriculum, and thinking from the Third World, such as Dependency Theory and Postcolonialism, began to register on the margins of mainstream IR. But IR, and to a considerable extent ir, nevertheless remained largely focused on the concerns and perspectives of the Western core. This happened partly because, after 1947, the obsession with great power war that dominated the interwar period was sustained and amplified by the risk of nuclear war between the two rival superpowers. Global nuclear war might destroy not only civilisation, but humankind as a whole, so it was a justified priority.

It was also the case that the periphery, while formally liberated politically, remained weak, and economically subordinated to the core powers,
mainly the West and Japan. Although the Third World had some independent play in world politics, it was heavily penetrated by the Cold
War competition between the United States and the Soviet Union. So,
although IR did incorporate the periphery into its concerns, it did so
mainly from the perspective of the core, seeing the Third World and its
events largely through the lenses of superpower rivalry and manipula-
tion. This orientation also reflected the singular dominance of the United
States within IR in terms not just of sheer numbers, but also in control
over finance, journals, academic associations and the theoretical debates
at the core of the field. American IR not surprisingly reflected American
ir: US concerns and interests about the Cold War, the global economy
and the ideological alignment of the Third World.

It is not until we get to the world after 1989, both post-Cold War and
post-decolonisation, that this imbalance between core and periphery
in both ir and IR begins to break down. During the 1990s the imbalance was briefly maintained while both ir and IR tried to figure out the
consequences of a seeming unipolarity of the United States and globalisation of the world. But this broke down quickly under several different
pressures. The rise of China, and to a lesser extent India and others,
exemplified what Fareed Zakaria (2009) calls 'the rise of the rest'. By the
early twenty-first century, the wealth and power gap between core and
periphery that was the legacy of the uneven and combined development
triggered by the revolutions of modernity during the nineteenth century
was visibly eroding. The United States shifted its security concerns first
towards a group of Third World 'rogue states', and after 2001 towards
global terrorism that mostly had its roots in the Islamic part of the Third
World. During the first two decades of the twenty-first century, and
especially after the economic crisis that started in 2008, China loomed
increasingly large as the main challenger to US dominance in ir. At the
same time, IR expanded and became institutionalised in more and more
countries. The United States retained more dominance in IR than in
ir, but was being challenged by Europe and Asia both in terms of IR
theory and institutions from academic associations to journals (Acharya
and Buzan, 2007a, b, 2017; Buzan and Hansen, 2009). Western IR, with
its core perspective, remained dominant. But increasingly others were
trying to get their own histories and political philosophies in play to
widen the historical and philosophical foundations of IR. By 2017 it was
increasingly apparent in both ir and IR that the global dominance of the
West was winding down. A post-Western world order was emerging in
which the West was no longer the only, or the dominant, centre of wealth,

power and cultural legitimacy. Yet especially in IR, the legacy of Western dominance hung on longer than it was doing in real-world ir.

To capture the unfolding of global international society (GIS) over the last two centuries we use a broad periodisation developed by Buzan and Schouenborg (2018): version 1.0 GIS, the first founding of modern ir taking Western-colonial form (from the nineteenth century up to 1945); version 1.1 GIS, the first major revision ending colonialism but still core-dominated and taking Western-global form (1945–2008); and the emergence of version 1.2 GIS after 2008, in which Western dominance increasingly gives way to a deep pluralist form in which there are many centres of wealth, power and cultural legitimacy. We use this historical trajectory of ir, in terms of the changing relationship between core and periphery, as a springboard to think about how IR now needs to become more global in order to reflect 'the rise of the rest'. Among other things, this means paying more attention to local histories additional to the Western one, and to world history told from a global perspective. Thinking about ir from other cultures and histories needs to be brought into both historical accounts and the process of theorising. And account needs to be taken of the historical grievances against the old core that still exist in much of the old periphery, and which continue both to poison contemporary ir and distort IR.

In order to capture the global evolution of IR as a discipline, we adopt the same broad view of what counts as 'thinking about IR' as in our earlier work (Acharya and Buzan, 2007a, b, 2010). In its early phases, thinking about international relations was as much an activity of political leaders and public intellectuals as it was of academics. Indeed IR did not become a primarily academic activity even in the West until after 1945, and rather later than that in the Third World. We take this non-academic thinking about IR seriously as part of the discipline's history, and show how it shaped subsequent academic developments in both core and periphery. Within the more academic IR that has evolved since the Second World War, we also take a broad view of what counts as 'theory'. The detailed discussion of this is in Chapter 2.

All of this has consequences for how the discipline is taught and institutionalised. We hope this book will open a debate for the whole discipline of IR about how and why it needs to make the transition from being mainly West- and indeed Anglosphere-centric, to being truly global, hence our term Global IR (Acharya, 2014a).

The argument sketched out above is organised around five pairs of chapters, each covering one time period: nineteenth century to 1919, 1919–45, 1945–89, 1989–2017 and looking forward from 2017. The first chapter of each pair sketches out the international history (ir) of the period, and the second sketches out the evolution of IR as a discipline, and how that evolution relates to the history of its time. As noted above, our argument is that the events of world history set much of the agenda for what IR thinks about: IR is to some extent a slave to current events. But it is also a two-way street. IR tries to capture this shifting reality, prioritises some things over others, and adds labels and concepts such as bipolarity, globalisation and international society, that in turn influence how people understand the world they are in and therefore shapes how they act.

1   The World up to 1919: The Making of Modern International Relations

Introduction

If IR as a discipline began, as the conventional mythology would have it, in 1919, we would still need to look back into the nineteenth century to see what the international history was that shaped its initial formation. In fact, as we will argue in Chapter 2, not only the roots, but also the practice of modern IR thinking extend back deep into the nineteenth century, which means that we need to get a sense of that century as a whole in order to understand its genesis.

This chapter unfolds four distinct but closely interlinked central themes:

(1) The impact of the revolutions of modernity on international relations.
(2) The consolidation of a hierarchical Western-colonial international society, and reactions against it.
(3) The rise of Japan as the first big move towards 'the rise of the rest'.
(4) The trauma of the First World War.

The Impact of Modernity on the World

Barry Buzan and George Lawson (2015a) argue that, during the nineteenth century, the revolutions of modernity transformed what had been an international system dominated by dynastic, agrarian empires, and laid the foundations for the set of ideas, actors, systems and processes which still define IR today. This section draws on that analysis to sketch out the transformation of the material and ideational landscapes of international relations.[1]

The Ideational Landscape

In ideational terms, the revolutions of modernity swept aside the conceptual foundations of the traditional agrarian world. Until the nineteenth

[1] Readers wanting more detail and deeper referencing should consult that work.

century, the closely linked ideas of religion and dynasticism dominated political legitimacy, making territoriality fairly fluid, and empire an attractive and often durable political form. This was complemented by economic thinking dominated by mercantilism: the idea that for any given state, exporting was much preferable to importing, and monopoly control of supply, obtained by direct seizure if necessary, preferable to open trade. Sovereignty was a well-established idea, at least in Europe, but was closely tied to the sovereign, and thus to the dynastic order. This was a system in which the different classes and ranks within societies were supposed to know their place and stay in it. Opportunity was thus shaped mainly by birthright.

During the long nineteenth century (1776–1914) this system of ideas and practices increasingly gave way to four ideologies of progress: Liberalism, Socialism, nationalism and 'Scientific' Racism. These four ideologies changed the meaning of war, territoriality, class, political legitimacy, sovereignty, law, individual and collective identity, and trade. They underpinned modern international relations, redefining what it was about, who practised it and how they practised it. These four ideologies generated many contradictions both within and between themselves, and with the traditional ideas they were replacing. Working out some of these contradictions was a key driver of the three world wars of the twentieth century.

Liberalism was associated with the leading edge society of the revolutions of modernity, Britain. It evolved into a complicated package of concepts that had its roots in two central ideas: that the rights of the individual should be foundational to society and politics, and that the relatively open operation of markets should be the basic principle for running the economy. These two ideas were mutually supportive to the extent that markets required individuals to have both private property and the freedom to innovate and interact, and that individualism would in turn be reinforced by the operation of markets and private property. For this package to work both economically and politically, individuals would have to be educated. Subjects would become citizens who collectively had the right of self-determination. Built into this was an emphasis on meritocracy and rationalism as alternatives to birthright.

Liberalism thus attacked several foundations of the traditional order. Its individualism and meritocracy undermined birthright and the rigid class structure, and invited individuals to seek wealth and power according to their capabilities. The same combination, along with self-determination, also undermined both dynasticism and the political role of religion. Individualism pushed towards popular sovereignty: ownership of the state by the people rather than by the sovereign. This idea potentially pulled some of the props from under the legitimacy of empire, though in practice Liberalism, especially its meritocratic line, quite easily accommodated the new imperialism of the late nineteenth century. Individualism also pushed for the internalisation or privatisation of religion, and a reduction of its role in politics. Liberal ideas about the market directly contradicted mercantilism, looking to make the pursuit of wealth and development a positive, rather than a zero-sum, game. This too pulled some of the ideational props from the legitimacy of empire. Although liberal individualism is now associated with democracy, this was less the case during the nineteenth century, when any thought of giving people the vote was heavily mediated by qualifications of education and property, and women need not apply. Only those men who had proved their 'merit' had the right to vote.

Socialism emerged as a reaction to the excesses of liberal capitalism in practice. It shared much with Liberalism, including antipathy to dynasticism, religion and birthright. Socialists too wanted to open up the class system, educate the people, encourage rationalism, allow class mobility and move people from being subjects to citizens. But Socialists were keener on the collectivity of citizens than on individualism, on egalitarianism rather than meritocracy, and on state command of the economy rather than the market. They saw private property and the market as means of exploitation rather than empowerment. Where Liberals saw a harmony of interests, Socialists saw exploitation and class war. They saw the consequences of liberal meritocracy, capitalism and, up to a point, free trade as generating unacceptable extremes of poverty and inequality. Socialists wedded themselves to the new political potential that industrialism had generated in the form of an expanding industrial proletariat. They sought either a fairer distribution of the fruits of capitalism, or in more extreme forms a replacement of capitalism by state-run command economies. Both Liberalism and Socialism had ambivalent views of the state, some embracing it as the desired political form, others pursuing more cosmopolitan visions. They were also ambivalent about political form. Nineteenth-century Liberals were not necessarily democratic if they gave more weight to meritocracy, and Socialists, while pushing for a wider franchise, could unfold in both democratic and authoritarian directions.

Nationalism came into prominence with the French Revolution. Its basic idea was to define people mainly in terms of some combination of shared language, culture, ethnicity and history, and then to make the resultant collective identity group the main foundation for political legitimacy. The French derived a lot of military power from this move, mobilising and motivating vast citizen armies, and this created huge pressure on others to follow suit. Nationalism supported the move from subject to citizen, and from dynastic to popular sovereignty, though some monarchies were able to adapt themselves to be expressions of it. It powerfully reinforced the state by wedding it to the nation, but severely disrupted the existing territorial forms, especially empires. Nationalism glued together the disparate dynastic polities within Germany and Italy, but acted as a solvent for the glue that held multi-national empires together. It created a problem for the fledgling United States, which initially had difficulty distinguishing itself from British identity in these terms. By creating a strong collective identity, nationalism offered not only a pathway to overcoming localisms and creating society on the larger scale required by industrialism, but also a counterweight to the divisive new class politics opened up by industrialism, and the Liberal and Socialist ways of dealing with it. Nationalism could go either way on trade, either liberal or protectionist, and could likewise go either way politically, underpinning both democratic and authoritarian regimes.

'Scientific' Racism became a powerful ideological strand of modernity between the middle of the nineteenth century and the middle of the twentieth. As Duncan Bell (2013: 1) notes: 'for the opening few decades of the [twentieth] century, race was widely and explicitly considered a fundamental ontological unit of politics, perhaps the most fundamental unit of all'. It grew mainly out of a combination of three things: the classificatory schemes that were defining the science of biology; the transfer from biology to society of the principle of 'survival of the fittest' (social Darwinism); and the hugely unequal encounters that were happening between 'civilised' European countries and 'barbarian' or 'savage' peoples around the world. That groups of human beings saw themselves as civilised and other groups as barbarian was nothing new. But this age-old and more or less universal practice was mainly based on judgments about culture and degree of civilisation. Within that form of discrimination there was room for social mobility. People could upgrade their culture, or adopt the culture of a more 'civilised' group. 'Scientific' Racism more or less closed this mobility. If inferiority and superiority were genetic, then there was little or no prospect of improvement, and the result was a racial hierarchy with whites at the top and blacks at the bottom. Progress was then defined as improving the racial stock and replacing inferior types with superior ones. As 'Scientific' Racism developed, it became more nuanced, opening the way for hierarchies within Europe among Aryans, Latins and Slavs. In this form, 'Scientific' Racism had obvious synergies with nationalism. It also gave a powerful justification for the new imperialism of the late nineteenth century.

As we will show in subsequent chapters, these four ideologies still dominate international relations, though some (nationalism, Liberalism – at least economic Liberalism) have been spectacularly successful, while others have been pushed towards the margins ('Scientific' Racism, and to a much lesser extent, Socialism). With the possible exception of the emerging ideology of environmental stewardship, no new ideologies of equivalent weight have come along to reshape international relations.[2]

The Material Landscape

In material terms, the revolutions of modernity had three distinct effects on international relations. First, they transformed the interaction capacity of the system by shrinking the time, cost and risk of moving goods, people and information around the planet. Second, they transformed the units, creating the familiar cast of modern characters in the play of world politics. Third, they introduced rapid technological change as a permanent feature of the system with major effects on both economic and military relations.

The first integration of the planet took place during the nineteenth century. It was largely the work of the new steamships and railways that broke down most of the historical barriers of distance and geography. At the beginning of the century it could take the best part of a year to send anything (goods, people, information) from London to Australia, with a substantial risk that all would be lost along the way. By 1914 information could be communicated in less than a day, and goods or people reliably transported in a few weeks. A network of telegraph cables tied most of the world together, and shipping and railways were able to move large numbers of people and massive quantities of goods cheaply, quickly and fairly safely around the planet. Interoceanic canals at Suez and Panama cut huge distances off shipping routes. This new interaction capacity was the backbone of the first version of the highly interconnected and interdependent international system that we have today. It enabled a truly global economy for the first time, which unlike the silk road links of classical times generated global markets in finance and trade, and involved bulk as well as elite goods. It also enabled mass migrations in which large numbers of people moved from Europe, South Asia and China to other continents. And it enabled the globalisation of war, as illustrated

---

[2] Fascism was simply a mix of nationalism and 'Scientific' Racism.

by Britain's defeat of China in 1840. With the exception of movement by air, all of the basic logistical features of the modern international system were in place by the end of the nineteenth century.

Also in place by the end of the nineteenth century was the whole set of actors that comprise the modern GIS. Among the core of modernised societies, the rational, national, bureaucratic state (in both its liberal democratic and authoritarian developmental form), had largely displaced the dynastic state. Nationalism had sacralised territory and tightened up borders (Mayall, 1990), and most of these modern states were the metropolitan cores of new overseas empires. Alongside the modern state was the rise of the transnational corporation (TNC). TNCs were enabled by the British Companies Act of 1862, which revolutionised the company, and substantially delinked it from the older form of chartered companies, which were both tied to the state and quasi-state-like organisations in themselves (Phillips and Sharman, 2015). TNCs both reflected and reinforced liberal ideas about trade, markets and investment, and played a large role in consolidating a global capitalist economy.

Another mainstay of contemporary GIS, IGOs, also took root at this time. During the last quarter of the nineteenth century, IGOs began to meet the functional demands for coordination and interoperability generated by the huge increases in global flows of trade and communication, and the rapid spread of new technologies such as railways and the telegraph. Given the general rule of divided sovereignty in the Western-colonial GIS at this time, an interesting feature of the development of IGOs was the success of some Non-Western states, including some under colonial rule, in gaining membership in them, which constituted a significant form of diplomatic recognition. This is explained by the greater emphasis on actual functional administration, rather than formal sovereignty, in these nineteenth-century international unions (Howland, 2016: 2). The following examples are indicative of the extent of this:

- International Telecommunications Union (founded 1865): Turkey joined in 1866, Egypt 1876, Iran 1868, India 1868, Japan 1879, Thailand 1883 and Sri Lanka 1896.[3]
- Universal Postal Union (founded 1874): Egypt joined in 1875, Turkey 1875, India 1876, Indonesia 1877, Iran 1877, Japan 1877, Liberia 1879, Thailand 1885, Tunisia 1888, Korea 1900, Algeria 1907, Ethiopia 1908 and China 1914.[4]

[3] www.itu.int/online/mm/scripts/gensel8 (Accessed 20 January 2013).
[4] www.upu.int/en/the-upu/member-countries.html (Accessed 20 January 2013).

• Permanent Court of Arbitration (founded 1899): Iran joined in 1900, Japan 1900, Thailand 1900, China 1904 and Turkey 1907.[5]

By 1913, there were 45 IGOs (Wallace and Singer, 1970: 250–1), a modest start, but establishing the foundations for the more ambitious developments that followed the First World War. The Hague Peace Conferences of 1899 and 1907 were also turning points in the widening of international society, bringing the states of the Americas into the core of inter-state diplomacy (Simpson, 2004: 135). These two conferences also founded the Permanent Court of Arbitration as a dispute settlement mechanism, and paved the way for the Permanent Court of International Justice that was part of the Versailles Treaties in 1919. IGOs both built on, and accelerated, the shift from natural to positive international law that also marked the revolutions of modernity.

Alongside the IGOs and the TNCs, the international non-governmental organisations (INGOs) that compose global civil society also arose at this time. Transnational INGOs covered a very wide range of concerns including transnational revolutionary movements, peace societies, anti-slavery associations, religious proselytising and lobbies that played into debates about the morality and practices of war, imperialism, intervention, public health, education, penal reform and market expansion. By the 1830s, transnational associations were taking part in vigorous public debates around issues as varied as trade policy and population growth. Several prominent INGOs, including the Young Men's Christian Association and the International Red Cross, were formed in the 1850s and 1860s, as were issue-based groups such as those seeking to improve animal welfare, promote the arts and formalise academic subjects ranging from botany to anthropology. The latter half of the nineteenth century saw a further growth in INGO activity. Labour movement groups formed in response to the inequities of industrialisation and the first industrial-era depression. The international organisation of sports included the International Olympic Committee, established in 1894 to revive the ancient Greek games in modern form. A transnational movement for women's suffrage emerged in the last quarter of the nineteenth century. The period leading to the First World War also saw the emergence of women's peace movements. The International Congress of Women held at The Hague in 1915 expressed itself strongly against nationalism and trade in armaments, called for displacing the balance-of-power approach with a concert of nations, creating an international force to displace national armies and addressing economic grievances

---

[5] www.pca-cpa.org/showpage.asp?pag_id=1038 (Accessed 20 January 2013).

that cause conflict. These demands were powerful precursors to the United Nations (UN) Women, Peace and Security agenda in the post-Cold War period (Tickner and True, 2018: 2–5).

At their pre-First World War high point, there were around 400 active INGOs around the world (Davies, 2013: 65–76; Osterhammel, 2014: 505–12). The global civil society that has been such a celebrated feature of the twentieth century has its origins in the long nineteenth century. The anti-slavery movement pioneered the lobbying activities of INGOs trying to affect the norms and practices of the society of states, and the peace movement advocates present at The Hague Conferences foreshadowed today's integration of IGOs into the processes of multilateral diplomacy (Buzan, 2017). Reflecting both the new thinking in the ideologies of progress, and the physical and social integration of the planet created by the vast improvements in interaction capacity, this new set of actors was tied together by the dynamics, and reactions to them, of industrial capitalism, war, revolution, imperialism and an emerging global economy and global culture.

The third material impact of the revolutions of modernity was to introduce rapid technological change as a permanent feature of the system. This new feature had huge consequences for both economic and military relations that started to unfold during the nineteenth century, and are still unfolding today. Continuous technological change constitutes a form of permanent revolution in human affairs that creates relentless upheaval in social, economic, political and military affairs both domestically and internationally. High-impact technological changes were of course not unknown in agrarian societies, as the stories of stirrups, iron, gunpowder and the compass all illustrate. But such changes were infrequent and usually separated by long periods of relative stability. The marriage of scientific method and industrialism changed all that. Although already visible in the improvements to steam engines during the eighteenth century, widespread and rapid technological change took off during the 1830s and 1840s and has remained at a fast pace ever since.

Rapid technological change had major synergies with capitalism. New technologies opened up new markets and new sources of profit. They made old goods cheaper and often of better quality (e.g. cloth, iron), delivered new goods (e.g. railways, automobiles, electric power) and massively eased the flow of goods and resources between primary producers, manufacturers and consumers. Between 1850 and 1913, the value of world trade (at constant prices) increased tenfold (Osterhammel, 2014: 726). The gross domestic product (GDP) of the industrial core countries increased by a factor of 9 between 1800 and 1913, and their GDP per capita by a factor of 3.3. By comparison, in what came to be known as the Third World, GDP increased by a factor of only around 1.5, and GDP per capita remained more or less the same (Bairoch, 1981: 7–8, 12). As these figures indicate, technological advance, in conjunction with the highly unequal distribution of the other revolutions of modernity, opened up the distinction between developed and underdeveloped countries that is still a major feature of international relations. A small group of states captured most of the wealth and power unleashed by the revolutions of modernity, and used that advantage to create a core–periphery system in which the core states set the rules according to their own interests, and the periphery states were exploited and often colonised. The new technologies also gave substance to the idea of progress embodied in the new ideologies.

Rapid and continuous technological change had a major impact on military relations. Most obviously, it opened up a huge gap in the mode of power between the modern core states and the underdeveloped periphery. As Britain demonstrated to China in 1840, those in possession of the modern, industrial mode of power had technological, economic and organisational capabilities that made it generally easy for them to defeat those still deploying the capabilities of the agrarian mode of power. This reinforced the core–periphery structure by creating a power gap that was both large and difficult to bridge. In addition to this, the new technological environment transformed the qualities necessary to be a great power, and added a highly disturbing factor – industrialised arms racing – to relations between the great powers in the core. During classical times, being a great power required a large population, a big treasury and reasonably good leadership. Military technology tended not to differ all that much among neighbouring polities. But once industrialism kicked in, the quality and type of weapons a country could put into the field began to matter hugely, as did whether it could make such weapons itself or not. And this was a continuous treadmill, because the quality of existing weapons such as rifles and cannon was improving all the time, and new types of weapons, sometimes transformative (e.g. machine guns, submarines, aircraft), were appearing all the time. On this basis it became increasingly necessary for great powers to be at the leading edge of development. Traditional great powers such as China, the Ottoman Empire and up to a point Russia, fell down the ranks, while successfully modernising and industrialising states such as Britain, Germany, the United States and Japan rose up them.

As illustrated by the little-known naval race between Britain and France during the middle of the nineteenth century, and the very well-known one between Britain and Germany in the run-up to the First World War, industrial arms racing created massive military insecurities among the great powers. Each had to fear that if it did not keep up, others would deploy superior weapons that might lead to its quick and decisive defeat. If France had deployed a navy of steam-powered ironclads before Britain, then Britain would have been unable to defend itself against invasion by the superior French army. There were synergies between civilian and military technological advances, as in the use of railways, steamships and the telegraph to transform the logistics of military operations. These new technologies also continuously transformed the nature of war, devaluing much of the wisdom learned from earlier conflicts.

Although colonial powers by and large sought to keep modern weapons out of the hands of their colonial subjects, there was also a spillover from capitalism into the military sphere in the form of the arms trade. Arms manufacturers wanted to sell their weapons not just to their own governments, but as widely as possible – in the post-mortems following the First World War, this earned them the label 'merchants of death' (Engelbrecht and Hanighen, 1934). New developments in weaponry began to generate efforts to control certain kinds of military technologies. The First Geneva Convention of 1864 and, later, The Hague Conventions of 1899 and 1907 contained a series of arms control measures that reflected responses to new military technologies. In conflicts between 'civilised' states, they banned bullets that flattened in the body (building on an earlier agreement on the non-use of so-called 'dum dum' bullets at the 1868 St Petersburg Conference), bombing from various kinds of aircraft and the use of gases as weapons. They also restricted the deployment of mines and torpedoes.

The rapid and continuous increase in the number and type of weapons, and in their destructive capability and cost, also generated the defence dilemma (Buzan, [1991] 2007: 217–33). This was a new phenomenon, different from the familiar security dilemma arising from fear of defeat by weapons in the hands of others. The defence dilemma challenged fear of defeat by fear of military competition (because of its expense and its treadmill quality) and fear of war (because rising costs and destructiveness combined with ever more intense mobilisations of society, meaning that societies might be destroyed by the process of war regardless of whether they won or lost). The defence dilemma, however, did not really gain traction until the First World War, on which more below.

Western-Colonial Global International Society

The material and ideational effects of the revolutions of modernity generated the first ever global-scale international society, which we refer to as version 1.0 GIS. International society is defined by Hedley Bull and Adam Watson (1984a: 1):

a group of states (or, more generally, a group of independent political communities) which not merely form a system, in the sense that the behaviour of each is a necessary factor in the calculations of the others, but also have established by dialogue and consent common rules and institutions for the conduct of their relations, and recognise their common interest in maintaining these arrangements.

The basic idea is quite simple: that states (or more broadly polities), like individuals, live in societies that both shape and are shaped by their identity and behaviour. Societies take the form of shared rules and institutions that define identity, membership and legitimate behaviour. Prior to the nineteenth century, distinctive sub-global international societies could be found in various places. There was a Westphalian international society in Europe based on dynastic sovereignty; an international society in the Indian Ocean based on trade between a mixture of entities including merchant cities, empires and European chartered companies; and a hierarchical international society in East Asia based around the Chinese tribute system (Suzuki, Zhang and Quirk, 2014; Phillips and Sharman, 2015). During the nineteenth century, the European international society both expanded to global scale and was itself transformed both by the revolutions of modernity and by encounters with other international societies.

The creation of version 1.0 GIS was driven by three main factors: the creation of a core–periphery world economy centred on Europe, the opening of a big power gap between the first round of modernisers and the rest, and the revolutions that created a host of new states in the Americas that were dominated by immigrants from Europe.

The creation of an integrated world economy made Europeans dependent on diverse sources of supply and global markets, and this drove a strong need to regulate and standardise behaviour across a wide variety of cultures and levels of development. As Gerrit W. Gong (1984: 7–21) notes, the European need for access (trade, proselytising, travel) was what drove the functional aspects of what became known as the 'standard of civilisation' (to protect the life, liberty and property of Europeans in other countries) and therefore the demand for extraterritoriality and unequal relations where the locals could not or would not provide these. The opening of a big and durable power gap between those states and societies at the leading edge of modernity and those not eventually empowered those at the leading edge to take direct control of the rest if they wished to do so. This development was signalled by Britain's easy defeat of China in 1840. After that, a new wave of imperialism saw the European powers, the United States and Japan take over large swathes of Africa and Asia, and reduce to subservience former great powers that had failed to come to terms with modernity, such as China and the Ottoman Empire. Finally, the late eighteenth- and early nineteenth-century revolutions in the Americas against colonial rule added new members to the emerging GIS. These new states were a mix of European and revolutionary culture, and by the 1890s the United States had become a great power in its own right.

It is not entirely correct to see the making of GIS as simply the expansion of European international society to global scale. European international society had itself received inputs from both Asia and the Islamic world in its own process of formation, and was therefore already in some senses a fusion. By the nineteenth century, this fusion was itself undergoing the revolutions of modernity, again a global process, and had become powerful enough to dominate the rest of the planet. That expansion did override the premodern international societies that existed in other parts of the world. Through processes of colonisation, and encounter-reform, the Europeans tried, and up to a point succeeded in, remaking the world in their own political and economic image, though far less so culturally.[6]

This first version of GIS was novel not only in the sense of being global, but also in the composition of its rules, norms and institutions. Parts of it were not specifically European. Dynasticism, for example, was a common form of government across many cultures. Likewise, human inequality was a common institution in many societies, justifying practices from slavery and gender discrimination to empire. Christian and Liberal ideas in Europe had to some extent undermined human inequality, most notably in the successful anti-slavery campaigns of the eighteenth and nineteenth centuries. But the surge of 'Scientific' Racism and social Darwinism during the nineteenth century largely kept human inequality in place as a key legitimiser of imperialism and colonisation, and gender discrimination (Towns, 2009, 2010). War was also a widespread institution in most societies, with relatively few restraints on reasons for going to war, and general acceptance that conquest conferred rights of possession.

Perhaps the main feature of version 1.0 GIS was that it was hierarchically divided between a privileged core, with one set of rules for itself, and a subordinated periphery to which quite another set of rules applied. It is reasonable to call this *Western-colonial* GIS because the core was mainly

---

[6] The key literature on the expansion of international society includes: Bull and Watson, 1984b; Gong, 1984; Watson, 1992; Keene, 2002; Buzan and Little, 2010; Dunne and Reus-Smit, 2017.

Western, although as Japan was to prove, membership of the core was open to those who could meet the 'standard of civilisation'. More on this in the next section. Within the core, the rules and institutions of international society were largely those taken from Westphalian international society, but adapted to the new needs and ideas of modernity (Buzan, 2014: 113–33). As noted above, sovereignty moved from dynastic to popular, with a stronger sense of legal equality, and international law became less rooted in natural law (made by God, and to be discovered by humans using reason), and more in positive law (made by humans as agreed rules of the game). Diplomacy moved from being driven by dynastic interests and hierarchies, to being increasingly multilateral, reflecting national interests and the need to find elements of cooperation in a more complicated and interdependent international system. The European core took on nationalism to replace dynasticism as the foundation for political legitimacy. And it consolidated the balance of power as a core principle for the conduct of great power relations, formalising this in the Concert of Europe. For some decades during the nineteenth century, the Concert institutionalised great power management, and gave great powers special rights and responsibilities above those of ordinary sovereign states, constituting a significant derogation from sovereign equality. As the leading industrial power, Britain tried to promote the market as an institution of GIS. But while this had some success, it gave too much advantage to British trade and industry, and was countered by infant industry protectionism in most of the other core powers. The United States was partly outside this core society because it eschewed the balance of power, pursuing instead a policy of political isolation, while remaining engaged in most other ways.

The periphery was denied sovereign equality, and subordinated in degrees ranging from complete absorption into the sovereignty of the metropolitan power, through protectorates having some domestic sovereignty, to dominions having a reasonable measure of domestic autonomy. Under the logic of social Darwinism and the 'standard of civilisation', it was also denied racial and cultural equality. Colonial economies were reshaped to serve both the resource needs of the metropolitan core, and to act as captive markets for its products. In places like India, this subordination to metropolitan interests led to substantial deindustrialisation. So, while there was what Hedley Bull (1977) nicely labelled an 'anarchical society' of sovereign equals in the core, the periphery had a hierarchical structure of divided sovereignty, and was exposed to exploitation, racism and intervention by the core.

In return, the periphery got, whether it was wanted or not, an encounter with the material and ideational resources of modernity.

In ideational terms, the four ideologies of 'progress' discussed above were drawn almost exclusively from the Western context and intellectual and policy debates. Their Western thinker-advocates rarely made any attempt to draw from similar or compatible ideas of the Non-Western world. They saw their ideas as a universal standard of 'civilisation' rooted in European history and agency, which could uplift the conditions of the periphery if properly learnt and assimilated by the 'uncivilised societies'. In material terms, and only up to a point, the periphery got some commitment from the colonial powers to promote development and move backward peoples towards being able to meet the 'standard of civilisation'. India may have lost its textile and steel industries, its cultural and racial dignity and its independence, but it did get railways and a taste of the machinery and ideas of a modern rational state.

Within this two-tier GIS, the European powers were, despite their overwhelming power and wealth, haunted by fear of revolution. Within the core, the fear was of revolutions arising out of the rapidly unfolding transformations of modernity. As noted above, the four ideologies of progress unleashed by modernity contained contradictions not only with dynastic and religious traditionalism, but also between themselves. Partly it was the fear of dynastic traditionalists, especially in Russia, Prussia and Austria-Hungary, against populist, nationalist, republican revolutions like that which had overthrown the French monarchy in 1789. As A. J. Grant (1916: 12) put it, the great powers, and especially the reactionary ones, 'had the French Revolution on their nerves'. Partly it was the fear of liberal capitalist elites of the new class dynamics unleashed by industrialism and mobilised by believers in Socialism. Revolutionary upheavals like those of 1848 made European elites uneasy in their seats. So too did the possibility of revolts in the African and Asian colonies. The independence revolutions in the Americas had shown the risk, as did the rebellion against the East India Company in South Asia in 1857–8. While the rebellions in the Americas produced states led by white elites, racists were concerned that rebellions in non-white colonies would empower 'inferior stock'. Such thought gave rise to the racist rhetoric of the 'yellow peril', and the injunction to 'let China sleep'.

This nervousness in the core even at the peak of its imperial pomp, was shadowed by the rise of anti-colonial movements in Asia, Africa, the Arab world and elsewhere during the late nineteenth and early twentieth centuries.

In India, the Indian National Congress Party, which some see as the 'first modern nationalist movement to arise in the non-European empire' (Marshall, 2001: 179), was founded in 1885. Its founders included Allan Octavian Hume, a British civil servant, and Dadabhai Naoroji, an

Indian educator who we will meet again in Chapter 2. The anti-colonial movement in India and elsewhere emerged from various sources, among them the growth of nationalism. But nationalism was not just a matter of the creation of 'imagined communities' (Anderson, 2006) by local elites. To be sure, some of the factors identified by Anderson, such as the homogenising effects of centralised colonial bureaucracies, the creation and use of a national language by the colonial power, and the proliferation of print medium, played a role in bringing people of varied ethnic groups together. But nationalism in the colonial world emerged fundamentally as resistance to foreign rule and dominance; in other words, nationalism was a by-product, rather than the cause, of anti-colonial resistance, although the two went hand-in-hand and were mutually reinforcing.

While Anderson talks of the 'creole' origins of nationalism, which accounts for the interplay of European influence and the role of local elites in developing the imagined community of the nation, his account has been criticised for taking nationalism as a universal idea that can be fitted into different colonial contexts and for its neglect of 'the complex place of subalterns in this story, in particular the place of "natives" coopted into colonial rule' (Calhoun, 2017). Moreover, the spread of nationalism and its effects in the colonies cannot be explained as the modular diffusion of a supposedly universal European idea (Nath and Dutta, 2014) which was 'learnt' by elites who studied and worked in Europe before returning to their homelands. Rather, as Partha Chatterjee (1993) argues, the development of nationalism and anti-colonial struggles took many forms; while local nationalists might have adopted material aspects of Western modernity, they also kept to their own cultural and spiritual beliefs in constructing nationalism. In short, the Non-Western world developed varieties of ideas and approaches behind anti-colonial struggles in accordance with local context and need: a classic case of active and 'constitutive localisation' (Acharya, 2004), rather than wholesale and passive adoption of a foreign idea by local leaders and societies.

The rise of Arab nationalism in the late nineteenth and early twentieth centuries had both secular and religious roots and was directed against Ottoman rule as well as Western imperialism, although it was more geared against the West in the Arab countries of North Africa. Much of the modern Middle East except Morocco was under Ottoman rule, at least nominally, in the nineteenth and early twentieth centuries. For long, Arabs had accepted Ottoman rule, thanks to their shared religion, as well as the power and authority of the Ottoman Empire that could challenge the West to the gates of Vienna and provide opportunities for local Arab rulers to serve in the Ottoman court. But with the decline of the Ottoman Empire in the nineteenth century, this changed. While local uprisings against Western-colonial powers did occur, such as the revolt led by 'Abd al-Qadir in Algeria in the 1840s, the true beginning of a wider nationalism in the Arab world could be traced to the 'Arab awakening' of the nineteenth century (Kramer, 1993). One source of this was secular; it was spearheaded by the *Nahda* (Revival) movement led by Lebanese Christian Jurji Zaydan (Jorge Zaydân) and the efforts of liberal Christian Arabs to adapt the Arabic language as a vehicle for the spread of Western modernity through education and literature. Another source was religious, reflected in the desire among Muslim Arabs to move away from the declining Ottoman cultural leadership and instead anoint the Arab civilisation as the standard bearers of Islam's glorious past and its future restorer (Kramer, 1993). There was also a political source of Arab nationalism, which found its strongest expression when Hussein ibn Ali, Sharif of Mecca, made an agreement with Britain in 1915 to revolt against the Ottomans in return for British support for the independence of the Mashreq (east of Egypt) Arabs. But the British made a deal with France (the 1916 Sykes–Picot Agreement) to divide up the region between themselves and did not fulfil their commitment. In addition, Britain's Balfour Declaration of 1917, calling for the creation of a Jewish national home in Palestine, aggravated suspicion of Britain and fuelled Arab anti-colonialism, which would find fuller expression after the First World War.

The growth of anti-colonialism in Africa was also marked by a variety of strategies and approaches, reflecting the size and diversity of the continent. Whereas the littoral states, which had come into contact with Europeans earlier (since the fifteenth century), were initially more accommodating towards colonial rule, the non-Christian interior societies came into contact with Europeans later and more superficially, and developed more militant struggles. Anti-colonial struggles were more violent in European settler colonies in East and North Africa, such as Kenya and Algeria, which were directly ruled by Europeans, than in non-settler colonies in the West coast, such as Nigeria and the Cameroons. European colonial rule in Africa expanded considerably following the 1884–5 Berlin Conference, which partitioned Africa among various European powers. This also inspired anti-colonial struggles aimed at both preventing further exploitation of Africa's resources and to overthrow European rule. Some of them took a militant character. But only Ethiopia was able to defeat a European power, Italy in 1896, and remain independent during this period. Anti-colonial struggles during early twentieth century included the Maji Maji Rebellion in Tanganyika in 1905; revolts in Madagascar in 1904–5 and 1915; the Mahdi revolts in Sudan

1900–4; Somaliland 1895–1920; and the Egba revolt in Nigeria in 1918.[7] Confronted with superior European power, Africans sometimes resorted to seasonal or permanent mass migration, especially in the French, Belgian, German and Portuguese colonies, leaving areas where colonial rule was especially oppressive and moving into relatively safer areas. The advent of print media helped anti-colonial movements in Africa.

Despite its divisions and insecurities, version 1.0 GIS did lay the foundations for what we now call global governance. As noted above, both global civil society in the form of INGOs and the novel institutionalisation of inter-state society in the form of permanent IGOs became prominent during the nineteenth century, and included some members from the periphery.

Japan Foreshadows 'the Rise of the Rest'

Except within specialist literatures on Northeast Asia and economic history, the story of Japan before the First World War is generally marginalised or ignored in IR accounts. It is worth drawing particular attention to it here, not only to redress this imbalance, but also because Japan's story embodies three themes that resonate in later chapters.[8] The first theme is that Japan was part of the first group of states that successfully embarked on modernisation before the First World War. The leading edge of modernity was therefore not a purely Western event, but one of which Japan was an integral part. The second theme is that already before the First World War Japan was playing a significant role in undermining the myth of invincible white power that was one of the important props of Western-colonial GIS. The third theme is Japan's role in questioning racism, which likewise helped to erode the legitimacy of colonialism as an institution of international society.

Japan As Part of the First General Round of Modernity

Where, when and how does Japan fit into the process of modernity that took off during the nineteenth century? Japan is usually considered as an exception, the one Non-Western country that somehow modernised a century before any other Non-Western state, and became recognised as a great power by other leading states. It does not fit the broader story about an Asia of 'stagnant' agrarian states either being colonised by

---

[7] The Boer War (1899–1902) was an unusual case of one white colonial elite in Africa rebelling against another.

[8] This section draws heavily on Koyama and Buzan (2018).

Western powers (South and Southeast Asia) or having violent and painful encounters with them from a position of weakness (China). Neither does it fit with the Western story, which likes to see the decisive emergence of a stable industrial modernity, whatever inputs might have come into Europe from the rest of the world, as something that happened in Western Europe and North America. A constant question that the Japanese case raises is whether Japan is part of the East or part of the West?

As shown by economic historians, Japan was a member of the quite small core group of countries that successfully responded to the British challenge and achieved durable industrial modernity before the First World War (Bairoch, 1982: 288; Maddison, 2001; R. Baldwin, 2016). Although starting late compared to France, Germany and the United States, Japan was part of a third subgroup of first round modernisers along with Russia, Italy, Spain and Austria-Hungary. Unlike most other Non-Western countries, and some Western ones, notably in Eastern Europe and Iberia, Japan had relatively favourable domestic conditions to facilitate its transformation to industrial modernity (Maddison, 2001: 27, 38, 46). It had a well-developed commercial economy, and its class structure, demography and land ownership were all favourable for modernisation (Curtin, 2000: 156–71; Totman, 2005: locs. 8028–56; Allinson and Anievas, 2010: 479–85). The Meiji reformers in Japan created a stable fusion of tradition (the emperor and Shinto) and modernity, and quickly put in place a modern rational state that could cultivate nationalism, pursue headlong industrialisation and resist foreign takeover (Jansen, 2000: chs. 11–12; Totman, 2005: locs. 8198–429).

Once started on the process of modernity, the Japanese leadership moved fast. They sent missions abroad, to observe how things were done in Western countries, and freely imported experts from abroad to help with all aspects of modernisation. The Japanese quickly learned that Western modernisation was a recent development, and the development gap therefore not as big or insurmountable as it might at first appear to be (Jansen, 2000: locs. 5364–438). During the period 1870–1913 Japan broadly caught up with rates of growth in Western Europe for population, GDP and GDP per capita (Maddison, 2001: 126). Japan's GDP tripled during this period, comparable to Germany and Russia, and better than Britain, France and Italy, and its GDP per capita doubled, slightly exceeding the rate in Western Europe (Maddison, 2001: 129, 206, 261, 264–5). Life expectancy in Japan also rose during this period, as it did in the other core countries, but not outside them (Topik and Wells, 2012: 602–3; Osterhammel, 2014: 170–2). Unlike other 'Third World' countries, Japan largely held onto its share of global manufacturing between 1800 and 1913 (Bairoch, 1982: 294, 296). During the same period, its per capita level of industrialisation (taking the United Kingdom in 1900 as 100) rose from 7 to 20, and between 1820 and 1913 Japan's share of the global GDP held fairly steady at around 3 per cent as it kept pace with the industrialising leading edge (Maddison, 2001: 127, 263). In terms of total manufacturing output, Japan ranked eighth by 1913, 20 per cent of the British level and 17 per cent of the German one (Bairoch, 1982: 284).

As the data show, Japan, despite being profoundly Non-Western, was clearly part of the nineteenth-century group of early modernisers. Like all those that followed Britain's lead, Japan reacted to the external pressure of the new configuration of modernity, and had the luck and the skill to both possess and create domestic conditions conducive to the pursuit of modernity. It also had models additional to Britain to draw on. It matched the later modernisers within the first round, and left behind those European countries that failed to respond effectively to the challenge of modernity. Japan generated its own distinctive fusion of culture and modernity, which became the template for the Asian developmental state. The idea that Japan was an integral part of the first round of modernisation is the foundation on which its position in international relations needs to be understood. On that basis, Japan quickly became the local model for modernisation in Northeast Asia, and was recognised as such by Chinese reformers (Koyama and Buzan, 2018).

Breaking the Myth of White Power

Like the other big industrialising powers of the time, Japan sought both great power status, and the accoutrement of empire that was the great power fashion during the nineteenth century. Its successful war against China in 1894–5 put Japan on the road to recognition as a great power, which was confirmed by the Anglo-Japanese Alliance of 1902, and reinforced by its defeat of Russia in 1904–5. The global significance of Japan's victory is little recognised now either by mainstream IR (Buzan and Lawson, 2014a), or by critics of Eurocentrism within IR, who focus more on Japan's own brutal colonialism than on its contributions to undermining the colonial system as a whole. But its importance was fully apparent to observers at the time. Alfred Zimmern, who became perhaps the leading academic in British interwar IR, was due to give a lecture to students at Oxford about Greek history, but instead began his talk by announcing that, 'I feel I must speak to you about the most important historical event that has happened, or is likely to happen, in our lifetime: the victory of a non-white people over a white people' (Vitalis,

2005: 168). This remark both illustrates the importance of race during the early twentieth century, which has been largely forgotten in IR, and underlines how Japan's military victories broke the myth of invincible white power that was established during the nineteenth century by relatively easy European and American victories over China, the Ottoman Empire and many parts of Africa. In so doing Japan gave both hope and a model to anti-colonial and modernisation movements around the world. A non-white people could indeed become a successful great power. The 'awakening' prompted by Japan's defeat of Russia was realised in nationalist revolutions against 'backwardness' in Iran, China and the Ottoman Empire, as well as in the emergence of a 'Pan-Asian' strand of thought whose leading voices, such as the Bengali poet Rabindranath Tagore, commanded large audiences (Collins, 2011). The Young Turks sought to make the Ottoman state the 'Japan of the Near East', praising its assertiveness and fashioning of a distinctly 'Asian modernity' (Aydin, 2007: 78). The early twentieth-century modernisers around the emperor in Ethiopia were called *Japanisers* (Westad, 2007: 253).

Racism

Japan's other contribution was, as the only non-white great power, to confront the other great powers with the issue of racism at the Versailles negotiations during 1919. This attempt to reform what was a key institution of colonial international society was mainly self-interested: it was about the standing of the Japanese, not about the principle of racism as such. As Naoko Shimazu (1998) argues, the issue of racial inequality threatened Japan's hard-won standing as a great power by casting it as inferior to white powers and placing it alongside the non-white subjects of the colonies. This humiliation was rubbed in by anti-Japanese and anti-Asian immigration policies in the United States, Canada and Australia. Without recognition of their equality as people, how could Japan avoid being seen as a second-class great power? As she argues, the consequence of this was that Japan was 'an arrogant, yet insecure power, dismissive of, yet sensitive to international opinion' (Shimazu, 1998: loc. 138). Even in these narrow terms, Japan failed to overcome the racism that underpinned Western-colonial order when its attempt to be accepted as racially equal was rejected by Western powers (Clark, 2007: 83–106). This humiliation resulted in an anti-Western turn in Japanese policy that laid the basis for geopolitical contestation during the interwar years (Zarakol, 2011: 166–73). Conrad Totman (2005: locs. 8960–82) makes the interesting link that this denial to Japan of an outlet for its surplus population fed into the justifications for empire building by Japan to solve this problem in a different way. Despite its self-interested approach, and its failure, Japan did at least mount the first significant challenge to the racial hierarchy of Western-colonial GIS.

The First World War

The 1914–18 war was the first major crisis of the modern era. There had been a couple of serious great power wars earlier (Prussia and Austria-Hungary in 1866, France and Germany in 1870, Russia and Japan in 1904–5), all short and decisive; and one substantial economic recession during the 1870s. But the First World War was far bigger and more destructive than any of these. Interestingly, the war was triggered neither by the ideological tensions generated by modernity, nor by any immediate economic crisis. Its main driver was the balance of power. Around the turn of the century, the global system had reached closure in the sense that all the territories and peoples who could easily be colonised, had been. As both Marxists and geopolitical analysts pointed out, this intensified imperialist competition by leaving redistribution as the only way for individual great powers to expand their empires (Lenin, [1916] 1975; Mackinder, [1904] 1996). Rising powers like Germany, Japan and the United States were all seeking their 'place in the sun', and could only do so at the expense of existing colonial powers.

The European power structure had polarised into two blocs, but both the Triple Alliance (Germany, Austria-Hungary and Italy) and the Triple Entente (Britain, France and Russia) were products of the balance of power, not ideological alignments. Japan was allied with Britain, the United States remained isolationist, detached from the European balance, and the Ottoman Empire allied itself to Germany at the outbreak of the war. The conventional story of the causes of the First World War emphasises inflexible alliances, industrial arms racing, rigid military planning and secret diplomacy. Britain and Germany had spent more than a decade before 1914 locked into an expensive naval arms race as German naval expansion threatened Britain's maritime supremacy (Marder, 1961). Germany worried about the pace of Russia's modernisation changing the military balance between them in the not too distant future. Given the alliance structure, Germany had to defeat Russia quickly, before the Russians could mobilise their large army, if it was to avoid a two-front war. Added into this potent brew was a sense of nationalist social Darwinism about the competition to be top nation, and the legitimacy and seeming practicality of war as an instrument of policy. The great power wars of the late nineteenth century did not offer any serious warnings about the cost and devastation of what was to come, and all the powers expected, and prepared for, another short, sharp war.[9]

One consequence of industrial modernity exposed by the First World War was to transform the pace, scale and cost of great power wars. The First World War was not only a war of production (who could produce the most troops and weapons), but also a war of technological innovation. New technologies created novel forms and conditions of warfare, rendering much traditional strategic and military wisdom obsolete. Although some aspects of these dynamics were present in nineteenth-century wars in North America and Asia, the First World War was the first major conflict in which submarines, aircraft, tanks, machine guns and chemical weapons played leading roles. On land, the new firepower created a protracted and bloody stalemate on the Western front, only broken by the development of combined arms modes of warfare, including tanks (C. S. Gray, 2012: chs. 6–7). At sea, submarines came close to winning the battle of the Atlantic for Germany.

In any event, what can be seen as the first all-out modern war between industrial great powers was a profoundly destructive and traumatic event. The First World War brought down empires, bankrupted great powers, fomented revolutions and produced unprecedented levels of death and destruction. To many it seemed that industrial war had outgrown the states that fought it, threatening to destroy European civilisation itself. The slogan of 'the war to end war' was a desperate attempt to conceptualise and justify a conflict whose duration, costs and casualties seemed to far outweigh any of the initial reasons for going to war. Casualties amounted to roughly 15 million, about four times the number for the French Revolutionary and Napoleonic Wars (Clodfelter, 2002), or double the per capita proportion given increases in population during the intervening century (Maddison, 2001: 241). The war was a catastrophe for all the states that engaged in it, apart from the United States and Japan. Although it was still better to have won than to have lost, two empires (Ottoman and Austro-Hungarian) were removed from the map, and a third (Russian) underwent a social revolution. Among the

---

[9] The American Civil War (1861–5), with its trenches, high casualties, long duration and exotic technologies such as ironclads and submarines, did offer some foreshadowing of the First World War, but its lessons were occluded by the more recent great power wars dominated by speed and mobility. The American Civil War mobilised half of all white male Americans, of which a third lost their lives (Belich, 2009: 331; see also C. S. Gray, 2012: ch. 4). The Taiping Rebellion in China (1850–71) also offered another unheeded warning. Between 1850 and 1873, something like 20–30 million people, and possibly as many as 66 million, died as a result of the protracted war, and China's population as a whole dropped from 410 million to 350 million (Phillips, 2011: 185; Fenby, 2013: 19; Schell and Delury, 2013: 45; Osterhammel, 2014: 120–1, 547–51).

'winners', Britain and France suffered huge casualties and economic forfeiture, and weakened the legitimacy of their empires by involving large numbers of colonial troops in the fighting.[10] The United States made big economic and political gains in return for relatively light casualties. But it turned its back on the international leadership role it had won, and returned to isolationism. Nevertheless, its engagement in the war marked the beginning of the end of the United States standing aloof from the responsibilities of balance of power and great power management. The main loser, Germany, underwent political humiliation and dislocation, territorial truncation, economic impoverishment and social upheaval.

The First World War generated three durable legacies for international relations. One was the Russian Revolution, which empowered the ideology of Socialism despite the apparent overriding of class identity by nationalism in most countries that participated in the war. The Russian Revolution embedded a new social organising principle within a powerful state, and thereby influenced the ideological make-up and conflictual alignment of the international system for the following seven decades. The second was the breakup of the Ottoman Empire and the creation of both a nationalist state in Turkey, and a politically fragmented Middle East subject to colonisation by the victorious British and French.

The third was the embedding of the *defence dilemma* mentioned above. The huge cost and carnage of the five years of intense fighting generated a fear of war and modern weapons that was strong enough to challenge the fear of defeat, and to bring the legitimacy and functionality of war into doubt. It was clear that no war would any longer resemble those that came before it, and that new weapons, particularly poison gas and aircraft, would make any new war hideously destructive. Foreshadowing the fear generated decades later by nuclear weapons, many Europeans began to fear that another war would destroy their civilisation. Germany was left angry, resentful and discriminated against, a legacy for which all would pay two decades later.

Yet other than these three big consequences, the First World War did little to change the basic structure of version 1.0 GIS, and on this basis Buzan and Lawson (2014a) classify it as a secondary benchmark date for IR. The power structure remained multipolar, and the roster of great powers did not change much. The war accelerated Britain's decline and heralded, but did not represent, a shift in power and leadership from

[10] Over one million members of the Indian Army fought for Britain in the First World War, as did a similar number of troops from the white dominions and nearly 150,000 troops from other colonies (Abernathy, 2000: 112).

Europe to North America. It made only marginal changes in the distribution of power, and almost none in social organising principles. Except for the Ottoman Empire, the periphery was mainly a passive object in the war: providing resources to metropolitan powers, and being possible spoils for the winners. The basic institutions of version 1.0 GIS, most notably colonialism/imperialism and human inequality, remained largely in place. The war accelerated the demise of dynasticism as a legitimate form of government, and strengthened nationalism. It weakened, but did not destroy, Europe's pretence to represent the 'standard of civilisation'. The success of both mass mobilisation for war as a model for Socialist governance, and of the revolution in Russia (offset by its failure in Germany), did boost the standing of Socialism. But it did little to resolve the tensions among Liberalism, Socialism and 'Scientific' Racism, merely pushing them to the fore to be resolved in later decades. Even the League of Nations (LN) was only an extension, albeit an ambitious one, of developments in standing IGOs started several decades earlier.

Conclusions

The century leading up to the First World War was profoundly transformational. Almost everything about international relations changed during this time, and most of the features of contemporary international relations originated during it. Powerful new ideational and material forces came into play, pushing aside older modes of production, destruction, power and governance. A closely interdependent world economy was established for the first time. But in conditions where racial discrimination and colonialism were still the order of the day, this took a starkly core–periphery form, reflected in the Western-colonial GIS. In a nutshell, a modern, global international system and society came into being for the first time.

At the close of this period, a huge war sent shockwaves through the system, leaving it weakened, but in most respects not fundamentally changed. There were two big shocks from this war. One was the unleashing into the arena of international politics of the contradictions inherent to the ideologies of progress. There had been a foreshadowing of this during the nineteenth century in the tensions between monarchical and republican governments, but the First World War set loose a three-way ideological rivalry between Socialism, Fascism and liberal democracy, with monarchies pushed to the background. The first round of the political struggle of modernity, between dynasticism and popular sovereignty, was largely over. The second round, defined by struggles within the ideologies of progress, was beginning. The other big shock was to the legitimacy and viability of great power war as an instrument of policy. The defence dilemma created a fear and unease about the resort to war that was not there before. This turn was to have large consequences both for interwar ir, and for the founding of IR as a recognised academic discipline.

2 International Relations up to 1919: Laying the Foundations

Introduction

Jeremy Bentham coined the term 'international' in 1789 to refer to the legal transactions between sovereigns. Yet the contemporary field, or discipline (opinion varies), of IR conventionally dates its origin to 1919, when its first university chairs and think tanks were set up, and 'International Relations' became one of several labels ('International Studies', 'International Politics', 'World Politics') for a specific field of study.[1] The question for this chapter is what happened during the 130 years that separate those two dates, and how does it relate both to the history unfolded in Chapter 1 and to the supposed formative moment in 1919? In what follows we divide the discussion into three main sections. The first covers that thinking and research within the core states that would today be labelled IR, but was not so called at the time. Taking the same perspective, the second section looks for this 'IR before IR' among voices in the periphery. The third section looks at the controversy over the 1919 founding date, and how that relates to what came before.

There are two main arguments underpinning this chapter. The first is that IR did not spring into being in 1919 as a specific reaction to the horrors of the First World War. E. H. Carr (1946: 1–2) carries some responsibility for propagating the 1919 foundation myth, asserting that before 1914, 'nowhere, whether in universities or in wider intellectual circles, was there organised study of current international affairs ... international politics were the business of diplomats'. Quincy Wright (1955: 26) is only slightly less wrong in his view that '[t]he discipline as a whole cannot be traced much back of World War I when the effort to organise the world through the League of Nations occasioned a more systematic examination of the contributory disciplines such as international law, international politics, international economics'. Our argument is

---

[1] This labelling debate is still ongoing today. For discussion of the meaning of these various labels see Albert and Buzan (2017: 900–1).

that the main foundations of IR, in terms of both its agenda of issues, and the theoretical approaches to the subject matter, were laid down during the several decades before 1919. The 'IR' that flourished during the nineteenth century covered a wide range of topics from Political Ideology, International Law and IGOs, and International Trade; through imperialism, colonial administration and Race Theory; to Geopolitics and War Studies. As Ole Wæver (1997: 8) astutely observes: 'Equipped with Ranke's essay on the great powers, Clausewitz, Bentham's works, maybe Cobden and finally Kant, it is difficult to be surprised by much in twentieth-century IR except for the form, the scientific wrapping, of much of it'.

The second argument is that nearly all of this IR thinking represented the view from the small group of industrialising countries that were the leading edge of modernity, and particularly Britain and the United States. The IR of the nineteenth century was very much a view of the world reflecting the concerns of the core powers, though we also note some early shoots of modern IR thinking outside the West. The trauma of the First World War facilitated a kind of reboot of this agenda in a narrowed, more focused way. The new IR that was founded in 1919 was obsessed with the trauma of the First World War and how to prevent such a catastrophe from happening again. It wanted to know the causes of that war, and it invested much hope that IGOs, particularly the LN, and arms control and disarmament, might be the solution. In short, the new IR devoted itself to the grand and noble problem of war and peace, and fixed its gaze firmly forward. In doing so, as we unfold in Chapter 4, it continued to marginalise and exclude the colonial world from IR.

IR before IR in the Core

This section sketches out the range and types of thinking during the nineteenth century that today would count as IR: a consciously ana-chronistic exercise of using present-day conceptions to structure the past. The writers we will cover did not generally see themselves as 'doing IR', though some sense of IR as a separate subject was beginning to emerge from the 1890s (Schmidt, 1998a: 70–121), and more clearly before and during the First World War (Olson and Groom, 1991: 47). Many of them were not academics in the contemporary sense, but some mix of public intellectuals and practitioners. Mostly they were doing other things (Economics, War Studies, Law, Political Economy, Political Science, Philosophy, Eugenics, etc.), which had spillovers into the inter-national realm. These bodies of thought contain elements of IR theory in

both the structural sense (how the world actually works) and the normative one (how it should work).

As we will show, these issues also apply to IR thinking in the periphery,
during both this period and subsequent ones. Our approach thus raises
questions we encountered in earlier work about what is IR, and more
particularly what counts as IR theory. We pointed to the

dichotomy between the hard positivist understanding of theory which dominates
in the US, and the softer reflectivist understandings of theory found more
widely in Europe (Wæver, 1998). Many Europeans use the term theory for anything that organizes a field systematically, structures questions and establishes
a coherent and rigorous set of interrelated concepts and categories. The dominant American tradition, however, more usually demands that theory be defined
in positivist terms: that it defines terms in operational form, and then sets out
and explains the relations between causes and effects. This type of theory should
contain – or be able to generate – testable hypotheses of a causal nature. These
differences are captured in Hollis and Smith's (1990) widely used distinction
between *understanding* and *explanation*. They have epistemological and ontological roots that transcend the crude Europe–US divide, and it is of course the
case that advocates of the 'European' position can be found in the US, and of the
'American' position in Europe. In both of these forms, theory is about abstracting
away from the facts of day-to-day events in an attempt to find patterns, and group
events together into sets and classes of things. (Acharya and Buzan, 2010: 3–4)

Stanley Hoffmann (1977: 52), invoking Raymond Aron, likens international relations theories to those of 'undetermined behavior' that 'can
do little more than define basic concepts, analyze basic configurations,
sketch out permanent features of a constant logic of behavior, in other
words make the field intelligible'. In a similar vein, we argued that
'Theory is therefore about simplifying reality. It starts from the suppos-
ition that in some quite fundamental sense, each event is *not* unique, but
can be clustered together with others that share some important similarities' (Acharya and Buzan, 2010: 4). We also argued that

Privileging one type of theory over others would largely defeat the purpose of our
enterprise, which is to make an initial probe to find 'what is out there' in Asian
thinking about IR. A broad approach to theory will give us a much better chance
of finding local produce than a narrow one, and those who take particular views
can apply their own filters to separate out what is of significance (or not) to them.
(Acharya and Buzan, 2007a: 291)

We also introduced the notion of what might be called 'pre-theory', or
'elements of thinking that do not necessarily add up to theory in their own
right, but which provide possible starting points for doing so' (Acharya
and Buzan, 2007a: 292; see also Acharya and Buzan, 2010).

This raises the relationship between theory and practice. Theory and practice are intimately linked, much more so in the early stages of the emergence of the discipline, than today. 'The realist regards political theory as a sort of codification of political practice', wrote Carr (1964: 12). For Hans Morgenthau (1948: 7), in the study of international politics one cannot 'divorce knowledge from action and ... pursue knowledge for its own sake'. Analysing the growth of the discipline in the United States, Hoffmann (1977: 47) notes: 'a concern for America's conduct in the world blended with a study of international relations ... To study United States foreign policy was to study the international system. To study the international system could not fail to bring one back to the role of United States'.

One does not have to be a Realist to recognise or accept that much contemporary IR is an abstraction from practice. As we noted in the Introduction, much of contemporary IR theory is just an abstraction from Western history. Theory often follows practice, that is, real-world developments. Hence ideas or worldviews of political leaders, whether in the West or the Rest, ought to count as thinking about IR, or even as IR theory, if they are powerful, impactful and sufficiently generalised or amenable to generalisation. Every policymaker, whether they admit to it or not, has a mental template within which they think and operate in the realm of policy. As Stephen Walt argues, 'there is an inescapable link between the abstract world of theory and the real world of policy'. 'Even policymakers who are contemptuous of "theory" must rely on their own (often unstated) ideas about how the world works', and to 'make sense of the blizzard of information that bombards us daily' (Walt, 1998: 29). It is with this understanding in mind that we approach what counts as IR thinking in both core and periphery, and in this and subsequent time periods.

In the space available we cannot make this a systematic and exhaustive survey. Our aim is to show the main outlines of the kinds of 'IR' thinking that were going on. The justification for doing this is threefold. First, we want to demonstrate convincingly that IR did not just spring from nowhere in 1919. It was not so much a new birth, as the repackaging and relaunching of things that had been going on for a long time. As William Olson and A. J. R. Groom (1991: 37–55) show, many of the main themes of modern IR from Realism and Liberalism, through peace movements, to revolutionism were all in play far back into the nineteenth century. Lucian Ashworth (2014: loc. 7) makes the nice differentiation of modern IR from earlier thinking: 'While the question of how to deal with strangers from other communities has been a constant throughout human history, it is only in recent centuries that the question of "foreign relations" (and especially imperialism and war) have become a matter of urgency for all sectors of society throughout the world'. Second, we want to show how deeply this emergent modern IR was a view from the core, drawing a sharp distinction between IR as relations between the 'civilised' states within international society on the one hand, and colonial relations between 'civilised' states and 'barbarian' and 'savage' peoples and societies on the other. Third, we want to set up for the argument in later chapters that the 'new' IR of post-1919 became relatively narrow in its focus. It was shaped by the impact of the First World War into an obsession with the core's problems of war and peace, and the military dynamics of industrial arms racing, among the great powers.

In getting to grips with this extensive literature of 'IR before IR' it is helpful to try to appreciate the context of the times. The extremely uneven development of industrial modernity, first in Britain, and then in a handful of other Western states and Japan, opened a huge gap in power and development between these core states and the rest. This gap was difficult to close, and the huge concentration of wealth and power in a small core quickly enabled it to dominate the global periphery. The handful of societies at the leading edge of modernity experienced a kind of euphoria at their new-found ability to exploit and overcome nature, and open up seemingly limitless resources of wealth and power. They saw themselves as representing the vanguard of both civilisation and progress. However reprehensible it may seem to us now, it is not surprising that this huge gap between the 'civilised' (mainly white) and the 'barbarian' and 'savage' (all yellow, brown or black) took on powerful racial overtones.[2] It was both easy and politically potent to link 'civilisation' and whiteness, and in the process justify the civilising mission and empire over the 'lesser breeds'.

For those thinking about international relations at the time, this huge development and power gap brought two issues into focus: (1) the problem of how the leading edge great powers should relate to each other in an era of both industrial modernity and rising interdependence and imperial competition; and (2) the problem of how the states and societies of the leading edge should relate to the backward peoples of the 'lesser races'. Options here ranged from extermination, through imperial exploitation, to some form of imperial tutelage in the arts of civilisation. As David Long and Brian Schmidt (2005) argue, the key debate for early IR was about the tension between imperialism and internationalism. That this formative era of IR has largely disappeared from the awareness

---

[2] Japan, also an early moderniser, was always a problem for this racist formulation. See Koyama and Buzan (2018).

of contemporary IR is partly due to the 1919 foundation myth, but also to the blatant racism inherent to much of the pre-1914 – and indeed the pre-1939 – literature. That is why the work of IR's key foundational thinkers, such as Paul S. Reinsch, remains largely unknown (Schmidt, 2005: 45–6; L. Ashworth, 2014: 107–9). To see the massive continuities between the concerns of nineteenth-century IR and the contemporary discipline, it is necessary both to break through the 1919 boundary, and to confront the fact that racism and the 'standard of civilisation' were foundational to IR and, although largely forgotten or repressed, remain influential still (Vitalis, 2005).

The obvious place to start looking at IR before IR are the four ideologies of progress discussed in the previous chapter: Liberalism, Socialism, nationalism and 'Scientific' Racism. While 'Scientific' Racism has fallen out of fashion as an explicit mainstream approach to IR, implicit racism has by no means disappeared from relations between North and South. Liberalism, Socialism and nationalism are still very much explicit parts of IR's normative and structural discourses. All four of these ideologies contained major strands of modern IR thinking, both structural and normative, and these strands were often woven together in various ways around the themes of imperialism and social Darwinism that dominated much nineteenth-century thinking about world politics. These four ideologies were complex mixtures. In part they were drivers of modernity that shaped the way things were understood, and in part they were responses to modernity, attempts to frame a new reality that was already emerging. This complex process took place alongside and in conjunction with the rise of public opinion and mass media as social and political forces during the later decades of the nineteenth century (Buzan and Lawson, 2015a). In relation to the emergence of IR thinking, we can group these ideologies into two pairs: Liberalism and Socialism were in many ways cosmopolitan, homogenising responses to the intensely globalising world that was happening during the nineteenth century. Nationalism and 'Scientific' Racism were parochial, differentiating responses to that same globalisation. But they were also drivers of, and responses to, the parallel intensification of social and political integration that was going on in the making of modern rational states.

Liberalism and Socialism

As Fred Halliday (1999: 73–5) notes: 'In many ways the internationalist perspective of Marx and Engels differed little from that of other Liberals of the first half of the nineteenth century'. Both groups of thinkers were highly aware of the rapid and unprecedented creation of a global market economy that was happening around them, and both understood this as a cosmopolitanising, globalising process. Summing all of this up at the end of this period, Arthur Greenwood (1916: 77) noted how the creation of a global economy had replaced the relatively self-contained economies of premodern times, generating systemic tension between free trade and protectionism, and pointing to the need for 'a political organization which shall control the cosmopolitan economic activity that has grown in modern times'. Halliday (1999: 80) argues that this cosmopolitan outlook was similar to that captured by 'interdependence' and 'globalisation' in the IR debates of the 1970s and 1980s. Contemporary globalisation, although mainly now liberal in perspective, also sees capitalism as a homogenising force on a global scale, increasingly penetrating, entangling and marginalising the state.[3]

Halliday (1999: 164–72) notes the generally cosmopolitan outlook of nineteenth-century Liberals, and their desire to replace dynasticism with popular sovereignty as a cure for war and mercantilism. The rise of Liberal understandings of economics and, in particular, the idea that both prosperity and peace arose from pursuing free trade, reinforced the idea that such political reforms within states would also beneficially transform relations between them. At some risk of oversimplification, the IR content of nineteenth-century Liberalism can be summed up as synergetic combination of democratic peace (states under popular sovereignty would be much less inclined to go to war than monarchies) and free trade (where the operation of open global markets would reduce incentives to seize territory for economic reasons). These ideas were embodied in both a string of classic Liberal writings and direct political activism, and it is no accident that most of this was concentrated in Britain, then the country by far the most advanced down the road to industrial modernity. A group of writers stretching from Adam Smith (1776), through David Ricardo (1817), to J. S. Mill (1848) both laid the foundations for the modern discipline of Economics and set out a Liberal view of international relations. Their ideas included individualism and the 'invisible hand', utilitarianism, the division of labour, comparative advantage and a relatively open operation of markets both within and between states. Political activists such as Richard Cobden and John Bright campaigned against mercantilist policies such as the Corn Laws in Britain (getting them repealed in 1846) and in favour of free trade internationally (L. Ashworth, 2014: 75–9). The nineteenth-century Liberal

---

[3] For an excellent review of the impact of the revolutions of modernity and the sense of a global transformation on a wide range of nineteenth-century writers, see Deudney (2007: chs. 7–8).

theory of international relations was thus that popular sovereignty plus free trade would go a long way towards eliminating the scourge of war from world politics. This view certainly had strong cosmopolitan and globalising elements, but it could also be compatible with the state and, up to a point, nationalism.

If anything, the Socialist embrace of cosmopolitan globalisation was even stronger, and that position goes some way towards explaining why early Marxism is generally thought to be weak on IR as now understood. Andrew Linklater (2001: 131–9) gives an insightful explanation of why this was so. In his account, Karl Marx and his followers gave primacy of place to industrial capitalism and the new dynamic of class that it was generating, and this is why their scheme of things discounted, and pushed to the margins, both the state and nationalism. They saw capitalism as an immensely powerful cosmopolitanising and globalising force, linking all the people of the world together far more deeply and intimately than ever before. Within that framing, traditional and segmenting elements like the state and nationalism could only be transitory and relatively unimportant. The overriding, homogenising force of industrial capitalism would soon incorporate and integrate everyone, and impose on all the overriding logic of class conflict that was intrinsic to the Marxian understanding of capitalism.

While Marxian thinking turned out to be wrong about the importance of the state and nationalism, and therefore diverged from the mainstream of IR thinking, it can still be seen as an early and in some ways insightful version of what would now be called a globalisation understanding of IR. Vladimir Lenin ([1916] 1975) explained imperialism as a kind of last gasp of nationalism before it would give way to a more globalised world. He famously interpreted the dynamics of capitalism as leading to competition to divide and then re-divide the territories, peoples, resources and markets of the world. He linked this essentially class dynamic to nationalism and the state, saw it as the 'highest stage of capitalism' (i.e. the last), called this *imperialism*, and used it to explain the First World War. This, along with Nikolai Bukharin's (1916) idea of a fusion of capital and the state, was about as close as early Marxism got to linking its understanding of globalisation to the more conventional IR analyses of inter-state power politics.

While there were some striking similarities in the Liberal and Socialist views of international relations, there was little to choose between them in terms of their attitude to relations between 'civilised' and 'barbarian'. The similarity of their attitudes confirms how widespread was the profoundly hierarchical attitude on racial and cultural grounds to 'inferior' peoples within colonial international society (J. M. Hobson, 2012: ch. 2).

Compare the following texts, the first from the Liberal thinker J. S. Mill and the second from Marx and Engels' *Manifesto of the Communist Party*:

To suppose that the same international customs, and the same rules of international morality, can obtain between one civilized nation and another, and between civilized nations and barbarians, is a grave error, and one which no statesman can fall into, however it may be with those, who from a safe and unresponsible position, criticize statesmen.

Among the many reasons why the same rules cannot be applicable to situations so different, the two following are among the most important. In the first place, the rules of ordinary international morality imply reciprocity. But barbarians will not reciprocate. They cannot be depended on for observing any rules. Their minds are not capable of so great an effort, nor their will sufficiently under the influence of distant motives. In the next place, nations which are still barbarous have not got beyond the period during which it is likely to be for their benefit that they should be conquered and held in subjection by foreigners. Independence and nationality, so essential to the due growth and development of a people further advanced in improvement, are generally impediments to theirs. The sacred duties which civilized nations owe to the independence and nationality of each other are not binding towards those to whom nationality and independence are either a certain evil, or, at best, a questionable good.

To characterize any conduct whatever towards a barbarous people as a violation of the law of nations, only shows that he who so speaks has never considered the subject. A violation of great principles of morality it may easily be, but barbarians have no rights as a nation, except a right to such treatment as may, at the earliest possible period, fit them for becoming one. The only moral laws for the relation between a civilized and a barbarous government are the universal rules of morality between man and man. (Mill, 1874: vol. 3, 252–3)

It was in this way that Liberal thinkers could square their commitment to individualism with a racist perspective on international relations and empire.

Marxian thinking at this time was similarly West-centric, seeing industrial modernity and capitalism as profoundly progressive forces. Notwithstanding its revolutionary vocation, it was a view of the world from a dominant Western core, looking at a passive 'barbaric' periphery.

First, the lower and lower prices of industrial products brought about by machine labor totally destroyed, in all countries of the world, the old system of manufacture or industry based upon hand labor. In this way, all semi-barbarian countries, which had hitherto been more or less strangers to historical development, and whose industry had been based on manufacture, were violently forced out of their isolation. They bought the cheaper commodities of the English and allowed their own manufacturing workers to be ruined. Countries which had known no progress for thousands of years – for example, India – were thoroughly revolutionized, and even China is now on the way to a revolution. We have come to the point where a new machine invented in England deprives millions of Chinese workers of their livelihood within a year's time. In this way, big industry has brought all the people of the Earth into contact with each other, has merged all local markets into one world market, has spread civilization and progress everywhere and has thus ensured that whatever happens in civilized countries will have repercussions in all other countries. (Marx and Engels, [1848] 2010: 45)

Like the Liberals, Marx and Engels saw the 'Asiatic mode of production', and premodern societies generally, as backward and static. Maxine Molyneux and Fred Halliday (1984: 18) note that Marx 'stressed the progressive character of capitalist development in expanding the productive forces of societies in Asia and Africa'. Charles Barone (1985: 12–13) argues that Marx saw the impact of imperialism as being both exploitative, in the way that capitalism was by its nature exploitative everywhere, but also progressive, and in some ways a necessary and positive force for development. Although the imperialists occupied places such as India for their own advantage, they could not help but tear down premodern political and social structures and plant the seeds of modernity. While revolution needed to be generated from within in the advanced industrial societies, it had to be imposed from above on premodern ones, which otherwise would not generate revolutionary potential.

Just how widespread such sentiments were within Western societies during the middle and late nineteenth century is underlined by Brian Schmidt's (1998a: 125) description of attitudes at meetings of the American Political Science Association during the decade before the First World War:

The discussion of the colonized regions of the globe, often described in language that most would today find offensive and inappropriate, fell outside the domain set by the early-twentieth-century discourse about the relations among sovereign states. Most political scientists believed that the colonized regions – the 'dark' places, the 'uncivilized', the 'backward' or 'barbaric' areas of the world – did not belong to the society of states. Rather than being viewed as constituent members of international society, the colonized regions were seen as falling outside of the society of nations and as places plagued by internal anarchy.

The prevalence of such views points strongly to the influence of the other two ideologies of progress, nationalism and 'Scientific' Racism.

Nationalism and 'Scientific' Racism

In contrast to the Liberal and Socialist imperatives to homogenise this globalising world according to their cosmopolitan readings of modernity, the imperative of nationalism and 'Scientific' Racism was to divide and differentiate the world. Nationalism and 'Scientific' Racism grew from quite different roots, but nonetheless shared some similarities, and could generate strong synergies. As described in Chapter 1, nationalism was about creating identity groups based on shared ethnicity, culture, language and history; while 'Scientific' Racism grew up later under the influence of biology, scientific classifications and the grossly unequal encounters between Europeans and the peoples of Africa and Asia during the late nineteenth century. Mass emigration from Britain to Australia, Canada, New Zealand and South Africa created states ruled by white elites who saw themselves as inherently superior to indigenous peoples, and who helped to construct racism as a primary institution of colonial international society. Yet nationalism had an ethnic component based on a similar biological logic to that of 'Scientific' Racism, and both were vulnerable to the influence of social Darwinism's 'survival of the fittest' way of thinking. Both offered ways of framing international relations that became increasingly influential as the nineteenth century wore on. The economic side of nationalism was represented by Friedrich List, who argued the need for states and peoples to protect their own process of industrialisation, which would otherwise be overwhelmed by those countries already leading the way towards industrialism and modern civilisation (L. Ashworth, 2014: 79–84).

There were many variations within both nationalist and Racist camps, ranging across a spectrum from essentialist zero-sum conflict on one end, through hierarchical orders, to egalitarian orders on the other. Nationalism was perhaps somewhat more inclined towards egalitarian orders on the grounds that its use as a foundation for political legitimacy associated it with the legal and sovereign equality of states. Within this there was room for some hierarchy between big and small nationalities paralleling that between great powers and ordinary states. But once infected with social Darwinism, nationalism, both ethno (e.g. Aryan) and civic (e.g. US), could and did become much more hierarchical. 'Survival of the fittest' logic opened the door to the domination and expropriation of weaker peoples by stronger ones. As F. F. Urquhart (1916: 40, 52, 60) notes, nationalism was a great disturber of international peace: 'Nationalities have proved as self-assertive and as acquisitive as the old kings'. 'Scientific' Racism was perhaps the more inclined towards hierarchical relations, and often lent itself to racial hierarchies with whites at the top and blacks at the bottom. At its extreme, it easily justified the domination or extermination of weaker peoples by stronger ones, though races could also be constructed as different-but-equal. Extreme ethno-nationalism of the kind that led to thinking about Aryans, Anglo-Saxons, Latins and Slavs within the general category of white/European could be thought of as a more finely subdivided form of 'Scientific' Racism.

As already noted, a great deal of IR's early thinking was mediated by the politics of race (Schmidt, 1998a: 125; Vitalis, 2005, 2010; Bell, 2013; J. M. Hobson, 2012). Benjamin de Carvalho, Halvard Leira and John Hobson (2011: 750–1) show how even the thinking of key figures generally thought of as Liberal, most notably Woodrow Wilson (see also Vitalis, 2005: 169), was also infused with racism. Robert Vitalis (2005: 161) argues that, in IR before the First World War, 'races *and* states were the discipline-in-formation's most important twin units of analysis'. He highlights how the institutional development of IR reflected this idea of racialism, showing how 'American territorial expansion led after 1900 to a wave of new courses, publications, popular and scholarly journals', which is where the 'real institutional origins of IR can be found', and not in the 1920s or 1940s as conventional wisdom dictates (Vitalis, 2005: 166). For Vitalis (2000: 333), there is a 'norm against noticing' IR's real history.

Especially in their hierarchical forms, both nationalism and race underpinned justifications for war and imperialism, creating a distinct and powerful counterpoint to the cosmopolitan globalism of Liberals and Socialists. Thinkers about race and world politics were divided on the question of imperialism. Some thought of it as a good way to elevate the backward races. Others thought of it as a good way to keep the coloured peoples down, and advance the cause of white supremacy. Yet others opposed imperialism either as an unnecessary interference in the natural development of other races, or as a threat to the purity of the white race through miscegenation or immigration (J. M. Hobson, 2010: 29–30; 2012). Its proponents therefore differed in terms of the levels of agency accorded to the East. Some 'defensive racists' such as Herbert Spencer and William Graham Sumner were anti-imperialist as they believed that imperialism would hinder the spontaneous development of the East. Others such as James Blair and David Starr were anti-imperialist not because they thought the East could develop independently, but because the East could not develop at all because of their racial inferiority, and the civilising mission was hence a futile exercise. Further, writers such as Charles Pearson and Lothrop Stoddard were concerned more with protecting the whites from the barbaric 'yellow peril', in the process according a very high level of agency to the East, albeit a 'regressive' and 'predatory' agency (J. M. Hobson, 2012: 8). Another strand of anti-imperialist racism was the idea that the East could develop on its own, but would follow the path of development and progress already delineated by the West. The East had 'derivative agency' (J. M. Hobson, 2012: 6), which would be suppressed by Western imperialism, thus making it undesirable. It is no surprise that one of the first IR journals, founded in 1910, was called the *Journal of Race Development*.

Even the now familiar tension between economic imperatives favouring migration, and social and political reactions against it, was established during the nineteenth century:

The immigrant labourer was accustomed to living on a lower scale of living. He was willing to accept far lower wages than the white labourer. He was outside the trade unions. He was usually of the labouring class, which is the most backward of all, and the one least susceptible of being assimilated into a civilization on European lines. He became, therefore, a grave menace to the white labouring class which saw their prospects of stable employment flitted away by strangers, for no other reason than they could live at a far lower standard, and could afford to accept a far lower wage. Further, the coolie labourer was accompanied or followed by the trader, and the Asiatic trader not only usually worked for longer hours, but was satisfied with smaller profits than the white trader. He therefore tended to get the custom not only of his own fellows, but of the white customer also. Thus the white trader as well as the white labourer suffered. (Kerr, 1916: 175)

But these four ideologies were by no means the only IR thinking going on during the nineteenth century. Woven through and alongside them were several other strands: Realism, Geopolitics, War and Strategic Studies, colonial administration and imperialism, and International Law and IGOs.

Realism

Realism has always made a fetish of its long intellectual pedigree going back as far as Thucydides. In that sense, Realist thinkers definitely do not see themselves as starting in 1919. That said, however, while they do remember Hobbes and Machiavelli as forbears, they tend to forget that part of their roots that lie in the starker, nineteenth-century German Realism of Heinrich von Treitschke (1899–1900) and his student Friedrich Meinecke (1908) (Wæver, 1997: 8). Treitschke's view of power politics as the basic reality of international relations was strongly tinged by social Darwinism and racism. It glorified war as a vocation of the nation, and was fully committed to the German struggle against the British Empire. Meinecke was likewise tinged with racism and committed to German expansionism.[4] Despite its neglect by IR, the German tradition of *machtpolitik* was, as noted by Michael Williams (2005), a potent source

---

[4] For a short summary of German Realism, see Deudney (2007: 70–3). For a summary of the impact of Darwinism on politics, see Carr (1946: 46–50).

for twentieth-century Realist thinking, particularly as this was carried via Treitschke to other writers influential in IR: Friedrich Nietzsche, Max Weber and Morgenthau.[5]

Geopolitics

Geopolitics is quite close to Realism in its focus on power politics, yet distinct from it in its specifically geographical drivers. The term *geopolitics* was coined in 1899 to capture an emerging body of thought that sought to marry geography and politics, and to look at world history as being driven by grand simplifications linking geographical positioning with world power. The use of massive and simple structural determinants gave Geopolitics as a theory of IR some of the same attraction that Neorealism was to enjoy eight decades later. Geopolitics also has other parallels with the attractions of Neorealism, not least its holistic view of the world as a single system. Since the new imperialism had, by the 1890s, actually made the world into a single system, all parts of which were to some significant degree known and connected, this was a timely and powerful perspective. Classical Geopolitics was very much focused on great power rivalry, also therefore closely linked to prevailing fashions of the day for social Darwinistic nationalism, imperialism and the assumption of the superiority of the white race and Western civilisation over all other peoples and cultures. Geopolitical thinkers in this period generally did not see international anarchy as a problem, but merely as an environment that required national strength if nations were to survive and grow (L. Ashworth, 2014: 106–7). It was, like most other perspectives on IR from this period, a view from the core.

Two of the key late nineteenth-century figures in Geopolitics were the German writer Friedrich Ratzel and the British Halford Mackinder (L. Ashworth, 2014: 98–102), though in both cases their work was to be more politically influential in the interwar years than in the run-up to the First World War. Ratzel's (1901) main contribution was the idea of *Lebensraum* (living space) attached to an organic concept of the nation (Ó Tuathail, 1998: 4). His work was particularly related to Germany, and was compatible with the thinking of German Realists. But it had wider relevance in a social Darwinist world of both competing imperial great powers, and nations and races competing for control of territory, and was not too concerned with the rights of the indigenous inhabitants.

---

[5] Morgenthau (1967) mentions neither Treitschke nor Meinecke. Waltz (1979) gives a passing mention to Meinecke. Mearsheimer (2001) mentions neither. Among the leading Realist texts, only Carr (1946: 14–15, 49, 88–9) gives both fair mention. Both Donnelly (2000) and Michael Williams (2005) give only passing references to Meinecke.

Mackinder's ([1904] 1996) work, particularly his idea of the 'heart-land', or 'pivot', was more globally cast, but aimed at informing the strategy of the British Empire (Ó Tuathail, 1998: 4, 15–18). Mackinder's (1919: 194) famous dictum was that:

Who rules East Europe commands the Heartland;
Who rules the Heartland commands the World Island;
Who rules the World Island commands the World.

This idea put Russia, and potentially Germany, at the centre of world power. Mackinder's holistic view gave him the sense that, by the late nineteenth century, the international system was moving towards terri-torial and political closure, with no 'unclaimed' spaces remaining. This idea was later taken up by Lenin ([1916] 1975) as an explanation for imperialism and the necessary competition over re-division of territory, as a crisis phase for capitalism. Mackinder displayed a racist-Realist theory that was offensive-imperialist in nature, blending Geopolitics and Eugenics. In the words of James Tyner (1999: 58): 'The confluence of geopolitics and eugenics foreshadowed a dangerous world, in which racial proximity and territorial expansion would lead to racial and social degeneration, with the potential for race wars'. Mackinder was fearful of a period of confrontation between the West and East after 1900, because the entire world had already been colonised and there was nothing more the Western powers could do to expand their territory and prevent the rise of the East (J. M. Hobson, 2012: 124–30).

Another British Geopolitical writer, J. R. Seeley (1883), was influen-tial in promoting the idea of 'Greater Britain' (Bell, 2007). Again, this had close links to empire and great power competition. 'Greater Britain' was a blend of Geopolitics (achieving critical mass in relation to rising continental-scale powers such as the United States and Russia); racism/ nationalism (consolidating the Anglo-Saxon race); and empire (consoli-dating the British Empire into some tighter form of polity). Whatever might be said about their racism and imperialism, the Geopolitical thinkers of the late nineteenth century were not afraid to think big. They were, however, almost entirely concerned with the great power politics of the core, and hardly at all with the periphery other than as an object of great power expropriation and rivalry.

War and Strategic Studies

Some argue that classical Geopolitics was the origin of what, after 1945, became Strategic Studies within IR (Olson and Onuf, 1985: 12–13). But while there are certainly overlaps, perhaps most notably Alfred Thayer Mahan (1890), the study of war and strategy were independently alive and well before and alongside Geopolitics. Despite the absence of world wars during the nineteenth century, this was nevertheless a time when some enduring classics in the study of war and strategy were written. As Grant (1916: 17–32) observed, these times were not necessarily perceived as particularly peaceful by those living within them. Despite the 40 years of peace after the 1870 Franco-Prussian war, Europe was marked by arms competitions on land and at sea, by colonial rivalries abroad, and, closer to home, by rivalries in the Balkans. These current events were not, however, the main focus of these classics, all of which looked back to the previous century, and all of which were written by professional military officers. Carl von Clausewitz's *On War* (1832) and Antoine-Henri Jomini's *The Art of War* ([1838] 1854) looked mainly to the Napoleonic Wars (see C. S. Gray, 2012: ch. 2). While Clausewitz wrote before the revolution in military technology had kicked in, he did capture the new political elements of warfare brought in by the French Revolution and nationalism, and also the ends–means rationality of modernity (Booth, 1975: 23–9). Mahan's *The Influence of Sea Power upon History, 1660–1783* (1890) was a study taken from Britain's maritime dominance in the age of sail. This backward-looking approach did not much register the massive changes in military technology taking place during the nineteenth century, but this weakness did not prevent all of them from having some timeless qualities.

Mahan's work contained elements of Geopolitics, both in its relating of maritime power to land power, and in its acceptance of social Darwinist assumptions (Ó Tuathail, 1998: 4, 18; L. Ashworth, 2014: 103–5). He exhorted the building of sea power, which included gaining control over the seas through building a strong navy and strategic defence capabilities, and control over strategic chokepoints in various parts of the world. One aim was to prevent the East from gaining any sort of foothold. Mahan, like Mackinder, worried about the rise of global interdependence or 'the closing of the world' (J. M. Hobson, 2012: 125), as it served to reduce the distance between the West and the East. He advocated the building of a strong US base in Hawaii to contain the rise of China. In John Hobson's (2012: 124–30) view, the solutions offered by Mackinder and Mahan were to nip the rise of the East in the bud through aggressive imperialist-racist projects.

By the turn of the century, only a few people had correctly foreseen what the technological revolution was doing to military capability. The most notable of these thinkers were Ivan Bloch (1898) and Norman Angell (1909). Bloch calculated in detail (six volumes!) the effects of increased firepower, and argued that an all-out war could not be won, and might well destroy the societies undertaking it (Pearton, 1982: 137–9). He anticipated the defence dilemma, and the First World War came close to proving his point. Angell argued an early version of the contemporary interdependence thesis, that under modern conditions, war no longer served the economic interests of society. For industrial societies, war destroyed more wealth than it created because it disrupted the global trade on which wealth and power had come to depend. These arguments broadly supported the Liberal line of interdependence. No longer could states gain in wealth by seizing territory and resources from each other as they had done during the seventeenth and eighteenth centuries (de Wilde, 1991: 61–90; Howard, 1981: 70–1; L. Ashworth, 2014: 116–19). Again, and not surprisingly, these theorists of war and strategy focused on relations between the core great powers.

Imperialism and Colonial Administration

The new imperialism of the West and Japan in Africa and Asia during the late nineteenth century was a major background fact for IR thinking during this period. As is already clear from the discussion so far, empire and imperialism infused much of the nineteenth-century IR debate, whether the perspective be from Liberalism, Socialism, nationalism, 'Scientific' Racism, Realism or Geopolitics. Olson and Groom (1991: 47) suggest that the 'discipline of international relations had its real beginnings in studies of imperialism'. Long and Schmidt (2005: 1–15) concur, though they argue that it was the twin concepts of imperialism and internationalism, and the debate around them, that defined the discourse of early IR. As John Hobson (2010: 28) argues, many leading Liberal intellectuals, including J. S. Mill, Richard Cobden, Norman Angell and J. A. Hobson, supported imperialism on the grounds of the necessity for the West to bring backward cultures up to the 'standard of civilisation'. Some Liberals opposed empire on the grounds of its contradiction with free trade (e.g. Bell, 1859). The best known of these is J. A. Hobson's (1902) Liberal critique of imperialism as both immoral and economically inefficient. J. A. Hobson rejected imperialism on functional rather than moral grounds, as a burden on the West and as something that is ultimately destined to fail. He also distinguished between 'sane' and 'insane' imperialism, and was willing to support the former (J. M. Hobson, 2012). Divided views could be found in most perspectives. 'Scientific' Racism, with its social Darwinist hierarchy of races, was without doubt one of the key legitimising props for imperialism. But as John Hobson (2012: ch. 4) argues, there was also a strong anti-imperialist strand in racist thinking that wanted to avoid both 'polluting' contact between the races, and wars between whites over imperial competition. Socialists were likewise of two minds about imperialism, seeing it as both progressive and exploitative. Empires and imperial competition were perhaps the major fact with which nineteenth-century IR writers had to deal: how to explain it, whether to oppose or support it, and how empires should best be managed?

As Buzan (2014: 153–6) has argued, there is a good case for seeing the post-1945 concern with development, and its emergence as an institution of GIS, as being the direct successor to the institution of imperialism/colonialism that collapsed after the Second World War. During the nineteenth century, debate about this was one of the major themes of IR thinking, and took place under the heading of *colonial administration*. Questions about how metropolitan powers should relate to colonial peoples, whether native or settlers, preceded the nineteenth century. But the nineteenth century saw a major shift in how imperialism was practised. During this period, most European powers assumed direct responsibility for their colonies from the Chartered Companies that had often served as the vanguard of European imperialism. As noted above, IR thinkers of the late nineteenth century made a sharp distinction between relations among 'civilised' states and those between such states and 'barbaric' peoples. From the 1890s this distinction was reflected in a burgeoning literature on colonial administration (Schmidt, 1998a: 136–40). At the first ever meeting of the American Political Science Association in 1904, 'Colonial Administration' was designated as one of the five fundamental branches of Politics (Vitalis, 2010).

An insight into the mind-set on this issue (and the language in which it was described!) can be found in P. H. Kerr's (1916) piece on 'Political Relations between Advanced and Backward Peoples'. Kerr was basically arguing for the necessity of colonial rule to deal with the problems created by encounters between peoples at very different levels of development. His perspective – illustrating the cross-currents of the time that seem alien now – was a blend of Liberal imperialism and 'Scientific' Racism, advocating the necessity of colonial administration, plus a form of apartheid to keep the races from mixing (Kerr, 1916: 174–9).

[D]eplorable results have invariably followed the appearance of the civilized trader among backward peoples … The individuals who engaged in trade entered upon it with no idea of helping the backward races but with the perfectly legitimate object of making profit out of the normal and materially beneficial process of commercial exchange … [It is a] general rule … that where there is a sufficient difference between the levels of civilization of two peoples, the more civilized power will be driven in the interests of justice and humanity to step in and regulate, at any rate for a time, the effects of contact between the two … The more advanced people having intervened in the interests of civilization, liberty, and progress, must conduct the government in order to promote those same ends. (Kerr, 1916: 144–5, 163, 166)

As with most other IR perspectives of the time, Kerr's was very much a view from the core. They fitted with the 'standard of civilisation' outlook of the day identified by Gong (1984: 24–53, 64–93), who notes how the Europeans' need for access (trade, proselytising, travel) was what drove the functional aspects of the 'standard of civilisation' (to protect life, liberty and property by exchanging reciprocal obligations in law). Where the locals could not or would not provide these, that triggered European demands for extraterritoriality and unequal relations (Gong, 1984: 24–53).

While this line of IR thinking did concern the periphery, it did so very much from a core perspective, and in a way that separated the study of relations among 'civilised' states from relations between 'civilised' and 'barbaric' ones.

International Law, Intergovernmental Organisations and International Society

During the late nineteenth century International Law was a major strand, and antecedent, of IR thinking (Schmidt, 1998a: 45). Ideas about the 'law of nations' had been around in Europe for several centuries, but under the pressure of a great increase in transportation and trade, the nineteenth century saw a shift away from the older mode of natural law, towards positive law (i.e. laws agreed by states, and guided by the idea that states were only bound by what they had agreed to). Henry Wheaton's (1866) influential *Elements of International Law* was first published in 1836. The development of positive international law went hand in hand with the spread of IGOs discussed in Chapter 1, with each feeding into the other. What might count as the pioneering text on IGOs (Reinsch, 1911) was written well before the First World War (Schmidt, 1998a: 118). If states still wanted to go to war, they certainly could. But if they wanted to pursue commerce and peace, then an ever-denser sphere of international rules and regulations over commerce, transportation and communications helped to coordinate inter-state behaviour (Koskenniemi, 2001; Davies, 2013). The rise of positive international law reflected the increasing dominance of Europe, for positive law was European law. The inclination within the natural law tradition to treat (most) non-Europeans as equals was replaced by an association of positive law with the hierarchy provided by the 'standard of civilisation'

(Gong, 1984: 5–32). In this sense, positive law contained a dual purpose: ordering conduct among sovereign equals in the core, and regulating 'difference' between core and periphery globally (Shilliam, 2013). In their encounters with European powers from the middle of the nineteenth century both China and Japan turned to Western writings on International Law and Diplomacy to try to work out how best to respond to the domineering powers that had arrived on their doorstep (Suzuki, 2009: 69–85; Howland, 2016).

International Law had by 1906 become a distinct enough subject for there to be an American Society of International Law, and the *American Journal of International Law*. The concerns of International Law were centred around the codification of customary law, arbitration, establishing international courts of justice and institutionalising multilateral diplomacy (Schmidt, 1998a: 110). By the late nineteenth century, international law was part of the practice of, as well as the thinking about, international relations.

International law easily led to the idea of international society, because if there was international law, then that must reflect the existence of an international society because law, especially positive law, cannot exist outside society. Schmidt (1998a: 124) argues that by the late nineteenth century American legal and political thinking about IR had clearly identified the existence of an international society among 'civilised' states, and captured this in the term *internationalism*. Elsewhere, the German historian A. H. L. Heeren's (1834) discussion of states systems set up the idea of international society picked up later by thinkers in the ES tradition (Keene, 2002; Little, 2008), and the term international society had been intrinsic to discussions of international law well back into the nineteenth century (Schwarzenberger, 1951). Torbjørn Knutsen (2016: 2) argues, indeed, that James Lorimer (1877, 1884) pretty much invented the concept of 'anarchical society', but that his pioneering work has been forgotten. This society of states was based on growing interdependence and shared interests around peace, commerce, and transportation and communication. Internationalism was increasingly visible in both the growing list of IGOs, and The Hague Conferences, and on this basis encouraged thinking about, and proposals for, some form of worldwide IGO to mitigate the effects of anarchy. By this time there was also the emergence of thinking about world federalism: Benjamin Trueblood (1899) and Raymond Bridgman (1905) (Schmidt, 1998a: 112).

Like the other perspectives on IR, all of this thinking was caught up with imperialism and racism, and was again decisively a view of the world from the core.

Conclusions

There can be no doubt that in the decades before the First World War an increasingly substantial and systematic discourse about international relations developed. Indeed, Knutsen (2016)[6] traces theoretical thinking about international relations all the way back to the fall of the Roman Empire. This first modern IR discourse was mainly located in Britain and the United States, and had fundamentally nineteenth-century concerns: the superiority (or not) of white peoples and the West; how to manage relations between more and less 'civilised' peoples; the role of Geopolitics in shaping international order; the rights and wrongs of imperialism; the increasing hold of notions of popular sovereignty and self-determination; the relationship of free trade and protectionism to international conflict; the rising dangers and consequences of military technology; and the capacity of war to be mitigated by international law and intergovernmental institutions. It is hardly surprising that the nineteenth century is so rich in thinking about international relations. As we showed in Chapter 1, the decades between 1840 and 1914 were imbued with massive transformations driven by the unfolding of modernity in both states and societies, and by a shift in the balance of what shaped economic, political and social life away from domestic and towards international factors. For much of the twentieth century, the principal driver behind IR was war and the fear of war. But the nineteenth century, at least for the states and societies of the core, was marked by a long peace, and it was in those core societies that thinking about IR developed. Consequently, the main drivers of IR thinking during the nineteenth century were the new global political economy of modernity; the new balance of power; and the new, highly unequal, racist and colonial, global core–periphery international society enabled by the huge gap in power and development between those in command of the revolutions of modernity, and those left behind by them. 'IR' thinking during the nineteenth century was, in Coxian terms, both by and for the core powers, with the periphery largely reduced to an object – or as Carvalho, Leira and Hobson (2011: 750) cutely label it, a 'West Side Story'.[7]

Although these developments had not yet cohered into a discipline or field of IR, there are clear signs of institutionalisation in terms of books,

---

[6] For shorter versions see Olson and Groom (1991: 1–15) and Dougherty and Pfaltzgraff (1997: 6–11).

[7] It might be argued that the intellectual space into which IR moved during the late nineteenth century was created by the failure of the emergent discipline of Sociology to engage effectively with the issue of war (Tiryakian, 1999; Joas, 2003).

journals and university courses. There are many 'IR' books from this period including:

Henry Wheaton ([1836] 1866) *Elements of International Law*.

James Lorimer (1884) *The Institutes of the Law of Nations: A Treatise on the Jural Relations of Separate Political Communities*.

Alleyne Ireland (1899) *Tropical Colonization: An Introduction to the Study of the Subject*.

Benjamin F. Trueblood (1899) *The Federation of the World*.

Paul Reinsch (1900) *World Politics at the End of the Nineteenth Century As Influenced by the Oriental Situation*.

Paul Reinsch (1902) *Colonial Government: An Introduction to the Study of Colonial Institutions*.

Raymond L. Bridgman (1905) *World Organization*.

Paul Reinsch (1911) *Public International Unions – Their Work and Organization: A Study in International Administrative Law*.

G. Lowes Dickinson (1916) *The European Anarchy*.

A. F. Grant, Arthur Greenwood, J. D. I. Hughes, P. H. Kerr and F. F. Urquhart (1916) *An Introduction to International Relations*.

David P. Heatley (1919) *Diplomacy and the Study of International Relations*.

What might count as the first professional IR journal, *International Conciliation*, dates from 1907 (Schmidt, 1998a: 101); the *American Journal of International Law* dates from 1907; and the *Journal of Race Development* (*Foreign Affairs* from 1922) from 1910. In Britain the earliest IR journal was *The Roundtable* (1910), which originally came with the telling subtitle *A Quarterly Review of the Politics of the British Empire*. Schmidt (1998a: 54–7, 70) gives some weight to the creation in 1880 of a School of Political Science at Columbia University as a milestone in the institutionalisation of IR, though he places the first identifiable IR course as being in 1899–1900 at the University of Wisconsin. In 1898, the George Washington University in Washington, DC, set up a School of Comparative Jurisprudence and Diplomacy, which would go through several iterations, including mergers with Political Science and Government departments, before becoming a Public and International Affairs school in the 1960s and later acquiring its current name as the Elliott School of International Affairs in 1988. The Women's International League for Peace and Freedom (WILPF) was founded in 1915 as a lobby group, but also became an influential focus for a group of Feminist thinkers during the interwar years (L. Ashworth, 2017). What is perhaps most conspicuously absent during this period is any academic membership associations organised around IR.

IR before IR in the Periphery

While it remains overwhelmingly true that IR at this time was an enterprise by and for the West, one can also find the first shoots of modern IR thinking emerging elsewhere in response to the encounters with both the West and modernity. The expansion of Western-colonial international society to global scale had, for better or for worse, and whether they wanted it or not, brought all peoples and polities into a global economy, a global system of power politics and a global hierarchy of race and development. The combination of global scale, intense interaction and political, economic and racial hierarchy were all new. Those in the periphery were both at the bottom of the hierarchies of wealth, power and status, and found themselves pressured by the homogenising force of modernity. At the time, it was difficult to separate modernisation from Westernisation, thereby posing to the peoples and polities of the periphery the acute dilemma of whether they had to lose their cultural identities in order to better their position in the global hierarchies. From this position, it is not surprising that early thinking about modern IR in the periphery was both heavily motivated by anti-colonialism, and strongly attracted to regional/racial identities to assert against the West.

Japan

Given what we argued in Chapter 1 about Japan being both part of the first general round of modernity and a great power by 1902, it is no surprise that we find its pre-First World War IR developments were somewhat similar to those in the West, i.e. clear precursors to the emergence of a systematic field of study. As Tetsuya Sakai (2008: 234–7) notes, Japan was fully aware of its odd position of being partly in colonial international society, but also aspiring to join the anarchical society of the Western great powers. He observes that there was by 1893 a systematic text on IR in Japan (Kuga [1893] 1968). Japan's international lawyers were active in its diplomacy around the Sino-Japanese War and published books on it (Ariga, 1896; Takahashi, 1899). A Japanese Association of International Law was set up in 1897. The works of the American IR writer Paul Reinsch (1900, 1902) were quickly translated, and influenced Japanese thinking on imperialism and colonial administration. The work of Yukichi Fukuzawa ([1875] 2009) on comparative civilisation and

Japan's need for modernisation also has IR elements.[8] Courses on diplomatic history were offered at several Japanese universities before the First World War (Hosoya, 2009: 22–3). As in its development generally, Japan was quick to catch up with Western IR thinking, especially International Law, and to establish its own brand (Howland, 2016).

Precisely because of its early success in development, Japan was the first in line to face the dilemma of modernisation/Westernisation. R. Taggart Murphy (2014: 63) brilliantly summarises the extent of the challenge posed to Japan, and by extension to all periphery states and peoples, by the 'standard of civilisation':

The Meiji leaders faced three urgent and intertwined tasks. They had to build a military strong enough to act as a deterrent to Western imperialism. They had to assemble the capital and technology needed to turn their country into an industrial power sufficiently advanced to equip that military. And they had to create the institutions necessary not only to accomplish these other tasks but to convince the West that Japan had accumulated the prerequisites for membership in the club of countries that were to be taken seriously. That meant not only a credible military – preferably evidenced by victories in imperialist wars waged on weaker lands – but also such institutions as parliaments, courts, banks, monogamy, elections, and ideally, Christian churches, not to mention familiarity with Western ways and appearances in such matters as architecture, dress, sexual mores, and table manners. It was only by governing as leaders of a convincing imitation of a modern imperialist nation that these men could persuade the West to revise the Unequal Treaties and thereby wrest back control over their country's tariff regime and security apparatus from the Europeans.

Japanese public intellectuals familiar both with the West and their own culture addressed IR issues. A famous editorial of 1885 attributed to Fukuzawa argued that Japan should leave Asia and join the West (Jansen, 2000: loc. 6450; Dreyer, 2016: 44). Okakura Tenshin (aka Kakuzō), another prominent Japanese scholar, was fully aware of the ironies of his country's international position. He wrote powerfully of this in his *Book of Tea*, first published in 1906 (cited in Suzuki, 2005: 137):

In the days when Japan was engaging in peaceful acts, the West used to think of it as an uncivilized country. Since Japan started massacring thousands of people in the battlefields of Manchuria, the West has called it a civilized country.

Okakura also contributed towards a Pan-Asianist vision that, as we shall see, also resonated in South Asia. As a successful early moderniser

---

[8] We are grateful to Takashi Inoguchi and Hitomi Koyama for their advice on these sources. We place Japan in the discussion of the periphery here because it was only at the end of this period, after its defeats of China and Russia, that Japan became clearly accepted as part of the core.

rapidly rising into the global ranks of the great powers, many, and not only in Japan, saw Japan as the natural leader of Asia (Okakura, 1903, 1904). Okakura anyway saw Japan as the best of Asian civilisation, as it 'mirror[ed] the whole of Asian consciousness' (Tankha and Thampi, 2005: 60). His Pan-Asian vision against the West was cultural:

Asia is one. The Himalayas divide, only to accentuate, two mighty civilisations, the Chinese with its communism of Confucius, and the Indian with its individualism of the Vedas. But not even the snowy barriers can interrupt for one moment that broad expanse of love for the Ultimate and Universal, which is the common thought-inheritance of every Asiatic race, enabling them to produce all the great religions of the world, and distinguishing them from those maritime peoples of the Mediterranean and the Baltic, who love to dwell on the Particular, and to search out the means, not the end, of life. (Okakura, 1903: 1)

Beyond Japan, IR thinking during this period was less in the form of an organised academic study, and, like much of the contemporary IR thinking in the West during the nineteenth century (e.g. free trade, anti-slavery), closely connected to public policy issues and the thinking of politicians and public intellectuals.

Latin America

Latin America, the first of the regions in today's 'Global South' to emerge from European colonialism, was not 'Non-Western' in the same sense as Japan and the other peoples and polities of Asia and Africa, but neither was it a rising great power. Although they achieved decolonisation in the late eighteenth and early nineteenth century, and thus membership of international society, its states were still part of the periphery in two senses: they were increasingly under the shadow of US regional hegemony, and were like colonies economically in being primarily commodity suppliers to an industrialising core, rather than being clearly on a track of modernisation themselves. They were the subjects of so-called 'informal empire'. From this perspective, it is hardly surprising that Latin American thinking during this period focused mainly on defending the right of sovereign equality, and its corollary, non-intervention. There was also a strong element of Pan-American regionalism, though this was riven by two contending purposes.

Pan-Americanism emerged in the nineteenth century initially to build cooperation between the states of the Western hemisphere, and was led by the United States (Lockey, 1920). Although the origins of Pan-Americanism go back to the first half of the nineteenth century, it was in 1890 that the First International Conference on American States was held. Notably, this was nearly a decade before the first Hague Conference.

Pan-Americanism, however, was confronted with a paradox. On the one hand, it was an idealist movement to foster cooperation between nations, later even eliciting comparisons with the LN owing to its legalistic structure. On the other hand, it was a movement by the Latin American states to counter American hegemony and the Monroe Doctrine. Because of the presence of the hegemon *inside* the movement, Pan-Americanism is different from those other pan-nationalist movements that were responses mainly to outside hegemons, though similar to East Asia, where Japan was also an insider hegemon. Inter-American relations were, in this sense, contingent on the 'abuse and non-abuse of political possibilities' open to the United States by virtue of its hegemonic position (Hula, 1942: 22). This problem notwithstanding, Pan-Americanism evolved to reflect notions of 'Latin American solidarity' and was anti-hegemonic in nature, similar to the other pan-nationalist movements across the globe.

Although the norms of sovereign equality and non-intervention are prominent all over the world, the early contributions of Latin America are particularly significant because these norms emerged there first, before travelling to other parts of the world. While sovereignty is stressed in the Peace of Westphalia of 1648, non-intervention is not. One of the most prominent Latin American norms is the doctrine of *uti possidetis juris*, or honouring inherited boundaries. This norm, which respected the Spanish empire's administrative boundaries, became 'a framework of domestic and international legitimacy in the otherwise bloody passage from the empire to its successor American states' (Dominguez, 2007: 90). This norm clearly supported and contributed to the global territorial integrity norm, or what Ian Brownlie ([1966] 1998) calls the 'creation and transfer of territorial sovereignty'. Another norm of Latin America is 'absolute non-intervention in the hemispheric community', both as an abstract principle and as a means to challenge the US Monroe Doctrine. Developed under the banner of Pan-Americanism, this norm responded to the perceived hypocrisy of a regional hegemon in dealing with its southern neighbours (Castle, 2000; Leonard, 2000).

The most prominent examples of Latin American thinking on non-intervention were the Calvo and Drago Doctrines, both of which were put forward by Argentines. The former is associated with diplomat and historian Carlos Calvo, who articulated in 1868 his doctrine that the 'authority to settle international investment disputes resides in the government of the country in which that investment is located' (Wood, 2008: 46–7). The doctrine was directed against intervention in the internal affairs of Latin American states by foreign powers (European and United States), and became a staple feature of constitutions and treaties in Latin America. The Calvo Doctrine remained legalistic, and was taken further by the Drago Doctrine, propounded by Argentine Foreign Minister Luis María Drago in 1902, who challenged the US and European position that they had a right to intervene to force states to honour their sovereign debts (Dominguez, 2007: 92). Specifically, the doctrine prohibited military intervention. On these foundations, Gerry Simpson (2004: 126–59) notes the strong representation from Latin America in defence of sovereign equality, and against US regional hegemonism, at the Second Hague Conference in 1907. He argues that this advocacy helped to pave the way for the compromise Assembly-plus-Council structure for twentieth-century IGOs, combining sovereign equality and hierarchy.

Perhaps a bit more surprising is that we also find elements of modern IR thinking emerging in China and India, which were neither first-round modernisers nor great powers. But in both cases, these are more in the nature of scattered elements, not yet suggesting the emergence of a systematic field of study.

China

While China unlike India was not formally colonised, it was heavily penetrated by outside powers including Japan. There was no systematic academic study of IR recognisable in China at this time, not least because of the sustained turbulence caused by a decaying Qing dynasty interacting with intensifying foreign pressure. But there were scattered elements of Pan-Asian thinking, and as noted in Chapter 1, by the late nineteenth century, many Chinese reformers were concentrated on Japan, and thinking hard about how to save China from being swallowed up by foreign imperialists.

Perhaps the most notable 'IR' work in China at this time was Kang Yuwei's ([1935] 1958) book *The Great Harmony*. Kang was strongly associated with the reformist, modernising movement in China at the end of the nineteenth century. Early versions of his book were written in 1884–5, and some of it was published in 1913. Kang's argument combined modernity and tradition. Its emphasis on harmony and a borderless, unified world reflected Confucian ideas, but much of its content about eliminating the boundaries of class, race, nation, gender and much else seemed to have roots in Utopian Socialism.

One of Kang's most notable followers was Liang Qichao (1873–1929), a journalist and intellectual of the late Qing Dynasty. Like Kang, he sought to reinterpret Confucianism to China, but was conflicted by a desire to emulate the West while still maintaining traditional cultural values and identity. Liang epitomised the desire of Chinese intellectuals of the period to reform and modernise their country to overcome the national humiliation and physical threat from Japan and the West, but failed to reconcile democracy with traditional Chinese values (Mishra, 2012: 123–215). During a visit to the United States in 1903, he became disillusioned with American democracy after witnessing its racism, corruption and inequality (Shepard, 2012).

One of the Chinese exiles in Japan was Sun Yat-sen, who was developing a 'state-based, anti-imperialist vision of Asia', but there were other forms of regionalism among Chinese intellectuals 'rooted in non-state-centered practices and non-national-chauvinist culturalism' (Karl, 1998: 1096–7). One example of this alternative regionalism was the activities of a little-known organisation called the Asian Solidarity Society, set up in Tokyo in 1907 by Chinese intellectuals, Japanese Socialists and Indian, Vietnamese and Filipino exiles. An interesting aspect of this regionalism was the recognition accorded to the 'first Filipino' José Rizal (1861–96), as 'the quintessential Asian patriot, from which China and other Asians must learn' (Karl, 1998: 1106). Although Rizal is better known as a champion of the unity of the Malay race, his message was appropriated by the non-state-centric variety of Asian regionalism. There is more on Rizal's nationalism later in this chapter.

India

As with much of the Non-Western colonised world, there was no systematic study of IR in India, but there was active IR thinking, both anti-colonial and Pan-Asian, among public intellectuals. Perhaps most notable was the fusion of modernity and tradition represented by Tagore who became Asia's first Nobel laureate in literature in 1913. Tagore's contribution to international thought centred on his stringent criticism and rejection of nationalism, while another strand of his thinking concerned Pan-Asianism. He ran an anti-nationalist, Pan-Asianist campaign which had its roots in Buddhism, and ironically saw Japan as the lead power for Asia. For Tagore, as he stated during his tour of the United States in the winter of 1916–17, 'The idea of the nation is one of the most powerful anesthetics that man has invented … Under the influence of its fumes the whole people can carry out its systematic programme of the most virulent self-seeking without being in the least aware of its moral perversion' (Tagore, [1917] 2002: 98). Tagore's anti-nationalism at a time when nationalism was becoming embedded as a key institution of GIS (Mayall, 1990) was not entirely eccentric. British historian Arnold Toynbee, director of studies at the Royal Institute of International Affairs (Chatham House) from 1924 to 1954, also condemned nationalism: 'Our modern

Western nationalism ... is a reversion to the idolatrous self-worship of the tribe' (cited in Brewin, 1995: 280).

Tagore believed that nationalism not only caused international conflict, but also domestic repression, or the suppression of individuality that he regarded as one of the major contributions of Western societies. With regard to international conflict, Tagore warned during a visit to Japan in 1916 that nationalism bred competition, or a 'survival of the fittest' mindset, or an extreme version of the self-help principle: 'Help yourself, and never heed what it costs to others' (Tagore, [1917] 2002: 33). Tagore warned Japan not to emulate the West, lest it also become as militaristic and repressive. He reminded an audience that 'where the spirit of nationalism prevails, the whole people is being taught from boyhood to foster hatreds and ambitions by all kinds of means – by the manufacture of half truths and untruths in history, by persistent misrepresentation of other races ... thus continually brewing evil menace towards neighbours and nations other than their own' (Tagore, [1917] 2002: 35). He saw nationalism as a blindness to the moral law that 'man becomes all the truer the more he realizes himself in others'. Moreover, 'nations who sedulously cultivate moral blindness as the cult of patriotism will end their existence in a sudden and violent death' (Tagore, [1917] 2002: 34). On the impact of nationalism on individual freedom, Tagore noted during his US tour, 'we cannot but acknowledge the paradox that while the spirit of the West marches under its banner of freedom, the nation of the West forges its iron chains of organisation which are the most relentless and unbreakable that have ever been manufactured in the whole history of man' (Tagore, [1917] 2002: 78).

There was also writing about India's exploited position in the inter-national economy of the British Empire, such as Dadabhai Naoroji's 'drain theory'. In his book *Poverty and Un-British Rule in India*, published in 1901, Naoroji attempted to examine statistically the net national profit of India, and concluded that most of India's wealth was being 'drained' by Britain, both by inhibiting the development of industry in India and by making the colony pay for the massive civil and administrative costs involved in maintaining the empire (Ganguli, 1965). Naoroji did not embark on an anti-colonial exercise, rather his project was to perform a scientific study. It is, nonetheless, true that Naoroji's theory gave heart to the Indian independence movement because of its repudiation of British rule, even if only the economic aspect.

IR in Other Colonial 'Regions'

One of the challenges in analysing the origins of IR in different parts of the world before the First World War was the absence then of the contemporary notions of 'region'. Terms such as the 'Near East', 'Middle East', 'Far East', 'South Asia' and 'Southeast Asia' were colonial constructions, created to serve the strategic and geopolitical purposes of imperial powers, especially Great Britain. For example, the region stretching from Afghanistan on the west to Indonesia in the east is now divided into South Asia and Southeast Asia, with Myanmar (Burma) serving as a dividing line. Yet, at the turn of the twentieth century, these regional concepts of South Asia and Southeast Asia were yet to be formed. In fact, Southeast Asia would emerge as a distinctive regional idea mainly after the establishment of the Southeast Asia Command by Allied powers during the Second World War (Acharya, 2013a: 38). The region was historically referred to by many Western scholars as Greater India, a term that would later in the 1920s inspire Indian nationalists in Calcutta to form a Greater India Society under the spiritual patronage of Rabindranath Tagore (Keenleyside, 1982; S. Bayly, 2004).

Much of the region known today as the Middle East was under Ottoman suzerainty during this period, and there was relatively little thinking about IR. Pan-Arabism did not open up until the First World War, but there was some IR thinking within the Islamic context. The idea of a unified Islamic Caliphate is old (Hashmi, 2009: 172–3). The distinction in classical Islamic legal sources (not the Qur'an) between *Dar al Islam* and *Dar al Harb* provides a basis for thinking about international relations, though not within *Dar al Islam* because there is only supposed to be one Islamic state (Tadjbakhsh, 2010: 176–84). The idea of Islamic unity emerged in a specifically anti-colonial context within the Ottoman Empire during the late nineteenth century as a way of countering European encroachments into the Islamic world. The Ottoman Sultan Abdülhamid II argued for some form of Islamic unity under the Ottoman Empire to strengthen resistance against the West. But this idea didn't really get anywhere.

Many intellectuals in the colonial world were inspired by Western ideas, including Liberalism, as a way to reform their society and fight colonisation and/or humiliation. But they did not always find Western ideas and approaches attractive or applicable to their own local context. Their efforts to reconcile Western modernity and indigenous values and identity sometimes led to failure in terms of political outcomes, but left a deep impact on nationalist movements in the colonial world. Aside from the aforementioned Qichao of China, a leading example of this is Jamal al-Din al-Afghani (1838–97), a Persian-born journalist and political activist who advocated a modernised Islam as the means to fight

Western dominance (Kedourie, 2018). He studied and travelled in Asia (India, Egypt and Turkey), as well as Europe (London and Paris) while developing and propagating Pan-Islamist political ideas which would inspire subsequent generations of Islamic nationalists in South Asia (including Pakistan's founder Muhammad Ali Jinnah), Egypt and Turkey (Mishra, 2012: 46–123).

If al-Afghani is seen as the founder of modern Pan-Islamist nationalism, the aforementioned Rizal, a European-educated ophthalmologist, writer and political leader, can be regarded as Asia's first secular nationalist or 'proto-nationalist' (Chong, 2017). While al-Afghani tried to reconcile traditional (Islamic) civilisation with Western modernity, Rizal epitomised the tensions between revolutionary and assimilationist nationalisms in the periphery. There is a debate over whether he was an assimilationist (reformist) or a revolutionary or both. His two novels *Noli Me Tángere* ('Touch Me Not') and *El filibusterismo* ('The Reign of Greed') contain armed revolutionary plots, but in both cases the efforts failed. Some see him as rejecting armed revolution in favour of liberal reform that would give the people of the Philippines a republican government, and equality and rights, including that of political participation and representation, and freedom of the press and of speech. Failing this, he opposed Spanish rule, which he saw as 'a government that has no concern for the people [and] becomes an anomaly in the midst of righteous people, just like a people with evil thoughts cannot stay under a righteous government' (Funtecha, 2008). What is unmistakable is that Rizal was among a few Filipinos who did not accept the Philippines under Spanish colonialism as a normal condition, and had the courage to stand up against it.

Sub-Saharan Africa was also both Non-Western and firmly in the grip of colonisation. Compared to China and India, it lacked widespread institutions and traditions of formal higher education other than those provided by the colonial powers. Nevertheless, the First Pan-African Conference was held in London in 1900, and received considerable international attention. At this stage, Pan-Africanism benefitted considerably from its links to the movement for black emancipation in the United States, and the influence of black American leaders such as W. E. B. Du Bois. The Pan-African conferences did not just restrict themselves to anti-colonialism or racial discrimination, but rather espoused larger concerns and causes in international relations. In his speech at the 1900 conference, Du Bois declared:

Let the world take no backward step in that slow but sure progress which has successively refused to let the spirit of class, of caste, of privilege, or of birth, debar from life, liberty and the pursuit of happiness a striving human soul. Let no color or race be a feature of distinction between white and black men, regardless of worth or ability.[9]

This is a clear indication that the conference embraced a cause broader than just black rights or race, and made allusions to ideas of equality and freedom at the international level. Interestingly, the First Pan-African Conference in 1900 was attended by Naoroji, the originator of the 'drain theory' of British imperialism.

The 1919 'Myth' of IR's Founding

Given both the rather impressive range and depth of IR thinking before the First World War, and clear signs not only of its institutionalisation in the core, but also of significant developments in the periphery, how do we account for the widespread understanding that IR only came into being in 1919? Like every nation or discipline, IR has its own 'foundational myths', which can be understood as 'part fictions/part truths' (Booth, 1996: 328). And like most myths, the origins of IR are shrouded in controversy. There is by now a vigorous critique of IR's 1919 'myth'. Schmidt (1998a: 149) opens the case with an empirical argument much like the one above, arguing simply that there was a lot of 'IR' before 1919:

Contrary to conventional orthodoxy, the field of international relations does not owe its origin or birth to the outbreak of World War I. The notion that the field did not come into existence until after the war is one of the dominant myths that informs most conventional accounts of the history of the field ... for the previous twenty years scholars had discussed the merits of creating some type of organizational structure that could mitigate international anarchy.

Knutsen (2016) also makes a detailed empirical case, and Carvalho, Leira and Hobson (2011) and John Hobson (2012: locs. 356–94) both firmly reject a 1919 founding story, and rightly focus on the neglect, or even complete forgetting, of modern IR's deep and substantial roots. Carvalho, Leira and Hobson (2011) and John Hobson's (2012) arguments feature the more political line of the convenience of forgetting IR's links to imperialism, colonial administration and racism (to which might be added Geopolitics) as part of the attraction of the 1919 myth. That forgetting has certainly influenced the way in which mainstream IR has developed, though, as will become clear in Chapters 4 and 6, most of that forgetting took place after 1945.

Nevertheless, there are two substantial reasons that explain the durability of the 1919 myth: institutionalisation and the trauma of the First

[9] 'To the Nations of the World', www.blackpast.org/1900-w-e-b-du-bois-nations-world (Accessed 27 May 2018).

World War. IR was clearly on the way to becoming institutionalised as an academic discipline or field of study well before 1914. But it was only in 1919, and after that, when this institutionalisation really took off, a phenomenon that was repeated again after the Second World War. The most frequently cited events are: the founding of the Department of International Politics and the Woodrow Wilson Chair in International Politics at Aberystwyth in 1919; and the creation of two IR think tanks, the Royal Institute of International Affairs in London in 1920 and its journal *International Affairs* in 1922, and the Council on Foreign Relations in New York in 1921. Further IR chairs, departments and institutes followed throughout the interwar years, and we elaborate these in Chapter 4.

This wave of institutionalisation was, however, considerably driven by the trauma of the First World War, and without the impact of that war, it would almost certainly not have happened so quickly or in the same way. The depth of the First World War's impact can still be seen in the way the Department of International Politics at Aberystwyth describes itself today:

The Department was founded in 1919 as a response to the horrors of the First World War, in which millions of people around the world lost their lives. It represented a normative project with the aim of understanding the dynamics of world politics in order ultimately to transcend war.[10]

The First World War was not the first one fought on a global scale: the French Revolutionary and Napoleonic Wars achieved that. Rather, the First World War was the first all-out conflict involving the whole array of industrialised great powers. It was fought with weapons unlike those used in earlier wars, and it was vastly more expensive, destructive and difficult to fight than had been anticipated. Those countries that entered it, as some did, with a degree of social Darwinist enthusiasm about proving which was the top nation, mostly exited from it, if they survived at all, deeply fearful of any repetition. As we described in Chapter 1, the war seemed to threaten the very existence of European civilisation, and left fear of war (what we called the *defence dilemma*) as widespread and strongly felt. It brought into question both diplomacy and the wisdom of allowing endless improvement in armaments to dominate relations between the great powers.

It was the impact of these overpowering considerations that, as the blurb from Aberystwyth shows, shaped the emerging discipline of IR. As James Joll (1982) argues, the First World War devastated all three nineteenth-century strands of thinking about how war could be

---

[10] www.aber.ac.uk/en/interpol/about/ (Accessed 28 May 2017).

tamed: conservatives' trust in the balance of power; Liberals' faith in the mediating effects of free trade and constitutions; and Socialists' belief that class solidarity would trump nationalism. Even the hopes of those, such as Bloch, who thought that the fear of using destructive new weapons would deter war were not met (Pearton, 1982: 137–9). As Buzan and Lawson (2015a: 62–3) argue:

> [F]rom the 1920s onwards, IR was almost obsessively focused on the present and near future which were, in turn, largely defined in terms of great power relations. This genesis launched IR as a presentist discipline whose primary concerns were the (dis)order of the great power system and how to understand the conditions that might lead to war or promote peace. The unfolding of the 20th century with its profound ideological divisions and its unremitting improvements in powers of destruction reinforced the centrality of these twin concerns. Under these conditions, it was easy to forget the world before 1914 other than as material for debates about the causes and possible alleviation of war … In the 20th century world, what mattered most was how to contain war from breaking out between ideologically polarised great powers.

Conclusions

Despite all the IR that came before, the First World War more or less drew a line under it. Rather than looking back to where it came from, IR fixed its gaze firmly on the future, and the noble problem of how to prevent war and cultivate peace. The need to manage the international anarchy of great power relations, arms racing and the world economy in order to prevent another war became the overriding priority of the 'new' discipline. What lay ahead looked far more urgent than the colonial issues that lay behind. The nineteenth-century balance in IR between managing the core on the one hand, and managing core–periphery relations on the other, largely gave way to concerns about managing relations within the core. It was the long great power peace in the core of the nineteenth century that had been overthrown by the war, and that needed urgent attention. The First World War had disturbed colonial relations, but not in ways that demanded immediate attention. The colonial order looked as robust in 1919 as it did in 1914, and could therefore be pushed into the background and kept largely separate from the study of ir in the core.

3   The World 1919–1945: Still Version 1.0 Global International Society

Introduction

The First World War can perhaps best be seen as the first round of a systemic crisis of modernity on a global scale. As we will show in later chapters, subsequent rounds of this crisis (the Second World War, the Cold War and decolonisation, the 'rise of the rest') occupied much of the twentieth century. As argued in Chapter 1, the causes of the First World War were generally rooted in the destabilisation of great power relations caused by modernity, and particularly in the destabilisation in military relations caused by both nationalism, and the dynamics of industrial arms racing. The war was not significantly caused by either ideological conflicts about forms of government, or an economic crisis arising out of modernity, though both of those were significant consequences of it. This chapter covers both the interwar years, as a failed attempt to recover and improve on the international society of the core from before 1914, and the Second World War, which was the consequence of that failure.

The next section picks up the main themes from Chapter 1, and looks at the continuities with, and discontinuities from, the period before 1914. We argue that the First World War was only a partial crisis of modernity, and that its consequences, though in some ways big, did not fundamentally change the structure of version 1.0 international society. The following sections look at the main themes of interwar international politics and the Second World War, finding it a much more substantial global crisis than the First. We build towards the argument that the First and Second World Wars and the Cold War, plus decolonisation were not really discrete events, but phases in a more general crisis unfolding from the consequences of the wholesale transformation in international relations generated during the nineteenth century by the revolutions of modernity (Buzan and Lawson, 2015b).

Continuities and Discontinuities from the Pre-1914 World

This section picks up the main discussions from Chapter 1 and sees how they carry forward, or not, into this period: the material and ideational impacts of modernity; the version 1.0 Western-colonial GIS; and the singular story of Japan, suspended between the West and the rest without being fully part of either.

In terms of material impacts, the revolutions of modernity continued to deliver a relentless pace of technological change both civil and military, and often both together. The existing technologies of steamships, railways and the telegraph that first shrank the planet during the nineteenth century continued to improve in speed, reliability, cost-effectiveness and coverage of the globe. With rising interaction capacity, the planet continued to shrink rapidly. One could now fly to many destinations, or use bombing from aircraft as a cheap way of controlling rebellious tribesmen in remote colonial locations. Radio made global communication more or less instantaneous, and also opened up a powerful new mass medium. Internal combustion engines, electricity and chemicals became the leading edge of industrialism. To the early breakthroughs in interaction capacity were added the mass production and widespread use of motor vehicles, aircraft and radios. In the military sector, the same mix of improvements and novelties applied. Things like submarines, aircraft carriers, poison gases, tanks, fighters, bombers and sonar were greatly improved, and novelties like radar were introduced. The permanent revolution in military affairs that kicked off during the nineteenth century carried on with no let-up.

The ideational landscape, by contrast, continued to be dominated by the same four ideologies of progress that had emerged during the nineteenth century. These evolved with the times, but there was nothing fundamentally new. The First World War was not caused by ideological rivalries about forms of government, though nationalism was a significant enabler of it, and it did hasten the demise of dynasticism as the main form of political legitimacy. But the war did little to address or resolve the contradictions among the ideologies of progress. It corroded empire, especially within Europe, though much less so overseas. Fascism, which emerged during the 1920s, might have looked like a new ideology but was not. It was simply a merger of 'Scientific' Racism and nationalism into a particularly extreme form of social Darwinism.

But while the First World War did little or nothing to resolve the ideological contradictions of modernity, it did much both to bring them into sharper focus and, by linking them to state power in the core, to make them a key factor in relations between the great powers. Before 1914, the ideologies of progress did not play much of a role in defining relations between the great powers, in part because dynasticism was still very influential. After 1919, the ideologies of progress became a, and arguably the, central factor in great power relations. Nationalism was strong everywhere, displacing dynasticism as the main foundation of the state. Forms of Liberalism already had state power in Britain, the United States and France, and this ideological closeness had played some role during the war. The first move to challenge Liberalism and its rise was the Bolshevik revolution in Russia in 1917. That move not only took Russia out of the First World War, but also set it up as the representative of an alternative, universalist idea of the political economy of modernity. The Soviet Union pitched a totalitarian state/society, and a command economy, against the individualistic, liberal-democratic capitalism of the West. This ideological dualism was quickly turned into a triad with the Fascist takeovers in Italy during the 1920s, and Germany, Spain and Japan during the 1930s.[1] Fascism also offered an alternative idea of the political economy of modernity, but a parochial rather than a universalist one, combining a totalitarian state/society with state capitalism, and adding a large dose of racist social Darwinism. Thus in addition to the normal pushing and shoving of the balance of power, great power relations during the interwar years were also driven by ideological competition between two contrasting universalisms, and between each of them and a set of ultranationalist parochialisms.

In a slower and more subtle way, these ideologies of progress also began to filter into, and corrode, the core–periphery structure of colonial GIS. The nationalist ideas about popular sovereignty pushed by President Wilson questioned the legitimacy of colonial rule. So too did Liberal ones about individual human rights, self-determination of peoples and freedom of markets. Racist ideas could be used to construct hierarchies in which Japanese, Chinese, Africans and others displaced whites at the top. Socialist ideas provided revolutionary tools not only for fighting capitalism, but also for the overthrow of imperial governments. There was thus during the interwar period a certain gathering of momentum in the anti-colonial movements in the periphery.

Latin America (excluding the Caribbean) was already formally independent, but during the twentieth century witnessed a revival of anti-colonialism. Anticipating the wider development of decolonisation after

---

[1] Japan's was more of a military government plus a god-emperor than Fascist in the Western style (Sims, 2001: 179–85; Totman, 2005: chs. 15–16), but otherwise fit the Fascist formula, and associated itself with Germany and Italy in the Axis alliance in 1940.

1945, this was recast more as ending economic and political dependency than as a demand for formal independence. Peruvian nationalist José Carlos Mariátegui was influenced by Mahatma Gandhi and Mao Zedong as well as Leon Trotsky, Lenin and Antonio Gramsci, and Irish revolutionaries. The anti-colonial movement in India was perhaps the most broad-based and transnationally influential among such movements of this period, but it was not a singular movement. The dominant strand of it was led by Gandhi, who returned to India in 1915 after leading his campaign of non-violence (*Satyagraha*, or 'love of truth') against white racism in South Africa. His doctrine of non-violence would inspire Nelson Mandela and Martin Luther King. But despite Gandhi's dominant influence, Indian anti-colonial thought and approach was not of a single variety. Other approaches were revolutionary, especially prominent in Punjab (Bhagat Singh) and Bengal (Aurobindo Ghosh) (dubbed 'terrorist' by the British); and Hindu nationalist (championed by V. D. Savarkar's *Hindutva* movement born in the 1920s). Moreover, challenging Nehru, Subhas Chandra Bose advocated cooperation with Fascist powers to speed up India's independence. At least some in the periphery were beginning to anticipate carving out a role in the balance of power within the core.

In Africa, anti-colonial resistance ranged from boycotts of trade in colonial products to outright armed struggles. In anglophone Africa – Ghana, Nigeria, Kenya, Uganda, Tanzania and South Africa – anti-colonial movements took shape in the 1920s, although they would not become powerful until after the Second World War. The situation in francophone Africa was different. Unlike the British, who regarded their colonies as separate, inferior civilisations and pursued a mix of direct and indirect rule, the French regarded their colonies as part of French civilisation, and pursued a policy of formal assimilation into the nation. Anti-colonial movements in francophone Africa were divided into those who accepted French cultural identity but called for formal equality, and those who rejected assimilation in favour of independence and identity with native African culture and values. Most of these were located in France itself, rather than the colonies, a situation that would not change until after 1945 (Goebel, 2015; Elam, 2017). The occupation of Ethiopia by Mussolini's forces in 1935–6, had a ripple effect in fuelling African nationalism. Ethiopia's defeat of an Italian invasion in 1896 had become a symbol of African resistance to colonialism.

During the interwar years, Arab nationalism took a more decisively anti-Western character, in contrast to the 'Arab awakening' of the previous century, which was politically directed against Ottoman rule but culturally sought to learn from the West (at least the element of it led by Christian Arabs). This had much to do with the creation of British and French mandates under the LN, after the First World War, with Britain receiving the mandate over Iraq, Palestine and Transjordan, and France over Lebanon and Syria. These mandates destroyed any immediate hopes for Arab independence and the British Balfour Declaration, envisaging the creation of a Jewish homeland, caused further opposition to Western colonialism.

These developments, however, did not generate enough pressure for independence during this period to threaten the structure of Western and Japanese imperial rule overseas. So in terms of the structure of GIS, the interwar years largely continued with the version 1.0 Western-colonial order that was set up during the nineteenth century. Considerable efforts were made to restore and strengthen this order, particularly by restoring the global economy, pursuing arms control and building a permanent structure of global IGOs. But divisions among the great powers, partly on ideological grounds and partly because of revanchism and weak leadership, undermined this enterprise. More on this in the next section.

The essential point to make here is that the First World War did not make all that big an impact on the structure of GIS. Its main impact, as noted, was on pushing ideological divisions to the forefront of great power relations. It also changed the distribution of power by destroying the Austro-Hungarian and Ottoman Empires, demoting Germany, weakening Britain and France, and strengthening the United States and Japan. But otherwise, the main features of version 1.0 Western-colonial GIS remained intact. The core–periphery structure, and the institution of colonialism, were a bit more under question, but still stayed legitimate. So too did the institution of racism (human inequality), which supported colonialism and was embraced by the Fascist powers, both as doctrine and in support of their own imperial aspirations. The changes in the distribution of power still left a multipolar structure overall. Although there were some changes of position within the multipolarity, Europe remained the central focus of power politics, with Japan and the United States still on the edges. There were no substantial changes in the organising principles of GIS. Divided sovereignty, territoriality, nationalism, diplomacy, the balance of power, international law and war all stood largely unaltered. Even the LN system was original only in the scale of its ambitions: the idea of standing IGOs was not new, making the LN an extension of existing practices rather than a novel departure (Reus-Smit, 1999: 145–9).

Japan's story during the interwar years continued in a fairly smooth trajectory from pre-1914.[2] Japan had an easy and profitable war. Afterwards,

---

[2] This discussion draws heavily on Koyama and Buzan (2018).

it functioned as a normal member of the great power club despite its failure in 1919 to get Western recognition as racially equal. This humiliation resulted in an anti-Western turn in Japanese policy that laid the basis for the geopolitical contestation with Britain and the United States during the interwar years (Zarakol, 2011: 166–73). In line with changes in its own domestic politics, Japan moved away from alignment with Britain, and towards both more self-reliance and an eventual alignment with Germany and Italy. At the Washington Naval Conference in 1921–2, Japan won designation as the third-ranked naval power, ahead of France and Italy. It continued to build its empire in Northeast Asia, aiming to construct a regional bastion capable of resisting the West. To this end it seized Manchuria in 1931, which was already a semi-autonomous warlord state, and constructed a quite successful developmental colonial state there (Duara, 2003). It invaded China in 1937, but despite many military victories was unable to defeat the Chinese, and got bogged down in a long and vicious war. In the run-up to the Second World War, Japan, like several other great powers, left the LN.

By the standards of the day, Japan's behaviour was not noticeably different from that of the other great powers, which also made alliances of both opportunity and ideology, and sought to build autarkic imperial spheres. Japan was, however, more than a little unusual as an interwar colonial power in that it put a lot of effort into modernising its colonies, imposing on them a version of its own Meiji reforms. As Jan Jansen and Jürgen Osterhammel (2017: 61) put it: 'Japan was the only colonial power prior to 1945 that saw an opportunity for strengthening the metropole in a planned industrialization of the imperial periphery'. Bruce Cumings (1984: 12–13) concurs: before 1945 Japan was 'among the very few imperial powers to have located modern heavy industries in its colonies: steel, chemicals, hydroelectric facilities in Korea and Manchuria, and automobile production for a time in the latter … By 1945 Korea had an industrial infrastructure that, although sharply skewed towards metropolitan interests, was among the best developed in the third world'. Atul Kohli (2004: 25–61) shows in detail how Japanese colonial rule was far more penetrative and modernising than British and French, reshaping Korean agriculture, transforming the class and political structures, abolishing slavery, and creating an export-oriented modern economy with a substantial industrial sector. Prasenjit Duara (2003) tells a similar story about Manchuria, where it is revealing that the large inward migration from China into Manchuria that had been going on since the 1890s continued apace during the Japanese occupation. While some Chinese resisted Japan's takeover, many others were drawn in by the expanding economic opportunities and the chance to escape the chaos of the warlords. Although these were undoubtedly coercive, repressive colonial states, Japan succeeded in co-opting substantial sections of their society, especially in Korea (Tudor, 2012: 19). Taiwan also got significant transport infrastructure and industrial development. Japan treated Taiwan, like Korea, in many ways as part of itself, including extending to the population its own system of mass education (J. Gray, 2002: 456). Japan's exploitation of its colonies, and its attempt to override their culture and identity, certainly generated opposition, but Koreans nevertheless played a significant role in Japan's colonisation and modernisation of both their own country and Manchuria; and between 1910 and 1940, both Korea and Taiwan had higher average GDP growth than Japan's 3.36 per cent, and Korea's manufacturing capacity grew at 10 per cent per annum (Cumings, 1984: 2).

Despite both its own colonialism, and eventually being defeated, Japan's early victories over the United States, Britain, France and the Dutch during 1941–2 had again broken the myth of white power in Asia and significantly paved the way for the decolonisation that followed (Westad, 2007: 88–9).

The Main Themes of Interwar International Relations

This section looks in more detail at how and why the attempt to recover and stabilise GIS failed despite efforts to control armaments and war, revive the global economy, and build more extensive global IGOs. This is a familiar story in IR, and needs only to be sketched here. It divides into two pretty clear phases: the attempt to rebuild an improved postwar order during the 1920s; and the progressive collapse of that order during the 1930s. In both phases the story is almost entirely about the core, which had been destabilised economically, politically, socially and militarily by the war. Despite the disruption in the core, there was no substantial threat from the periphery to the core–periphery colonial order during this period, though, as noted, foundations were being laid down for stronger resistance later. Anti-colonialism became more organised in Vietnam, India, Indonesia and many parts of the Middle East, and the colonial powers had to deal not only with intellectual and political opposition fuelled in part by Wilsonian rhetoric of the right of self-determination, but sometimes with fierce protests and insurgencies (Jansen and Osterhammel, 2017: 35–70). But during the interwar years, colonial concerns were much more along the geopolitical lines of competition between the great powers to re-divide the colonial spoils, with Britain, France and the United States as the status quo powers, and Germany, Italy, Japan and, up to a point, the Soviet Union as the revisionist ones. The colonial powers still enjoyed a big advantage over the periphery in power and development, and up to a point, within the norms of GIS, legitimate authority. Within the core, colonialism was still a fully legitimate institution of GIS.

The attempt to restore and strengthen GIS after the First World War was centred around building a system of global IGOs, reviving the global economy, controlling the arms race, and banning war. In all of these areas there were some notable successes.

The LN and its associated family of functional IGOs established a permanent multilateral forum on a global scale for the first time. Although domestic politics prevented the United States from joining what its own president, Woodrow Wilson, had created, the LN nonetheless institutionalised multilateral diplomacy at the core of GIS. It hoped to replace the discredited balance of power with a system for collective security. It made room for public opinion, and aimed to create a legal framework to support world peace. Like the earlier IGOs mentioned in Chapter 1, the LN's members were not only the leading powers, but also many Non-Western states, some still under colonial rule. Among the founding members were China, India, Liberia, Persia/Iran and Siam/Thailand; and joining later were Abyssinia/Ethiopia (1924), Turkey (1932), Iraq (1932), Afghanistan (1934) and Egypt (1937). In some of the great powers, most notably Britain, there was strong public support and hope for the LN. The LN Union in Britain amassed over 400,000 members, and was a leading expression of the idea that democratic public opinion should henceforth play a large role in the promotion and preservation of peace.

The attempt to revive the global economy had some success during the 1920s. World trade recovered somewhat after the war, and the reinstitution of the gold standard as the basis for a global financial regime was moderately effective. This nineteenth-century regime had collapsed during the First World War, but by the late 1920s many countries had returned to it.

The major successes in arms control were the Washington Naval Treaty (1922) and the Geneva Protocol (1928) prohibiting the use of chemical and biological weapons in wars. Both of these addressed issues arising from the First World War: the naval arms race that had preceded the war and was partly held responsible for it, and the use of chemical weapons during the war. The Washington Treaty fixed ratios of capital ships among the five major naval powers, allowed large-scale scrapping of existing battleships and largely halted ambitious naval building programmes that still had momentum from the war. The Geneva Protocol effectively reinstated a ban first set up at The Hague

Conferences before the war. There was also preparatory work during the 1920s for a World Disarmament Conference to implement the promises made in the Treaty of Versailles. In 1925, the Treaties of Locarno went some way towards normalising relations with Germany, and affirming the territorial settlement of the war. In 1928, the Kellogg–Briand Pact gained wide support for banning war as a legitimate instrument of state policy, and was accompanied by the General Act for the Pacific Settlement of International Disputes. This was seen as idealistic even at the time. But it did reflect the trauma caused by the First World War and the fear of such an event being repeated, and it did provide a foundation for later laws of war and war crimes.

During the 1930s, the key elements in this attempt to strengthen GIS largely collapsed. The LN had been weakened from the beginning, mainly by the vetoing of US membership by American isolationists, but also by the punitive peace against Germany, which was not admitted to the LN until 1926. Several Latin American states withdrew from it during the 1920s and 1930s. The Fascist great powers withdrew during the 1930s: Japan in 1933 over the refusal of others to recognise its client state in Manchukuo; Germany in 1933 ostensibly because of the failure of the LN Disarmament Conference; and Italy in 1937 because of sanctions over its invasion of Ethiopia. The Soviet Union was expelled in 1939 because of its invasion of Finland. In part because of weak and divided great power leadership, and in part because of unrealistic expectations and weak enforcement capabilities, the LN failed to stand up as a mechanism for conducting collective security. Public opinion was not as universally pacifist as had been hoped, and in some countries it supported aggressive nationalist policies. Divergent interests among the great powers quickly destroyed any chance of the consensus that would be necessary to pursue collective security.

The same weakness that afflicted the LN with the absence of the United States also affected the world economy. Britain was too weakened economically by the war to be capable of resuming financial and trading leadership, while the United States, which had been greatly strengthened financially and industrially by the war, was politically unwilling to take the leadership role (Kindleberger, 1973: 28, 292). The market crash of 1929 in the United States quickly triggered protectionism and the collapse of both world trade and the gold standard, with even Britain being forced out of the gold standard in 1931, and abandoning free trade in 1932 (W. Ashworth, 1975: chs. 8–9; Foreman-Peck, 1982: chs. 7–8; Gilpin, 1987: 127–31).

The momentum behind both arms control and the banning of war drained away during the 1930s. The World Disarmament Conference, finally convened in 1932, broke up quickly in 1933, partly because of the complexities of distinguishing between offensive and defensive weapons, and partly because Germany refused to accept ongoing military constraints and inferiority while others refused to disarm to its level. The new Nazi government in Berlin started to re-arm, and others followed suit. Constraints on numbers and types of weapons were abandoned, and an arms race somewhat like that preceding the First World War got underway. Notwithstanding the still-strong fear of war in the status quo countries, fear of defeat unleashed the industrial arms dynamic of rapid qualitative and quantitative improvements at full tilt. The ban on war merely caused countries such as Italy and Japan to forego declaring war when they invaded others. Strong pacifist movements in places such as Britain were undermined when events such as the Spanish Civil War forced many Socialist pacifists to choose between their pacifism and their opposition to Fascism.

In sum, by the mid-1930s, the attempt to rebuild the prewar order was in full retreat. The LN was conspicuously failing to stop great powers from invading other countries. Germany was breaking out of the restraints and penalties imposed upon it by the Treaty of Versailles. The world economy had broken down, with the gold standard abandoned and tariff barriers being raised almost everywhere. Increasingly, the great powers all entered into the zero-sum game of trying to create autarkic economic blocs. The attempt to restrain the arms dynamic was falling apart, and one by one the great powers embarked on rearmament programmes. The idea that war could be banned looked hopelessly naïve, and among the Fascist powers war was increasingly celebrated as the destiny of the nation.

Weak leadership of GIS explains some of this breakdown, but so too does the powerful synergy between the introduction of ideology into great power relations, and the relentless pressure of the industrial arms dynamic. The three-way ideological division made balance-of-power, and balance of threat, calculations very tricky and complicated. Were the liberal democracies more threatened by communism or by Fascism? Was Fascism more threatened by communism or by liberal democracy? Were communists more threatened by Fascists or by liberal democracies? Under such conditions, could the enemy of my enemy be my friend? Such questions did not have clear answers leading to an easy consensus. Complicating such calculations were the rapid changes in the military balance being created by German, Japanese and Soviet rearmament, and the responses to them in France, Britain and the United States. These changes were not only quantitative (how many aircraft, ships, tanks, troops), but also qualitative. New generations of weapons were much more effective than older ones, and some entirely new things such as radar could change the game entirely.

Adding to this toxic brew was the breakdown of the global economy and the race to construct autarkic economic blocs. This essentially mercantilist move strongly re-established the link between prosperity and control of territory. In so doing, it sharpened the tensions within the core between the status quo and revisionist powers. The 'have' powers, such as Britain, France and the United States, were early modernisers that already had spheres of influence and/or empires that they could turn into economic blocs. The 'have not' powers, such as Germany, Italy, Japan and Russia, were later modernisers that needed to acquire (or in the case of Germany and Russia re-acquire) their own empires in order not to be squeezed out. Under such conditions, collective security was impossible. The logic of system closure that some geopolitical analysts used to explain the First World War was thus operating far more intensively in the run-up to the Second. By the 1930s, this combination had ignited a competitive imperialism of re-division of the colonial periphery by the core great powers that set the world firmly on the path to the Second World War.

The Second World War

As noted in the Introduction, in some ways the Second World War can best be seen as round two of the crisis of modernity kicked off by the First World War. The two wars together could be seen as a kind of European civil war (Preston, 2000: 153–4). There were a lot of continuities and similarities. Once again, Germany was at the centre of the European problem. The First World War had solved neither the problem of Germany's power in the heart of Europe, nor of its dissatisfaction with its status within GIS. Indeed, the harsh settlement at Versailles had worsened the latter, and helped pave the way for the rise of revanchist Fascism in Germany. The alignments for the Second World War took a quite similar form to those of the First, with Britain, France, Russia and eventually the United States lining up against Germany, Italy and various remnants of the Austro-Hungarian Empire. The failure of the attempt to strengthen GIS during the 1920s unleashed the same dynamics of development and armament that had destabilised great power relations before the First World War. Russia, Germany and Japan rapidly increased their industrial and military strength, and new weapons such as bombers promised to make a new war very different from the previous one. The Second World War was also, like the First, very much an event of the core, with the periphery serving mainly as a source of supply, including substantial numbers of troops, and as an object of competition between the great powers. Social Darwinism and nationalism remained powerful influences on the conduct and rationalisation of international relations, and in Fascism took an even more extreme form than they had prior to 1914.

There were some differences in the alignments. Japan joined the Axis powers rather than Britain, Turkey stayed neutral and Italy did not defect from Germany at the beginning of the war. But this difference was relatively minor compared to two others: ideology and scale. Whereas the First World War had mainly been a straightforward struggle over the balance of power and nationalism between the great powers, the Second World War was, in the end, a battle about ideology: what version of the political economy of modernity was going to own the future? While nationalism had pretty much triumphed everywhere, the contradictions inherent in the other three nineteenth-century ideologies of progress had not been resolved. Socialism, Liberalism and Fascism were all legitimate heirs to the revolutions of modernity. By the 1930s, all were firmly embedded in competing great powers, with the issue between them to be resolved by combat. On one side was the parochial ideology of Fascism, which threatened to bring the colonial hierarchies of race and imperial domination into the core. On the other were two universalist ideologies, liberal capitalism and totalitarian communism, which promised different visions of how humankind as a whole might be organised to take modernity forward. This alignment happened almost by chance. Japan tried attacking the Soviet Union in 1939, but was defeated, made peace with it and turned south, and eventually against the United States. In 1941, Hitler broke his pact with Stalin and not only invaded the Soviet Union, but declared war on the United States.

The Second World War was much larger in scale and intensity than the First. It was, in effect, the merger of two regional wars: one in Europe, which was round two of the First World War, and the other in Northeast Asia. The latter came about as a result of Japan's alienation from the United States and Britain during the interwar years described above, and its attempt to build a regional bastion in East Asia that could withstand Western pressure. This East Asian war began in earnest in 1937 with Japan's invasion of China, and merged with the European war in 1941 when Japan attacked the United States and Hitler took that opportunity to declare war on the United States. Despite its merged, global nature, the Second World War still remained Europe-centred. Germany was much more powerful and threatening than Japan, because it had the possibility of unifying the whole industrial core of Europe and becoming a global superpower. Japan had neither the intention nor the capability to invade the United States, threatening mainly to reassign the vulnerable Western colonies in Asia and the Pacific to itself.

This merger of two regional wars nevertheless made for a truly global world war with much larger imperial stakes. During the First World War, only the Middle East was seriously contested, whatever wider dreams Germany might have had about getting the British out of India. Elsewhere, as in Africa and East Asia, the mopping up of German colonies was a relatively minor affair. But during the Second World War, not only were the Middle East and North Africa at stake, but also the colonial empires in South and Southeast Asia. For a time, Germany and Italy threatened Britain's position in the Mediterranean and Egypt, and Japan took control of Southeast Asia and threatened India. New and improved weapons extended the range of military operations, and, except for the United States, brought the home front much more intensely into the conflict, most notably by the heavy bombing of cities. Some idea of the difference that both the wider scale and the new technologies made to great power war can be seen from the comparable casualty figures: roughly 15 million for the First World War and 41 million for the Second (Clodfelter, 2002).

Because of these differences, the consequences of the Second World War were also much larger than those of the First. As Buzan and Lawson (2014a) argue, the cluster of events around the Second World War deserve the status they have as a primary benchmark date for IR, whereas the First World War only ranks as a secondary benchmark date. The First World War changed relatively little in either the material or normative structure of GIS, whereas the Second World War changed a lot. After 1919, version 1.0 GIS carried on. After 1945, the changes were big enough to justify calling what resulted version 1.1 GIS. The main consequences of the Second World War were:

- The removal of France, Germany, Italy, Japan and, a bit later, Britain from the top rank of powers.
- The elevation of the United States and the Soviet Union to superpower status and the shift from an ideologically and materially multipolar structure to one that was bipolar both in distribution of power and in its narrowing of the ideological rivalry driving world politics to that between two versions of universalism: liberal-democratic capitalism and totalitarian communism.
- The downgrading of Europe from being the core of the core to being the principal object of contestation between the two superpowers.
- The ending of US isolationism, and a willingness within the United States to take over economic and political leadership from Britain. A corollary of this was a major shift towards multilateral diplomacy and

rebuilding an improved set of global IGOs. Although there were two superpowers, in reality the United States was vastly ahead of the Soviet Union in terms of wealth and material capability. The Soviet Union competed seriously only in military capability and ideological punch.

- The reunification of China as an independent power under communist rather than nationalist rule.
- The delegitimation of racism and human inequality as primary institutions of GIS, and their replacement by human equality and human rights. A corollary of this was the delegitimation of Fascism as a form of modern government on the grounds that it had moved the racism and unrestrained use of force previously reserved for the periphery into the core.
- The delegitimation of colonialism/imperialism as a primary institution of GIS, and its replacement by development. A corollary of this was the rapid abandonment of formally divided sovereignty, its replacement by universal sovereign equality, and the beginning of a great expansion in the membership of GIS. But while this ended the political side of the core–periphery structure of version 1.0 GIS, it left its economic side firmly in place.
- The arrival of nuclear weapons, and the consequent return in amplified form of the defence dilemma (fear of war outweighing fear of defeat). The state of military technology reached by 1945 promoted the idea that war was irrational because it would be impossible to distinguish between winners and losers. Nuclear weapons created for the first time the possibility of human species suicide. As after the First World War, only this time much more powerfully, the idea was in play that a new war would threaten the existence of civilisation, and that the problem was not how to fight such a war, but how to stop it from ever being fought.

Conclusions

The outcome of the Second World War set up the main features that were to dominate international relations right up to the end of the 1980s:

- An intense, global-scale ideological and material rivalry between the two superpowers.
- The emergence of China as a third wheel in the great game of power and ideology.
- A largely unconstrained arms dynamic that would continue to pump new and improved weapons into the system, creating a continuous destabilisation of superpower relations.

- A very major problem about how to deal with the massive impact of nuclear weapons on the purposes and practices of war.
- How to adjust to the breakup of colonialism, and the rapid tripling of the membership of GIS, with most of the new members being politically and economically weak, and a long way from having internalised and stabilised the revolutions of modernity in their domestic affairs. Having delegitimised colonialism, how was the still highly unequal and core–periphery economic reality of version 1.1 GIS to be managed under the new institution of development?

4   International Relations 1919–1945: The First Founding of the Discipline

Introduction

We argued in Chapter 2 that throughout the nineteenth century and through the First World War, there was a great deal of thinking and theorising that would, by today's standards, count as IR. Much of this was concentrated in the core countries and reflected their perceptions and concerns, including a strong distinction between relations among 'civilised' states and peoples within international society, and relations between 'civilised' peoples and those they had colonised. Thinking in terms of racial and developmental hierarchies played a central role in much of this 'IR before IR'. There were some early signs of institutionalisation in terms of books, journals and university courses, and most of these developed only in the decade or two before the First World War, and only in a handful of core countries and Japan. There was IR thinking in the periphery too, much of it motivated by anti-colonialism and anti-(white)racism, and mainly not yet taking academic form. This 'IR before IR' did not yet have a collective label, but the thinking involved covered much of the agenda of contemporary IR. We concluded by arguing that the 1919 founding 'myth' was at best a half-truth. It is true that from 1919 IR became a self-conscious field of study, and acquired a significant degree of institutionalisation. It is also true that the trauma of the First World War refocused the priorities of the new field towards the core's problem of war and peace between the great powers in a world of sharp ideological divides. It is not true that systematic thinking and theorising about modern IR began in 1919.

As argued in Chapter 3, while the First World War disrupted many things, it did not break the structure of either colonial GIS or the racial and developmental hierarchies that underpinned it. Since ir remained in version 1.0, Western-colonial GIS, the main differences in IR were in its institutionalisation and in the core's obsession with the problem of war and peace between the great powers. Indeed, the trauma of the war further marginalised concern with core–periphery relations as part of both ir and IR. During the interwar years, there is, therefore, very considerable continuity with the pre-1914 agenda of IR thinking, and this is true both within the core and within the periphery. We can therefore use the same general structure in this chapter as we did for Chapter 2, looking at IR thinking in the core, and then in the periphery. But first we look at the institutionalisation of the discipline worldwide, which is the core of the 1919 founding claim.

The Institutionalisation of IR

We look first at the institutionalisation of IR in the core countries, which is a fairly well-covered story, and then at the beginnings of its institutionalisation in the periphery, which is much less well-covered.

The Core

There is no doubt that the First World War triggered a step change in the study of IR, marking its emergence as a formal, recognised field of study, or even academic discipline (opinion on this varied then, as it still does now, with narrower and broader interpretations of the subject matter). This formalisation and institutionalisation took place against the background not just of a hugely destructive and costly war, but also alongside the Versailles Peace Conference and the formation of the LN. The establishment of IR was thus entangled with anti-war sentiments and hopes for the new LN as a guarantor of world peace that crystallised into a robust form of idealism. The rise of public opinion and mass media from the late nineteenth century played an increasing role in both ir and IR, especially after 1919, and were a big element in the 'Utopian' schemes for world peace and collective security (Seton-Watson, 1972). It was only after the First World War that there emerged a desire to take international relations out of the hands of professional diplomats. Carr (1964: 2) notes the change of mood, with the 'agitation' against secret treaties being 'the first symptom of the demand for the popularisation of international politics [which] heralded the birth of a new science'. Both Michael Banks (1985: 10) and Ekkehart Krippendorff (1989: 34) echo the familiar view that the war, the 1919 Peace Conference and the creation of the LN were closely linked to the emergence of IR as a new discipline.

As noted in Chapter 2, the symbolic first move in the institutionalisation of IR was the endowment of the Woodrow Wilson Chair in International Politics at Aberystwyth in 1919 (Booth, 1996: 328, 330). The aim of the new department was 'repairing the shattered family of nations'[1] and instilling support for the LN. There is much to support the view that the United Kingdom was as important, if not more, to the birth of modern IR as the United States. After the founding of International Politics at Aberystwyth, the Royal Institute of International Affairs, commonly referred to as Chatham House, was founded in 1920 (Olson, 1972) and started publishing its journal *International Affairs* in 1922. The Ernest Cassel Chair of International Relations was established in 1924 at the London School of Economics, with Philip Noel-Baker as the first holder. This was followed by a full-fledged Department of International Relations at the school in 1927, with the Cassel Chair becoming the Montague Burton Chair from 1936.[2] In 1930, the Montague Burton Chair of International Relations was established at Oxford.

The institutionalisation of IR during the interwar years in the United States was even more prolific, including departments, institutes and think tanks on international relations.

In 1918, the League of Free Nations Association was founded to support Wilsonian 'just peace' ideals. Among its founders were John Foster Dulles and Eleanor Roosevelt. The year 1921 saw the establishment of the Council on Foreign Relations (CFR), founded with a mission to 'afford a continuous conference on international questions affecting the United States, by bringing together experts on statecraft, finance, industry, education, and science'.[3] The CFR was a 'sister house' of London's Chatham House, and, similarly, served as a policy-oriented think tank (Olson, 1972: 13). This was followed in 1923 by the reconstitution of the League of Free Nations Association into the Foreign Policy Association, which was fairly progressivist and served as an alternative to the conservative CFR (Vitalis, 2005: 175). The association's major foreign policy analysis publications include *Foreign Policy Reports*, *Foreign Policy Bulletin* and *Headline Series*.

Universities followed research institutes. In 1919, Georgetown University launched its Edmund A. Walsh School of Foreign Service and the University of Chicago's Committee on International Relations was co-founded in 1928 by Quincy Wright and Hans Morgenthau, and claims to be America's 'oldest graduate program in international affairs'.[4] This was followed in 1930 by Princeton, who set up their School of Public and International Affairs (later named after Woodrow Wilson in 1948). Tufts University's Fletcher School of Law and Diplomacy was founded in

---

[1] www.aber.ac.uk/en/interpol/about/history/ (Accessed 29 September 2017).
[2] http://blogs.lse.ac.uk/internationalrelations/2017/04/26/foundation-and-history-of-the-international-relations-department/ (Accessed 29 September 2017).
[3] www.cfr.org/who-we-are (Accessed 29 September 2017).
[4] https://cir.uchicago.edu/content/about (Accessed 29 September 2017).

1933. In 1935, the Yale Institute of International Studies was founded, led by Nicholas Spykman and Frederick Dunn,[5] and in 1936 the Graduate School of Public Administration was set up at Harvard. The School of Advanced International Studies was established in 1943 in Washington, DC (it became part of the Johns Hopkins University in 1950). Schmidt (1998a: 155–7) notes that by the early 1930s in the United States there were 204 college courses on IR, 67 on International Organisation, 196 on International Law, and several IR textbooks to choose from.

Another milestone was the establishment of the Institute of Pacific Relations (IPR) in 1925 in Honolulu, the 'first formal regional studies center in the United States' (Vitalis, 2005: 177). Unlike the CFR, the IPR sought to be a more inclusive grouping. It was composed of national councils of nations of the Pacific, although in practice dominated by the American national council (known as the American IPR). It held conferences in Japan (1929) and China (1931). Wilsonian Idealism was a strong influence, as reflected in its flagship journal *Pacific Affairs*. The Social Science Research Council created its first Advisory Committee on International Relations in 1926.

Although the main action of institutionalising IR was in Britain and the United States, there were also wider, but mostly thinner, developments elsewhere. Chatham House and its journal *International Affairs* were widely imitated in parts of Europe (initially in Germany in 1921 and 1923, and then in Hungary, Poland, Denmark and Czechoslovakia); and the British Empire (Australia, South Africa, India and New Zealand) (Riemens, 2011: 914–16). The Graduate Institute of International Studies was founded in Geneva in 1927.

The interwar years did not see institutionalisation in the form of the academic membership associations of IR, which became a feature of the field after the Second World War. Instead, the main focus was a variety of national coordinating committees on IR, mainly European and American, working through the International Institute of Intellectual Cooperation (IIIC) in Paris. The IIIC was French-sponsored, but linked to the LN. From 1928 until the Second World War, it facilitated the annual International Studies Conference (ISC), which considered various themes and published reports of its proceedings. In the beginning, it was called the Conference of Institutions for the Scientific Study of International Relations, which more accurately captures both its federal structure and its sense of purpose. The delegates were from many countries, and the conference grew to more than a hundred participants.

---

[5] The institute shut down in 1951 after a mass defection of the faculty to Princeton after encountering issues with Yale's new president.

The ISC devoted much of its time to trying to define the scope and content of the new discipline. It was suspended during the Second World War, but revived briefly afterwards, being wound up in 1954 (Long, 2006; Riemens, 2011). The ISC was the forerunner of the institutionalisation of academic IR that took off during the 1950s. It was a mainly US/European/white dominions affair, with national bodies being the members. But delegates from India, China, Egypt, Japan and Turkey also participated (Riemens, 2011: 920).

An interesting twist to all this is the role of American foundations in funding this early institutionalisation of IR (Kuru, 2017). These foundations had a broadly Liberal Internationalist outlook, were opposed to US isolationism and wanted to promote a practical 'engineering approach' to the social sciences (Kuru, 2017: 50–3). Rockefeller and Carnegie funded the meetings of the ISC: Carnegie funded IR chairs in Berlin and Paris in the mid-1920s; and Rockefeller funded a foreign policy institute in Hamburg in 1923, and the Yale Institute of International Studies in 1935. Thus at a time when American politics had turned away from international responsibilities, capitalist American foundations were doing the opposite.

Despite this institutionalisation, there was still no agreement on the name of the field. The Aberystwyth Chair was 'International Politics', not 'International Relations'. Others, such as Carr and Morgenthau, also used the term 'International Politics', and 'International Studies' was strongly in play too. Where IR was considered to be a branch of Political Science, as most obviously in the United States (Schmidt, 1998a: 55; L. Ashworth, 2014: 13; Kuru, 2017: 46), 'International Politics' or 'World Politics' was perhaps the more obvious label. Some early books did carry the term 'international relations' in their titles, such as Grant et al.'s *An Introduction to the Study of International Relations* (1916), D. P. Heatley's *Diplomacy and the Study of International Relations* (1919) and Edmund Walsh's *The History and Nature of International Relations* (1922). These books dealt with diverse topics including economics, history and law, but were particularly focused on diplomacy. American scholar Raymond Leslie Buell, in 1925, wrote a book entitled *International Relations*, perhaps the first textbook on IR. At the time, it was the 'best-selling American textbook devoted to a new political science of *International Relations*' (Vitalis, 2005: 159). Frederick Schuman's 1933 text was, however, titled *International Politics* (Schmidt, 1998a: 213).

The Periphery

We have not been able to find evidence for the institutionalisation of IR in Latin America, Africa or the Middle East, though this might be a research opportunity for others. There were, however, significant developments in Japan, and to a lesser extent in India and China, and possibly also elsewhere. We noted above that delegates from India, China, Egypt, Japan and Turkey participated in the ISC, and that fact suggests that those countries had at least rudimentary institutionalisation of IR. The same logic applies to the IPR conferences held in Japan (1929) and China (1931). Michael Riemens (2011: 925) cites an LN study in which Japan was ranked in the second tier of countries (after Britain and the United States in the first tier, and alongside Australia, France, Italy and Canada), in terms of the quality, depth and institutionalisation of its IR studies; India was ranked in the third tier, between Japan and China; and China was ranked in the fourth tier, which meant that some individual IR experts were active, but with little or no institutionalisation.

In Japan, there were institutions where 'International Politics' was taught, such as the faculty and chair at the University of Tokyo (then called Imperial University of Tokyo), set up in 1924, and Waseda University, which introduced a course in 1932 (Kawata and Ninomiya, 1964: 193–4). In India, the first institute dedicated to the study of IR was the Indian Institute of International Affairs, formed by the British government in the 1930s. However, this institute was set up by, and composed of, members of the colonial authorities. The Indian intelligentsia's response was to set up a think tank, the Indian Council of World Affairs (ICWA), in 1943, which as we show in Chapter 6 was in many ways the genesis of the development of the field of IR in India.

The story of interwar IR in China is controversial and under-researched. Most scholars tracing the historiography of IR in China take 1949 as their starting point (Song, 2001; Zhang, F., 2012a). However, they ignore the fact that IR in China existed during the pre-communist period. Chinese scholars mostly do not yet recognise this legacy. The development of IR in China before the Second World War is obscured by political developments after the communist revolution in 1949. Lu Peng (2014) argues that the field of International Studies was well-established in China during the nationalist regime, with the help of scholars trained in the West, but after the communist revolution, scholars renounced that legacy. Pre-1949 IR followed themes and approaches, such as International Law and Organisation, that were commonplace in the West, with universities such as Tsinghua (then called National Tsinghua University), Peking and St John's in Shanghai (founded by American missionaries in 1879 but closed by the government in 1952) taking the lead in the field. At these universities, there was a distinct focus on studying China's place in the world, and China's relations with the world, although the discipline remained separate from domestic Chinese politics, despite being housed in departments of Political Science (Lu, 2014).

IR Thinking in the Core

The dominance of the Anglosphere in the institutionalisation of IR came at a cost. As Schmidt (1998a: 13) rightly notes, 'the academic study of international relations is marked by British, and especially, American parochialism'.[6] Out of this parochialism came another foundational IR 'myth', that of a 'great debate' between Realism and Idealism during the interwar years. That any such debate took place structured as a zero-sum contest between two incompatible positions has been pretty much debunked (Schmidt, 1998a; Wilson, 1998; L. Ashworth, 2014: 134–7). Schmidt has challenged the widespread characterisation of the interwar development of IR as one of Idealist dominance. He points to a pluralism of views and perspectives during the interwar period in Europe and North America. For example, G. Lowes Dickinson, though viewed as an Idealist, argued, 'in much the same way as neorealists, that the existence of independent sovereign states recognizing no higher authority other than themselves was the single most important cause of war' (Schmidt, 1998b: 444). The 'Utopians' were fully aware of the power politics aspect of IR, and were trying to find ways of controlling and managing it (Long and Wilson, 1995; Wilson, 1998; L. Ashworth, 2002). Yet Peter Wilson (1998) shows that, despite being strongly criticised when it was first published in 1939, Carr's *The Twenty Years' Crisis* was a powerful polemic with a big influence both then, and after 1945. And like all such myths, the Idealist–Realist debate was not without consequence or value. As Scott Burchill and Andrew Linklater (2013: 9) put it: 'the myth of a great debate between the realists and the idealists gave the discipline its identity in the years following World War II'. The first great debate is thus more a construct of IR after 1945 than a representation of what happened during the interwar years (L. Ashworth, 2014: 134–7).

In understanding this 'first great debate' it is important once again to take into account the link between ir and IR. The new field of IR arose in the wake of the catastrophe of the First World War, which had toppled empires, bankrupted nations and laid waste to a generation of young men. The war had (eventually) been fought by Britain and the United States under the slogan of 'the war to end war', and the new IR was substantially motivated by this aim. It sought to understand the

---

[6] Olson and Groom (1991: 74–5) make the good point that: ' ... in authoritarian states the study of international relations or foreign policy could only exist as an explanation and justification of state policy'. This provides some explanation for the dominance of the Anglosphere, and democracies, in IR, and is relevant both to the story of Japan below, and to the Soviet Union and China in later periods.

causes of the First World War in secret diplomacy, arms racing and the balance of power. In the game of two halves that was the interwar period (see Chapter 3), the first half was dominated by the hopes vested in the LN that the problem of war could be solved by means of arms control, informed public opinion and intergovernmental institutions. In the second half, when these hopes were crumbling, the realities of power politics reasserted themselves. While there was no 'great debate' as such during this period, there was certainly a broad spectrum of opinions on how to deal with the anarchy problem in the wake of the First World War. These ranged from those hoping that public opinion would be a new force against war, through those hoping that stronger intergovernmental institutions could mediate the causes of war, to those looking to the balance of power despite its failure in 1914. During the 1920s, those of the Liberal (and up to a point Socialist) end of this spectrum largely held sway in IR.[7] As one retrospective on Sir Alfred Zimmern, the first holder of the Woodrow Wilson Chair at Aberystwyth and the scholar who was the main target of Carr's critique, puts it:

There was an apocalyptic mood, symbolised by the creation of the Woodrow Wilson chair of International Politics in the University College of Wales, Aberystwyth, in 1919, the first such university chair anywhere in the world. It shows vividly how the optimism and brave new world idealism of the immediate post-war period focused on the creation of the new League of Nations at the Paris Peace Conference in 1919. The naming of the chair after Wilson reflected the fact that the idea of a League of Nations was in practice very much an Anglo-American one. (Morgan, 2012)

Zimmern was a good example of the often deep interplay between IR thinkers, and those who were advocating and promoting the LN. During the 1930s, the Realist voices became stronger. Carr's polemic bundled the whole Liberal end of the spectrum together under the labels 'Utopian' and 'idealist', which as Wilson (1998: 1) observes were little more than 'a realist category of abuse'.

The impact of Carr's work was more after 1945 than during the interwar years, and did much to establish the Realist view that 'Utopian' schemes to control war were foolish and dangerous. But in some ways the idea of a 'first great debate' does capture the character of the new IR as it grappled with the problem exposed by the First World War, that industrialisation had made war too costly and too destructive to be a

---

[7] As Lucian Ashworth (2014: 147–71) points out, attitudes towards the LN were much more complicated than any simple left–right divide. Many conservatives were strong supporters of the LN, and many on the left opposed it. It is impossible to extract any simple Realist/Idealist divide out of the actual politics of the day.

normal instrument of great power policy. The founding of IR took place at a time when there was a strong sense among both elites and publics that the world (or more accurately Western civilisation) was in crisis, with real chances for either catastrophe or the making of a new world order (L. Ashworth, 2014: 138). There is so much written about Carr's critique of Utopianism (and its various mis/interpretations) that it is unnecessary to revisit it in any detail here (M. Cox, 2001). The positioning of him as an avowed Realist has itself been challenged. Carr, at times, is as critical of Realism as he is of Idealism, arguing that 'the abrupt descent from the visionary hopes of the first decade [1919–29] to the grim despair of the second [1929–39]' marked a shift 'from a utopia which took little account of the reality to a reality from which every element of utopia was rigorously excluded' (Carr, [1939] 2016: 207).

In his critique of Utopia, Carr especially targeted the 'harmony of interests', the doctrine of free trade and international institutions then represented by the LN and its underlying doctrine of collective security. He argued that through the writings of the 'Utopians', such as Norman Angell, the already obsolete laissez-faire doctrine was reintroduced after the First World War in the form of the harmony of interests (Carr, [1939] 2016: 49), especially in the United States. He viewed this as impractical and even dangerous. Carr stressed Realism as an alternative. Although his work was mainly a repudiation of the Wilsonian Idealism that informed much of the development of IR in the interwar period, he believed that politics is a combination of power *and* morality. The degree of divergence between Idealism and Realism can be overstated: it did not imply fundamental differences in worldviews. In recent re/interpretations, Sir Alfred Zimmern has been recast as a 'Cautious Idealist', who disagreed with and criticised more extreme Utopians and Socialists such as Harold Laski, did not dismiss the importance of power and great power primacy, and recognised the limits and failures of the LN (Rich, 1995).

Most of Carr's examples of the fallacies of Utopianism and the logic of Realism are drawn from the European experience. His argument that early IR theory is idealistic partly because it emerged from English-speaking countries (the United States and the United Kingdom) that had never 'profited' from war (Carr, [1939] 2016: 50) may seem objectionable to those outside the West. The victims of Western colonialism saw Britain as well as the other colonial powers of Europe as having greatly profited from colonial wars.

Within this obsession about how to deal with the problem of great power war, all of the themes and approaches that marked IR before 1914 continued to be in play. This is hardly surprising given that many of the key figures from IR before 1914 remained active during the interwar years: J. A. Hobson, Mackinder, Angell and others (L. Ashworth, 2014: 137). To the extent that 'Idealism' was essentially Liberalism, as Carr's attack on ideas of a natural harmony of interests suggests, then the great debate was about the ongoing tension between globalising Liberalism and the *raison d'etat* of Realism. After the First World War, Realist logic was more seen as the problem than the solution, allowing Liberal thinking a decade of dominance. But as the approach to war became more obvious during the 1930s, these positions reversed, culminating in Carr's polemic.

The impetus behind Liberal 'Idealism' during the 1920s generated International Organisation as a distinct sub-field of IR as it developed in the United States and the United Kingdom in the interwar period. Couched in idealist and normative language, work in International Organisation often involved in-depth studies and analyses of the working and functions of international organisations, with the LN being the primary focus. Indeed, Pitman B. Potter (1922), in his book *An Introduction to the Study of International Organization*, argues that International Organisation, conceptualised as 'a procedure of facilitating international harmonisation and coordination between states' is different from International Politics or International Law precisely because of its Idealist orientation (Schmidt, 1998b: 449–52). The number of books examining the prospects for, but also indirectly appealing for, an 'international government', such as J. A. Hobson's *Towards International Government* (1915), Leonard Woolf's *International Government* (1916) and Clyde Eagleton's *International Government* (1932), bear testimony to the Idealist strain in International Organisation. Likewise the concept of international society also remained strong during this period. Among the books covering this approach were: T. J. Lawrence, *The Society of Nations: Its Past, Present and Possible Future* (1919); Philip Marshall Brown, *International Society: Its Nature and Interests* (1923); S. H. Bailey, *The Framework of International Society* (1932); Felix Morley, *The Society of Nations: Its Organization and Constitutional Development* (1932); and Alfred Zimmern, *The League of Nations and the Rule of Law* (1936).

Although somewhat neglected in accounts of the great debate, 'Scientific' Racism, nationalism and Geopolitics all played into it, mostly on the side of Realist power politics. Racism and Geopolitics, as they had been before 1914, were often mutually reinforcing. 'Scientific' Racism was reaching its peak during this period, particularly so in the Fascist states, where it was merged with hypernationalism. The pre-1914 attitude of racial hierarchies as defining relations between core and periphery remained largely unaltered. The new development was the intensification of race politics within the core, with whites now being differentiated into racial hierarchies of Aryan, Latin and Slav. Writers on race and world politics, such as Lothrop Stoddard (1923: 12), reverberated the point noted in Chapter 1 that the Japanese victory over Russia in 1905 meant that 'the legend of white invincibility lay, a fallen idol, in the dust'. As Vitalis (2005: 159–60) notes, there was 'a flood of new writings and theorizing in the 1920s on both race and race war'. Du Bois, whom we met in Chapter 2 as an exponent of Pan-Africanism, wrote (e.g. in *Foreign Affairs*) on race in international relations (Vitalis, 2005: 172–3). Du Bois provides an interesting insight into the pervasiveness of racism at the time. As a student at Harvard, he was to write later: 'it was not easily possible for the student of international affairs trained in white institutions and by European ideology to follow the partially concealed and hidden action of international intrigue, which was turning colonial empires into the threat of armed competition for markets, cheap materials and cheap labor. Colonies still meant religious and social uplift in current propaganda' (Du Bois, [1940] 1992: 232).

Geopolitics also remained influential in imperial thinking before 1919 and remained so until the end of the Second World War (L. Ashworth, 2013; Guzzini, 2013). In Germany, Karl Haushofer picked up on, and combined, the pre-1914 work of Mackinder and Ratzel on the heartland theory and *Lebensraum*. He founded the *Zeitschrift für Geopolitik* in 1924, and had some influence on Hitler's thinking about a grand strategy for Germany (Ó Tuathail, 1998: 4, 19–27; J. M. Hobson, 2012: 154–9; L. Ashworth, 2014: 203–6). Mackinder remained active with a less geographically deterministic view in his 1919 book *Democratic Ideals and Reality*. In the United States Isaiah Bowman's influential 1921 book *The New World: Problems in Political Geography* also blended material and ideational factors in understanding world politics. Both Bowman and Derwent Whittlesey cultivated a more open Geopolitics to counter the German version, and to pave the way for the more globalist US grand strategy after 1945 (L. Ashworth, 2014: 141–7, 206–9). Also in the United States, Nicholas Spykman (1942) picked up geographical determinism and the theme of land versus sea power from both Mackinder and Mahan, to argue for a Rimland Geopolitics against Mackinder's continentalist heartland approach, and that the United States should not revert to isolationism after the Second World War (L. Ashworth, 2014: 206–13). Both Spykman and Haushofer were influenced by the ideas from pre-1914 Geopolitics and 'Scientific' Racism about the protection of the white races, and the use of imperial containment to prevent the 'yellow peril' from taking over the West. Others did not see the same threat from the East as Mackinder and Mahan did. Tyner (1999: 58) describes Geopolitical scholars including Haushofer, Ratzel and Rudolf Kjellén as propounding an 'organic-state theory', because of the emphasis on space required by the state for survival, as opposed to the 'eugenicist' theory of Mackinder and Mahan.

Another illustration of the pervasive influence of racism is Woodrow Wilson. The conventional view of the development of IR paints Wilson as a champion of Idealism and self-determination and free values. But Wilson, despite his Liberal credentials, was an active exponent of race politics and white supremacy both domestically and internationally (Vitalis, 2005: 168). Paul Rahe (2013) and John Hobson (2012: 167–75) argue that Wilson was not as progressive as portrayed by IR historiography, but was in fact deeply racist. Wilsonian self-determination was another way of expressing 'the need for a Western imperial civilizing mission in the primitive East' (J. M. Hobson, 2012: 168). Liberals such as Wilson did not want to instil change but rather wanted to maintain the status quo, as reflected in the design and functioning of the LN. The mandate system of the LN was basically colonialism by another name. The starkest indication of Wilson's racism at the international level was his sustained effort to deny the inclusion of Japan's racial equality clause at the Paris Peace Conference. Domestically, Wilson sought to justify the racist activities of whites in the South, including the Ku Klux Klan, stating that they had little choice because of 'the sudden and absolute emancipation of the negroes' (cited in J. M. Hobson, 2012: 171). Tyner (1999) identifies how the United States, including under Wilson, excluded Filipinos from immigration because of the racial difference. Wilson also justified the colonisation of the Philippines, arguing that Americans could teach the Filipinos how to govern, saving self-determination for *after* this instruction in the superior Western style of governance (J. M. Hobson, 2012: 172–3).

The 'great debates' approach to studying IR fails to recognise that during the interwar period 'Scientific' Racism and Geopolitics continued the pattern from pre-1914 IR thinking of being both influential and mutually reinforcing. In addition, both were within the framework of, and were bound by, the general Eurocentrism of IR. John Hobson (2012) argues that all the IR theories, irrespective of which side of the debates they were on, were focused on preserving and propagating Western ideas and values. This West-centrism easily took on racist content. Hobson is quite right to consider the thinkers of 'Scientific' Racism and Geopolitics as part of a 'strong continuity between pre-1914 international theory and its interwar successor' (J. M. Hobson, 2012: 15).

Socialism, which after 1917 was embodied in a great power, is another neglected part of the great debate. As Lucian Ashworth (2014: 7) notes, there was a 'raging debate in 1930s IR over the role of capitalism as a cause of war'. Many Socialists refused to fight for capitalism and comprised one strand of anti-war pacifism during this period. The left, indeed, was quite fragmented in its attitude towards the LN, with some opposing it as a tool of capitalism, others opposing any idea of an international police force or army, and yet others wanting to reform and strengthen it to help domesticate international politics (L. Ashworth, 2014: 159–71). To the extent that Stalin's foreign policy goals influenced thinking on the left, there was also another link between ir and IR. Stalin's policy was to prevent Japan and Germany from aligning against the Soviet Union. To do this he encouraged France and Britain to align against Germany, and Japan to get bogged down in China and be at odds with the United States (Paine, 2012: loc. 5672, 2017: 149–56).

There was also a continuation of a distinctive literature on War and Strategic Studies. As in the pre-1914 period, military professionals dominated this literature. The difference was that during the interwar years there was much more focus on the new technologies of tanks and aircraft as ways of restoring mobility to warfare. Basil Liddell Hart (1946) advocated combined arms warfare, and J. F. C. Fuller (1945) explored armoured warfare (both being more taken up by the Germans as *Blitzkrieg* than by Britain). Giulio Douhet ([1921] 1998) wrote on air power in his classic, *The Command of the Air*. In a sign of what was to come after 1945 (Buzan and Hansen, 2009), there were also works in this area by civilians; not just the extensive propaganda of peace organisations, but also the work of academics such as Philip Noel-Baker on disarmament and the arms trade (Buzan, 1973).

Another point worth making about interwar IR is its strong inter-weaving of international politics and international economics. As Lucian Ashworth (2014: 253–4) observes, this blending was largely natural and unconscious, and carried forward from pre-1914 IR. It was expressed in the works of writers such as Norman Angell, Karl Polanyi, David Mitrany and Albert O. Hirschman.

One new line of thinking not present in IR before the First World War opened up during the interwar years: Feminism. This perhaps dates from Helena Swanwick's 1915 pamphlet *Women and War* written for the Union of Democratic Control (L. Ashworth, 2008, 2014: 125–6). Lucian Ashworth (2017) argues for the existence of an influential early Feminist movement in IR, centred on the WILPF. Women writers associated with WILPF developed a 'maternalist' perspective on war and collective security, arguing that as givers of life women had a different perspective on these issues from men. This position was accepted, and influential, in the IR discourses of the day. This early Feminist development in IR has been forgotten, making Feminism in IR seem to be a more recent development than it is.

Despite all their many differences, the interwar thinkers on IR were mainly similar in dealing with imperialism not as the central issue of IR but as a sideshow, and offered only a partial or conditional rejection of it. This is another blindness of the 'great debate' understanding of interwar IR. Carr's trenchant criticism of Utopianism did touch on imperialism, but, reflecting the times, did not consider it as a central issue. Carr viewed imperialism mainly as an example of Utopian hypocrisy or as a critique of the Idealist 'harmony of interest' thesis, rather than as a moral evil itself. In his view, 'The harmony of interest was established through the sacrifice of "unfit" Africans and Asiatics' (Carr, 1964: 49). However, the colonial angle was not central, but marginal, to his overall case against Utopianism. Many on the left, such as H. N. Brailsford, and some Liberals, were opposed to imperialism, but given the strong shadow of the First World War there was more concern in these quarters about the relationship between capitalism on the one hand, and war and Fascism on the other, than about imperialism (L. Ashworth, 2014: 213–21). Given the influence of 'Scientific' Racism and Geopolitics in interwar IR, and the linkage of both to imperialism, Vitalis (2005, 2015) is partly right to refute the view that imperialism was neglected by IR at this time. He argues that race relations and colonial administration were central concerns of American IR scholars. As it had been before 1914, colonial administration continued to be an important branch of study, but also as before 1914, it was not considered to be part of IR, but a separate field. Arthur Berriedale Keith (1924), for example, looked at the layering of legal and political powers within the British Empire, including the participation by the dominions, including India, in various IGOs; the negotiations between Britain and its colonies over the provision and payment for defence; the tensions between the demands of white settlers, and the responsibility of the empire to develop the native peoples towards civilisation; and the tension within the empire about non-white migration into white settler colonies. But while imperialism was present in interwar IR, it was very much a view of it from the core, and largely continued the practice from pre-1914 of not seeing colonial relations as part of IR.

Conclusions

To sum up, the field of IR is commonly understood to have been born during the interwar period, with the specific aim of preventing the outbreak of another large-scale, devastating and debilitating world war.

In this context, IR at its first founding is credited with the normative purpose of avoiding war and improving the conditions of people around the world so as to make it a better place to live. This view is embodied in the myth of the Realist/Idealist debate. Neither of these myths is true. The IR of the interwar years was much more complex, wide-ranging and interdisciplinary than implied by the 'great debate' formulation, and, as both Schmidt (1998b) and Lucian Ashworth (2014) show in detail, much less clearly polarised between 'Idealist' and 'Realist' camps. The setting up of Idealism as a strawman was a successful ruse largely done by Realists after 1945 (Kahler, 1997: 27). Interwar IR also featured a lot of continuity with IR from before 1914, most notably the background assumptions of West-centrism, imperialism, Geopolitics, International Political Economy (IPE) and racial hierarchy that remained largely unaltered. Following the trauma of the First World War, and with the great experiment of the LN in front of them, it is no surprise that interwar IR showed a particular interest in IGOs as a possible way of managing the anarchy problem. So, IR had dark legacies and roots as well as the altruistic one of understanding war and pursuing peace. IR, and 'international theory' more generally, was inextricably intertwined with the project of the advancement and protection of the West and Western ideas, resulting in Eurocentrism at best and Geopolitics and 'Scientific' Racism at worst. The critiques of racialism and imperialism from a normative perspective and from the vantage point of the oppressed came mainly from the nationalist leaders and thinkers in the colonies. These contributions were the original foundations of the Global IR project that this book is about.

IR Thinking in the Periphery

The foundational IR writings from the core largely neglected IR thinking and debates in the Non-Western world. Carr briefly acknowledges ancient China as one of the two locations where attempts to create a 'science of politics' were made, the other being ancient Greece (Carr, 1964: 6). In his view, 'current theories of international relations … emanated almost exclusively from the English-speaking countries' (Carr, 1964: 52). Non-Western (non-European and US) contributions to the study of international relations during the interwar period have been seriously understudied. Yet, the interwar period saw the emergence of a number of key ideas outside the West that would shape not only the foreign policy of Non-Western countries after the Second World War, but would also have a major impact on world politics as a whole.

As we did in Chapter 2, we use the broad criteria set up in our earlier work as to what counts as IR. Given the extreme environment created by the First World War, the interwar period was marked by an especially strong nexus between theory and practice even in the core. It is impossible to make sense of the origins and ramifications of the Idealist–Realist debate without looking at policy debates surrounding Wilson's Fourteen Points, the LN, the Kellogg–Briand Pact and the efforts at disarmament, and suchlike. The Realist critique of Idealism was powerfully framed within the critique of the expectations about and failures of the LN. Zimmern was not only the author of an important book on the LN, he was also deeply involved in promoting the idea of the LN both as a UK government official and as part of an advocacy group. Much the same was true in the Non-West. The ideas of nationalist leaders and the movements and institutions they inspired were equally influenced by the realities, both hopeful and dark, of international life as they saw them. The nationalist and anti-colonial ideas and movements of the interwar years also left a rich and long-term legacy for the foreign policy behaviour and global and regional interactions of the Cold War and decolonisation era after 1945. Indeed, they shaped and continue to shape the foreign policy beliefs and practices of emerging powers such as China and India. If anything, they are making a comeback as these states become more powerful and influential on the world stage.

The Non-Aligned Movement (NAM), which was formally established in Belgrade in 1961, grew out of the Asia–Africa Conference in Bandung in 1955, which in turn was influenced by the First International Congress against Imperialism and Colonialism held in Brussels in 1927 (Prasad, 1962: 79–99). India's Jawaharlal Nehru was a key participant in all three: Brussels, Bandung and Belgrade. Regional organisations such as the Organization of African Unity (OAU) drew inspiration from the Pan-African ideals and movements of the early twentieth century, including the interwar period. IR thinking in the periphery during the interwar years was not just about anti-colonialism, but also contained ideas about internationalism, world order, international development, cooperation and justice. It extended well beyond anti-imperialism, although that was often a central organising theme. Interwar IR had multiple and global origins, not just Western ones, and this matters to understanding how IR has arrived at its current form, and where it should go from here. As we did in Chapter 2, we approach IR thinking in the periphery in terms of the major states and regions.

Japan

Whether to place Japan in the core or the periphery during this period is a difficult question. We leave it in the periphery partly because Japan was on a different trajectory from the West, having been a consider-able beneficiary of the First World War, but mainly because it still had to struggle with the race question projected against it by the West. IR thinking in Japan evolved from its pre-1914 roots (Kawata and Ninomiya, 1964: 190; Sakai, 2008: 237–44). Japan's interwar international thought was strongly influenced by the German *Staatslehre* and Marxist traditions (Inoguchi, 2007). Early Japanese IR scholarship corresponded with the rise of Japan as a great power, and sought to understand Japan's place in the world, but was not entirely Japan-centric. There was work on World Politics (Royama, 1928, 1938) and also on colonial administra-tion (Yanaihara, [1926] 1963). Similar to the West, Japanese scholars in this period studied subjects such as International Law, International Organisation, Diplomatic History, Regional Integration and IPE (Kawata and Ninomiya, 1964; Inoguchi, 2007). Takashi Inoguchi (2007, 379–80) even identifies Nishida Kitaro as an 'innate constructivist', because of his focus on identity. Japan had a presence in the international legal system, for example with Mineichiro Adachi, an international legal scholar, who was a diplomat and then Chief Judge of the Permanent International Court of Justice (The Hague), and also wrote on the LN (Adachi and De Visscher, 1923). Japan still had to face the problem of racist 'yellow peril' reactions in the West, and responded with the Kyoto School's philosophy of 'post-white power' (D. Williams, 2004; Shimizu, 2015). 'Yellow peril' racism played against both Japanese emigration to the Americas, and against its reception as a new member of the great power club (Shimazu, 1998).

During the 1930s, the emphasis shifted towards 'hegemonic region-alism' as Japan dropped out of the LN and began pursuing its vision of a Japan-led Greater East Asia Co-Prosperity Sphere (Acharya, 2017: 6–7). Asia's rise was equated with Japan's rise. Japan espoused Pan-Asianism to counter Western dominance, but in that process staked a claim, as the only modern state in Asia, to its own centrality and empire (Koyama and Buzan, 2018). The increasing predominance of these imperial policies eventually retarded the growth of academic IR, which was suppressed by the authorities (Kawata and Ninomiya, 1964: 194).

China

While international relations became a thriving field in China from the 1990s, Chinese IR scholars, as noted above, have been reticent about acknowledging the legacy of the pre-1949 development of IR in China. According to the current founding myth, Chinese IR is said to have begun around the mid-1960s. For example, Zhang Feng divides the history of IR in China into four phases. The first phase was from 1949 to 1963, when IR was not an academic discipline yet, and scholarly research was forbidden. 'International study was largely synonymous with policy analysis, in the form of annotated policy reports or advice' (Zhang, F., 2012a: 69). The specific 'power–knowledge interaction mode' (Lu, 2014: 133) that interrupted the growth of Chinese IR during the 1950s is not unique to the Non-Western world, although the revolutionary political transition in China and the effect of the Cultural Revolution, as well as persisting political restrictions on Chinese academia, might have had a special bearing on how and why Chinese IR continues to refuse to acknowledge its pre-1949 origins. The communist government sought to impose its own narrative on international affairs that the scholars defied at their peril. Some prominent scholars were denounced after the 1957 revisions to the academic disciplines. The 'silenced memory' of pre-war IR in China, as Lu (2014: 149) puts it, is important for political reasons, and continues to be so, as it attests to our general framing that Non-Western IR exists but is not visible, and that local circumstances can be a key factor, not just international ones or the hegemony of Western IR. It also suggests that development of Non-Western IR was shaped by two sources: indigenous ideas (especially of nationalist leaders) and Western-trained academics.

In a less formal sense, Sun Yat-sen was a key source of international thought in China. Sun's internationalism was both cosmopolitan and Sinocentric. He championed cooperation with Japan and other countries of Asia, but stressed the superiority of Chinese traditions of statecraft. Sun stressed the past glory of Asia and spoke of 'not only China and Japan but all the peoples in East Asia … unit[ing] together to restore the former status of Asia' (Sun, 1941: 144). However, for that to happen, the countries of Asia had to first be rid of the colonial yoke and gain independence. Sun (1941: 144) was hopeful of that happening as he saw 'concrete proofs [sic] of the progress of the nationalist idea in Asia'. Yet, Sun's Pan-Asianism, like that of Japan, was also hierarchic. Sun (1941: 146) invoked the tributary system, recalling how the 'weaker nations … respected China as their superior and sent annual tribute to China by their own will, regarding it as an honor to be allowed to do so'. Sun emphasises the voluntary nature of the relationships in the tributary system, arguing that China ruled by 'Right', that is, by good principles of friendliness and reciprocity, and not by 'Might'.

The broader purpose of Sun's Pan-Asianism was 'to terminate the sufferings of the Asiatic peoples and … to resist the aggression of the powerful European countries' (Sun, 1941: 151), revealing a strong anti-colonial strand that is a common thread running through international thought in the Non-Western world. Sun's (1941: 151) writings made sure to include Japan; indeed, one may say they were targeted towards Japan, despite that country having 'become acquainted with the Western civilization of the rule of Might'. Sun (1941: 151) maintained that it 'retains the characteristics of the Oriental civilization of the rule of Right', and was key to ensuring the fruition of the Pan-Asian movement. Sun did speak of Asian virtues, but in juxtaposition to both European and Japanese colonialism. He urged Japan not to develop Pan-Asianism through empire, but through Asian virtues, such as ethics, righteousness and benevolence. He also contrasted European materialism and militarism (the ways of a hegemon) with these Asian virtues. But the opening issue of the journal *Xinyaxiya* (New Asia), launched in China in 1930 to advance Sun's nationalist cause, argued: 'the regeneration of China is the starting point of the regeneration of the Asian peoples' (cited in Tankha and Thampi, 2005: 108). It claimed Sun to be the only leader who can come to the rescue of the Asian peoples. Sun was a strong proponent of Pan-Asianism, but yearned for the continued supremacy of China. However, there did exist competing ideas of Pan-Asianism from within China as well as from other countries in Asia (Acharya, 2017).

In addition, according to Eric Helleiner (2014, 376–8), it was Sun Yat-sen who was the originator of the idea of international development. Analysing the origins of international development cooperation, Helleiner contests the commonly held view that the norm of international development originated with a speech in 1949 by US President Harry Truman. He credits the norm to Sun, dating back to 1918, as articulated in a book published in 1922 entitled *The International Development of China*. In this book, Sun describes an 'International Development Organization' that would help China to develop. While his ideas are admittedly Sinocentric, i.e. aimed at developing China, they perhaps influenced the Bretton Woods institutions.

India

Possibly the signature achievement of academic IR theory in India was that of Benoy Kumar Sarkar (M. J. Bayly, 2017a). In 1919, he published 'Hindu Theory of International Relations' in the *American Political Science Review*. He analysed a number of Indian concepts, including *Mandala* (sphere of influence) and *Sarva-Bhauma* (world sovereign), drawing on the work of classical writers such as Kautilya, Manu and Shookra, and the text of the *Mahabharata*. Out of these, he claimed that

The conception of 'external' sovereignty was well established in the Hindu philosophy of the state. The Hindu thinkers not only analyzed sovereignty with regard to the constituent elements in a single state. They realized also that sovereignty is not complete unless it is external as well as internal, that is, unless the state can exercise its internal authority unobstructed by, and independently of, other states. (Sarkar, 1919: 400)

Sarkar (1921) wrote another essay, for the *Political Science Quarterly*, 'Hindu Theory of the State', in which he compared Indian concepts of the 'state of nature' with those of European political philosophers and found that they were similar, in the sense that both called for suppressing strife with the help of a higher authority capable of wielding sanction and punishment. Sarkar (1916) also wrote an essay, entitled *The Beginning of Hindu Culture As World-Power*, which examined ancient India's international, especially Pan-Asiatic, connections, including commerce, conquest and the flow of ideas. The timing of these publications paralleled the nascent years of IR as a field, and, in so far as they drew on the Indian tradition, were substantially independent of Western debates. They may be the first major IR contributions by an Indian, and one of the first modern efforts to develop an indigenous Non-Western theory of IR.

As Martin Bayly (2017b) argues, some Indian IR scholars also engaged with Western IR. M. N. Chatterjee (1916) 'turned the corpus of "western" peace studies, including Norman Angell, Victor Hugo, John Bright, Cobden and Kant, against the supposedly "civilized" warring European powers' (M. J. Bayly, 2017b: 22). S. V. Puntambekar (1939) articulated Realistic, Idealistic and Utopian lines of IR thought at the same time as Carr.

On the less academic side, there were plenty of successors to Tagore's work, discussed in Chapter 2. Nehru, the fast-rising leader of the Indian National Congress, espoused anti-colonialism along with a strong dose of internationalism. Some Indian thinkers took a relativist stance, highlighting the difference between Western and Eastern thought, and some even asserted the relatively more inclusive nature of the latter. Like others in Asia, they distinguished Eastern spiritualism from Western materialism. One position held that the world needed Eastern ideas and approaches, even dominance, to cure it of the scourges of competition and war. During the debates of the Indian Legislative Assembly in 1936, Pandit Krishna Kant Malaviya said that 'the domination of the East' was the 'only panacea for all the ills of this world'. 'We with our love of peace, spiritualism and goodwill for all can only bring peace on this earth' (cited in Keenleyside, 1982: 211). But others were more moderate, advocating East–West synergy. In 1933, the Indian philosopher (later the president of India) Sarvepalli Radhakrishnan, who was also a professor at Oxford University, argued that Asians were 'pacific by tradition and temperament', and could 'supply the necessary complement and antidote to the pragmatic nationalism of the West' (cited in Keenleyside, 1982: 211). In 1940, Nehru argued that the postwar order should combine the 'best elements of the East and the West', wherein Western science would be tempered by the 'restraining influence and cultural background of India and China' (cited in Keenleyside, 1982: 212). Examples of the kind of Utopian thought found in the West could also be found in Gandhi's presidential address to the Indian National Congress in 1924, where he stated, 'the better mind of the world desired not absolutely independent states warring one against another, but a federation of friendly inter-dependent states' (cited in Prabhu, 2017).

But Idealism was not the dominant or even the main element of international thought in interwar India. It is interesting that even before Carr's attack on Utopianism, and at a time when Indian nationalists were preaching both resistance to Western colonialism and the unity of the world, Indian Political Scientists were drawing upon the recently discovered *Arthasastra* to lay out a doctrine of realpolitik. Sarkar, for example, laid out the key ideas about international relations drawing from classic Indian texts. The Hindu concept of *Matsya-Nyaya* (the Logic of the Fish), contained in several Indian texts, both secular and religious, including the epic *Mahabharata*, the *Arthasastra*, the *Manu Samhita* (the Code of Manu) and the *Ramayana*, explained the creation of the state from the state of nature. The *Mahabharata* holds that in the absence of a state or ruler with the authority to punish, society will be governed by the logic of the fish whereby 'the stronger would devour the weak like fishes in water' (cited in Sarkar, 1921: 80). The same logic also applied to international relations.

Several aspects of this Indian thinking on international relations stand out. The first is that it represented an attempt to identify and elaborate on concepts of international relations, both with reference to domestic politics as well as exclusively to the international sphere, to explain how states relate to each other. Second, it contained a diversity of positions, compatible if not identical with both Utopianism or Idealism and Realism in the Western sense. Third, some Indian scholars and leaders often drew comparisons with Western thinking on these subjects. Sarkar not only frequently drew parallels between classical Western political and international thought (including ancient Greek as well as modern), but even claimed that Indian ideas could help understand the contemporary Western context. Comparing the logic of the fish with the ideas of Hobbes, Spinoza and Mill, he argued that 'the Hindu answer was identical with the European' (Sarkar, 1921: 79). Similarly, in the international realm, 'the diplomatic feats conceived by the Hindu political philosophers could be verified almost to the letter by numerous instances in European and Asian history' (Sarkar, 1919: 407). This reference to

European thought and context anticipated a widespread practice in the later development of IR, where Non-Western scholars often began their scholarship on IR by invoking Western ideas, and using them as referent points to highlight and validate indigenous concepts and practices. While this might have stunted the development of purely indigenous theories, it did, in principle though not in practice, provide the basis of a global conversation on the theories of International Relations.

An important statement of Nehru's approach to International Relations can be found in *The Discovery of India*, written in prison in 1944. There, under the heading of 'Realism and Geopolitics: World Conquest or World Association?', Nehru forcefully criticised an idea proposed by Spykman and Walter Lippmann (also backed by Winston Churchill) that the postwar world order be organised around regional security systems under great power 'orbits'. Nehru characterised them as 'a continuation of power politics on a vaster scale ... it is difficult to see how he [Lippman] can see world peace or co-operation emerging out of it' (Nehru, [1946] 2003: 539). Apart from rejecting power politics, it also signalled his desire and hope for greater international cooperation, not in the form of military alliances that would reflect power politics, but of a 'commonwealth of states', or a 'world association'. It is significant that this was written before the Second World War was over.

Two years later, in a speech delivered on 7 September 1946, he offered a further elaboration of his normative beliefs:

We propose, as far as possible, to keep away from the power politics of groups, aligned against one another, which have led in the past to world wars and which may again lead to disaster of an even vaster scale. We believe that peace and freedom are indivisible and that denial of freedom anywhere must endanger freedom elsewhere and lead to conflict and war. We are particularly interested in the emancipation of colonial and dependent territories and peoples and in the recognition in theory and practice of equal opportunities for all peoples ... We seek no domination over others and we claim no privileged position over other peoples ... The world, in spite of its rivalries and hatreds and inner conflicts, moves inevitably towards closer cooperation and the building up of a world of commonwealth. It is for this one world free India will work, a world in which there is free co-operation of free peoples and no class or group exploits another. (cited in Mani, 2004: 66)

Yet, Nehru's critique does not find a place in IR texts dealing with the Idealist–Realist debate or the Realist–Liberal debate.

Latin America

We noted in Chapter 2 the distinctive nineteenth-century Latin American contributions on regionalism, sovereign equality and non-intervention.

During the interwar years, other major concepts, now staple in IR, originated in the Pan-American movement. The most significant among these is the concept of declarative statehood contained in the Montevideo Convention on the Rights and Duties of States that was adopted at the Pan-American Conference in Montevideo in 1933. This convention codified in international law, perhaps for the first time, the definitional components of the state in IR: population, territory, government and recognition. Latin American advocacy eventually led the United States to formally, if not always in practice, abandon the Monroe Doctrine in 1933 and accept non-intervention as a basic principle in its relations with the region. After an initial gestation period, the norm of non-intervention not only became robust in Latin America, but also spread to other parts of the world, notably Asia after decolonisation.

While Latin America is known for developing Dependency Theory in the post-Second World War period, Eric Helleiner and Antulio Rosales (2017) highlight prior and more general contributions from the region on Eurocentrism, imperialism, Dependency and regional cooperation during the interwar period. The work of two Peruvian thinkers, Víctor Raúl Haya de la Torre (1895–1979) and José Carlos Mariátegui La Chira (1894–1930) is especially important. Haya felt that political ideas in Latin America were being borrowed from Europe without much regard for Latin American (or what he called 'Indoamerican') context and conditions. He rejected the view that European ideas, including the Marxism that he believed in, were as universal as their champions claimed; different parts of the world had developed different worldviews reflecting their local history and condition. Hence, 'it is imperative to recognize that the global and simplistic application to our environment of European doctrines and norms of interpretation should be subject to profound modifications' (cited in Helleiner and Rosales, 2017: 673). Haya's thinking was regionalist, calling for 'Indoamerican' economic nationalism that incorporated the marginalised indigenous people. Moreover, he challenged Lenin's thesis of imperialism being the highest stage of capitalism. While that might be so in Europe, for Latin America, it was the first stage. However, this view was challenged by Mariátegui, who accepted Lenin's position. Both developed early versions of Dependency, but Mariátegui was especially concerned with Peru's heavy reliance on commodity exports controlled by foreign interests and hence its vulnerability to fluctuations in commodity prices. Mariátegui went further than Haya to argue that Socialist development thinking in the region should incorporate the values of the region's indigenous peoples, thereby adding more local context and agency to development concepts in Latin America. But Mariátegui opposed Haya's preferences for a 'united front' of revolutionaries and bourgeoisie elements to fight imperialism. Mariátegui's position was similar to that of international Marxist thinker and activist from India Manabendra Nath Roy (1887–1954), who was a founder of the Mexican Communist Party and who had earlier challenged Lenin's position, articulated in 1920, of developing a broad anti-imperialist coalition. These ideas and debates were antecedents to the subsequent development of Latin American IR thinking, including but not limited to Dependency Theory. As Helleiner and Rosales (2017: 671) note, Haya's rejection of European 'monistic' universalism and his sensitivity to regional variations and adaptations are a powerful precursor to our ideas of localisation and pluralistic universalism in Global IR.

It was also in Latin America that the concept of international development emerged in a concrete form. In the 1930s, Latin American countries developed ideas about development, and sought to establish an Inter-American Bank (IAB) to facilitate the flow of funds from the United States for the purposes of the development of these countries. While the IAB was stillborn, the proposals for it certainly influenced the initial US drafts of the Bretton Woods institutions of the International Monetary Fund (IMF) and the International Bank for Reconstruction and Development (World Bank) (Helleiner, 2014). In fact, Helleiner shows how the Latin American countries, along with China and India, were key contributors at the Bretton Woods Conference of 1944.

Another area of Latin American contribution to IR was human rights. In discussing the key milestones in Latin America's contribution to human rights, Kathryn Sikkink (2016: 122–33) mentions the 1945 Inter-American Conference on Problems of War and Peace, attended by 19 Latin American nations and held at Mexico City. Three years later, 21 countries, including the United States, had signed the American Declaration of Rights and Duties of Man at Bogota, Colombia, in April 1948, seven months before the passage of the Universal Declaration of Human Rights (UDHR) on 10 December 1948. Although these Latin American initiatives came in 1945–8, first in the lead up to the drafting of the UN Charter in 1945, and then the UDHR in 1948, Paolo Carozza (2003: 282, 311) argues that they reflected 'a long and deep tradition of the idea of human rights in the region', which had evolved through the region's struggles against Spanish conquest, the liberal republican revolutions in the continent and the Mexican constitution of 1917, which placed a strong emphasis on social and economic rights. Carozza (2003: 311–12) further argues that the evolving Latin American thinking on human rights 'was strongly universalistic in its orientation, founded on the equal dignity of all'. Latin American nations 'produced a constitutional rights language with a strong devotion to both liberty and equality'.

The Middle East

During the interwar period, Pan-Islamism and Pan-Arabism were two major 'isms', or strands of thought in the Middle East that interacted closely with nationalism to shape international thought and actions in the Arab world. Pan-Arabism and Pan-Islamism might have shared similar goals in advancing decolonisation, but Pan-Arabism was a much more secular phenomenon. The idea of the Arabs as a nation, both culturally and politically, mainly emerged during the First World War with the Arab Revolt against the Ottoman Empire. Among its most prominent advocates at that stage was Hussein ibn Ali, Sharif of Mecca, who got British support against the Ottomans and championed 'a united Arab state spanning from Aleppo to Aden'.[8] But because of his reliance on British support, Ali downplayed the religious aspects of Pan-Arabism. Pan-Arabism displayed affinity with Western-style secular nationalism. A major role in developing Pan-Arabism was played by Lebanese and Syrian intellectuals who were influenced by Western thought and Western institutions, such as the Syrian Protestant College (later the American University of Beirut) (Antonius, [1938] 2001). In the 1930s Pan-Arabism acquired a greater intellectual force, as it came to be influenced by Marxism. The founding of the Baath or 'renaissance' party in the 1940s by Michel Aflaq and Salah al-Din al-Bitar was another highpoint of the Pan-Arab movement, although it did not become very effective. Interestingly, interest in Pan-Arabism remained low in Egypt, despite its historic importance as an intellectual and political centre in the Arab world. Egyptian nationalism, rather than Pan-Arabism, was the dominant strand of 1930s and 1940s nationalism in Egypt. Yet, Egypt would emerge as the source of a more militant and international form of Pan-Arabism after the Second World War, under the leadership of Gamal Abdel Nasser.

The Western influence on Pan-Arabism and its secular undertones were rejected by Pan-Islamism, which presented itself as an alternative. Pan-Islamism generally stands in opposition to nationalist projects because of the different identity base. The Turkish abolition of the Caliphate in 1924 generated political fragmentation over who might inherit the title, thus weakening Pan-Islamism compared to Ottoman times (Hashmi,

---

[8] 'The two "isms" of the Middle East', *Aljazeera News*, www.aljazeera.com/focus/arabunity/2008/02/200852518534468346.html (Accessed 5 October 2018).

2009: 181–6). In contrast to Pan-Arabism, Pan-Islamism was concerned about the erosion of Islamic values, and rejected Westernisation and secularism. A highpoint in its evolution was the founding of the Muslim Brotherhood by the Egyptian Hassan al-Banna in 1928.

The shared goal of Pan-Arabism and Pan-Islamism was the rejection of the Westphalian nation state. This would lead to major political struggles and regional conflicts in the post-Second World War period, shaping international thinking and approaches in the Middle East, although the idea of the nation state would remain resilient and prevail over both Pan-Arab and Pan-Islamist currents (Barnett, 1995).

Africa and the Caribbean

Pan-Africanism differed from other pan-nationalist movements in that, as noted in Chapter 2, the initial impetus was not from leaders from the continent of Africa but rather from African-Americans in the United States and the Caribbean. W. E. B. Du Bois continued to be an important figure. Du Bois was concerned with the 'problem of the color line' that was not only an internal problem of the United States but a larger problem for the whole world, including Africans in Africa. Pan-African leaders from the 1920s such as Jamaica-born Marcus Garvey (1887–1940) stressed the collective past and shared experience of the black people on both sides of the Atlantic. Garvey championed black nationalism and Pan-Africanism and believed that communism would benefit whites more than blacks. The Universal Negro Improvement Association and the African Communities League that he founded emerged as the organisation that propelled such thinking onto the international stage (Kuryla, 2016). The interwar period saw the convening of no less than four Pan-African congresses, starting in 1919 in Paris and ending in 1927 in New York. Not all of these were effective, but they allowed socialisation and passing of the torch from outsiders to Africans. As the movement progressed, the centre moved away from African-Americans to Africans in Africa and African states. The conferences were strongly anti-colonial, and adopted resolutions that clamoured for decolonisation and independence, while still focusing on racial discrimination.[9] The Pan-African movement also echoed this note of underdevelopment and inadequate international efforts to address the problem. Du Bois flitted between advocating for 'black capitalism' and more Socialist and

---

[9] 'Anticolonial Movements, Africa', http://what-when-how.com/western-colonialism/anticolonial-movements-africa/ (Accessed 27 May 2018).

Marxist-oriented ideas about the institutionalised difference in development of blacks and whites.

The intimate human and intellectual connection between activists and thinkers in Africa, the Caribbean and the black nationalist movement in the United States was also manifest in the pioneering work of C. L. R. James from Trinidad. His pamphlet *The Case for West-Indian Self Government* (James, 1933) was the first important manifesto calling for national independence in the British West Indies (Fraser, 1989). *World Revolution* (James, [1937] 2017) analysed the history of the Communist International with a focus on its internal contestations. Despite his sympathy for and involvement in the Trotskyite movement, he would challenge Trotsky's position by calling for the black emancipation movement to be organised independently from a vanguard Troskyite communist party. James's *The Black Jacobins* ([1938] 1989) remains a classic account of a Marxist study of the Haitian slave revolution of the 1790s. Another important work of this period is *Capitalism and Slavery* by Eric Williams ([1944] 1994), who would become the first prime minister of Trinidad and Tobago from 1962 to 1981. It examined how slavery contributed to Britain's massive capitalist accumulation and industrial revolution, and argued that Britain's ultimate abolition of the Atlantic slave trade in 1807 and slavery in 1833 was motivated not by humanitarian concerns, but by economic reasons, as Britain's industrial economy with its growing reliance on wage labour made slavery economically inefficient and redundant.

Conclusions

Anti-colonialism was a common theme and motivation for much of the IR thinking in the periphery. This was especially so in those places still colonised or highly penetrated by the Western powers, and was often interwoven with a combination of regionalism and pan-nationalism, which could, and commonly did, have a tricky relationship with nationalism. Pan-nationalism could complement more narrowly based nationalist movements by providing a support framework for anti-colonialism. But even where there was some kind of racial (e.g. Africa), national (e.g. Arab world) or cultural (e.g. Latin America, Islamic world) homogeneity, pan-nationalism and the nation state could fall into tension. Pan-Asianism contained no obvious homogenising factor at all except a huge and diverse shared geography, and a desire to escape from Western domination. These pan-national and regionalist movements were, like most strands of interwar Western IR, normative/Idealist. But they were against imperialism, not great power war. Imperialism took the same place for intellectuals in the colonies as the problem of war did for Western IR scholarship during the interwar years. Interwar pan-nationalism was not just about liberation, but also a vision of how the world should be organised. Even at this early stage there were the beginnings of concerns about development, as noted in Latin American and China. Unsurprisingly, the thinkers of the Non-Western countries from the interwar period and before had much to say about the idea of international development, some of which pre-dated Western thinking on the subject. The ideas from the Non-Western world did not always conform with, indeed they were often in opposition to, Western ideas. This was partly because these ideas were largely anti-colonial in nature and origin. These movements contained a variety of positions, including Idealism and Realism. They often stressed a cultural escape from, and alternative to, Western culture. But sometimes, most obviously with Japanese – and to some extent with Chinese – Pan-Asianism, they suggested a regional hegemony as a necessary counter to Western domination. The longstanding interest in sovereign equality, non-intervention, human rights and anti-hegemonism in Latin America can be seen, as it would become more generally after decolonisation post-1945, as the natural follow-on position from anti-colonialism for the periphery.

Most current Western texts on IR ignore these regional and pan-nationalist ideas as a source of IR. It is interesting to note the attitude towards them of a widely used interwar text by Buell (1925: 91), which equated these ideas with racialism, or 'racial nationalism', and thus saw them as reactionary or ethnocentric. This acknowledgement of race as an important force in the international relations and thought of the pre-First World War and interwar period is important, suggesting that IR emerged not only from an Idealist–Realist divide in the West, but also from a racial, economic and political divide between the West and the Rest. Interestingly, Buell scarcely distinguishes between such movements in Europe, such as Pan-German or Pan-Slavic, or notions of Aryan, Teutonic and Nordic supremacy, and the pan-nationalism in the Non-Western world, such as in Asia, Africa, Latin America and the Arab world. He does not distinguish between the reactionary and emancipatory motivations that separated them. In reality, both reactionary and emancipatory streams were represented in most of the pan-nationalist movements. Even Japan, which had developed an extreme version of the former since the late nineteenth century under the guise of Pan-Asianism (and Asia for Asians), developed a more emancipatory vision of the same, represented by Okakura Tenshin and others.

Buell (1925: 92) views pan-nationalist movements in the West as sources of conflict, more important than conflict provoked by purely economic or political causes, thereby anticipating a Huntingtonian 'clash of civilizations'. As regards pan-nationalist 'colored movements of the world', in which he included the Pan-African, Pan-Islamic, Pan-Arab, Pan-Turanian (Turkish) and Pan-Asiatic movements, while race was important to their creation, these had little to sustain themselves except shared 'resentment toward European and American imperialism, and the exploitation of the white man' (Buell, 1925: 93). These movements, he believed, would fade away once the external sources, imperialism and dominance, were removed. While Buell correctly identifies imperialism as a major source of these pan-nationalist movements, their motivating factors and impact were in reality more multidimensional and longer-lasting than he anticipated. The movements not only contained visions about organising the world and the region, they also provided the basis for developing the norms of conduct for postcolonial international relations, and the ideas underpinning the later founding of globally significant movements such as the Bandung Conference in 1955 and the NAM from the 1960s (Acharya, 2009, 2011a).

Conclusions

During the interwar period, IR became significantly institutionalised as an academic discipline, mainly in the West, and particularly in the Anglosphere, but also to some extent more globally. It nevertheless retained a lot of continuities with its nineteenth-century antecedents. In line with the actual practice in ir, these included a pretty stark separation between IR in the core, which was largely focused on the perspectives and problems of the core, and IR in the periphery, which was mainly driven by anti-colonialism. There was also a lot of continuity in the main types of themes, approaches and theories in IR, including Liberalism, Socialism, Realism, 'Scientific' Racism, nationalism, International Organisation, IPE and Geopolitics in the core, and anti-colonialism and regionalism in the periphery. Colonial administration/development remained a topic for both core and periphery, albeit from different perspectives. Most of the main subjects and theories that would compose IR after 1945 were already in place, and some, most notably Feminism and IPE, were fully in play, and would not reappear in post-1945 IR until the 1970s. Also, in both core and periphery, and despite the academic institutionalisation, there remained very substantial non-academic elements engaged in the debates about IR, including public intellectuals, advocacy organisations and political discourses.

The conventional accounts of IR during the interwar period not only overstate the dominance of Idealism, but also the differences *between* Idealists and Realists, while masking the differences *within* each camp

(Long, 1995: 302–3; L. Ashworth, 2014). These accounts also privilege the core, and largely neglect the IR thinking in the periphery. Taking into account the latter shows that the origins of IR were even more diverse and complex. In some cases, Non-Western contributions followed dominant trends in the West, in others they were independently developed. For example, Tagore's criticisms of nationalism and imperialism predated Toynbee's and J. A. Hobson's theories of imperialism. The interwar period laid the groundwork for the Dependency and Postcolonial approaches to IR that made their way into the IR of the core once decolonisation began to break down the separation of core and periphery, and the exclusion of the latter from both ir and IR by the former.

A global investigation into the origins of IR suggests a diversity and complexity that has not been captured in available texts in the field, including those which have sought to question the idea of a first debate. First, categories such as Idealist–Realist debate or Idealism, Utopianism and Realism are too simplistic to fit the variety of thinking and approaches that could legitimately form the source of IR. Neither would they easily fit the categories of revolutionary or Postcolonial as they came to be known in the post-Second World War evolution of the field. Nehru, generally perceived in the West as an Idealist (a label which he rejected) or even a Liberal Internationalist, was briefly deeply attracted to Marxism, and he dismissed great power alliances.

International thought during the interwar period transcended the Idealist–Realist debate. While many Non-Western thinkers and leaders agreed with the Western 'Idealists' on the moral repugnance and physical dangers of war, they also agreed with those Realists who saw hypocrisy in Western Liberalism/Idealism when it came to colonialism in the Non-Western world. They would not accept the harmony of interests perspective, criticised by Carr. Nor did they accept the interwar Idealist view that war could be prevented through interdependence or institutions in the absence of efforts to eradicate colonialism. Western Idealists and Realists were more concerned with war between the Western nations, and the international anarchy problem, and only peripherally with imperialism. But thinkers in the Non-Western world were primarily concerned with imperialism and colonialism. This does not mean they were not worried about world peace, but they did not believe that world peace or order could be achieved simply by eliminating war between the European powers. It would also require addressing imperialism and in some cases nationalism.

5   The World after 1945: The Era of the Cold War and Decolonisation

Introduction

This chapter picks up the story of international history from where we left it in Chapter 3 at the end of the Second World War. We argued there that the Second World War produced many major changes in GIS both normative and material, enough to count as a transition from the version 1.0 Western-colonial GIS established during the nineteenth century, and continuing after the First World War, to version 1.1 Western-global GIS after 1945. We call it version 1.1, rather than 2.0, because although the changes were many and big, they were changes *in* the system/society rather than changes *of* it. International relations was still set up as a system of states, and many of its defining primary institutions remained in place.

The next section summarises briefly the continuities and discontinuities from the pre-1945 GIS. The one following looks in more detail at the main themes of version 1.1 GIS during the period from 1945 to 1989: the era of the Cold War and decolonisation.

Continuities and Discontinuities from the Pre-1945 World

As argued in Chapter 3, there was a lot of continuity between the period before 1914 and the interwar years. The main discontinuity came from the First World War itself, with the scale of death, destruction and cost creating a great shock wave that amplified the defence dilemma to a sufficient extent to call into question the viability of great power war. By contrast, the Second World War generated several major changes to the material and ideational structure of GIS (Buzan and Lawson, 2014a). It also far outpaced the First World War in the scale of death, destruction and cost, but added to this the spectre of nuclear weapons, which massively further amplified the fear of war, and made the possibility of humankind committing species suicide clearly apparent to all. While the

First World War raised the possibility that a new world war would destroy Western civilisation, nuclear weapons raised the possibility of the extinction of the human species. The consequent strengthening of the defence dilemma was perhaps the major continuity between the interwar period and the Cold War. Otherwise the story is mostly one of changes within the structure of GIS.

The Cold War order that emerged quickly in the years after 1945 is commonly summed up by the term *bipolarity*, and in some ways there is a good case for doing so.[1] The United States and the Soviet Union were the big winners of the Second World War, and quickly emerged as the two dominant centres of military power and ideological competition. The ceasefire lines between them in Europe and Northeast Asia became the boundaries delineating the new world order. This was an East–West formation defined as a global ideological competition between liberal-democratic capitalism and a totalitarian communist command economy for which would dominate the future of modernity. The development of large arsenals of nuclear weapons, and the long-range delivery systems necessary to carry them over intercontinental distances, quickly differentiated these two 'superpowers' from great powers. The traditional set of great powers all faded into the second rank of merely great powers, or worse. Germany and Japan were occupied, disarmed and subordinated to the two superpowers. While they quickly recovered economic strength, they largely lost not only the political will and the international legitimacy but also the political independence to be fully fledged great powers. The German problem was solved by dividing the country between the Soviet and US blocs. Britain was also among the winners, and briefly played a role as the third superpower, but was quickly reduced to mere great power status by its economic weakness and loss of empire. France struggled to overcome its defeat and to reassert its great power status. Europe fell from being the core of world politics and the balance of power to being the main prize in the rivalry between the superpowers. The main focus of the remaining powers in Western Europe shifted from playing global empires to finding

---

[1] There is also a case against using bipolarity. Polarity theory distinguishes only between great powers and the rest. It neglects the distinction between great powers and superpowers, which arguably remains of considerable consequence to how GIS works. Following this thinking, during the Cold War GIS had two superpowers and several great powers: China, the European Community, arguably Japan. The same error was repeated after the implosion of the Soviet Union. Unipolarity was widely declared, but in fact the structure was one superpower and four great powers. There is a massive structural difference between a system with only superpowers and minor or regional powers, and one in which there are great powers standing between the superpower(s) and the rest. See Buzan (2004a).

a path to regional integration, and keeping the United States in the North Atlantic Treaty Organization (NATO) to protect them. Japan became America's subordinate ally and forward base in the western Pacific.

But while bipolarity tells a powerful story, it was not the only story in play that defined this era, and seen in long historical perspective may not even be the main story. The other big story was the North–South one of decolonisation. While bipolarity defined two superpowers and their camps, and two rival ideologies for the future of modernity, decolonisation defined a Third World, and a position of non-alignment, outside the bipolar structure. Bipolarity mainly tells the story of the core powers, privileging the core and marginalising the periphery. This is in continuity with the great power story from the interwar period, where the main focus was on great power competition, and ongoing colonialism allowed the periphery to be largely written out of international relations. But from 1945, decolonisation changed the version 1.0 GIS picture in a fundamental way. Racism and colonialism were delegitimised as institutions of GIS, and its membership quickly tripled with the addition of more than a hundred newly sovereign countries mainly from Africa and Asia. Western-colonial GIS morphed into version 1.1 Western-global GIS: international society remained core–periphery in terms of dominant and subordinate economic positions, but the periphery now had its own political standing and voice. The world political economy was now doubly divided: East–West and North–South. After 1945, the sharp separation between international relations as what happened among the states of the 'civilised' core, and colonial relations as what happened between the metropolitan core and the colonial periphery, broke down, and these two elements increasingly merged into a single story.

While these East–West and North–South stories are distinct, and have their own dynamics and consequences, they are also linked. The two superpowers and their allies competed for influence and allies within the Third World, and saw their successes and failures there as indicators of who was winning, and who was losing, the great ideological struggle between them. In the other direction, the countries of the Third World played the superpowers off against each other in order to maximise their leverage in getting access to economic and military resources. China sat awkwardly within both the East–West and North–South stories. It acted more like a great power towards the Third World than as a member of it, despite being a developing country; and it increasingly became a third wheel in the bipolar ideological and power structures.

Version 1.1 Global International Society: The Main Themes of International Relations 1945–1989

To capture the main themes of Cold War international relations we need to look in more detail not just at bipolarity, but at the transformation in core–periphery structure and relations generated by decolonisation. This section therefore focuses on the key themes in the core, the periphery and the relationship between the two. Like Japan earlier, China needs to be told as its own story somewhat apart from, but related to, that framing.

The Core

Two key themes dominate the international relations of the core between 1945 and 1989, and differentiate it from the interwar period: the shift from a multipolar to a bipolar distribution of power and the revolution in military affairs precipitated by nuclear weapons.

As Alexis de Tocqueville ([1835] 2006) noted presciently in his book *Democracy in America*, Russia and America were emerging as two giant powers that would one day dominate the world even though they were following very different paths of development. In 1945 his geopolitical prediction came true. The war had broken and demoted all of the other traditional great powers. Germany and Japan were defeated, smashed and occupied. Britain, France and Italy were damaged, depleted and teetering on the brink of bankruptcy. The United States was undamaged, and financially, industrially, militarily and politically dominant. The Soviet Union was badly damaged economically and had taken huge casualties, but it remained militarily and politically strong. It was in durable occupation of Eastern Europe and East Germany, and in Manchuria for long enough to loot the industry that Japan had planted there.

This shift in polarity was marked by the new term *superpowers*, but bipolarity was about much more than a new material disposition of power. Despite their strong ideological differences, the United States and the Soviet Union had eventually cooperated to defeat Fascism. The success of this project transformed the ideological tripolarity of the interwar period into a simpler, but more intense dyad between democratic capitalism on one side, and a totalitarian command economy on the other. The question was still what form the political economy of modernity would take, but the options were now down to two – at opposite ends of the spectrum. The elimination of Fascism also eliminated the parochial, racist version of modernity from the competition. The United States and the Soviet Union may have been at opposite ends of the ideological spectrum, but unlike the Fascist powers both represented universalist ideologies. In principle, anyone could accept, and be accepted into, their way of life and political economy, and both thought of themselves as owning the future of modernity. This made the rivalry between them acutely zero-sum, quickly manifesting itself not just in the bipolarity of two superpowers, but also in the bipolarisation of the core into two coalitions (NATO versus Warsaw Pact) and two economies (Organisation for Economic Co-operation and Development (OECD), General Agreement on Tariffs and Trade (GATT) and IMF versus Council for Mutual Economic Assistance).

The Soviet Union had the ideological advantage that, despite Russia's longstanding occupation of Central Asia, and Stalin's postwar attempt to gain footholds in Turkey, Iran and Libya (Westad, 2007: 57–66), the Third World countries did not associate its form of modernity with colonialism. Western capitalism, by contrast, was widely seen in the Third World as a direct continuation of colonial inequality and exploitation, and a threat to the newly acquired sovereignty of the Third World states. Yet both superpowers were in their own way anti-colonial. Both opposed the old imperialism of the European powers and Japan, marking a major ideological shift in the character and outlook of the dominant powers in the core compared to that of the interwar years. The United States gave independence to its colony in the Philippines in 1946. But given that both superpowers actively pursued versions of informal empire, seeking clients, bases and protectorates, there was more than a little hypocrisy in their anti-colonial stance, particularly so on the Soviet side given its thinly disguised imperial military and political occupation of Eastern Europe after 1945. But the rhetoric mattered because it was one of the several forces that brought down colonialism and racism as institutions of GIS.

Despite its attractive simplicity and superficial appropriateness, bipolarity was, as noted above, always a somewhat inaccurate way of defining the structure of the core. Not only did it exclude a set of old powers that were still 'great' if not 'super' (Western Europe and Japan), but it also excluded a rising China that increasingly looked and behaved like a third 'pole' in the system. As Germany and Japan rebuilt their economies, and began to rival (and in the case of Japan surpass) that of the Soviet Union, the distinction between 'great' and 'super' also began to fray. Germany and Japan became massive 'civilian powers' (Maull, 1990), and Britain and France had both nuclear weapons and some ability to conduct military operations globally. Bipolarity was also blind to the steady emergence of the European Economic Community (EEC) as a new kind of power on the world stage.

Even between the United States and the Soviet Union, the parity implied by both being superpowers did not stand up to close scrutiny (Dibb, 1986). It was perhaps most justified in military terms. Although the Soviet Union was often behind the United States technologically, it strove mightily to get and maintain military parity. Initially, this was done by remaining mobilised after the war, while the United States quickly demobilised its huge wartime forces and rested on its monopoly of nuclear weapons. The Soviet Union tested its own nuclear weapon in 1949, and for a time during the 1950s seemed to have a lead in missile delivery systems. The Korean War (1950–3) forced the United States to remobilise, and from that point onwards, the two engaged in across-the-board arms racing in conventional and nuclear weapons, and delivery systems for the latter. The Soviet Union successfully achieved nuclear parity with the United States during the 1970s. It kept larger ground forces than the West throughout the Cold War, but despite its naval expansion, the Soviet Union never achieved the capability to operate as a global naval power comparable to the United States. The Soviet Union had to work very hard to maintain military parity. It was a fair comment that while the United States *had* a military-industrial complex, the Soviet Union more or less *was* a military-industrial complex (Buzan and Hansen, 2009: 76–7). Its economy produced little else other than basic goods, and it had to spend a larger proportion of its smaller GDP on defence to keep up with the United States.[2]

It was in the economic sector that the Soviet claim to superpower status was weakest. For a time during the 1950s and 1960s, the Soviet claim looked good. Recovery from the war gave it a strong rate of growth, and the command economy looked like a credible challenger to Western capitalism in terms of things such as steel and energy production. Nikita Khrushchev's famous boast that 'we will bury you' on his visit to America in the early 1960s was not a military threat but one about production of consumer goods. This was given credibility not just by Soviet achievements in military technology and production, but also by its early successes in the space race, signalled by the launch of Sputnik in 1957. But by the 1970s, the hollowness of Khrushchev's boast was

---

[2] Given the high level of Soviet secrecy, and the difficulty of interpreting the statistics it did make public, there was much debate about how to calculate both Soviet GDP and military expenditure. Statistics given by the International Institute for Strategic Studies (1971: 62) suggest that between 1951 and 1970, the United States regularly outspent the Soviet Union on defence by between a quarter and a third. The Stockholm International Peace Research Institute (1979: 36–9) suggests the gap was more like a third to a half, and that the Soviet Union regularly spent between 1 per cent and 3 per cent more of its GDP on defence than did the United States.

becoming apparent. The Soviet economy failed to produce much in the way of consumer goods, and other than in the military sector it was failing to innovate and to keep up with technological advances elsewhere. By the late 1970s, Japan had become the second-biggest economy,[3] start-ling the world with its innovations in consumer electronics, motorcycles, cars, high-speed trains and production techniques. For a brief period in the 1980s it looked like it might even overtake the United States as the biggest economy (Vogel, 1980). By comparison, the Soviet motorcycle industry was still producing the Ural, a (cheap, but poor quality) copy of a 1940s BMW based on designs and equipment looted from German factories after the war. The GDP of the Soviet Union, which in 1970 was a bit less than half that of the United States, was down to a third by 1980, and with the stagnation of the Soviet economy during the 1980s, down to less than one-seventh by 1990.[4] The writing was on the wall when China abandoned the command economy model in the late 1970s and embraced the market. Although successful in the military sector, the Soviet economic model singularly failed to keep up with the capitalist economies in terms of wealth, consumer production and innovation. By the late 1980s, it was clear that capitalism was the winner in the struggle for the economic future of modernity.

The story is somewhat similar in the political sector. Initially, the Soviet Union did well and looked strong. It gained a lot of kudos for being a winner in the war against Fascism, and also for its early successes in challenging the economic and technological lead of the United States. Its command economy model of authoritarian development was attractive to many leaders in the Third World, as was its opposition to capitalism and the West, both still strongly associated with colonialism and exploitation. The Soviet Union gained major allies in China, India, Vietnam, Egypt and Cuba, and its revolutionism, Socialism and developmentalism also sold well in much of Africa, and parts of the Middle East. Marxist polit-ical parties were strong in many parts of Western Europe, and Marxist-inspired revolutionary movements were common in Latin America.

But the Soviet Union's initial political lustre quickly began to fade. Its harsh suppression of uprisings in Poland and Hungary (1956), and Czechoslovakia (1968), made it look more like an empire than a foun-tainhead of ideological inspiration, and the turn to ideological confron-tation with China in the late 1950s split communist loyalties worldwide.

---

[3] United Nations National Accounts Main Aggregates Database: all countries for all years, https://unstats.un.org/unsd/snaama/dnllist.asp (Accessed 5 July 2017).
[4] United Nations National Accounts Main Aggregates Database: all countries for all years, https://unstats.un.org/unsd/snaama/dnllist.asp (Accessed 5 July 2017).

From the 1970s, its relatively poor economic performance was becoming increasingly obvious, undermining its claim to own the future of modernity. Its leadership was an uninspiring succession of doddery old Party apparatchiks, and its invasion of Afghanistan in 1979, and the decade-long war that followed, again made it look like an imperialist power in the eyes of many in the Third World. Apart from some notable achievements in sports and high culture, Soviet society seemed grey and dull when compared with the pop culture, fashion, mass entertainment, open debate and cornucopia consumerism of the capitalist societies. The rapid crumbling of the Soviet empire in Eastern Europe once Mikhail Gorbachev lifted the threat of intervention was the death blow to Soviet political plausibility, and was quickly followed by the disintegration of the Soviet Union itself.

By the mid-1980s it was becoming widely apparent that the Soviet Union had lost the Cold War, or, put the other way around, that the political economy of capitalism was winning it. Increasingly, its large nuclear arsenal, and broad nuclear parity with the United States, was the only remaining foundation for the Soviet Union's claim to be a superpower.

By comparison with the Soviet Union, the United States actually was a full-spectrum superpower. All of its armed forces, and not just its nuclear weapons, had truly global reach. The United States had demonstrated this capacity massively during the Second World War, and did so again with its military deployments in Europe and Japan, and with the distant wars it fought in Korea and Vietnam. With its network of bases around the world, its deployment of fleets in several oceans and its huge sea and air-lift capability, the United States could and often did operate militarily, both in the Third World and all around the periphery of the communist bloc. Economically, the United States was the core of a financial and trading system that included all of the major capitalist economies, and which penetrated deeply into the Third World. While the OECD, GATT and IMF could, as suggested above, be seen as instruments of a Western economic bloc, they were perhaps better seen as the institutions of a global economy from which the communist bloc countries chose to exclude themselves. As the economy of the Soviet Union weakened, the global nature of the Western economic system became more apparent. That the Western economic system was the global one was certainly apparent to Deng Xiaoping when he decided in the late 1970s that China should join it.

Those in the Third World who were seeking to reduce economic exploitation and improve their own development were in little doubt that they were still operating in a core–periphery world economy, and doing so from a disadvantaged position of dependency. They complained about the terms of trade between the industrialised core and the raw-material-supplying periphery, and they were caught up in the various instabilities and crises (debt, oil) that afflict capitalist systems. Many Third World countries were badly affected by the increase in the price of oil during the 1970s, and, especially in Latin America, by the debt crisis of the 1980s. Despite this turbulence, and some domestic ups and downs, the US economy remained fundamentally strong, innovative and prosperous throughout the Cold War. As Europe and Japan recovered during the 1950s and 1960s, the United States lost the rather extreme economic dominance that it had in 1945, but it remained the core that linked together the liberal international economic order. As the Asian Tigers, and from 1978 also China, prospered under capitalist develop-ment, the United States, unlike the Soviet Union by the 1980s, could still plausibly claim to own the future of modernity.

The United States also had an ideology and a society that were attractive to many. Like the Soviet Union, it started out with huge credit for being the major force behind the defeat of Fascism. As the postwar world quickly polarised into a zero-sum ideological battle, the United States set itself up as the bastion and defender of the so-called 'free world'. Ideologically, the United States offered individualism, cap-italism, democracy and human rights against the collectivism, command economy, totalitarianism and primacy of the party/state offered by the communist bloc. As a society, the United States offered the idea of social mobility: that individuals should and could have the right to prosper according to their talent and their hard work, and not on the basis of birthright or ideological loyalty. Despite the ongoing racism within American society, this idea attracted millions of migrants to the United States to pursue 'the American dream'. While US foreign policy often triggered strong opposition in both the West and the Third World, American society remained attractive. People might have demonstrated against the Vietnam War and other US interventions, and against US pol-icies on nuclear weapons and deterrence, but they still wore American sweatshirts, admired inspirational US leaders such as John F. Kennedy and Martin Luther King, and often wanted to emigrate to the United States.

In terms of the core, then, bipolarity was real but uneven, and, except in the military sector, increasingly so. The picture is nicely captured by Ian Clark (2011: 123–46), who argues that the United States was broadly hegemonic only within the West, where it was able to provide security, control nuclear proliferation and create a liberal economic order. It nevertheless presented its hegemony in global and universalist terms, and had some success in getting that view accepted. To a significant extent, it created multilateral practices and institutions, and bounded its own power, enough to make that claim look real, even though its leadership was always contested both by the communist bloc and many in the Third World. From this perspective, it is easy to see how, during the 1990s, *unipolarity* became the successor term to bipolarity to capture the basic structure of the system, a topic we return to in Chapter 7.

The second key theme of the international relations of the core during this period was the revolution in military affairs precipitated by nuclear weapons. From the first nuclear test in 1945, the development of the technology for both the weapons themselves and for their delivery systems was very rapid. As with the fast changes in late nineteenth-century naval technologies, this industrial/scientific/military dynamic destabilised relations between the leading powers. Partly these were technologies that were ripe for fast development, and partly they developed fast because the superpowers and others poured vast resources into them. The explosive yield of nuclear warheads jumped from being measured in thousands of tons of TNT (trinitrotoluene) equivalent, to millions of tons, quickly exceeding the maximum size of explosion for which anyone could think of a military use. Greater accuracy of delivery made large warheads unnecessary. By the 1960s, such weapons could be delivered by missiles to anywhere on the planet within 30 minutes. By the 1970s accuracies had fallen from the few kilometres of the 1950s missiles, to a few metres. The numbers of nuclear warheads deployed by the superpowers soared into the tens of thousands, making the power of destruction, which had historically been in short supply, now available at levels that might easily change the planetary climate and exterminate all higher life forms.

The extraordinary potency of nuclear weapons had two big impacts on the international relations of the core during this period. First, it amplified hugely the logic of the defence dilemma, and the imperative to avoid great power war, that had kicked in after the First World War. Second, it made preventing the spread of nuclear weapons beyond a very small circle of great powers an imperative embraced by both superpowers despite the depth of their other differences. Even without nuclear weapons, the massive death, destruction and cost of the Second World War would have intensified the defence dilemma. The losers in the Second World War lost more heavily than in the First, and once again many of the winners suffered badly. But the winners still won in a significant way, and some, such as the United States, won big. What was clear to even the earliest thinkers (e.g. Brodie, 1946) about the significance of nuclear weapons was that any all-out war fought between superpowers using large numbers of nuclear weapons would have no meaningful winner. The puzzle posed by the nuclear revolution was how to avoid such a war, while still pursuing a zero-sum ideological struggle about who would shape the future of modernity. The solution to that puzzle was deterrence, and the pursuit of a 'war' that was to be 'cold' rather than 'hot'.

Deterrence was the defining logic of superpower nuclear relations. The aim was to convince the other side that there were no circumstances in which they could attack first and not suffer a devastating blow in return. This principle was simple enough in itself, but implementing it plausibly under conditions in which the relevant technologies were changing quickly, and in which life-or-death decisions might have to be made within a few minutes, was very far from simple. The complexities of great chains of 'if-then' reasoning about provocation and response generated a vast literature on deterrence logic (for a review of it see Buzan and Hansen, 2009: 66–100). The need to cover all of the contingencies drove the accumulation of huge and varied arsenals of nuclear weapons. In addition to being fearsomely expensive, this system of deterrence carried real risks that either accident (a false radar reading of incoming missiles) or miscalculation (one side getting the logic wrong or seeing a weakness where a first strike might work) could trigger a nuclear war. In the event, the 'balance of terror' did work, though there were occasions when it was sorely and dangerously tested, most notably during the Cuban missile crisis of 1962, when the world spent several days poised on the brink of the nuclear abyss.

By holding back superpower nuclear war, deterrence opened the way for the United States and the Soviet Union to pursue their struggle by other means: economic competition; seeking friends and allies around the world; subverting the friends, clients and allies of the other side where possible; and sometimes using local conflicts as an opportunity to fight limited wars. Because bipolarity was uneven, the Cold War got constructed as a game of containment, in which the United States tried to prevent the Soviet Union from making any further inroads into the Western-global GIS. For its part, the Soviet Union tried to break out of containment and increase its ideological influence wherever it could. The nuclear stalemate made it too dangerous for the United States to try in any major military way to roll back the Soviet sphere. Deterrence largely preserved the ceasefire lines from 1945, diverting the superpower competition into other sectors and areas.

As already noted, the United States and its allies eventually won the economic competition, in the process gutting the legitimacy of the Soviet Union's ideological project. Both sides had success in seeking friends, clients and allies, though over the duration of the Cold War the United States was more successful. The Western alliance system was more consensual than coerced, while the Soviet system tended to be the other way around. The Soviet Union quickly lost China, but did succeed in sustaining a consensual friendship with India. The consensual weight of US alliances was confirmed by their continuation after the fall of the Soviet Union. Neither superpower had great success in proxy wars. The United States got expensively bogged down in Vietnam during the 1970s and was humiliatingly defeated there, being forced to withdraw in 1975. The Soviet Union got expensively bogged down in Afghanistan during the 1980s and was humiliatingly defeated there, being forced to withdraw in 1988–9. Both superpowers expensively backed clients in the Middle East, but without gaining much leverage over their clients' behaviour. America's investment in Iran as a key ally blew up in its face in 1979, and the Soviet Union lost Egypt after 1973. Their interventions in Africa's civil wars raised the level of local bloodshed, but did not durably reshape the region to either side's advantage. Even the Soviet Union's big success in bringing revolutionary Cuba into its camp generated the stomach-churning missile crisis of 1962, followed by an expensive dependency. Superpower intervention and competition in the Third World also added a threat of destabilising their core deterrence relationship. There was a fear that conflicts involving clients, particularly in the Middle East, might get out of control and draw the superpowers into an unwanted direct confrontation. Concern about this became part of deterrence thinking about how to control escalation from lower to higher levels of conflict that might result in unstoppable pressures to use nuclear weapons.

Within the question of the defence dilemma and war avoidance was the problem of how to stop the spread ('proliferation' was the chosen term) of nuclear weapons. The imperative against proliferation was partly about superpower status, because large nuclear arsenals were a key marker for that status. The superpowers tolerated, and even up to a point helped, a handful of their major allies acquiring nuclear weapons: Britain, France and China. These second-rank nuclear weapon states (NWSs) kept their arsenals small, so allowing the superpowers to keep large arsenals as a marker of their status. Beyond that, however, the superpowers gen-erally opposed nuclear proliferation, and during the 1960s jointly set up a non-proliferation regime. By controlling nuclear technology and trade, and separating military from civilian uses of nuclear technology, this regime was designed to make it difficult for lesser states to acquire nuclear weapons. In addition, the superpowers, especially the United States, used the technique of providing a 'nuclear umbrella' ('extended deterrence') to their allies in order to reduce their clients' and allies' incentives to acquire nuclear weapons of their own.

Non-proliferation was partly about superpower interest both in defending their special status, and in avoiding the complexities that the spread of nuclear weapons would have on the stability of the already very complex and delicate nuclear deterrence relationship between them. But it was also partly about the interests of the non-nuclear weapon states (NNWSs). There was widespread acceptance of the idea that the more fingers there were on nuclear triggers, the more likely it was that, whether by accident or design, such weapons would be used. Nuclear war was palpably in nobody's interest, so this was an argument of some force, albeit one whose legitimacy was constantly under pressure by the formalisation of the distinction between NWS and NNWS in the Non-Proliferation Treaty. That treaty obliged the NWSs to pursue nuclear disarmament, an obligation they paid lip-service to, but never pursued seriously. Many NNWSs also accepted the non-proliferation regime because they did not want the expense and risk of having to acquire nuclear weapons if their neighbours might do so. The regime did not work perfectly. Some second-rank NWSs leaked the technology to third parties: France to Israel, China to Pakistan – and from Pakistan to several other places in the Islamic world. Some developing countries (India, Brazil, Argentina, South Africa, North Korea, Iran) were capable over time of building up their own nuclear expertise. Nevertheless, by raising costs and reducing incentives, the non-proliferation regime almost certainly slowed down the spread of nuclear weapons significantly. It made it easier for Germany and Japan to accept NNWS status, and for countries such as Sweden, Switzerland, South Korea and Taiwan to decide not to acquire nuclear weapons.[5]

The Periphery

The key theme of international relations for the periphery was decolonisation. In the three decades following 1945, the vast bulk of the colonial world achieved political independence, and the anti-colonial movements discussed in previous chapters came into their own. They did so by many routes, both violent and peaceful, and by 1975 colonialism as a formal political structure of unequal core–periphery relations was over. After the Second World War, Arab nationalism took on a more militant character, much of it directed against the newly formed state of Israel. As Martin Kramer (1993: 184) puts it, 'Arab nationalism, which became "anti-imperialist" after 1920, became "revolutionary" after 1948'. In Asia, however, anti-colonial struggles were more mixed, with armed struggles being the case in Indonesia, Vietnam and Burma (especially during war

---

[5] There is a vast, and ongoing, literature on nuclear proliferation. For overviews, see Greenwood, Feiverson and Taylor (1977); Sagan and Waltz (1995); Buzan and Hansen (2009: 114–17).

time), while Malayan nationalists took on a more moderate and diplomatic approach. India's independence in 1947 gave a powerful boost to political and diplomatic pathways to independence. With many Asian nations, including India and Pakistan (1947), Ceylon (1948), Burma (1948) and Indonesia (which declared independence in 1945 but was recognised by the Dutch only in 1949), attaining independence immediately after the Second World War, Africa assumed the centre stage of anti-colonial struggles, with the first sub-Saharan nation to gain independence being Ghana in 1957. Factors in Africa contributing to anti-colonial efforts included: the 1941 Atlantic charter, which recognised the right of self-determination of countries that supported the Allied Powers (but which the United States wanted to apply universally); the weakening of European colonial powers; inspiration from and effects of independence gained by Asian countries in the 1940s; use of the UN General Assembly to mobilise diplomatic pressure; and international public opinion, human rights and self-determination norms.

In shaping anti-colonial movements, nationalism, anti-colonialism and regionalism went hand-in-hand. In Western Europe after the Second World War, regionalism was seen as a necessary means to tame the curse of nationalism that was blamed for two world wars. But leaders in the Non-Western world throughout the twentieth century viewed regionalism exactly in the reverse; it was a helpful tool for attaining national independence and sovereignty they had lost to the West. This explains the fundamental variation between the EEC/European Union (EU) model of regionalism and those found in the Third World, including the League of Arab States, created in 1945, the OAU, created in 1963, and the Association of Southeast Asian Nations (ASEAN), established in 1967. Many nationalist leaders saw regionalism as a way to advance decolonisation not only in their own countries but also more generally. This nexus was especially evident in the link between Pan-Africanism and anti-colonial struggles in Africa and the Caribbean. It would also be evident in India's support for Indonesian independence at the Second Asian Relations Conference (ARC) in New Delhi in 1949, as well as at the 1955 Asia–Africa Conference in Bandung, which made a strong push for an end to the remnants of colonialism, especially in Africa. Like the EEC, Third World regionalism was about reducing regional conflict and creating stronger positions in world politics. Unlike the EEC, these organisations bolstered nationalism, sovereignty and non-intervention.

As Jansen and Osterhammel (2017: 1) observe, decolonisation was a massive ideational and behavioural shift from the version 1.0 Western-colonial GIS that structured international relations up to 1945: it was 'the disappearance of empire as a political form, and the end of racial

hierarchy as a widely accepted political ideology and structuring principle of world order'. Under version 1.1 Western-global GIS, the former
colonial world morphed into the bipolar structure of the Cold War as
the new 'Third World'. These countries now had the political freedom to
make their own way in world politics, though, as Marx ([1852] 1963: 1)
famously noted, not in circumstances of their own choosing. The leaders
and peoples of the Third World had won or been given their political independence. But their states were mostly poor and underdeveloped, with
weak economies that remained significantly dependent on the former
metropoles. Their domestic politics were often turbulent and unstable,
and the ideas of nationalism and self-determination that had facilitated
their struggle for independence often destabilised the multi-ethnic and
multi-cultural successor states. Most kept their colonial boundaries,
and these had seldom been drawn with any idea of containing a nation
in mind, especially in Africa. As Jansen and Osterhammel (2017: 177)
note: 'almost 40 percent of the length of all international borders today
have been originally drawn by Great Britain and France'. The lack of
a consolidated demos, and the consequent problems of secessionism,
and/or struggles by different groups to capture control of the state, were
endemic. Although they were no longer toyed with as prizes in colonial competitions among distant great powers, they were subject to the
superpowers' global ideological and military competition over their mode
of development and political alignments. As Odd Arne Westad (2007: 5)
notes, the Cold War could be seen as 'one of the final stages of European
global control'.

So, while the leaders of the Third World were finally sitting as sovereign equals at the table of GIS, they were holding weak cards. In some
ways, they were playing a familiar game of core–periphery relations, in
which they now at least had an independent voice. But in other ways the
game was new, with bipolarity and the Cold War posing a quite different
set of challenges and opportunities from those of the colonial era. The
leaders and peoples of the Third World had to play multiple games on
several different fronts.

Domestically, they had to try to consolidate and stabilise their new
states, and find both a political direction and a development strategy that
would enable them to modernise as quickly as possible in order to meet
the aspirations of the people and leaders for wealth and power (Westad,
2007: 90). The capitalist and Socialist development models offered (and
either supported or opposed) by the two superpowers differed starkly: capitalism came with Western aid, but was easily associated with much-
resented exploitative colonial practices; Socialism seemed to suit the
desire of many Third World leaders for a simple, quick and authoritarian

path to development (Westad, 2007: 91–3). Given the fragmented demos that was the political legacy for many postcolonial states, for many of their leaders, regime security against internal challengers was as much or more of a problem than worrying about threats from neighbours. Being mostly weak both as states and powers, Third World states were generally not in a position to threaten their neighbours militarily. The credibility of guerrilla war, honed during some of the decolonisation struggles, was a plausible deterrent against any threat of occupation. There were some exceptions to this, most notably in the Middle East and South Asia, where many new states did see their neighbours as posing existential military and political threats.

At the regional level, Third World states had to work out economic, political and security relationships with their newly independent neighbours, and develop policies for operating within their regions. This was often far from easy. Many of the new regions were born into conflict (Buzan and Wæver, 2003). South Asia, for example, had to transition from being a unified hub of the British Empire to being a fractious regional security complex riven by religion and history. The Middle East moved from Ottoman control, to being divided up into European colonies and mandates after the First World War, to being a highly conflictual regional security complex, divided against itself along many religious, ethnic and political lines. Former colonies within a region often had little in the way of economic relations to give them a shared interest, and much in the way of political, religious, cultural and boundary disputes to set them at odds with each other. Ironically, one widely accepted strategy for dealing with both the domestic and regional challenges was to agree to keep colonial boundaries unchanged. Third World states, often with the support of the UN system, generated many regional, sub-regional and super-regional IGOs – not just the ones already mentioned above, but also the Organization of American States (1948), the Organisation of Islamic Cooperation (1969), the Economic Community of West African States (ECOWAS) (1975), the Gulf Cooperation Council (1981) and the South Asian Association for Regional Cooperation (1985).

At the global level, the new states of the Third World also had to play in the game of world politics now dominated by the two superpowers. At this level too, IGOs played a crucial role both in enabling Third World states to play an active role in diplomacy, and in providing them with at least some ways in which they could use their numbers to compensate for their economic weakness. In this sense, there was an important synergy in version 1.1 GIS between the US commitment to promoting multilateral diplomacy and IGOs on the one hand, and the Third World's need to get into the game of global politics, and try to influence it, on the other.

The United States was not, of course, directly interested in promoting the influence of the Third World. It wanted to create a stable order and pursue its struggle against communism, and was prepared up to a point to bind its own power in institutions in order to do that. Nevertheless, the UN system provided both a forum and a moral framework within which the Third World states could have their say. At least in the General Assembly, it also provided them with a forum in which their numbers mattered when it came to winning votes.

The creation of an inclusive system of IGOs was more fundamentally important to the function of version 1.1 GIS than is immediately apparent. As Barry Buzan and Richard Little (2010: 317–18) argue, the great expansion in the number of states brought about by decolonisation created something of a crisis for the standard bilateral practices of diplomacy. Especially for poorer countries, it was impossible, both on cost grounds and because of the lack of enough trained people, for every state to have even an embassy in the capital city of every other state. Regional and global IGOs were thus not only useful forums for discussing collective problems, but essential machineries for concentrating diplomacy in a way that enabled poorer countries still to play a full role.

Yet, many Third World countries came to view certain international institutions as instruments of coercion in the hands of the North, contributing to the power disparities in the international system, and being geared to American strategic goals. One conspicuous example was the IMF's ability to enforce structural adjustment in Africa despite its immense human and political costs. Robert Cox's assessment of international institutions was suggestive, especially when viewed from the perspective of Third World countries: 'international organization can now be redefined as the process of institutionalization of hegemony. International institutions universalise the norms proper to a structure of world power, and that structure of power maintains itself through support of these institutions. In that sense, institutions are ballasts to the status quo' (R. W. Cox, 1980: 377). In response, Third World states sought to create institutions which would be more supportive of their interests and aspirations. At the global level, they developed three institutions. The Group of 77 (G77) (1964) harnessed their voting power in IGOs and multilateral global negotiations on issues such as the Law of the Sea and the proliferation of nuclear weapons. The UN Conference on Trade and Development (UNCTAD) (1964) contested and counterbalanced the dominance of the West in the global financial institutions (IMF, World Bank, GATT). The NAM (1961) tried to create political space outside the ideological bipolarity of the superpowers.

During the 1970s, a small group of oil-exporting countries found and exploited a powerful economic lever that they could use against the West. By restricting supply, they were able to use the Organization of the Petroleum Exporting Countries (OPEC) to greatly increase the price of oil. The political and security space opened up by the competition between the superpowers allowed them to get away with this. Their success, however, turned out to be a one-off. Other commodity exporters failed to construct similarly successful cartels, and the high price of oil did a lot of damage to other developing countries that had to import it and could not deal with the higher price as easily as wealthier countries could.

More successfully, the Third World states played moral cards, using the normative framework embedded into the UN system's constitutional documents and statements of purpose. So long as decolonisation remained incomplete, they relentlessly pressed for the remaining cases. In parallel with that, they campaigned tirelessly against racism, making particular play against the apartheid regime in South Africa, and accusing Israel of pursuing colonialism and racism against the Palestinians. The Third World lobby also promoted aid and development as a matter of right, and defended its newly won sovereignty against both old and new forms of intervention.

Despite the Cold War, the Third World states did succeed in opening up significant political space for themselves. Although they were heavily penetrated by the dynamics of the Cold War superpower rivalry, they also used the bipolar division to create bargaining leverage for themselves over everything from aid to anti-racism. The Cold War might have been 'one of the final stages of European global control', but compared to the Western-colonial period it was also a very considerable liberation. The overriding concern of most Third World countries, however, was to pursue modernisation and development, and here the often high hopes that accompanied decolonisation were mostly met with bitter disappointments. Many on both the metropolitan and ex-colonial sides had assumed that independence-plus-aid would fairly quickly solve the problem of underdevelopment. In the event, only a handful of Asian Tigers (South Korea, Taiwan, Singapore) successfully made the full jump into industrial modernity. Most of the experiments with Socialist, autarkic and/or 'import substitution' development strategies were expensive failures.

Across much of Africa, Asia and Latin America, development was stalled by various mixtures of conflict, kleptocracy, misguided ideology, bureaucracy, corruption, weak government, poor education and poor health. The weak states of the Third World struggled to maintain their independence in the face of the globalisation of finance and production in the world economy. They found themselves engaged in an unequal struggle not only with the strong states and powers of the North, but also with powerful transnational firms and global trade and financial structures over which they had little leverage or control.[6] What was striking about this period was not the success of Third World development, but how quickly and thoroughly those industrialised countries that had been devastated by the war recovered. Japan and Germany speedily became modern industrial giants once again, and the West as a whole prospered (Westad, 2007: 91). The gap between developed and developing was not closing, and in many places and in many respects was getting wider.

Reconstruction of an already modernised society was vastly easier than developing one not yet modernised, and any analogy between the two was false. As some colonial thinkers had argued, and as had been embedded in the LN mandate system, not all of those who gained independence were ready for self-government under the highly penetrative and demanding conditions of modern world politics. As in the previous periods, development required undergoing the revolutions of modernity while retaining political stability, and this task had not got any easier with the shift from colonial control to independence. The obligation of the colonial powers to raise their charges up to the 'standard of civilisation' had morphed into an obligation to provide aid and promote development. But the range of cases and conditions was very wide, and the highly uneven starting places in the race for development were matched by highly uneven degrees of success. At one end of the spectrum were the Asian Tigers, such as Korea and Taiwan, whose societies had been forcibly, but effectively, modernised by Japan when they were its colonies. This handful of countries, including Singapore, did succeed in developing quickly, albeit mostly under authoritarian regimes. In the middle of the spectrum were countries such as India, which had reasonably effective governments, and some elements of industrialism and modernity. These were a complex mix of successes and failures, with some progress towards modernisation, but slow and patchy. In India and elsewhere, many rural parts of the country remained largely agrarian and premodern. At the other end of the spectrum were many countries in Africa, where decolonisation had not been expected to happen anything like as soon as it did, the legacy of colonial boundaries was particularly difficult, and the educational, social, bureaucratic and financial resources

---

[6] For useful overviews of the developments within the world economy during this period see Gilpin (1987); Hurrell and Woods (1995); Stubbs and Underhill (1994).

to run a modern state were often lacking. Some of these regressed in development from colonial days, having less political order and worse conditions for investment, and being unable to maintain some of their inherited infrastructure such as railways. Even some successes in development, such as improved health care and disease control, had problematic consequences in the form of high rates of population growth.

The problem faced by colonial administrators of how to find fair, stable and progressive ways of relating strong, industrial economies to weak, unmodernised ones was not solved by decolonisation. It was exposed as a very long and difficult job. While it might have become possible by the end of this period to imagine that one day all of the world would be equally developed, it had become difficult or impossible to imagine that this would happen either quickly or evenly. At best, it was going to be a long, drawn-out process in which a trickle of states would move across the boundary from developing to developed status, and in which such states might spend a long time in a middle zone between the two. It was deeply politically incorrect to express such thoughts, but that is where all of the experience of the decolonisation/Cold War era pointed.

Restructuring the Core–Periphery Relationship

In the decades following the end of the Second World War, both core and periphery were transformed. The core shifted to an intensely contested bipolarity in which the option of great power war was closed off by the nuclear defence dilemma. The periphery shifted from colonial status to independence, and a both collective and individual struggle to find workable pathways to development from a huge variety of starting conditions. These stories were causally entangled. As colonies became states, empires also had to become states. The Second World War created the superpowers in part by weakening or demolishing the European great powers and Japan, and it was that weakening of the main imperial powers that facilitated decolonisation. But the two stories also have their own distinct dynamics. The rise of the United States and the Soviet Union, as Tocqueville noticed, had been in the making for a long time. So too had decolonisation, which had roots stretching well back into the nineteenth century in both local resistance, and local culture and religion, and in the ideologies of Liberalism, Socialism and nationalism. As Westad (2007: 86–97) observes, while it might have been the Second World War that destroyed colonialism, the First World War had significantly inspired and opened up resistance to it in the periphery.

The Cold War and decolonisation occurred side by side and played into each other in myriad ways. From our perspective, perhaps the

most important point is that it was during this interplay that international relations became truly global for the first time. Decolonisation
steadily dissolved the separation dividing colonial relations between
metropoles and their peripheries on the one hand, and international
relations between the 'civilised' states on the other, that had so strongly
marked version 1.0 GIS. The unexpected speed and scale of decolonisation between 1945 and 1975 transformed Western-colonial GIS into
Western-global GIS. Although relations of power and wealth, and levels
of development in terms of modernisation, remained highly unequal,
legal and political relations on the basis of sovereign equality became
effectively universal. What had been formal relations of inequality for
the previous century or more, now became formally equal, albeit with a
lot of informal inequality remaining. Racism was formally, and to a considerable extent informally, eliminated as basis for determining political
and legal relations.

It was on this basis that the Cold War rivalry of the superpowers played
into the newly minted Third World. For the United States and the Soviet
Union, the Third World became a key arena in which they played out
their struggle. They offered strikingly different strategies for modernisation, and their ability to attract clients and allies, and to shape the political economy of modernisation in the Third World, became an important
marker of how they were doing in their overall competition. These superpower interests intersected with the many fault-lines within and between
Third World countries, leading to competitive interventions with aid,
arms supply and sometimes direct political and military support to one
side or the other. As well as scoring ideological points off each other,
the superpowers were also interested in more parochial great power
concerns such as access to resources (e.g. oil in the Middle East and
Africa, uranium in the former Belgian Congo) and bases (e.g. in the
Philippines, Cuba, the Gulf, the Levant, the Indian Ocean). Under Cold
War conditions, it was difficult for Third World countries to avoid superpower penetrations into their domestic and regional relationships. Each
superpower tended to interpret the Third World not in terms of the local
dynamics, but by seeing events in terms of machinations by its superpower rival. When the superpowers got engaged directly in Third World
conflicts, as the United States did in Vietnam, and the Soviet Union in
Afghanistan, each made life as difficult and painful as possible for the
other by supplying and encouraging any and all forms of local opposition
to it. The meaning of 'Cold' in Cold War was that the United States and
the Soviet Union could not take the risk of fighting each other directly.
In the North, 'Cold' meant arms racing and the creation of military and
political standoffs in Europe and Northeast Asia. In the South, 'Cold'

meant a wide-spectrum competition across the military, political and economic sectors, and a willingness to engage in proxy wars.

The Cold War thus transformed the colonial obligation of metropol-itan powers to bring their charges up to the 'standard of civilisation' into a global ideological struggle about which was the best and quickest path to modernisation and development. Before 1945, how well or badly (or at all) the colonial obligation was implemented varied greatly, and it was not really well done anywhere. The Cold War politicised develop-ment, which increased both the aid resources made available for it, and the levels of dispute, conflict and confusion about how such resources should be used. The Third World's obsession with achieving develop-ment intersected with the superpowers' ideological point-scoring to reshape the role of IGOs in world politics. While the LN had attempted to manage great power relations through collective security, the Cold War quickly sidelined the UN from that function. Instead, with decolon-isation, the UN system became the main forum for North–South politics over development, nuclear proliferation, the management of the global economy and a host of other issues. For the Third World, the UN system was the preferred forum because it was the one place where they had any political and moral power.

During this period, the periphery remained largely weak and dependent on the core. Development by whatever path proved to be slower, more difficult and less stable than expected. Only a handful of Asian Tigers made the jump fully into modernity. By the end of the Cold War, with the big exception of China and the Tigers, the gaps between developed and developing states remained much as they had been at the beginning. While the war-damaged states in the core had reconstructed themselves quickly, most of the Third World remained in a state of eco-nomic dependency. The new Third World had in some significant ways reshaped international politics, not least in transforming the main pur-pose and functions of IGOs. During this period, international relations became truly global in the sense that all peoples – or more accurately all governments – now participated in it independently. But GIS was still dominated by the West, and the Third World was still weakly placed within a core–periphery global economy. With the demise of the Soviet Union, the Third World lost influence against the West.

There is one further feature of this development that is relevant not only to this period, but also to the ones before and after it. This concerns the way in which history is remembered – and forgotten – differently in the North and in the South. Most of the peoples and governments in the North mainly remember this period as 'the Cold War era', and think of decolonisation – if they think of it at all – as a side-show to that. And looking back deeper, they hardly remember the colonial era, and the role of their countries in it, at all. If they do remember, it is mainly with a prideful glow about past glories and legacies.[7] Apart from a handful of historians and leftists, they have largely forgotten how complicit their own states and societies were in racism, and how violent and coercive the practice of empire was. By contrast, most of the peoples and governments in the South, especially in Africa and Asia, mainly remember this period as the time of decolonisation and liberation. Their memory of the earlier colonialism and racism, and the violence and indignity it inflicted on them, remains strong, and is often actively cultivated and reproduced. The ongoing economic inequality between the North and the South facilitated this reproduction, as did the need for Third World governments to find someone other than themselves to blame for their failure to achieve rapid development. This disjuncture between metropolitan forgetting and remembered postcolonial resentments in the periphery emerged as a key feature of global politics during this period, and echoed forward strongly from there in issues ranging from aid and terms of trade, through human rights and peace-keeping, to non-intervention and terrorism.

China As an Enigmatic Outsider

China does not fit comfortably into either side of this story. It was not a superpower, yet played independently in the superpower game both materially and ideologically. It was a developing country with a strong resentment against the West, Russia and Japan for its 'century of humiliation' at their hands. It thus shared the anti-imperialist and anti-racist sentiments of the Third World. It also shared their passion to find a quick path to modernity in order to recover its wealth and power. Yet China was not itself a former colony. Like other Third World states it clung onto its designation and identity as a developing country, but unlike most of them, it also saw itself as a major power, albeit one in a temporarily weakened position. It shared this combination with India. But China's combination of vast size, long-established civilisation and state traditions, relatively coherent ethnicity, and ruthlessly controlling central government differentiated it sharply from all the others in the Third World, including India.

---

[7] The United States is something of an exception here because it was a relatively minor colonial power before 1945. Its 'colonial' experience was largely internal because of the importation of African slaves, the racism associated with that, and the ongoing problem of how to handle the race issue in American domestic politics.

After the end of its civil war in 1949, China briefly aligned itself with the Soviet Union and accepted Soviet aid and the Soviet development model. It had clashed with the United States in Korea, and saw the United States as preventing the final reunification of the country by protecting the rump Kuomintang (KMT) regime that had retreated to Taiwan. Despite continuing to feel threatened by the United States, Mao's regime split with the Soviet Union during the late 1950s, promoting its own ideology both within the Soviet bloc and the Third World, and seeking its own accelerated path to development. It began to play an independent role opposing and challenging both superpowers. Yet although China played a significant role at the 1955 Bandung Conference, it did not join the NAM, and the Sino-Indian border war of 1962 was a major blow to the cohesion of the Third World (Westad, 2007: 107). In the 1970s it formed a strategic partnership with the United States against the Soviet Union, but abandoned this in the 1990s once the Soviet threat had diminished.

Mao's regime chalked up some notable accomplishments, not least in unifying the country after decades of devastating civil and foreign war, and quickly acquiring its own nuclear weapons. But it also extended China's lamentable history of self-harm stretching back into the nineteenth century. His attempt to destroy China's traditional culture and social structure, and to find a fast-track to development, inflicted huge material and social damage on the country. His abortive 'Great Leap Forward' in the late 1950s both damaged the economy and resulted in the deaths of some 35 million Chinese from violence and famine (Rummell, 1991: 12–13; J. Gray, 2002: 310–15; Shirk, 2007: 18; Dikötter, 2011: locs. 61–74, 5602–784; Westad, 2012: loc. 5188; Schell and Delury, 2013: 236–40; Fenby, 2013: 396, 415, 481). His 'Great Proletarian Cultural Revolution' in the mid-1960s killed many fewer people, but ruined lives and disrupted development on a vast scale (Kissinger, 2011: 181–4; Westad, 2012: loc. 5482; Fenby, 2013: 560; Dikötter, 2016: loc. 4070).

Yet just as it had done in the late 1950s, in the late 1970s China once again broke the mould of this era by embarking on Deng's policy of 'reform and opening up'. In effect, the Chinese Communist Party (CCP) retained its own dictatorship while switching from the Socialist to the capitalist model of development. In the short run, this dramatic turnaround signalled the death-knell for the Soviet challenge to the West for the future of modernity, and the impending end of the Cold War. In little more than a decade the Soviet Union itself was gone, and China was joining the Asian Tigers in a rapidly rising trajectory of export-led development. In the longer run it signalled a deeper challenge to the West as the CCP committed itself to creating a form of stable authoritarian capitalism that would break the liberal linkage between capitalism and democracy. In pursuing this agenda, the CCP abandoned Mao's attempt to destroy traditional Chinese culture, and began instead to revive and re-legitimise those elements of Confucianism that could support this third-way model of development. The phrase 'Chinese characteristics' began to become a staple way of talking about the fusions of tradition and modernity that the CCP needed in order to stabilise this model.

One of the main reasons for putting China into a category of its own as an enigmatic outsider to the broader patterns set by both the Cold War and decolonisation was the extreme volatility of its foreign policy. As described above, it flip-flopped in alignment with the superpowers while at the same time seeking the strength to stand alone. It was unclear whether China wanted to play for leadership of the Third World, or was one of the great powers competing for ideological and political dominance there. Despite its poverty, Mao's China gave generous aid to many Third World countries (Fenby, 2013: 423). Sometimes China intervened ruthlessly in its Southeast and South Asian neighbours, backing revolutionary regimes and movements, and helping Pakistan to become a NWS in order to make trouble for India. At other times, it sought harmonious relations. On the spectrum of status quo to revisionist, China swung from being a dedicated revolutionary revisionist under Mao, to presenting itself as a stability-seeking status quo power under Deng.

In retrospect, and with an eye to the future, Deng's revolution is already beginning to look like a more important event than the demise of the Soviet Union.

The Ending of the Cold War and Decolonisation

The Cold War ended between the late 1980s and 1991, beginning with Gorbachev's failed attempt to do his own version of reform and opening up, passing through the disintegration of the Soviet empire in Eastern Europe, and ending with the implosion of the Soviet Union itself into 15 new states. Whether that was also the end of decolonisation, or whether that happened in the mid-1970s (independence of the Portuguese colonies in Africa) or the mid-1990s (South Africa and Hong Kong) is a matter of debate (Jansen and Osterhammel, 2017). Either way, the Soviet Union and its ideology were clearly the big losers of the Cold War. In one sense the United States specifically, and the West and Japan more generally, can be said to have won the Cold War. The Soviet Union lost the battle over the future of modernity, and the price of independence for the Third World was both to take on the Western political form of sovereign, territorial, national states, and to participate in the Western-led global economy as a periphery. In a more specific sense, however, the big winners were ideational: capitalism and nationalism (Buzan and Lawson, 2015a: 280–91). In terms of working out the ideational tensions unleashed in the nineteenth century, nationalism became the almost universal foundation for state legitimacy, and capitalism became the accepted best path to development, and thereby to wealth and power. In the process of winning the Cold War, however, capitalism had both fragmented into several varieties, and become delinked from democracy, most notably in China.

The ending of the Cold War brought both bipolarity and the nuclear defence dilemma to an abrupt end. The United States seemed to stand alone as the sole superpower, and defusing of the ideological and military tensions between East and West both reduced nuclear arsenals, and moved them from hair-trigger alert status to the remote possibility of uncontrolled escalation or use. The post-Cold War period seemed to offer *unipolarity*, and a more-or-less unopposed run for US-led neoliberal capitalism and economic globalisation. The Third World had mostly not solved the problem of development and dependency, and had lost both the political space and leverage opened up for it by bipolarity, and one of its development models. This is the story we will pick up in Chapter 7.

Conclusions

When looked at in long historical perspective, decolonisation might well come to be seen as the major defining feature of this period, with the victory of capitalism (though not democracy) as a close second. The Cold War might look more and more like just another episode in the ever-changing kaleidoscope of great power politics. Bipolarity itself may not look particularly significant. What might stand out about the Cold War are two things. First, it looks significant because it was a major round in the game of working out the ideological choices about the future political economy of modernity that was set rolling during the nineteenth century. Capitalism was going to carry modernity forward, but, if the Chinese could work it out, not necessarily in conjunction with democracy. Second, it was the first time that humankind faced the threat that it might commit species suicide, and with the help of some good luck, our species survived that first test.

6 International Relations 1945–1989: The Second Founding of the Discipline

Introduction

This chapter picks up the story of the discipline of International Relations from where we left off in Chapter 4. We use roughly the same structure of looking at IR thinking in the core and in the periphery, and sketching out the institutionalisation in both. We note continuities where they exist, but as the subtitle of this chapter indicates, we are more impressed with the differences. Krippendorff (1989: 34) sees 1945 as a second founding for IR as a discipline, and as 'more serious' than the one in 1919. We agree. And given our overall argument that IR reflects ir, this is not surprising because, as we argued in Chapter 5, the Second World War marked a significant transformation in ir from the version 1.0 GIS first set up during the nineteenth century to version 1.1 GIS. The key changes defining version 1.1 were:

- A shift from a multipolar system with several great powers to a bipolar one with just two superpowers each promoting a rival universalist ideology.
- The introduction of nuclear weapons and intercontinental delivery systems generating a sharp intensification of the defence dilemma and concern about war.
- The delegitimation of racism and colonialism, and a tripling of the membership of GIS as decolonisation brought in the former colonies as the new periphery of Third World 'developing countries'.

The first two of these changes propelled the United States to the forefront of IR, both because it shifted from isolationism to global engagement and because it became the leading nuclear weapons power. The combination of an intense, ideologically driven, global bipolar rivalry, and the world-destroying potential of nuclear weapons, ramped up the obsession of IR in the core, already established during the interwar years, with great power relations and war. Decolonisation was a very radical transformation in political relations between core and periphery, yet it did not impinge all that much on the great power concerns of IR thinking in the core. As Arlene Tickner and Ole Wæver (2009b: 7) note, the concern with East–West relations dominated IR during this period, pushing concern with both North–South and South–South relations to the margins. Decolonisation weakened the anti-colonialism and anti-racism themes of IR thinking in the periphery, but not by much. Instead opposition shifted to the neocolonialism of economic inequality, and the Eurocentrism and hidden racism of much Western IR thinking.

The idea that IR had a 'second founding' after 1945 rests on several developments that we explore in more detail below:

- A massive expansion of institutionalisation in terms of teaching, research and publications.
- The demise of the ISC, which was centred on the LN, and the rise of independent academic IR associations.
- Especially in the core, a notable shift from being a broader intellectual and political subject to being a more professionalised, theorised and academic one (L. Ashworth, 2014: 256).
- A major exercise in forgetting or dismissing much of what had come before.
- The rapid rise of new sub-fields, most notably Strategic Studies with its focus on the unique problems posed by nuclear weapons.
- The beginnings of recognition in the core for IR thinking from the periphery.

Most of these changes can be explained by the shift of the centre of gravity of both ir and IR to the United States. As a globally engaged superpower and leader of the Western world, the United States had an urgent need to know more about international relations. It already had strong foundations from the interwar period to build on, and now it had the incentive, the people and the money to do so. The longstanding practical tradition in American social science lent itself to this new need, and in terms of the quantity, and up to a point quality, of its IR the United States quickly become by far the most prolific and influential country in the discipline. Krippendorf (1989: 33) argues that IR as a discipline in the United States originated as a government initiative not only to produce policy-relevant research but also to train highly qualified government personnel tasked with understanding the outside world. Britain fell to a distant second place, while Germany and Japan were subordinated and under American influence. The Soviet Union made little impact on IR thinking other than within its own bloc, falling victim to the reality, as pointed out in Chapter 4, that 'in authoritarian states the study of international relations or foreign policy could only exist as an explanation and justification of state policy' (Olson and Groom, 1991: 74–5; see also Sergounin, 2009). Mao's China, interestingly, became somewhat of an exception to this rule.

The shift of IR's centre of gravity to the United States after 1945 in one sense just perpetuated and reinforced the existing dominance of the Anglosphere in the discipline inherited from the interwar years. But while it brought many advantages, such as US funding for foreign IR scholars, it also pushed some American peculiarities to centre stage. As already remarked, IR in the United States was tightly bound to Political Science (Schmidt, 1998a: 55; L. Ashworth, 2014: 13; Kuru, 2017: 46), and in its early days as an academic discipline IR was generally housed as a specialisation within Political Science departments (Richardson, 1989: 287–8). This feature was prevalent throughout the Cold War period and remains so to this day. One key consequence of this linkage was that American IR was both narrowly focused, understanding the subject to be a subset of the political sphere, and deeply predisposed to formal 'scientific' methods. This strong linkage of IR to Political Science was not generally true elsewhere. IR in Britain had its main roots in History, International Law and Political Theory, while on the continent there were strong links with Sociology.

In famously calling IR an 'American social science', Hoffmann (1977) identified three 'institutional factors' that led to IR bearing a distinctively American stamp, but that had 'not existed, and certainly not simultaneously, elsewhere'. The first was 'the most direct and visible tie between the scholarly world and the world of power: the "in-and-outer" system of government, which put academics and researchers not merely in the corridors but also in the kitchens of power'. A second and related factor was 'relays between the kitchens of power and the academic salons', or the close connection, some would say nexus, between the academic and policy worlds. Universities formed the third institutional factor, being 'flexible; because of their own variety, which ensured both competition and specialization' and evincing an 'almost complete absence of the strait jackets of public regulations, quasi-feudal traditions, financial dependence, and intellectual routine which have so often paralyzed the universities of postwar Europe' (Hoffmann, 1977: 49–50).

American primacy nevertheless substantially imposed its standards onto the rest of the discipline after 1945. As Tickner and Wæver (2009c: 329) put it: 'The US form of IR is simultaneously a single local instance of the field and an integral component of everyone else's universe'. Yet while the United States set the standard for IR globally both by its relative size and command of resources (finance, academic organisations, top journals), it was also true that the rational choice and quantitative methods that increasingly dominated American IR were 'almost totally absent in the rest of the world': 'it is striking how the currently dominant forms of US IR do *not* travel' (Tickner and Wæver, 2009a: 5, 339; Maliniak et al., 2018). The academic professionalisation of IR by US standards also deepened the exclusion of the non-academic IR from the periphery from the disciplinary debates in the core: 'few contributions from the non-core are recognised as legitimate ways of thinking about international politics' (Tickner and Wæver, 2009b: 3).

Perhaps also linked to US primacy in IR was the major forgetting that took place in the discipline. While IR before the Second World War was born with some degree of diversity in the sense of having different thematic concerns and with a certain multidisciplinary orientation, IR after the Second World War became notably narrower and less multidisciplinary. Having flourished during the nineteenth century and the interwar years, Geopolitics was delegitimised after the Second World War, sunk by its association with Fascism, conveniently allowing the rest of the West to forget that they too were part of its heritage. So deep was this break that Geopolitics (mainly in the form of Critical Geopolitics) only began to re-emerge in Anglo-American IR during the 1990s (Ó Tuathail, 1996; Ó Tuathail, Dalby and Routledge, 1998; Guzzini, 2013). The promising line of Feminist thinking that had opened up during the interwar period likewise did not re-emerge until the 1990s. IPE, except for Dependency Theory (on which more below), which was a purely Non-Western idea, got dropped from IR post-1945 as the field focused on the security problems of the Cold War, not reappearing until the oil and financial crises of the 1970s and 1980s impacted on the United States. The general absorption of IR by Political Science in the United States, and Morgenthau's separation of the political sphere as the discrete focus for IR study, became key moves in the three-decades silencing of IPE (L. Ashworth, 2014: 253–4). As the old formal empires quickly disappeared in the two decades following 1945, so too did IR's links to colonialism. The successor topic to colonial administration – development – was not a major issue within IR. Partly this was because it was taken up in other disciplines (Development Economics, Comparative Politics), and partly because it was one of those North–South issues that got subordinated to East–West ones. IR's roots in racism were also forgotten, especially in the United States (Vitalis, 2005: 161–5), which is not to say that a less overt racism did not continue to play a significant role in much IR thinking (J. M. Hobson, 2012). In addition, the nineteenth-century roots of the discipline were more or less forgotten. The first 'great debate', as noted in Chapter 4, was mainly constructed after 1945 as a way of dismissing the IR of the interwar period, with its big focus on the LN as mainly

Utopian, and totally unsuited to the Realist world of the Cold War that was opening up during the later 1940s.

The Institutionalisation of IR

A key feature of the 'second founding' of IR after 1945 was both the great expansion of its academic institutionalisation in terms of teaching, university departments, think tanks, textbooks and journals, and the founding of mostly national, academic associations of IR (or more commonly the broader 'International Studies') to replace the ISC. These developments were mostly in North America and Western Europe, though for this period we move Japan and Korea from the periphery to the core. As during the interwar years, no consensus emerges about what to call the discipline, with several labels remaining in play.

The Core

In many ways, the institutionalisation of IR in the core followed a similar pattern to that of the interwar years. In those countries where IR was, or became, established, there was a general increase in the number of places teaching it, the number of journals and think tanks, the number of people doing IR teaching and research, and the setting up of academic IR associations. This expansion was most marked in the places where IR had already developed during the interwar years and earlier, but there was also broadening into additional countries. In line with its size, wealth and new global roles, the United States mainly led in these developments, and was certainly the biggest in most respects.

The already significant development of IR in American universities and think tanks, discussed in Chapter 4, continued and gathered greater momentum in the postwar period. As Norman Palmer (1980: 348) notes, 'Courses in international relations ... proliferated in American colleges and universities', with 'a growing recognition and acceptance of international relations as a field of study'. He estimated that, as of 1980, there had been a 'fivefold increase in the number of international relations courses' as compared to the 1930s. Significantly, there was a surge in both undergraduate- and graduate-level courses. Aside from Political Science departments, courses in or relevant to the study of IR became available through History, Economics and Area Studies departments and programmes in universities, as well as in other law and business faculties. Separate IR schools emerged, such as the School of International and Public Affairs at Columbia (founded in 1946), the School of International Service at American University (1957) and a similar school at Denver (a graduate school of International Studies in 1964). As a corollary to the growth in university departments and courses, IR textbooks, associations and journals also proliferated in the United States more than any other country. A majority of IR textbooks used by IR students at all levels the world over are published in the United States.[1]

Neil Richardson offers several reasons behind the surge in undergraduate student interest in IR in the United States: Ronald Reagan's 'high profile' foreign policy posture, employers looking for college graduates with knowledge of international affairs, and the changing content of IR curricula (Richardson, 1989: 288–9). The increase in PhD IR graduates must also be taken into account as must the qualitative features of graduate programmes that attract graduate student interest – programmes which have been 'unique in attempting to balance academic rigour with pragmatic, vocational training suited to a variety of careers in public and private sectors' (Richardson, 1989: 290).

Similar institutional expansions took place elsewhere, albeit mainly in the Anglosphere, and places such as Scandinavia where English was strong as a second language. In Britain, IR quickly spread to most universities, with dedicated departments at City University, St Andrews, Warwick, Keele, and Bradford (Peace Studies). Similar expansions took place in Australia (with Australian National University as a particular centre), Canada (mostly in Political Science departments) and New Zealand (Cox and Nossal, 2009: 295–301). Scandinavia also developed a strong position in IR, with a particular emphasis on Peace Research (Friedrichs and Wæver, 2009). Peace Research was also the leading strength of IR in Germany at this time. IR teaching, again including a strong emphasis on Peace Research, also expanded in Japan and Korea, but in the absence of Political Science departments in Japan, its institutionalisation remained somewhat diffuse and weak in terms of universities (Inoguchi, 2009: 94, 97). Think tanks also underwent a boom during this period. In Western Europe, 19 IR think tanks were formed, in the United States another 18, and in Japan, 3.[2]

A natural corollary of this was an expansion in the number of people involved in academic IR, and this ties into one of the big institutional shifts following the Second World War: the demise of the ISC and its replacement by independent academic associations mostly organised along national lines. The ISC was wound up in 1954 when American

---

[1] See Sandole (1985) for a review of post-1945 textbooks.
[2] For detailed information about the associations and think tanks, see McGann (2018); www.wiscnetwork.net/about-wisc/members; www.isanet.org/ISA/Partners (Accessed 14 February 2018).

foundations and academics turned their interest to the International Political Science Association (IPSA) founded by the UN Educational, Scientific and Cultural Organization in 1949 (Long, 2006: 607–12). Shortly after the demise of the ISC, several national academic IR associations were formed: the Japan Association of International Relations (JAIR) and the Korean Association of International Relations in 1956, the (American) International Studies Association (ISA) in 1959, and the British International Studies Association (BISA) in 1975.[3] These associations were much alike in form and purpose, and similar to associations set up by other disciplines. Generally, they were independent professional membership organisations. Their main tasks were to run academic conferences, support specialist working groups,[4] publish one or more journals and award prizes, and generally cultivate a sense of identity and participation among the members of the discipline. They funded themselves through membership fees, conference profits, support from foundations and income from their journals. These organisations grew along with the general expansion of IR in universities as a subject for teaching and research, and they rapidly outgrew the relatively small-scale membership of the ISC. By the late 1990s, JAIR had over 2,000 members; BISA had over 1,000 members by 2006; and ISA's membership grew from 200 in 1959 to over 2,000 by the end of the Cold War.[5]

ISA was without doubt the biggest, wealthiest and most influential of these new academic IR associations, and its particular story is told by Henry Teune (1982), Ole Holsti (2014) and Michael Haas (2016). ISA sought to move beyond Political Science and embraced a degree of interdisciplinarity, in a sense therefore challenging the close and longstanding institutional (much less so the epistemological and methodological) association between IR and Political Science in the United States. ISA's size also raised a perennial question of internationalisation. Unlike most other academic IR associations ISA's name did not show a national affiliation, leaving open the possibility that it was, or would be, a global body. There is, of course, something of an American penchant for this kind of universalist ambiguity – think, for example, of the 'World Series' in what is largely the American game of baseball. ISA allowed Canadian and later European membership, and from the 1970s (although the exact timing of this is not clear) accepted non-North

---

[3] At least in the case of BISA there was a connection to the ISC because the British Coordinating Committee generated the Bailey Conferences which ran from 1960, and were the precursors to BISA (Long, 2006: 619).

[4] For a comparison of these between BISA and ISA see Cox and Nossal (2009: 293–4).

[5] www.isanet.org/ISA/About-ISA/Data/Membership (Accessed 18 September 2017).

American participation. The relative underdevelopment of communication technology at that time might have hampered participation of Global South scholars in ISA in its early years (information on the participation of Global South scholars in ISA conventions is very scarce). Towards the end of the 1980s, ISA seemed to embark on a campaign to expand into Europe. That triggered opposition, particularly from Britain, which in turn led to a significant reshaping of the institutional landscape of academic IR associations, a story we pick up in Chapter 8.

ISA's relative size, wealth and openness to participation might support Michael Haas's (2016: 10) contention that 'American ISA scholars launched a truly international field'. But as noted above, the ISA's promotion of the American approach to IR, especially once the 'scientific', behavioural revolution of the 1960s was underway, did not travel well to the rest of the world. As Haas (2016: 10) argues, ISA's founders

sought metatheories or paradigms with empirical research involving proposition testing (mid-level theories) that would operationalize concepts from propositions derived from macro-theories in the form of low-level hypotheses. Known as 'behavioralists,' they could be found at Michigan, Northwestern, Stanford, and Yale. They sought to supersede traditional international relations scholarship and provide policy guidance based on scientific research.

If ISA as an organisation gave a powerful impetus to the distinctively American quest for a 'science' of IR and contributed to the 'behavioural' revolution in the discipline, this desire and focus were not shared by Europe or other developing regions, as would be evident in the debate between Bull (1966) and Morton Kaplan (1966) (see also Tickner and Wæver, 2009a). Hence, the early ISA might have furthered the gulf between the 'American social science' and the development of the field in the rest of the world, including the Global South.

Accompanying all this was a very substantial expansion in the number of IR journals (Palmer, 1980: 349–50), many US-based, but many also in Europe and the rest of the Anglosphere. Some of these were associated with university departments or institutes (*Journal of International Affairs* [Columbia, 1947]; *World Politics* [Princeton, 1948]; *Mershon International Studies Review* [Ohio State, 1957]; *International Relations* [Aberystwyth, 1960]; *Asian Survey* [Institute of East Asian Studies at the University of California, Berkeley, 1961]; *Millennium* [LSE, 1971]; *International Security* [Harvard. 1976]; *Cambridge Review of International Affairs* [Cambridge, 1986]). Some were affiliated with think tanks and independent research institutes (*Australian Journal of International Affairs*, originally *Australian Outlook* [Australian Institute of International Affairs, 1946]; *International Journal* [Canadian

International Council and the Bill Graham Centre for Contemporary International History, 1946]; *Journal of Conflict Resolution* [Peace Science Society, 1957]; *Orbis* [Foreign Policy Research Institute, 1957]; *Survival* [International Institute for Strategic Studies, 1959]; *Journal of Peace Research* [Peach Research Institute Oslo, 1964]; *Security Dialogue*, originally *Bulletin of Peace Proposals* [Peace Research Institute Oslo, 1970]; *Foreign Policy* [Carnegie Endowment for International Peace, 1970]). Some were generated by the new academic IR associations (*Kokusai Seiji* [JAIR, 1957]; *International Studies Quarterly* [ISA, 1959]; *Cooperation and Conflict* [Nordic International Studies Association, 1965]; *Review of International Studies*, originally *British Journal of International Studies* [BISA, 1975]). And some were independent (*International Organization* [1947]; *International Politics*, originally *Co-Existence: A Journal of East–West Studies* [1963/2000]; *Journal of Strategic Studies* [1978]; *Contemporary Security Policy* [1980]).

As during the interwar years, and in a similar pattern, American foundations continued to be influential funders of IR. The Ford Foundation funded the Center for Studies in International Relations at Sciences Po from the early 1950s. Rockefeller and Ford funded the Free University in Berlin. Rockefeller funded the British Committee, and IPSA was funded by the Ford Foundation (Kuru, 2017: 56–8). US foundations also played a considerable role in funding IR development in the Third World (Tickner and Wæver, 2009a: 232).

During the Cold War period, the development of IR in the Soviet Union and Eastern Europe bore similarities (as well as differences) with the core as well as the periphery. IR in the Soviet Union was shaped both by Area Studies and by some of the similar domestic factors that constrained the discipline in Asia and other parts of the periphery. The Institute of World Economy and World Politics, founded in 1924, was closed in 1947 by the government, which felt challenged by the writings of its head that pointed to the survival of capitalism. Moscow State University established its Faculty of International Relations in 1943, whose curriculum focused on diplomatic history in a manner similar to the initial development of IR in Western Europe (Lebedeva, 2004: 263). Think tanks also flourished. In 1956, the Soviet Academy of Sciences created the Institute of World Economy and International Relations, which would take the lead in studying substantive issues in world affairs, while the academy also established a number of Area Studies institutes to study different regions of the world, including the Institute of Africa (1959), the Institute of Latin America (1961), the Institute of the Far East (1966) and the Institute for the Study of the USA and Canada (1967). The study of the economics and politics of other communist countries was undertaken at the Institute of the Economy of the World Socialist System (1960) (Lebedeva, 2004: 264–5). This showed a clear orientation towards Area Studies in the development of IR in the Soviet Union, which was also the case with some developing countries, especially India. But unlike India, the study of IR in the Soviet Union was constrained by an official ban on English language texts from the West, official censorship and lack of contact with Western scholars. This particularly affected scholarship on IR theory. The development of IR in Central and Eastern Europe (CEE) countries faced similar resource and ideological constraints, and its research orientation was mostly empirical rather than theoretical and overall it remained underdeveloped (Drulák, Karlas and Königová, 2009: 243). In some respects, IR research in the CEE countries was influenced by the German model, which gives much authority to heads of institutions and senior professors in scholarly publications (Drulák, Karlas and Königová, 2009: 257).

During the 1945–89 period, whatever theoretical underpinnings IR had in the Soviet Union were a mixture of both Marxism-Leninism and 'Realism'. Some see Realism as the dominant strand, in the sense of being state-centric. If so, this was also a characteristic of IR throughout the periphery. But in the Soviet Union it developed without much direct influence of Western Realist and Neorealist scholars, because of the non-availability of their writings (Lebedeva, 2004: 268). The underlying Realist view would account for the rise of Geopolitics in post-Soviet Russian IR, even as scholarship there turned more theoretical and embraced a variety of theoretical approaches.

The Periphery

It is much more difficult to track the institutional development of IR in the periphery. From what we can find, there was not yet all that much when compared with the core. In terms of teaching and research, IR courses were being taught in Turkey (Ankara University) in the 1950s, and there was a department of IR at the Middle East Technical University by 1984. In Israel, the Hebrew University was offering IR degrees by 1946, and an independent department of International Relations was created in 1969. In India, the developments discussed in Chapter 4 led to the formation of the Indian School of International Studies in 1955, which, in 1959 launched *International Studies,* one of the earliest academic journals dedicated to IR in Asia and the Third World in the English language (*India Quarterly,* a more policy-oriented journal, had started publishing in 1954 under the auspices of ICWA). In 1969, the Indian School of International Studies joined the newly formed Jawaharlal

Nehru University as the School of International Studies (Batabyal, 2015: 137–63). In China, the educational reforms in 1952 subordinated higher education to the CCP, resulting in the elimination of Political Science from the curriculum, and the dismantling of IR as a coherent subject. In 1963, the CCP ordered the strengthening of the study of IR and set up IR departments at Peking University, Renmin and Fudan, but these mainly served the needs of China's foreign policy, and the IR there was largely framed within Marxist ideology (Lu, 2014: 133–4, 144–9). The first IR Chair in Africa was established in 1977 at the Nigerian University of Ife (Ofuho, 2009). Think tanks did somewhat better, with one in Africa, one in Latin America, three in the Middle East, three in South Asia and ten in East Asia, mostly in China.

The academic study of IR in the periphery did not yet have sufficient coherence or scale to follow the institutionalisation pattern in the core. Academic IR associations were scarce, although a notable exception was the formation of the Mexican International Studies Association (Asociación Mexicana de Estudios Internacionales) in 1967. There were also a couple of journals based either in universities (*International Studies* [taken over by Jawaharlal Nehru University in 1969]; *Issues & Studies* [National Chengchi University, 1964]) or institutes (*Contemporary Southeast Asia* [Institute of Southeast Asian Studies, 1979]).

IR Thinking in the Core

The story of IR's development up to the First World War, and during the interwar years, told in Chapters 2 and 4, is not all that widely known within the discipline. But the story of IR's theoretical development, 'paradigm' wars and 'great debates' during this period is a standard part of almost any induction into the subject, and does not need repeating in detail here. It is available in the many IR textbooks that introduce the subject to new students, and in the many self-reflections on the discipline. In this section, our main concern is therefore to link this familiar story to our main themes:

- To what extent and in what ways did the development of IR reflect the main developments in the real world of ir?
- Did IR continue to reflect the interests and perspectives of the core, and to marginalise the periphery?

As noted above, the key developments in ir were the package of bipolarity, the Cold War and nuclear weapons on the one hand, and decolonisation on the other. The first of these played very powerfully from ir into core IR, but the second did not. Decolonisation, as we show in the next section, played strongly into IR in the periphery. We will also explore the contradiction, mentioned above, between American hegemony in IR and ir on the one hand, and the diversity and differentiation of IR thinking within the core on the other. We start by looking at the diversity and differentiation within the core. The next subsection looks at Hoffmann's claim about IR as an American social science. Subsequent subsections look briefly at mainstream developments in Realism, Strategic Studies and Peace Research, Liberalism and Marxism, and the ES as the new face of a re-founded IR that had, as set out above, forgotten or pushed aside much of what had comprised the field in the years before 1939.

Diversity and Differentiation within Core IR

Diversity and differentiation within core IR was considerable. While not much commented on at the time, or indeed now, this was an important harbinger for the development towards Global IR that we discuss in Chapters 8 and 10. There was quite a lot of similarity within the core in terms of institutionalisation, but not nearly so much in terms of either the academic linkages or the methods, and there were also significant differences in topics and approaches. Korea, Canada and, up to a point, Germany followed the United States in basing IR within Political Science. But this was not generally the case elsewhere. In France and Germany, IR was more closely linked to Sociology. In Britain and the rest of the Anglosphere except Canada, IR was often organised in its own right, and had its main roots in History, International Law and Political Theory. In Japan, there were no Political Science departments, but neither did IR develop with independent departments (Inoguchi, 2009: 94). As Jörg Friedrichs and Ole Wæver (2009: 262) put it, the situation of IR thinking in the core during this period was that: 'all Western European IR communities stand in a center–periphery relationship to the American mainstream'. Yet as noted above, there was little interest in Europe or Japan in the 'scientific' approaches of the United States, with Wayne Cox and Kim Richard Nossal (2009: 303) arguing that the other Anglosphere countries, including Canada, were the major source of challenge to the positivist, Rationalist epistemologies favoured by American IR. In coping with their marginal position in the centre–periphery relationship, European IR communities developed three different coping strategies: academic self-reliance (France), resigned marginality (Italy and Spain) and multi-level research cooperation (Nordic countries and Dutch- and German-speaking areas) (Friedrichs and Wæver, 2009: 262). Curiously, Japan's academic style of thick description fits more within the periphery in terms of the division of labour noted by Tickner and Wæver

(2009c: 335), in which the core does theory and the periphery doesn't. Europe and the rest of the Anglosphere did theory, but not always the same theory that the Americans were following.

There was some unity around the 'great debates' between Europe and America, and also quite a bit of commonality around the main 'paradigms' of Realism, Liberalism and Marxism. That said, Japan took little interest in the 'great debates', and largely ploughed its own self-referential furrow in thinking about IR, as did France (Inoguchi, 2009: 90; Friedrichs and Wæver, 2009: 263–4, 267–8). Given the focus of core IR on East–West relations and nuclear security issues, it is not surprising that security issues and theories (Strategic Studies) provided common ground, but, that said, Peace Research was more prominent as an approach to security in Europe and Japan than in the United States. Marxism was more prominent in thinking about IR in Europe and Japan than it was in the United States. The Anglo-core also developed the 'English School' or 'international society' approach to IR theory, a social alternative to the mainstream, materialist Realist and Liberal approaches that dominated in the United States. Neither Europe nor Japan were heavily penetrated by US PhDs, but Korea was, and structured itself more along the Political Science model and formal methods approach of US IR (Cox and Nossal, 2009: 300–1; Inoguchi, 2009: 95–7). There was not much crossover of PhDs between the United States and both the rest of the Anglo-core and Japan (Korea is the exception), though both the United States and the Anglo-core exported PhDs elsewhere. And as long ago demonstrated by Wæver (1998), while US IR thinking was widely read in the rest of the core, the United States itself remained relatively impermeable to IR thinking from Europe, Japan or indeed the periphery. Yet while it is easy to accuse the United States of both hegemony and insularity, neither charge is an accurate reflection. The United States is hegemonic mainly because it amounts to such a large part of IR in global total. It is not hegemonic in either epistemological or substantive terms. And while it is true that the United States is insular, it is hardly less so than Japan, or France, or Italy. Resentment about US insularity is more because of its relative size than out of principle.

American Power, American Social Science?

Given the great weight of the United States in both IR and ir, Hoffmann's claim that IR was 'an American social science' was an accurate view of the discipline as seen from the United States, but a contested one in other parts of the core. The insularity of American IR, and the high priority given to the country's new engagement as the leader of the West facing a major ideological and military challenger, certainly made this view sustainable for the United States. The Cold War was the central concern of US foreign policy, underpinning the theoretical development of IR there. The other major stories of this period – decolonisation, the emergence of the Third World, development of regionalism in the postcolonial areas and core–periphery relations in general – played a relatively minor role in the development of IR and IR theory in the West.

Hoffmann claims that IR was 'born and raised' in the United States (Hoffmann, 1977: 50). This of course ignores the British origins of IR except the contribution of E. H. Carr, whom Hoffmann recognised as having written, in his *The Twenty Years' Crisis*, the 'first "scientific" treatment of modern world politics', even though he insisted that it was in America, and not in England, where Carr's Realist critique made most impact (Hoffmann, 1977: 43). Not only did Carr influence Nicholas Spykman's *America's Strategy in World Politics*, his work also, more importantly, gave birth to Morgenthau as the 'founding father' of IR in America. What seems clear is that Morgenthau, like Carr before him, was intent on developing a type of IR scholarship which he considered scientific, not in the methodological sense as with subsequent behavioural or Rationalist approaches that emerged in IR from the 1960s, but in the sense of being distinct from Utopia or Idealism. Hoffmann took little notice of the development of IR scholarship elsewhere, mentioning only Australian Hedley Bull and French scholar Pierre Hassner for their 'brilliant individual contributions', which in his view did not 'make a discipline' (Hoffmann, 1977: 49). For Hoffmann, the rise of the United States, manifest through rapid economic growth at home and foreign policy success abroad, was a foundational force underpinning the rise of IR and the American dominance of the field: 'a concern for America's conduct in the world blended with a study of international relations … To study United States foreign policy was to study the international system. To study the international system could not fail to bring one back to the role of United States' (Hoffmann, 1977: 47).

Morgenthau (1948: 8) shared this sentiment: 'To reflect on international politics in the United States, as we approach the mid-twentieth century, then is to reflect on the problems which confront American foreign policy in our time'. Through its links with Political Science, American IR was also influenced by the success of Economics as a science, and sought to emulate Economics in a bid to become more 'professional'. Hoffmann pointed to some other notable tendencies in American IR such as a quest for certainty, presentism (fear of history) and ignoring the weak due to a focus on bipolarity.

American IR was dominant because it was big, and rich, and centred in the leading power of the West. And there is no doubt that American fashions in Realism, Liberalism and Strategic Studies generally led the way for much of IR thinking elsewhere in the core. But it was not hegemonic epistemologically, because few others shared American obsessions about 'science' understood as positivist method. And it was far from being universally hegemonic in approaches to IR either, with challenges coming from both the ES and Peace Research.[6]

Realism

To observers of world politics, the prominence of Realism in the immediate post-Second World War period is ironic, if not puzzling. It is ironic because the wartime period (1939–45) was also a period of intensive global institution building, including the IMF and the World Bank, culminating in the 1945 San Francisco Conference that drafted the UN Charter. All this should have made the early postwar years a 'Liberal moment' in IR theory, since Liberal theory had made so much out of the idea of a postwar 'Liberal international order' (Deudney and Ikenberry, 1999; Ikenberry, 2011) around a system of multilateral institutions created under American initiative and direction, and providing global public goods of security, stability and economic openness. As Lucian Ashworth (2014: 237–9) observes, Realism was indeed not immediately dominant in American IR after 1945, but was an artefact of the late 1940s and 1950s (i.e. the onset of the Cold War). There was not any obvious 'win' by Realists in the supposed 'great debate' of the interwar years. If anything, IR thinking during and immediately after the Second World War, especially in the United States, was quite Idealistic in the sense of once again looking to international institutions to promote peace. As Michael Williams (2013) argues, many of the key figures in American Realism, such as Morgenthau, Niebuhr, Lippman and Herz, were in fact trying to transcend the either/or problem of Realism or Utopianism set up by Carr, by developing a middle ground position (see also Hacke and Puglierin, 2007). They wanted to save Liberalism from Utopianism, and save Realism from the methodological strictures of American Political Science, which they thought could not deal with the necessarily normative study of Politics.

---

[6] Peace Research in Europe challenged Strategic Studies on normative grounds, but, especially in Scandinavia (see the *Journal of Peace Research*), it was often also an exemplar of the positivist, quantitative methodology that was popular in the United States but largely rejected in the rest of European IR.

But the evident limitations of the UN in maintaining peace, combined with the outbreak, escalation and subsequent regulatory aspects of Cold War bipolarity, deterrence and crisis-management (especially after the Cuban missile crisis) fuelled a more materialist type of Realism, and later the rise of Neorealism. The prominence of Realism during the Cold War is of course not puzzling. Instead of multilateral institutions and liberal order, the core theme of IR from the late 1940s was bipolarity and super-power rivalry. The Cold War seemed to vindicate the core assumptions of Realism that anarchy, or the absence of any higher form of authority above the state, is the basic feature of the international system; and that international relations is a zero-sum game in which international institutions play a marginal role. Instead the key to international order is the maintenance of a balance of power, with power defined primarily in economic and military terms. In the second edition of *Politics Among Nations,* published in 1954, Morgenthau added a section on 'six principles of political realism' that are seen as a clear statement of real-politik.[7] Whatever his intentions, in the unfolding context of the Cold War, his work was read mainly as making the case for a power politics approach to both ir and IR.

While Morgenthau's classical Realism had much impact, it was not the dominant theorisation of the Cold War or bipolarity, the major themes of American IR. That came with the emergence of Neorealism. This version of Realism, pioneered by Kenneth Waltz in the 1970s, stressed the importance of the structural properties of the international system, especially the distribution of power (aka *polarity*), as the chief determinant of conflict and order. Neorealism downplayed both the impact of human nature (emphasised by classical Realists) and the influence of domestic- and regional-level politics in international relations. Since the notion of system structure refers to the distribution of capabilities among the units, only those units that occupied the upper rungs of the power matrix could affect system structure by virtue of their conflictual or cooperative behaviour. The extreme materialist simplification of polarity put the two superpowers at the centre of IR theory and marginalised all others. Not only the Third World, but also Europe and Japan, simply

---

[7] Especially principle 4: 'Realism maintains that universal moral principles must be filtered through the concrete circumstances of time and place, because they cannot be applied to the actions of states in their abstract universal formulation', and principle 5: 'Political realism refuses to identify the moral aspirations of a particular nation with the moral laws that govern the universe'. These quotes are from the fourth edition (Morgenthau, 1967: 9–10). The addition of a chapter entitled 'A Realist Theory of International Politics' is mentioned in the preface to the second edition of 1954, which is also reproduced in Morgenthau (1967: xii).

became the battleground on which the two superpowers fought out their zero-sum game of ideology and power. There were big, but inconclusive, debates about polarity theory and the relative stability, or not, of bipolar versus multipolar systems (Deutsch and Singer, 1969; Rosecrance, 1969; Gilpin, 1981; Levy, 1989; Gaddis, 1992/93). But what was very clear was that Neorealism and its debates sidelined the security predicaments and local dynamics of the Third World, largely reducing them to being seen as artefacts of superpower rivalry. The historical evidence used to support the arguments of both sides came from the evolution of the European states system. These system-level generalisations ignored the consequences of decolonisation, and the emergence of the Third World, for the maintenance of international order. In effect, by ignoring the relationship between the North and the South as a factor in systemic order, Neorealism maintained the exclusion of the periphery from the concerns of mainstream IR that had been a feature of IR since the nineteenth century. In Waltz's theoretical position, the high incidence of Cold War conflicts in the Third World did not challenge the essential stability of bipolar international systems, so long as the central balance and its European strategic core remained war-free. A few scholars sought to reassert the importance of the regional level, and its autonomy from the global bipolar one (Buzan, 1983; Ayoob, 1986), but the grand simplification of Neorealism generally swept all before it.

Strategic Studies and Peace Research

The dominance of a bipolar superpower rivalry perspective on the world, when combined with the advent of nuclear weapons, not surprisingly amplified the concerns with armaments and great power war that had marked interwar IR. Fears of an apocalyptic 'next war' had also haunted the interwar years, but with nuclear weapons in play the fear that the next war would not just destroy civilisation, but perhaps wipe out humankind became very real. The Realist side of IR responded to this in pragmatic fashion by trying to work out rationally how to incorporate nuclear weapons into superpower strategy while minimising the risk of major nuclear war. The core of this was deterrence theory, giving rise to a new subfield of Strategic Studies. Although classical writers on strategy such as Clausewitz remained influential, one of the striking things about Strategic Studies was that it was mainly done by civilians.[8] Nuclear war was so different from anything that had come before that military tradition

---

[8] Civilian strategic thinkers were not unknown in earlier periods, notably Angell (1909) and Bloch (1898).

and precedent provided little wisdom or guidance. Throughout the Cold War period, thinking about deterrence theory had to keep pace with the rapid and relentless developments in the technology of nuclear weapons and their delivery systems. Broadly opposed to Strategic Studies was Peace Research, which generally rested on the view that nuclear weapons posed an unacceptable risk to human survival and should be eliminated. Whereas Strategic Studies was mainly working to inform and improve defence policies that incorporated nuclear weapons, Peace Research was more linked to the popular activist movements that wanted nuclear weapons eliminated. For most Peace Researchers, the nuclear weapons themselves posed more of a threat than the enemy superpower. Strategic Studies was dominant in the states possessing nuclear weapons (the United States, the rest of the Anglosphere and France [in its own way of course]), while Peace Research dominated in those countries more on the front line of any superpower nuclear war (Scandinavia, Germany and Japan).[9] Given its constitutional renunciation of war, pacifism has been an important element of Japanese IR studies, linking also to the idea of comprehensive security (later human security). But these ideas have not coalesced to produce a distinctive Japanese approach to the study of IR.

Deterrence theory was almost obsessively East–West in its concerns, but there were two exceptions that brought in a North–South dimension. One was the fear that conflicts in the Third World would draw in the superpowers and trigger escalations that might lead to global nuclear war. This was particularly so concerning the Middle East, and was part of the general habit of core IR to think of the periphery mainly as an arena for superpower rivalry.[10] The other exception was nuclear proliferation, and the desire of both superpowers to keep the nuclear club as small as possible. Non-proliferation was aimed partly at nuclear-capable core states (mainly Germany, Japan, Sweden, Switzerland), but mainly at the Third World. Partly it served the superpowers' status needs to differentiate themselves as a special club above the rest, but partly also they could credibly claim that proliferation would increase the chances of nuclear weapons being used. More fingers on more triggers equals a higher

---

[9] Peace Researchers and Strategists could be found on both sides of this divide. For a comprehensive view of these literatures and their development, see Buzan and Hansen (2009).

[10] The Third World was excluded even here. The 'Correlates of War' project at the University of Michigan, led by Singer and Small, used criteria for defining war which excluded imperial and colonial wars. As a consequence, as Vasquez observes, while the project's data set for interstate wars from 1816 to the then-present (1972) involving 'nation-states' was definitive, the data for 'extra-systemic' wars, i.e. imperial and colonial wars, remained 'woefully incomplete for non-national entities … usually the victims in this historical period' (Vasquez, 1993: 27).

probability of nuclear war. But there was also an element of prejudice in the backing of non-proliferation by the core. A key element in deterrence theory was the requirement for those in control of nuclear weapons to think rationally about their use and non-use, and there was certainly a strand of thinking behind non-proliferation resting on the assumption that many Third World states did not have the quality of leadership or government to meet that standard. This view was held not just by many Western nuclear strategists, but, as Hugh Gusterson's (1999) ethnographic study of Lawrence Livermore Laboratory confirms, by American nuclear scientists and weapon designers as well. K. Subrahmanyam (1993), an Indian strategist, called this tendency 'racist'.

Another North–South link in this literature was about wars fought by the North in the South, and core interventions into the South more generally. Most of this literature was instrumental and from the perspective of the North in the context of superpower rivalry in the Third World. It was about guerrilla war and how to counter it, about the dangers of escalation when the superpowers were supporting opposing sides, and about limited war, with all of its constraints on weapons and tactics, as opposed to the more all-out, unrestrained style of the Second World War. The periphery here was largely an object in the overriding struggle between the superpowers.

Liberalism

With the onset of the Cold War, the scope for Liberal IR to focus on global IGOs was sharply constrained. It is therefore perhaps not surprising that a good deal of postwar Liberal theory focused on regional integration (Nye, 1988: 239). The most important point of reference of this theory was provided by the EEC, which was the most successful example of a regional integration and security community to emerge in the post-Second World War period. Other examples included Canada and the United States, Europe and North America, and the United States and Japan. In contrast, such communities were virtually non-existent in the Third World, with the limited exception of ASEAN and the Southern Cone of Latin America.

Regional integration theory was in part a crossover from interwar to post-1945 IR in the form of David Mitrany's Functionalism (L. Ashworth, 2014: 221–5). The vast literature on regional integration theory (E. Haas, 1964, 1973; Hansen, 1969; Lindberg and Scheingold, 1971; Puchala, 1984; Mace, 1986) largely revolved around the influential school of Neofunctionalism led by Ernst Haas, and to a lesser extent transactionalism, whose main intellectual proponent was Karl

Deutsch (Puchala, 1984: 186). But there was 'little agreement on how the dependent variable ("integration") is to be defined, or on whether it is a process or condition' (Hodges, 1978: 237).

While both approaches assumed a progressive dilution of state sovereignty, the Neofunctionalist approach envisaged that exchanges and cooperation among states starting with issues of 'low politics' or lesser political sensitivity (such as trade and resource management) could have a 'spill-over' effect, leading to broader and more political and security cooperation. The transactionalist approach focused on increased social communications leading to a 'security community', where relations are marked by 'the absence or presence of significant organized preparations for war or large-scale violence among its members' (Deutsch, 1961: 99; see also Yalem, 1979: 217). Security communities could either be 'amalgamated' through a formal political merger of the participating units, or remain 'pluralistic' in which case the members would remain formally independent. While transactionalism ignored the role of institutions in political unification, for Neofunctionalists, institutions would be of central importance.

Although some Third World subregional groups such as the East African Community and the Central American Common Market initially sought to emulate the EEC, they fell far short. While the Neofunctionalists envisaged a 'spill-over' from economic integration to political and security cooperation, the Third World experience turned out to be quite the reverse; political understanding and cooperation was a prerequisite for economic integration (Axline, 1977: 103). In general, regional economic integration in the Third World proved to be 'much more rudimentary than in Europe, more obscure in purpose and uncertain in content' (Gordon, 1961: 245), thereby raising questions regarding the applicability of the regional integration theories to the Third World (Duffy and Feld, 1980: 497). Ernst Haas (1973: 117) would acknowledge that the 'application [of his Neofunctionalist model] to the third world ... sufficed only to accurately predict difficulties and failures of regional integration, while in the European case some successful positive prediction has been achieved'.

Through his extensive research into regional integration in Latin America and Africa, Joseph Nye concluded that the causes of integration failure in the Third World had much to do with domestic conditions: paternalistic leadership, weak bureaucratic and political institutions which are susceptible to military takeover, economic disparity, absence of organised interest groups, cultural gaps between urban and rural areas, and lack of adequate trained manpower (Nye, 1968: 381–2). But perhaps the real reason why EEC-style regional integration did not take off in the Third World was the postcolonial leaders' normative preference for keeping sovereignty undiluted. While West European regionalism sought to move regional international politics beyond the nation state, Non-Western proponents of regionalism, after centuries of colonial rule, sought the creation and consolidation of nation states, however artificially conceived. Hence, unlike the EEC, the OAU and the Arab League functioned more as 'instrument[s] of national independence rather than of regional integration' (Miller, 1973: 58) and embraced an expanded version of non-intervention.

From the mid-1970s, there was a clear shift of focus in Liberal IR theory towards Neoliberal Institutionalism and interdependence. Ernst Haas (1975: 6) admitted that regional integration was becoming 'obsolescent' in the face of widening economic linkages that were increasingly global in scope and impact. Beginning in the 1970s, as interdependence discourse displaced the regional integration paradigm, Neoliberal Institutionalism and its popular offshoot, regime theory, increasingly challenged the traditional dominance of the Realist/Neorealist paradigm. Unlike classical Liberalism, which took a benign view of human nature, Neoliberal Institutionalism accepts the Realist premise that the international system is anarchic and that states are the primary, if not the only, actors in international relations. But it disagrees with Neorealism's dismissal of international institutions. Neoliberals maintain that international institutions, broadly defined – including regimes and formal organisations – can regulate state behaviour and promote cooperation by reducing transaction costs, facilitating information-sharing, preventing cheating and providing avenues for peaceful resolution of conflicts (Keohane, 1984: 15; 1989: 10).

Neoliberal Institutionalism challenged the Hegemonic Stability Theory (HST), which had grown out of the work of Charles Kindleberger (1973), with further contributions and modifications by Stephen Krasner (1976), Robert Gilpin (1987) and Robert Keohane (1984) himself, that also led to the emergence of the sub-field of IPE. HST draws upon the global role of Britain before the First World War and that of the United States after 1945 in supporting free trade and security (especially maritime) as international public goods. Simply put, HST maintains that order and cooperation requires the initiative of a preponderant power, or a hegemon. Two such actors in the recent history of the world were Great Britain in the nineteenth century and the United States after the Second World War (Grunberg, 1990: 431). Such a power creates economic or security institutions and regimes to serve its interests, but also offers benefits, or international public goods, to others. The maintenance of this order depends on the hegemon's superior material (economic and military) power and coercive capacity as well as its ability to forge ideological consensus and consent. The hegemon's rule seeks to discourage cheating and encourage others to share the costs of maintaining the system.

But HST has been criticised not only for its limited ability to explain order and change in world politics (Snidal, 1985), but also for its ethnocentrism (Grunberg, 1990: 444–8). Keohane (1984) would depart from HST by arguing that international institutions would persist after the decline of US hegemony, because they continued to provide benefits such as information-sharing and lowering of transaction costs, and because it was more difficult to create new institutions than reform old ones in a world 'after hegemony'. But while regional integration theories could be accused of Eurocentrism, Neoliberal Institutionalism is rather Americacentric. Keohane admitted to the 'distinctively American stamp that has been placed on the international relations field', acknowledging how that shaped his own theoretical contribution. As he conceded in a footnote to a chapter on 'Theory of World Politics':

An unfortunate limitation of this chapter is that its scope is restricted to work published in English, principally in the United States. I recognize that this reflects the Americanocentrism of scholarship in the United States, and I regret it. But I am not sufficiently well-read in works published elsewhere to comment intelligently on them. (Keohane, 1989: 67, note 1)

There was very little that the institutionalist theories had to say about the role of the periphery as a contributor to the growth of multilateralism, and the ideas underpinning that growth. Liberal thinking overlooked the agency of the Third World. The same can also be said of the more general understandings of multilateralism and global governance. For example, one of the most influential books on multilateralism (Ruggie, 1993) did not contain a single chapter dealing with multilateralism in the Third World, seeing multilateralism as a distinctively American way of organising GIS.

Although work on international interdependence and regimes proliferated in the 1980s, it was mostly concerned with the relationships between the Western countries. As Robert Cox noted,

regime theory has much to say about economic cooperation among the Group of 7 (G-7) and other groupings of advanced capitalist countries with regard to problems common to them. It has correspondingly less to say about attempts to change the structure of world economy, e.g. in the Third World demand for a New International Economic Order (NIEO). Indeed, regimes are designed to stabilize the world economy and have the effect, as Keohane has underlined in his work, of inhibiting and deterring states from initiating radical departures from economic orthodoxy, e.g. through socialism. (R. W. Cox, 1992a: 173)

Liberal institutionalist theorists paid scant attention to the Third World's principal cooperative institution in the Cold War period, the NAM.[11] Moreover, these theories would 'assume, rather than establish, regimes as benevolent, voluntary, cooperative and legitimate' (Keeley, 1990: 90), a highly questionable assumption when one considers, as mentioned in Chapter 5, the exclusionary nature of some regimes and the coercive role of certain multilateral institutions as perceived by the Third World countries. Yet Liberalism's focus on US hegemony and its benefits in providing public goods such as free trade, international institutions and collective security laid the basis for the idea of a benign global liberal hegemonic order, which would become prominent after the end of the Cold War (to be discussed in Chapter 8).

The 1980s saw a debate between Neorealism and Neoliberalism. The major points of their contention have been well-enough summarised (D. Baldwin, 1993: 4–8; S. Smith, 2000: 381) to require no further elaboration here. Generally speaking, while both professed belief in anarchy, Neorealists took the constraints it imposes on state behaviour more seriously, while making light of the possibility of international cooperation and the impact of international regimes and institutions that are recognised by Neoliberals on the basis of national self-interest. As such, Neorealists stressed the importance of concerns about relative gains over those about absolute gains. Although both recognised the importance of the interplay between economics and security, Neorealists put a premium on national security concerns, while Neoliberals emphasised economic welfare. For Neorealists material capabilities and their distribution would matter more than intentions, interests or information. But the differences in this debate were a matter of degree of faith in anarchy and cooperation that could be reconciled with conceptual jugglery. This common ground manifested itself in the so-called 'Neo-Neo' synthesis. As Wæver (1996: 163) explains, both 'shared a "rationalist" research programme, a conception of science, a shared willingness to operate on the premise of anarchy (Waltz) and investigate the evolution of co-operation and whether institutions matter (Keohane)'.

International Political Economy

Among the most important developments in IR in the 1970s and 1980s was the growing popularity of IPE. Unlike the heavy East–West orientation of Strategic Studies, IPE emerged with a strong North–South

---

[11] An exception is Willetts (1978).

dimension. This had partly to do with its links with Marxism and Dependency Theory. In a more practical way, it had also to do with the origins of IPE in the oil crisis of the 1970s, in which boycotts by the Third World members of OPEC exposed the economic vulnerability of the United States and the West, giving rise to concerns about economic security and interdependence. In the United States and the United Kingdom, where the sub-field developed relatively independently, both Gilpin (1987) and Susan Strange (1988) gave reasonable place to the Third World, and IPE might be the most Third-World attentive of the core approaches to IR.

Some of the interdependence theorists, especially Nye and Keohane, contributed to the rise of IPE in the United States. But IPE also saw major interventions from Realist scholars such as Krasner and Gilpin. In his 1975 book, Gilpin defined IPE as 'the reciprocal and dynamic interaction ... of the pursuit of wealth and the pursuit of power' (Gilpin, 1975: 43). He would go on to write one of IPE's most widely used texts (Gilpin, 1987). Gilpin's classification of IPE theories into nationalist, Liberal and Marxist remained influential: Gilpin's own approach, as he would put it later, was state-centric Realism (Gilpin, 2001). But alternatives to the US approach emerged elsewhere, in the United Kingdom and Canada. Compared to the dominant strand of IPE thinking in the United States, Strange took a much more critical view on the working of the global economy, stressing the volatility of international financial capital (Strange, 1986) and the challenge posed by the rise of global markets to the authority of the state (Strange, 1988). In Canada, Robert Cox (1987) and Stephen Gill (Gill and Law, 1988; see also Gill, 1991) developed neo-Marxist and Gramscian approaches to IPE.

Marxism

IR thinking from the Soviet bloc made almost no impact on IR thinking in the Western core and Japan. But Marxism was an influential framework for thinking in the social sciences generally, and also about IR, often as a form of Critical Theory (see section on 'Critical Theories' in Chapter 8). It was an important strand of IR in Japan at least up until the 1960s (Inoguchi, 2009: 88–90). In Britain, the University of Sussex developed a tradition of Marxist IR, and mainstream IR scholars such as Robert McKinlay and Richard Little (1986) organised a paradigmatic approach to the subject around Liberal, Socialist and Realist models of world order. Marxist-influenced scholars such as E. H. Carr, Robert Cox, Fred Halliday and Immanuel Wallerstein were substantial figures in IR. It was not uncommon for introductory readers and textbooks to include discussions of Marxist approaches to IR, perhaps especially in IPE: e.g. Little and Smith (1980); Gilpin (1987). Marxist thinking continued to suffer from the marginal-isation of the state in its framework, but it had useful things to say about capitalism and exploitation (and therefore neocolonialism), and was in principle, and up to a point in practice, more open to the problems and perspectives of the Third World than either Realism or Liberalism.

It is fair to say that the most significant impact of Marxism on IR has been indirect, i.e. through theories such as the Dependency, World Systems and neo-Gramscian literature and to a lesser extent Postcolonial approaches to IR. This may have to do with what some scholars bemoan as the 'geopolitical deficiency' in traditional Marxist thought (Teschke, 2008: 166) or its 'ambivalence towards the polit-ical, its simultaneous negation and retention' (Davenport, 2011: 42). But major elements of Marxist and Leninist thought, especially the role of economic forces in shaping politics and security, the place of inequality, injustice and dominance, and the prospect for resistance and transformation in world politics, have been incorporated into a range of alternative conceptualisations of world politics. Marxism has been especially influential in challenging state-centric conceptions of IR in mainstream IR theories and the benign portrayal of capitalist interdependence in Liberalism (Davenport, 2011: 35), especially by offering an alternative conception of hegemony through both coercion and consent (R. W. Cox, 1987). Moreover, Marxist and Gramscian-inspired scholarship influenced epistemological debates, one of the most important examples being Robert Cox's famous line that 'theory is always *for* someone and *for* some purpose', and his distinc-tion between 'problem-solving' and 'critical' theory (R. W. Cox, 1981: 128–30). The former, which include Realism, Liberalism, the ES (and some versions of Constructivism), accepts the present order and seeks reform and change within its existing parameters, along 'with the prevailing social and power relationships and the institutions into which they are organised' (R. W. Cox, 1981: 128). Critical Theory, by contrast, calls into question the existing order and its institutions. It concerns itself with how they came about and 'how and whether they might be in the process of changing' (R. W. Cox, 1981: 129), thereby seeking their fundamental transformation. While problem-solving approaches help 'legitimate an unjust and deeply iniquitous system', Critical Theory 'attempts to challenge the prevailing order by seeking out, analyzing, and where possible, assisting social processes that can potentially lead to emancipatory change' (Hobden and Wyn Jones, 2008: 151). We have already discussed Cox's critique of Liberal Institutionalism and will dis-cuss Dependency and World Systems theories later in this chapter.

The English School

The ES got going in the late 1950s when the Rockefeller Foundation funded the meetings of the British Committee on the Theory of International Politics. From an early stage it diverged from the thinking about IR going on in the United States. The essence of the difference was that American thinking, both Realist and Liberal, was mainly focused on the idea of *international system*, whereas the ES developed mainly around the idea of *international society*.[12] Systems thinking represented international relations in essentially materialist and mechanical terms: balance of power, polarity, interdependence and suchlike. Thinking in terms of international society represented international relations in more social, and sociological, terms, as about the shared rules, values and institutions that compose a society of states. In this sense, the ES anticipated what was to become Constructivism (and influenced one of its leading exponents, Alexander Wendt). It has generally been a more explicitly normative approach than mainstream American IR theory. Rather than posing Realist and Liberal analyses as opposites, the ES takes a holistic approach, seeing ir as an ongoing and ever-changing debate between the imperatives of order (represented by the *pluralist* wing of the ES) and those of justice (the *solidarist* wing). The idea is not that either side should win this debate, but that what is at stake is a balance between them that makes the best of the circumstances available at the time. Like the early American Realists discussed above, the ES can be understood as an attempt to transcend the paralysing either/or choice of Carr's opposition between Realism and Utopianism. The ES contains no teleology, accepting that international society waxes and wanes, and is in continuous evolution.

But the ES also contains a strong structural approach (Bull, 1977; Holsti, 2004; Buzan, 2004b). It sees *primary institutions* – a set of durable norms and practices that evolve over time – as the social structure of international society. In the classical ES work during this period the main primary institutions discussed were: sovereignty, territoriality, balance of power, war, diplomacy, international law and great power management. The emergence of nationalism during the nineteenth century was added by James Mayall (1990). These primary institutions were understood as constitutive of both the members of international society (sovereignty + territoriality + nationalism = the modern state) and of legitimate behaviour within that society (rules about how states communicate, manage the system and fight with each other). Primary institutions could be tracked

---

[12] For a comprehensive overview of the ES's history, ideas and literature, see Dunne (1998); Vigezzi (2005); Buzan (2014).

in terms of emergence, evolution and sometimes decay and obsolescence. The ES differentiated between a society of states (aka *international society*) and a more notional, but normatively important, *world society* of humankind as a whole.

The ES was much more markedly historical than other mainstream IR theories at this time. It had a particular focus on how the GIS that came into being with decolonisation had evolved and expanded from an originally European international society, that had itself evolved from the medieval period in Europe and begun to emerge in modern form by 1648 (Wight, 1977; Bull and Watson, 1984a; Watson, 1992). This historical approach did much to differentiate the ES from Neorealism (which subordinated the significance of history to the universality of the rules of power politics) and Liberalism (which did not have much history, and did not want to revisit its supposed 'Utopian' failure in the interwar years). But in relation to the Third World, it put the ES in much the same Eurocentric place as other Western IR theory at this time. Classical ES thinking marginalised the Third World in three ways. First, it interpreted European international society as a pristine development then imposed upon the rest of the world. There is some force to this in terms of the processes of colonisation and decolonisation, but the classical ES story mainly ignored the inputs that the rest of the world made to Europe in its formative stages. Second, the classical ES, like Neorealism, took a 'like units' view of states seeing them as alike in form, function and sovereign equality, and not differentiating them except by the criterion of power separating great powers from the rest. This created a double discrimination against Third World states: since none of them were great powers, they dropped out of great power management; and it ignored the huge differences in domestic and international politics that resulted from these states being postcolonial, and often artificial, states that were mostly poor and underdeveloped. Third, the classical ES's main response to decolonisation was to worry about the weakening of international society by the entry of many new states that were weak, poor and did not share Western culture. Bull's (1984) analysis of the revolt against the West at least recognised the strength of anti-colonial sentiment there, and opened up the justice claims of the Third World. But the ES mostly saw decolonisation as a problem because it weakened the established order by undermining its (Western) cultural coherence.

IR Debates Itself Again

As during the interwar period, core IR during the Cold War had another 'great debate'. The second great debate actually happened during the late 1950s and 1960s. Taking place within the context of the behavioural revolution in the 1950s and 1960s that significantly shaped American IR, this debate was summed up in the exchange of polemics between Bull (1966) and Kaplan (1966) already mentioned above, and nicely symbolised the growing rift between the methodological obsessions of American IR and the relative lack of enthusiasm for this approach in most of the rest of the core. Bull desired a 'classical approach' – using an interpretivist framework based on Philosophy, History and Law – to pursue *understanding* of world politics. In contrast, behaviouralists like Kaplan demanded a 'scientific approach' – using an explanatory framework based on positivism, pursuing *explanation* of world politics by producing nomothetic knowledge anchored on a hypothetico-deductive model (Bull, 1966: 361–2).[13] The second debate 'concerned methodology, not theory or the sources of theoretical innovation' (Kahler, 1997: 30). As noted above, some Realists joined Bull in arguing against the use of the scientific method in American IR. As Miles Kahler notes, Realist stalwarts in the field such as Morgenthau were 'squarely on the antibehavioral side and launched a vigorous attack on works by Lasswell and Kaplan' (Kahler, 1997: 30; see also M. Williams, 2013). The second debate was not brought about by cataclysmic events in the way that the First World War propelled the first debate. But it helped to forge the 'scientific identity' of subsequent American IR (Schmidt, 2002: 11), and it might be said that the behaviouralists won this debate in the United States, but not in most of the rest of the core. Although evidence is scanty, the second debate had practically no direct impact on the periphery, where the academic study of IR was still at its infancy. But based on our survey of the development of IR in the periphery, it is reasonable to suppose that IR scholarship there was much more in tune with the classical approach than the scientific one.

IR Thinking in the Periphery

As discussed in Chapter 4, IR thinking in the periphery during the interwar years was a mixture of academic work and the thoughts of public intellectuals and leaders, with the balance strongly favouring the latter. One explanation for this was the weak or non-existent institutionalisation of the new field of academic IR in most of the periphery. During the period of the Cold War and decolonisation this general pattern remained the same. Despite some strengthening of institutionalisation of academic

[13] On the distinction between *understanding* and *explanation*, see Hollis and Smith (1990).

IR, it still remained generally weak, and where it did exist, it was often focused mainly on the policy and personnel needs of the state. The intellectual hegemony of a burgeoning Western IR was strong. As Tickner and Wæver (2009c: 335) argue, there emerged something of a division of labour with the core doing IR theory, and the periphery not. Even in China, when IR opened up again after the death of Mao and began to grow rapidly, it took some decades just to absorb and master the Western opus of IR before any thought could be given to the possibilities for a Chinese school of IR (Qin, 2010, 2011a). Much of the fledgling academic IR in the periphery was poorly resourced and tasked mainly with teaching/training rather than research. Resource constraints also meant that it was largely cut off from direct participation in the conference circuits of the new Western and Japanese academic IR associations, even when these opened themselves to wider participation.

The thinness, weakness and newness of academic IR in the periphery left the field open for influential political leaders to make much of the running in thinking about IR. Decolonisation gave political leaders in the periphery both louder voices and more scope for action. Some of these leaders also put forward ideas about regional and international order. For example, Burma's Aung San, who at first collaborated with the Japanese, later repudiated the idea of great power blocs (such as the Japanese Greater East Asia Co-Prosperity Sphere) as a means of achieving regional peace and well-being. He advocated regional cooperation on the basis of sovereign equality and interdependence, thereby both echoing older themes in periphery IR thinking and anticipating the principles of regionalism in much of the periphery in the post-Second World War period, including those developed by ASEAN, founded in 1967. In the 1960s, Indonesia's Sukarno expounded a radical conception of North–South conflict by arguing that the main division of the world was not through the Cold War, but through the struggle between the 'Old Established Forces' (OLDEFOS) and the 'New Emerging Forces' (NEFOS). The OLDEFOS comprised the Western colonial powers, which still threatened the newly independent countries through their military bases and economic exploitation. The NEFOS included forces aligned against colonialism and neocolonialism, including the 'anti-imperialist axis' of Indonesia, Cambodia, North Vietnam, People's Republic of China and North Korea (Weinstein, [1976] 2007: 167). There were also examples of the diffusion of regionalist ideas about sovereignty, equality and economic self-reliance across regions. Kwame Nkrumah, prevented from attending the 1955 Bandung Conference by Ghana's colonial ruler Britain, adopted the Bandung Conference's principles (such as abstaining from superpower-led regional blocs and economic self-reliance) in organising the first official gathering of newly independent African nations: the Conference of Independent African States in Accra on 15–22 April 1958. A subsequent conference held in Addis Ababa in 1960 further developed the principles of decolonisation, arms control and control over natural resources, laying some of the groundwork for the establishment of the OAU in May 1963.

At least while decolonisation remained incomplete, from the late 1940s to the mid-1970s, such leaders could continue the anti-colonial and anti-racism themes from the interwar years and earlier. As formal colonialism became history, the rhetoric turned more to opposing neocolonialism, especially in the form of the economic and developmental inequalities that remained long after most peoples had acquired political independence. Anti-racism remained a robust theme, especially against the apartheid regime in South Africa, and against Israel, both perceived by much of the Third World as colonial states. In the Middle East, Nasser picked up and reinvigorated the Pan-Arab theme from the interwar years. In India, Nehru's ideas about non-alignment and non-exclusionary regionalism had a substantial impact on Third World foreign policy approaches, most notably the NAM, though they received little attention in the IR theoretical debates of the core (Behera, 2009: 143). Gandhi's ideas about non-violent resistance had both practical and intellectual influence worldwide, inspiring Martin Luther King and Nelson Mandela. Mao's thoughts about Socialist politics and development resonated widely among the far left in many places. His 'three worlds theory' from the mid-1970s was both a political project against the hegemony of the two superpowers (the first world), and a way of understanding the dynamics of world politics overall (Garver, 2016: 327–8).[14] Mao, along with Che Guevara and Régis Debray, also developed, promoted and practised the idea of guerrilla warfare as a strategy for the militarily weak to use against the militarily strong – what today would be called 'asymmetric warfare'.

Overall, as shown above, mainstream IR theory in the core continued to be focused on bipolarity, Western problems and great power relations. Even though decolonisation was one of the key developments defining post-1945 ir, the changing dynamics of core–periphery relations received far less recognition in IR theory. The main sign of change, as we hinted in Chapter 4, was that two perspectives on IR emerged from

---

[14] Mao's typology of three worlds was different from the standard one, which had the Western developed countries as the First World, the Socialist bloc as the Second World, and the underdeveloped states as the Third World. Mao's scheme agreed with this for the Third World, but had the Second World as being the developed states other than the two superpowers.

the periphery to challenge the debates in the core: Dependency Theory (*dependencia*) and Postcolonialism. Dependency Theory was born in Latin America, a region where decolonisation had happened much earlier than in Asia, Africa or the Middle East. Yet, the latter, especially Asia, could claim to be the stage for the birth of another Non-Western IR theory: Postcolonialism. While scholars generally view Postcolonialism as having come after Dependency, its ideational and practical roots were arguably laid earlier. Dependency Theory and Postcolonialism have similar points of origin, as both link colonies to former colonial powers in a negative sense.[15]

Postcolonialism

Postcolonialism's roots are embedded in the whole half-millennium of European overseas expansion and empire. It is about seeing that process not only as one of domination and anti-colonial struggles, but also of cultural encounters and mutual reshapings.[16] As an academic approach to thinking about IR, it belongs mainly in the post-1989 period, but some important beginnings occurred during the Cold War. Much of the early Postcolonial inspiration has to do with the interplay between the practitioner and academic worlds of IR, and the re-evaluation by academics of the 1955 Asia–Africa Conference at Bandung. Postcolonialism has embraced Bandung as one of its foundational moments. As Mustapha Kamal Pasha puts it, while the Bandung Conference might not have achieved all its stated political or economic goals, it did mark a '*discontinuous* moment in the universal story recounted at the behest of IR' (Pasha, 2013: 146, emphasis original).

The Bandung Conference was the outgrowth of two ARCs, held in New Delhi in 1947 and 1949. The agenda of the 1947 conference covered eight issues: national movements for freedom, racial problems, inter-Asian migration, transition from colonial to national economy, agricultural reconstruction and industrial development, labour problems and social services, cultural problems, and status of women and women's movements (Appadorai, 1979). The second ARC was specifically tied to the demand for Indonesia's independence from Dutch rule (Acharya, 2009: 34–5). The Bandung Conference went beyond the ARCs, its

---

[15] Readers wanting a more detailed review of IR thinking in the periphery should see Tickner and Wæver (2009a); Tickner and Blaney (2012, 2013).

[16] This includes the story of blacks in the United States, whose slavery was linked to colonialism and racism, and whose struggle for emancipation was, as shown in earlier chapters, linked to Pan-Africanism.

purpose being not only 'to continue the struggle toward a full materi-alization of national independence', but also 'the formulation and establishment of certain norms for the conduct of present-day inter-national relations and the instruments for the practical application of these norms' (Abdulghani, 1964: 72, 103). The Bandung Conference's goal was to bring about an 'agreement on general principles' of con-duct in international affairs (League of Arab States, 1955: 23). It marked the shift from opposing colonialism to staking out a place for the Third World in GIS. Participants in the Bandung Conference would regard the Declaration on World Peace as a 'most important resolution', because it defined 'the principles regulating their relations with each other and the world at large' (League of Arab States, 1955: 151).

After Bandung, the move towards a rising consciousness in the Third World countries and a quest for greater participation and say in GIS reached a peak in the 1960s and 1970s with the founding of the NAM in 1961, the subsequent call for NIEO and the formation of G77. The Vietnam War and other interventions by the United States, particularly in Latin America, throughout the 1960s and 1970s raised the question of whether the United States was acting as a neo-imperial power (Viotti and Kauppi, 2011: 211). Hopes for greater engagement and cooper-ation between the North and the South were undermined in the 1970s, which aggravated the perception of inequity and injustice in the inter-national capitalist economy (Darby, 2004: 2). These events were a factor in stirring Postcolonial IR theory.

The foundational scholars of Postcolonialism such as Frantz Fanon, Edward Said, Gayatri Chakravorty Spivak, Homi Bhabha and Ngugi wa Thiong'o came from a wide variety of professions and disciplines and were influential in the work of those bringing the Postcolonial perspective into IR. Some of the key arguments of Postcolonialism are Aimé Césaire's (1955) rejection of colonialism's alleged 'civilising' mission, Fanon's (1965) work on its dehumanising effect and Said's (1978) exposure of 'orientalism', or the representation of the colonised as inferior, exotic, despotic, mystical by Western literary works. Fanon's (1965) *Wretched of the Earth* explored how colonialism inflicted on its subjects a sense of dependency, and political, psychological, economic and social inferiority, so profound that it can only be redressed through resort to violence. Said's (1978) *Orientalism* sought to demonstrate the extent to which what was becoming, and has come to be known as, the 'West', is very much derived from an 'othering' of the 'East' (the 'West' is all that the 'East' is not, and cannot be, and via imperi-alism, seeks to ensure the fulfilling of that prophecy).

Because Postcolonial thought draws from a wide variety of perspectives, literary, Marxist, Gramscian and a range of Postmodern thinkers, it has been criticised as 'theoretically promiscuous' (Kennedy, 1996: 347–8). Because of the heavy influence of literature scholars, such as Said and Spivak, Postcolonialism's link with IR has been regarded as somewhat tenuous by traditional IR scholars, despite the work of Postcolonial IR scholars to locate Postcolonialism firmly within IR debates. Because of its origins in literature studies, Postcolonialism, unlike Dependency Theory, often exhibits a focus on ideational forces that shape society, over material forces. Dependency Theory 'is primarily an economic theory of under-development which does not lend itself easily to an analysis of issues of race, culture, language and identity' (Tikly, 2001: 251). Yet these issues are among the central concerns of Postcolonialism, partly arising out of the identity themes in literature from the former colonies, and partly out of the roots of Postcolonialism in Area Studies, to which it became in some senses a successor (Harootunian, 2002).

As a political idea, Postcolonialism views the origins of the modern international system not from 1648, or the Peace of Westphalia, but from 1498, the 'discovery' by Columbus of the New World. Postcolonialism argues that because the knowledge of international order and the world system was produced largely in the period of Western colonial expansion and domination, this production of knowledge must be questioned and problematised (Grovogui, 2013: 249). Postcolonialists, thus, are suspicious, to say the least, of colonial ethnography and anthropology, and indeed of any Western-generated universalisms, including capitalism and Marxism (Chibber, 2013). Postcolonialists are especially concerned with how the prevailing knowledge is accepted without much critical scrutiny by IR theory.

Dependency Theory

Dependency Theory is based on a materialist understanding of the inter-national economic structure, and highlights the inequality between the developed Western economies and the underdeveloped or developing Third World economies. Dependency Theory argues that the division of the international economic structure into the 'core' and the 'periphery' makes the latter dependent on the former, and causes it to suffer from a chronic disadvantage in the terms of trade.

The core economic aspects of ideas that came to be associated with Dependency Theory were developed in the 1930s and 1940s by Argentine economist Raúl Prebisch, well before it became an issue in international politics. Prebisch's ideas were particularly influential on the international stage because he served as the head of the Economic Commission for Latin America at the time of its formation in 1948, and turned it into a launch pad for his ideas. After this, Prebisch moved on to become the first director-general of UNCTAD, where he spearheaded the call for NIEO (*The Economist*, 2009). Later strains of Dependency Theory, especially the work of Fernando Cardoso and Enzo Faletto (1972), slightly shifted focus from purely economic concerns to a Political Economy approach. In this sense, Dependency Theory anticipated the re-emergence of IPE in mainstream Western IR during the 1970s and 1980s. Dependency Theory, especially in its later works, had a discernible Marxist strain. Some of this was influential in mainstream IPE, though that had more Liberal leanings. Development, underdevelopment and dependency were, according to Cardoso and Faletto, effects of the international economic as well as political structure. Moving away from purely economic arguments, Cardoso and Faletto thought it necessary also to analyse social forces and ideologies. Apart from the aforementioned scholar-practitioners from Latin America, other key contributors to Dependency literature include Andre Gunder Frank (1966, 1971), who has a Marxist Political Economy focus, as well as Samir Amin (1972), an Egyptian-French Marxist scholar, who has analysed Africa among other regions. Related to Dependency Theory is Johan Galtung's (1971) structural theory of imperialism. Galtung sought to highlight the inequalities between the centre and the periphery at the international level, but also between centres and peripheries within nations. Galtung defines imperialism as 'a system that splits up collectivities and relates some of the parts to each other in relations of *harmony of interest*, and other parts in relations of *disharmony of interest*, or *conflict of interest*' (Galtung, 1971: 81, emphasis original). Galtung develops the theory with the aim of attaining 'liberation' from 'structural violence'.

The initial focus of Dependency Theory was quite narrow in that it focused solely on the economic aspects of dependency. Drawing from the experience of Latin America, and specifically of Argentina, Prebisch argued that the periphery could never develop because they were reliant on exports of raw materials as a source of income, whereas the core was dependent on manufacturing. This comparative disadvantage to the Latin American economies was not likely to change under the Western liberal order that enforced free trade. Prebisch instead advocated for protecting the national economies of the periphery through adopting policies of import substitution industrialisation. As Helleiner notes, Prebisch believed that the countries of the periphery 'needed to insulate themselves from the powerful shocks emanating from the industrialized countries and to carve out policy options to promote state-supported industrialization and economic development' (Helleiner, 2017: 89). This was required for protection of infant industries to allow for local industrialisation. Prebisch drew this conclusion from his observation that 'the price of primary products tended to decline relative to those of manufactured goods (which embodied higher productivity), and thus that industrialised countries derived more benefit from trade than developing ones' (*The Economist*, 2009). Therefore, structural change was required for economic development. German-born British economist Hans Singer reached the same conclusion independently, and their idea became known as the 'Prebisch–Singer' thesis (Toye and Toye, 2003). In this sense, Dependency Theory is a critique of modernisation theory.

Dependency Theory acquired prominence in IR at a time when there was angst among the countries of the developing world about the lack of economic development after decolonisation. During the 1970s and 1980s, the problems of IMF and World Bank debt faced by many Third World countries, especially in Africa, because of the harsh conditionalities exacerbated this angst. Dependency theorists saw this as a structural issue where the former colonial powers practised a form of neocolonialism through economic dependence, as opposed to direct colonial rule. The high point of Dependency Theory in terms of its impact on international affairs was in 1974 when the UN General Assembly adopted the Declaration for the Establishment of a New International Economic Order, with much of the impetus coming from UNCTAD. While NIEO was not successful in terms of implementation of the provisions in it, it was significant as it voiced the concerns of the developing world about the ill-effects of imposed free trade.

After the initial enthusiasm, which peaked in the 1970s, Dependency Theory segued into World Systems Theory (WST), which shares almost all the characteristics of the former but with important distinctions. WST is most closely associated with the work of Immanuel Wallerstein (1974, 1979, 1983, 1984). It had a strong IPE structural theme built around the dynamic interplay of core, semi-periphery and periphery. It resonated with both Marxist and Liberal approaches to IPE, and became an influential theory across the social sciences and History. It was broadly compatible with Dependency Theory but had a much grander history and theoretical scope. WST was structural and materialist, and focused on the core and periphery. While Dependency Theory focused primarily on short-term effects for the Third World, specifically Latin America, WST theorised about international economic relations and structure in a truly global sense.

One of the main criticisms of Dependency Theory is its excessive, even exclusive, focus on economic issues. Its materialism prevented it from incorporating issues of race and gender. Thus, despite the focus on marginalised nations of the world, or the periphery, the theory did not lend itself to analysis of other kinds of marginalisation, such as marginalised communities within countries. Dependency Theory's structuralist focus did not allow for theorising about the role of elites within the periphery, specifically their interest in and action towards maintaining the unequal economic relations with the Western core. Another criticism is the disjuncture between theory and practice. While NIEO did gain significant exposure and momentum in the 1970s, its provisions proved impracticable and were left unenforced. When Cardoso became president of Brazil, he backtracked from his theory and instead implemented policies that contradicted his Socialist-oriented writings (Viotti and Kauppi, 2011: 202). Perhaps the biggest criticism is the focus on the economic structure at a particular time in history as well as particular regions in the world, which prevented generalisation. For instance, when the East Asian economies started rising from the 1970s onward, and experienced rapid economic growth in the 1980s and early 1990s, they did so not on the basis of import substitution, but rather through export promotion. This phenomenon made Dependency Theory lose much of its relevance.

From the 1980s, much of the momentum in theorising about the Non-Western world moved to WST and Postcolonialism. Dependency Theory nevertheless made a significant impact. It was seemingly the first IR theory from the periphery to register, and be discussed in, the core. It anticipated both WST and the later reintroduction of IPE into core IR, and was taken up by influential core scholars such as Galtung. As Banks (1985: 18) argues, structuralism, including imperialism, always 'loomed in the shadows of IR' throughout its formative period. As we argued in Chapters 2 and 4, IR in the core did indeed marginalise it. But it was finally 'brought into light' in core IR by the works of Dependency theorists in the 1960s and 1970s. There was a certain division of labour between Dependency Theory and Postcolonialism. As Ilan Kapoor (2002: 647–8) notes, 'Dependency chooses a structuralist and socioeconomic perspective, seeing imperialism and development as tied to the unfolding of capitalism, whereas Postcolonial theory favours a post-structuralist and cultural perspective, linking imperialism and agency to discourse and the politics of representation'. Chapter 8 discusses Postcolonialism in greater detail.

IR in the Regions

Systematically tracing the development of IR in different Non-Western regions is made difficult by the generally weak institutionalisation of IR in most periphery countries (discussed earlier), political restrictions on academic work and the consequent paucity of information. While it is in the post-Cold War period that IR scholarship around the world began to mature and articulate key ideas, important conceptual foundations were laid during the Cold War.

Asia

Studying the evolution of Asian IR suffers from some of the problems of intra-regional diversity and variations found in other regions, albeit at a higher scale, especially due to the fact that the region's three major IR powerhouses, Japan, India and China, have developed the field in different and distinctive ways (Alagappa, 2011) and without any links with each other. Additionally, Japan was more part of the IR core than the periphery. The development of IR in these countries is also a dynamic process, responding to the shifting domestic politics and geopolitical currents facing a country.

The 'master narrative' of IR in India was non-alignment, although later it was joined by pursuit of security in the traditional sense (Alagappa, 2011: 204). In China, the narrative was its position as a Socialist country which identified with the developing world. Ironically, in India, despite the country's role as a founder of NAM and a champion of Third World solidarity, the IR community failed to build the concept of non-alignment as a robust theoretical contribution to IR from the Non-Western world (Mallavarapu, 2009). This was in contrast to China where Mao's three worlds theory (explained above) could be used as a Chinese contribution to IR (Alagappa, 2011). But for most of this period, academic Chinese IR was either under the tight ideological control of the Party, or was consumed, along with most university life, by the chaos of the Cultural Revolution.

While some Western theories, especially classical Realism, were influential in both India and China, Postcolonialism and approaches inspired by Subaltern Studies have been hugely popular in India and could be India's most important contribution to IR theory. Yet, some prominent Indian IR scholars reject the existence of any distinctive Indian approach to IR (Mallavarapu, 2009: 166; Behera, 2010: 92).

During the Cold War, Indian thinkers/scholars contributed to ideas of global order and justice from the vantage point of the Indian experience. But these contributions did not constitute a single monolithic understanding of global order. It may also be possible, with some risk of oversimplification, to describe Sisir Gupta as a 'sturdy Realist', A. Appadorai as a Liberal Internationalist, Nehru as a Liberal-Realist, and Ashis Nandy as a Postcolonialist. Siddharth Mallavarapu (2018: 169–70) finds 'considerable eclecticism in the manner in which order has been theorised within the fold of Indian International Relations thinking

… It would be misplaced to attribute or impose any single essentialist or monolithic view of political order emanating from India'. At the same time, 'these perspectives have often been in conversation with each other either by endorsement or by way of critique' (Mallavarapu, 2018: 170). Moreover, he detects a strong normative ethos as a shared feature of these Indian contributions (Mallavarapu, 2018: 170). Navnita Chadha Behera advocates creating alternative sites of knowledge construction, which can be done by using different perspectives, as a way to build a new IR. It should draw on post-positivist emphasis on culture and identity (Behera, 2007: 355).

Latin America

During the 1970s and 1980s, the Latin American interest in Dependency gave way to autonomy, drawing from classical Realism its ideas on the role of political elites and the role of power. Autonomy, as Arlene Tickner (2009: 33) explains, was 'viewed as a precondition for both internal development and a successful foreign policy strategy … as a mechanism for guarding against the noxious effects of dependency on a local level, and from the inside out as an instrument for asserting regional interests in the international system'. Brazilian epistemic thinking was especially influential in developing the concept of autonomy. Like their counterparts in other regions, Latin American IR scholars found imported IR theories deficient in explaining local reality, but instead of completely abandoning them, they have localised them. This has led to the emergence of what Tickner calls the Latin American 'hybrid' model (A. B. Tickner, 2009: 33). Works by Helio Jaguaribe and Juan Carlos Puig represent such synthesis or 'hybridisation', or the 'creative incorporation' of traditional IR principles into regional analyses of international relations, leading to the 'fusion of concepts from dependency theory, realism, and interdependence … that became fundamental to the analysis of global issues in many countries of the region' (A. B. Tickner, 2003a: 331).

Africa[17]

As in other regions, African IR both adopted and adapted Western IR concepts and theories. IR scholars in sub-Saharan Africa (SSA) have

---

[17] We are conscious of the fact that our sources on Africa mainly have a post-Cold War dating. A good deal of IR scholarship on Africa is of relatively recent origin, especially compared with Latin America and Asia, but as with sources on IR scholarship and debate on other regions, much of which are also relatively recent, they do cover the main themes of IR as it developed during the Cold War.

been critical of dominant strands of Western IR, such as the Neo-Neo synthesis. In one view, 'the neo-neo synthesis not only fails to explain political realities in SSA and that the neo-neo synthesis allows for the exploitation of SSA', but also 'legitimizes exploitation by emphasizing power politics' (Claassen, 2011: 182). African IR scholars have combined modernisation, Dependency and statist perspectives. Arguing against the state-centric nature of modern IR theory, Assis Malaquias (2001: 27) suggests that the nation or sub-state actors, instead of the Westphalian state, should be the unit of analysis for African IR.

A divide between those who favour a Western-based universalist framework and an African-based contextualist framework has also characterised IR scholarship in the region (Ofuho, 2009: 74). African IR scholarship has been from the very outset more geared to challenges facing the continent, such as 'conflict and ethnicity, refugee crises, insecurity, corruption and bad governance, lack of democracy, militarism and coups d'état, poverty and underdevelopment, famine and food insecurity, HIV/AIDS, international aid and debt crises, gender and environmental issues, terrorism, the collapsed infrastructure, and gross human rights abuses' (Ofuho, 2009: 76). Here, like in other regions, the utility of Western-based IR theories is a major concern for IR scholars.

A second focus of African IR, similar to other regions of the periphery, has been on regionalist ideas that stressed the importance of Pan-African solidarity and action. Following Thomas Tieku (2013: 15), one might attribute this to the belief among African rulers that proper behaviour is anchored on the 'feeling of oneness and support towards other Africans, at least in public'. Despite the importance of nationalism and the territorial integrity norm, African writings on IR tended to emphasise a collectivist worldview, which is often neglected in Western writings on Africa (Tieku, 2013: 16). This worldview led to proposals for peace and security, such as Nkrumah's call for an African High Command (Adebajo and Landsberg, 2001) to secure Africa's peace and security without outside assistance and intervention.

A major contributor to African IR thinking during the late Cold War period was Ali Mazrui, who may be described as Africa's great conceptual synthesiser and hybridist thinker. Hence we consider him separately here, although some may think that he belongs to the category of Postcolonial thought discussed above. Though influenced by Pan-Africanism (Mazrui, 1967), Mazrui (1986) stressed Africa's triple heritage: indigenous African culture, Islam and Christianity. In ideology, Mazrui stood outside of both Marxism and capitalism. Unlike Africa's first postcolonial rulers such as Algeria's Ahmed Ben Bela and Tanzania's Julius Nyerere, he did not see Socialism as a better alternative to capitalist development. But

Mazrui also recognised the ills of capitalism, and in a famous argument against Guyanese intellectual and Pan-Africanist Walter Rodney called for a mix of liberal capitalism and African values (Rajab, 2014). This belief in hybridity might explain why he backed Nyerere's programme of 'Ujamaa' (familyhood), a concept that combined Socialist principles with African values. A staunch critic of Israel, Mazrui promoted the concept of 'Afrabia', the merger of Africa and the Arab world (Rajab, 2014). Mazrui's work, with its recognition of cultural and civilisational diversity and its pluralistic understanding of ideology, identity and approaches to development, has led some scholars to view it as a precursor to the idea of Global IR that informs our book (Adem, 2017: 247).

The Middle East

During the Cold War, the development of IR throughout the Middle East remained theoretically weak and focused on practical/policy issues and training of diplomats. In Turkey, the study of IR under the direction of the *Mekteb-i Mülkiye* ('Palace School', or the School of Government), founded in 1859 but merged with Ankara University in 1950, focused heavily on Diplomatic History and International Law (Aydinli and Mathews, 2008). Realism applied to practical problems dominated any attempt at theoretical framing. In the Arab world, as Karim Makdisi (2009: 183) puts it, the study of IR was defined by an 'amalgam of pressing current affairs and short-term public policy concerns'. Before the 1979 Khomeini revolution, IR in Iran was neither methodologically nor theoretically rigorous. Realism was dominant. But after the revolution, Iran not only saw growing attention to theory and methodology, especially among the younger generation, but also the adoption of competing conceptual frameworks in understanding their country's foreign policy, including Liberal and Realist orientations and a mix of ideological and non-ideological (positivist, empirical, integrative) approaches (Sariolghalam, 2009: 160–1). Israel has always been closely integrated with European and American IR, and was therefore more part of the core than of the periphery. This did not change, and perhaps because of its greater exposure to and closer interaction with Western IR, Israel lacks the potential for a distinctive theoretical approach to the study of International Politics (Kacowicz, 2009).

Conclusions

By the end of the Cold War, IR was beginning to spread the more academic approach from core to periphery, becoming more of a formal discipline there. But the discipline remained overwhelmingly dominated by the West, because of the predominance of core power and core concerns about bipolarity and nuclear weapons as well as a host of other factors such as limited resources, lack of interest in theory and method, and the largely policy and empirical orientation of scholars in the periphery (to be discussed in Chapter 10).

Yet, there was the beginnings of engagement between IR in the core and in the periphery, helped by the emergence of Dependency and WST, responses in the core to them, and their impact on IPE and Development Studies. However, during this period, Postcolonialism remained mostly a dialogue among like-minded scholars from the periphery. Even though IR theory in the West was not a monolith, and by the 1980s Realism, Liberalism and their variants were already beginning to encounter challenges from Feminism and other Critical Theories (we will take these up in Chapter 8, as they really came into their own in the 1990s), IR theory was basically geared to constructing the Western experience in universalist terms. Although decolonisation was a big change in ir, and a key part of the shift from version 1.0 to version 1.1 GIS, in this first phase it remained largely marginal in both ir and IR. To be sure, the periphery now had independence and a bigger political voice. But it had neither wealth nor power in material terms. Seen from the core it looked vastly less important than the huge zero-sum game of the Cold War's ideological and nuclear rivalries. Yet the worm was beginning to turn. Some IR from the periphery was beginning to register in the core, and this trend was to pick up significantly during the 1990s and beyond when IR's focus turned away from ideological rivalry and nuclear weapons and towards interdependence, globalisation, human rights and IPE.

7 The World after 1989: 'Unipolarity', Globalisation and the Rise of the Rest

Introduction

This chapter covers the period from the end of the Cold War, through the economic crisis that began in 2008, to the time of writing (2017–18). The first two decades of this period, the nineties and most of the noughties, mark the high point of the version 1.1 GIS that began after the Second World War. The third decade, the teens, saw the beginnings of the transition of GIS from the Western-global structure of version 1.1 to the post-Western structure of version 1.2. The next section summarises briefly the continuities and discontinuities from the Cold War/decolonisation GIS. The one following looks in more detail at the main themes of version 1.1 GIS and how they play into the gathering pace of the transformation to a post-Western, version 1.2, GIS.

Continuities and Discontinuities from the Pre-1989 World

As argued in Chapter 5, the ending of the Cold War seemed to mark the triumph of the West's democratic Neoliberal capitalism over the Soviet Union's totalitarian command economy version of modernity. Within this there was to some extent also a victory of Neoliberal capitalism over more social democratic, Keynesian forms of capitalism such as those in Scandinavia, continental Europe and Japan. During the early 1990s, the United States and its principal allies all looked strong. Their partnerships showed real depth by surviving intact after the demise of the shared Soviet ideological and military threat that had bound them together during the Cold War. The United States convincingly asserted its military might by defeating Saddam Hussein and ousting his forces from Kuwait in 1990–1. Its economy revived from the slump of the 1980s and looked robust.

Like the United States, the EU also seemed to be regaining momentum. The Single European Act of 1987 and the '1992' project of reforms and integration generated a real sense of progress. The Maastricht Treaty of 1993 promised monetary union within a decade, and the Schengen Treaty of 1995 dismantled internal borders. The EU was not only getting deeper, but also wider: Spain and Portugal joined in 1986; Germany achieved reunification in 1990, bringing the former East Germany inside the EEC; Sweden, Finland and Austria joined in 1995; and the prospect of eastward expansion opened up after the liberation of the Baltic states and Eastern Europe from Soviet control. This sense of momentum was embodied in the change in 1993 from being the EEC to the EU. At least in the early 1990s, the other key US partner, Japan, was enjoying the momentum of its long economic boom, and was seen by some as the likely challenger to the United States (Huntington, 1991: 8; Layne, 1993: 42–3, 51; Waltz, 1993: 55–70; Spruyt, 1998). It had a leading role in the 'flying geese' formation of fast-developing economies in East Asia (Cumings, 1984), and was playing a major role in the modernisation and expansion of China's newly unleashed 'market Socialism' (Yahuda, 2014: locs. 627, 2258; S. A. Smith, 2015: 35–6; Kokubun et al., 2017: 95–121). Capitalism, and to a lesser extent liberal democracy and human rights, looked to be in a commanding position in GIS as the 1990s began to unfold.

And at least initially, the victorious West faced no powerful challengers. After the implosion of the Soviet Union, Russia went into sharp economic, political and military decline, barely hanging on to its status as a great power. The three Baltic states plus the former Soviet satellite states in Eastern Europe all quickly pointed themselves westward, and most of them were within NATO and the EU by 2004. China had given up the command economy for capitalism in the late 1970s, and had done well in economic reforms during the 1980s. But it started the new era under a cloud, with the CCP in a deep panic over the collapse of communist regimes throughout the Russian empire, and the country under sanctions for its ruthless crushing of pro-democracy demonstrations in Tiananmen Square in 1989. Beijing wanted and needed stability and access to the global economy, and it followed Deng's advice to keep a low profile, bide its time and seek to join the World Trade Organization (WTO) on the best terms it could get. The only other possible challenger was India, but until the late 1990s India seemed to be mired in slow growth and inward-looking politics.

Given all this, it is not surprising that the structural transition after 1989 was generally captured by two big simplifying concepts: *unipolarity* and *globalisation*. So comprehensive did this victory for liberal capitalist democracy seem that Francis Fukuyama (1992) boldly declared 'the end of history'.

In the Neorealist formulation that was influential in the United States and elsewhere in both academic and policy circles, bipolarity had shifted to unipolarity (Huntington, 1999; Kapstein and Mastanduno, 1999; Wohlforth, 1999, 2009). What had started as a three superpower world in 1945, reduced to two between 1947 and 1989, and then to one. From 1990, the United States stood alone as the only superpower. Its crushing of Saddam's army in 1990–1 seemed to point towards a military ability to intervene without either competition from, or restraint by, other powers. With the post-Soviet command economy in collapse, and China converted to the market, Neoliberalism seemed to stand as the sole remaining ideological flag-carrier of modernity, opening the way to a full globalisation of the capitalist world economy. In addition, the threat of imminent nuclear war that had hung over the Cold War world evaporated with remarkable speed. The United States and Russia both wound down the high levels of military alert and sensitivity that had built up between them over the four decades of the Cold War, and began to shrink the enormous arsenals of nuclear weapons and delivery systems that both of them had accumulated. Even nuclear proliferation seemed to be under control, with Russia taking back the surplus nuclear arsenals from some of its successor states, most notably Ukraine, and South Africa dismantling the small nuclear arsenal that had been built by the apartheid regime. The grand simplification of unipolarity centred on the United States was reinforced when Japan's economic bubble burst, and the briefly popular speculation that it might overtake the United States disappeared into the dustbin of history.

The state-centrism of unipolarity played somewhat oddly with globalisation, which became the other popular way of seeing the post-Cold War world (Hirst and Thompson, 1996; Clark, 1997; Armstrong, 1998; Held et al., 1999). Globalisation generally pointed away from understanding IR purely as a system of states, and towards seeing it as a system of flows embodying many types of actors including states. The essence of it is to track the increasing links and interdependencies between states and peoples on a global scale. Since economics has been the leading sector in such linkages and interdependencies, the globalisation perspective favours economic dynamics over political ones. It tends to see states and peoples as increasingly entangled in webs of economic interdependence woven by TNCs and IGOs. These economic linkages, when added to shared fates, such as the environment and global disease issues, and to a growing array of transnational INGOs linking people together across state borders for a wide variety of purposes, pointed towards a deterritorialising world order in which states are less relevant to the scale of policy issues, and world politics drifts towards global governance (Held et al., 1999; Weiss, 2013).

Even if one took the view that globalisation was a longstanding process, it seemed unarguable that the unipolarity of the 1990s, because it was led by a liberal power, had given it a freer reign than ever before. Capital could now be unleashed within a rule-bound system, integrating production on a global scale, and deepening the interdependence of all within world trade and finance. The leading liberal states promoted economic globalisation (though much more for capital and goods than for labour) even though it weakened their domestic control and territoriality. The bargain was to trade economic autarchy for global markets and higher rates of growth, and this bargain was accepted even by the CCP. The idea that linked globalisation and unipolarity was hegemonic stability: the theory that a liberal global economy worked best when there was a leading liberal power strong enough to hold the ring, provide security, and promote and support the institutions necessary to govern world trade and finance so that the global economy remained stable (Kindleberger, 1973; Gilpin, 1981, 1987). Globalisation pointed towards rising interdependence in the generation of wealth, and a hoped-for diminution in the utility of war and military power as a consequence (Keohane and Nye, 1977). Less obviously it pointed towards the rise of shared fates as an increasing factor in world politics. The clearest of these was the shared fate of all being entangled in a global capitalist economy, and dependent on its smooth operation for wealth and welfare. Less clear were the shared fates of living on a small planet that was increasingly under stress from the demands of rising human numbers and standards of living.

Both unipolarity and globalisation flattered the United States, and were unsurprisingly popular there. They were broadly accepted elsewhere, though not always with enthusiasm, and often as things to be opposed. The focus on these two concepts drew attention away from the fact that the era of decolonisation had also come to an end. Some thought of the breakup of the Soviet Union, and the emergence not only of Russia and 14 other successor states, but also the liberation of its six satellite states in Eastern Europe, as being the last round of decolonisation. But others (Jansen and Osterhammel, 2017: 13–22), though acknowledging that both Third World and post-Soviet decolonisation involved delegitimising the practice of alien rule, saw the post-Soviet case as different from the dismantling of empires in which core metropoles dominated Third World peripheries. With the implosion of the so-called 'Second World' after 1989, GIS became more starkly divided between a

First World core of advanced industrial economies, and a Third World periphery of developing countries. China was initially still ambiguously in the middle ground between core and periphery.

Within this core–periphery framing that was dominated by a coalition of a liberal superpower and its great power allies (EU and Japan), there was, not surprisingly, a revival of the 'standard of civilisation' after 1990, though not using that colonial-era language. The 'standard of civilisation' morphed into the politer liberal terminology of human rights, 'good' (i.e. democratic) governance and conditionality. Many writers noted how human rights had become a new 'standard of civilisation' (Gong, 1984: 90–3; 2002; Donnelly, 1998; Jackson, 2000: 287–93; Keene, 2002: 122–3, 147–8; Clark, 2007: 183; Bowden, 2009). The practices associated with the promotion of the Washington Consensus before the 2008 financial crisis also reflected 'standard of civilisation' attitudes. So too did the idea, which became prominent in the United States during the nineties and noughties, that a 'league' or 'concert' of democracies should assert managerial responsibility over international society (Ikenberry and Slaughter, 2006; Geis, 2013). This reflected not only a longstanding tradition of American foreign policy, but also a post-Cold War US policy of expanding the sphere of democracy that was initiated by Bill Clinton and carried forward in a more aggressive fashion by George W. Bush (Bouchet, 2013; Lynch, 2013).

But what seemed at the beginning to be an opening towards the fulfilment of liberal teleology quickly turned into something much more complex and challenging. After the end of the East–West ideological war, the globally pervasive tension between totalitarian communism and democratic Liberalism that had dominated GIS for half a century collapsed. In its place, there was a resurgence of nationalism, religion, civilisationalism and identity politics. This heady brew was often mixed with postcolonial resentments, and sometimes accompanied by extreme violence. In some ways and in some places Islam emerged to replace communism as the ideational counter-pole to the liberal project. In other places, most notably China and Russia, capitalism was accepted, but not democracy, once again creating an authoritarian/democratic divide within the capitalist world. China's meteoric rise to wealth and power began to question Western dominance more profoundly than Japan's earlier rise had ever done. The hoped-for reconciliation between the West and Russia soon turned sour, and the rising powers began to assert themselves against Western dominance. Fukuyama's liberal hubris about the 'end of history' was quickly proved wrong.

The Peaking of Version 1.1 Global International Society and the Transition to Version 1.2: The Main Themes of International Relations 1989–2017

In this section we use the same structure as in Chapter 5, looking at the core, the periphery and the interplay between them, and picking up the threads from where we left them. One key difference is that China becomes part of the core, and so we discuss it there rather than as a separate outlier.

The Core

During the Cold War era, the core was dominated by superpower bipolarity and the rapid evolution of nuclear weapons. After 1989, concern about great power nuclear weapons and wars faded into the background, though concern about nuclear proliferation to other states remained strong (Buzan and Hansen, 2009: 239–43). 'Bipolarity' gave way to 'unipolarity', but just as we argued in Chapter 5 that bipolarity failed to capture much of the structure of the Cold War GIS, so unipolarity was never an accurate description of the post-Cold War international structure. The idea of a single differentiation between great powers and all other states simply left out too much. A better characterisation of the post-1989 GIS was that there was one superpower (the United States), several great powers (the EU, China, Russia and more arguably Japan and India) and quite large numbers of regional powers (e.g. Brazil, Indonesia, Iran, Nigeria, Pakistan, South Africa, Turkey) (Layne, 1993, 2006; Huntington, 1999; Buzan and Wæver, 2003; Buzan, 2004a). If the United States had been a sole superpower in a world with no great powers and only regional powers, it would indeed have been relatively unconstrained. But with a set of great powers also in play, one of which, China, was rising fast, the United States had a dominant, but far from commanding, position. Nevertheless, during the 1990s, in the immediate afterglow of the victory of capitalism in the Cold War, unipolarity did have some credence. It supported liberal hopes and plans for expanding the liberal-democratic sphere, and underpinned a fatal drift towards unilateralism in the United States that came to full flower under the Bush administration (2001–9).

The affirmation that something like unipolarity was indeed in play was the rhetoric of calls for a more 'multipolar' world order from Russia, China, France, Iran, India and others opposed to US dominance (Ahrari, 2001; Ambrosio, 2001). These powers had quite different reasons for wanting more multipolarity, though none bothered to lay out any coherent vision of what kind of GIS they had in mind. The common thread was that they wanted more autonomy, and/or more status and voice, for themselves and their regions within GIS. In the case of some, notably Russia, China, Iran and India, the not-so-hidden subtext was that they wanted more influence within their own regions, and less subjection to American rules and interventions. While unipolarity as a characterisation of the structure of GIS may have confused more than it clarified, it nonetheless remained true, at least until 2008, that for all of the great powers their relationship with the United States was more important than their relationships with each other. On that basis, it is worthwhile in this subsection to review briefly each of these bilateral relationships of great powers with the United States. Such a review reveals not only the substance behind the claim for unipolarity, but also the mechanism behind its ongoing erosion. We start with those most opposed to the United States (Russia and China), then look at those closely allied with it (Europe and Japan), and finish with India, a rising power that had for long tried to steer a more neutral course.

Russia

The story of the Russia–US relationship is a game of two halves. The first half covers the period of Russian weakness following the implosion of the Soviet Union in 1991, and the second centres around Russia's recovery in the noughties and teens. During the 1990s Russia was in political and economic disarray, trying to find a transition from communism to some form of democracy and capitalism. Its economy and military power imploded, and its political leadership was weak. Some illusion of Russia's former superpower status was maintained by the ongoing negotiations with the United States over nuclear arms reductions, but Russia's position was weak because it could not now afford to maintain even those weapons that it had. Russia lost its sphere of influence in Eastern Europe in 1989, and it was clear right from the beginning that its former vassals, and indeed some of the constituent parts of the former Soviet Union, would align themselves with the West. The 1990s and early 2000s saw this massive readjusting of spheres of influence between NATO/EU and Russia take place (MacFarlane, 1993; Fierke, 1999). Germany reunified in 1989, bringing the former East Germany into both NATO and the EU. After due preparations, Poland, the Czech Republic and Hungary joined NATO in 1999; Bulgaria, Estonia, Latvia, Lithuania, Slovakia, Slovenia and Romania in 2004; and Albania and Croatia in 2017. The Czech Republic, Estonia, Hungary, Latvia, Lithuania, Poland and Slovakia joined the EU in 2004; and Bulgaria and Romania in 2007. The United

States withdrew from its Anti-Ballistic Missile Treaty with Russia in 2002, and NATO then began moving towards installing missile defences, ostensibly against Iran, but strongly opposed by Russia on the grounds that they undermined its deterrent. Under US unipolarity, a weak Russia was barely hanging onto its status as a great power. Its sphere of influence had been rolled back, it had not received the expected economic assistance from the West, and NATO's flirting with Ukraine and Georgia penetrated ever deeper into Russia's traditional sphere.

The second half began in the noughties, as Russia, benefitting from the commodities boom fuelled by the growth of China, began to recover some of its strength under Vladimir Putin's leadership. Its way forward was to be authoritarian state capitalism, combined with an increasingly nationalist, anti-Western outlook on policy. While Russia recovered some of its former strength, it was most definitely not, despite its inclusion in the BRICS (Brazil, Russia, India, China, South Africa), a 'rising power' like China or India. It was at best a recovering power, remaining largely a commodity exporter, particularly vulnerable to market fluctuations in the price of oil. Unlike China, its capitalism was shallow, and not really capable of generating wealth and power as a fully fledged modern economy. Its population was shrinking, and in contrast to 1945, when it was surrounded by weak neighbours, now it was surrounded by states most of which were doing better than it in coming to terms with modernity in ways that were effective in generating wealth and power.

Nevertheless, Russia's recovery under Putin from 2000 was sufficient to enable it to begin to assert itself within its region and to fight back against the United States and the West. It used both military and ideational means, the latter seen in an upsurge of nationalism and redefining its identity outside of the West (this would reshape Russian IR thinking, as will be discussed in Chapter 8). Russia was not anywhere near strong enough to challenge the West economically or politically, and only in a limited way militarily. But it was strong enough to make itself a considerable nuisance, and proceeded to do so as soon as it was able. One part of Russia's fight-back was to probe and unsettle the NATO/EU expansion into its former sphere. This it did by such actions as the 2007 cyberattack on Estonia, the resumption of regular military probing of NATO defences by its air and sea forces, and subtle meddling in European politics by supporting far right political parties. Another, firmer, part was to halt any further eastward expansion of NATO/EU. Russia invaded Georgia in 2008, detaching Abkhazia and South Ossetia from it, and making clear its strategic dominance in the Caucasus.

A much bigger move came in 2014, when Russia partially invaded Ukraine, and annexed Crimea. It did so in conjunction with pro-Russian separatists in eastern Ukraine, creating ongoing uncertainty as to whether it wanted to weaken the country, further break it up or create conditions by which Ukraine as a whole might be incorporated into the Russian Federation. This move was seen in the West as a major violation of the sanctity of borders as a general principle of GIS. It led to a sharp deterioration of relations with the West. Russia was expelled from the Group of 8 (G8), the economic club of leading capitalist powers, of which it had been a member since 1998. In addition, the West imposed sanctions against Russia and NATO activity in Ukraine increased. In effect, Ukraine became the subject of a tug of war between NATO and Russia. With this move, Russia essentially broke the ties with Europe that had been built up during the 1990s, and set itself as once again a hostile power threatening NATO, especially the Baltic states, and the EU. This break pushed Russia to deepen its ties with China, where it was increasingly a junior partner in Beijing's anti-US hegemony project. Russia continued in this vein by mounting a substantial intervention in the Syrian civil war in 2015 in support of the Assad government. It is widely thought to have tried to influence the US presidential election of 2016, a subject of ongoing investigations at the time of writing.

Russia's weakness for more than a decade after the end of the Cold War was part of what made GIS look unipolar. Its recovery during the noughties, its increasingly strong stand against the United States and the West, and its shift to a strategic partnership with China as its key international relationship are part of a pattern that points towards the emergence of a post-Western era.

China

In Chapter 5 we characterised China as an enigmatic outsider that did not fit comfortably into either bipolar or Third World framings. Once China had recovered from the temporary setback of 1989, its steady and very rapid economic growth quickly made it not only one of the great powers in the 'unipolar' system, but also increasingly the one thought most likely to challenge the United States, both materially and politically. This created a strange dualism in US–China relations. On the one hand, the two countries became increasingly closely tied economically. The United States opened its markets to China, allowing Deng and his successors to pursue a highly successful export-led growth strategy. China thus became a major beneficiary of globalisation by being able to link its economy into the US-led trading and financial orders. The trade deficit this created for the United States was offset by both China's massive purchases of US treasuries (Shirk, 2007: 25; Foot and Walter,

2011: 18) and by cheap Chinese imports lowering consumer costs and keeping inflation down. Even though China was a rival to the United States, Washington basically struck the same kind of economic deal with Beijing that it had made with its ally Japan during the Cold War.

On the other hand, in terms of political and strategic relations, there are interesting parallels between interwar Japan and post-Mao China in how they related to the United States. Both interwar Japan and contemporary China wanted primacy in Asia, and could not avoid rivalry with a United States on which they were economically dependent, and which was also a major player in the region (Buzan, forthcoming). During this period, China moved clearly into the core in terms of great power calculations, as its tremendous economic growth made it the most obvious possible challenger to the United States. It moved further away from the periphery as its development took off, though continuing to self-identify in important ways as a developing country. It is generally true to say that policy in China is driven primarily by domestic political considerations, most obviously the desire and need of the CCP to quash any challenges to its rule and to stay in power forever. This domestic factor drove the curious dualism in China–US relations. The CCP needed economic growth to bolster its legitimacy once most of its class war, and Marxist economics, had been thrown overboard, and this made it dependent on Washington's global economic order. But it also needed nationalism to reinforce national unity during the turbulence of economic transition, and that paved the way for a tense and irritable political relationship with the United States. The United States was equally torn, welcoming China as a major addition to the capitalist world economy, but worrying about it as both an economic and military/political rival, and increasingly as a challenger for global primacy.

A clear example of this messy dualism was the process that took China into the WTO in December 2001, thus formalising its integration into the Western economic order. China had first applied in 1995, the year in which the WTO replaced the GATT (where China had been an observer). China hoped to be a founder member of the WTO, but this was blocked by the Western powers and Japan, who required more reforms to the still heavily protected and state-managed Chinese economy. The Clinton administration bungled a chance for a deal early in 1999, humiliating Chinese premier Zhu Rongji in the process. Washington had to accept a less advantageous deal with China later in the year, after the US bombing of China's embassy in Belgrade had further soured relations between the two (Shirk, 2007: 192, 228–31). The process was difficult and demanding for China, requiring it to open up its economy more than most other developing countries and reform many institutions and practices before it could join (Shirk, 2007: 132; Westad, 2012: loc. 6179). Entry to the WTO was a major step for China's reform and opening up, committing it to a multilateral world trading order, and giving a big boost to its economy and development.

Despite the successful outcome, there was plenty of room for differences of perspective about this whole process. The United States saw itself as having generously accommodated an illiberal rising power by letting it into the global trading and financial system (Shirk, 2007: 25; Kissinger, 2011: 487–503; Westad, 2012: locs. 5962, 6150). China was divided, with some embracing the commitment to globalisation as reinforcing China's reform and its pursuit of wealth and power. The more nationalist-minded, however, saw China as having been bullied into concessions while it was still weak, and having an order imposed on it that was not of China's making. There was considerable resentment in China about the length and the terms of its entry process with some comparing it to the humiliation of China by Japan's infamous 'twenty-one demands' during the First World War (Shirk, 2007: 230). The consequence of China's accession was to increase the US trade deficit with China to the point where it became 'politically explosive' in US domestic politics (Shirk, 2007: 249). As China got stronger this nationalist sense of resentment at having been forced into rules that it did not participate in making increased. China entered into the WTO as a non-market economy, which subjected it to numerous claims for dumping (Shirk, 2007: 276–7; Shambaugh, 2013: 160). When that status ended automatically in 2016, it opened up an ongoing contestation between China's claim that it had now to be treated as a market economy, and US and EU claims that it did not yet meet that standard.

The testy China–US rivalry was more obviously on display in a series of spats in the military and strategic sector. Despite the dropping of revolutionary rhetoric from China's foreign policy after Mao, there was a lot of continuity to the military/strategic shoving and pushing that had marked US–China relations throughout the Mao period. The temporary reprieve in the 1970s and 1980s, when China and the United States had aligned against the Soviet Union, quickly dissipated once the Soviet Union was gone. Tensions between the United States and China over Taiwan remained a durable feature, as did the US alliances with Japan and South Korea. China had its own history problem with Japan, and the CCP found that cultivating an anti-Japanese nationalism among the Chinese people through sustained programmes of 'patriotic education' was a useful way of reconciling China's domestic political history divisions, closing the gap between the KMT and the CCP in their shared opposition to Japanese imperialism (Wang, 2008, 2012). Beijing was torn over whether the US–Japan alliance was a good thing (because it constrained any revival of Japanese militarism) or a bad one (because it was part of a US plot to contain the rise of China). Complex entanglements ensued in which the United States got drawn into China–Japan disputes over the Senkaku/Diaoyu islands, and Japan got increasingly committed to supporting the United States in defending Taiwan.

The main military/strategic frictions between the United States and China during this period have been:

- Taiwan Straits 1996. After a row between the United States and China (and within the United States) in 1995 over the granting of a visa to Taiwanese President Lee Teng-hui, China conducted missile tests off the Taiwan coast in 1995–6, some of them close enough to disrupt shipping at Taiwan's ports, and in part aimed at intimidating the electorate in Taiwan's 1996 elections. The United States responded by sending two carrier groups to the region, and sailing one of them through the Taiwan straits. China lost this crisis. Not only did the United States demonstrate naval superiority, but Lee's majority was increased, and security relations between the United States, Japan and Taiwan were deepened.
- Embassy bombing in Belgrade 1999. In May 1999, the United States bombed the Chinese embassy in Belgrade during its air war against Serbia. There was much Chinese popular outrage, encouraged by the government, at the act and the deaths. American claims of an accidental mistargeting were given little credence in China. Eventually, this incident was settled diplomatically with the United States paying compensation for the damage to the Chinese embassy and for the killed and wounded, and China paying compensation to the United States for the damage to its embassy in Beijing as a result of public protests not contained by the police.
- Aircraft incident in April 2001. A Chinese fighter harassing a US EP-3 intelligence aircraft over the South China Sea collided with it, killing the fighter pilot, and so damaging the EP-3 that it had to make an emergency landing on Hainan Island. China detained the aircrew for more than a week, and only returned the dismantled EP-3 in July. This issue was settled diplomatically after some heated rhetoric.
- South China Sea island-building by China 2010–present. In 2010, China redefined the South China Sea as a core national interest comparable to Taiwan. From 2014 to 2016 there was rapid Chinese construction of several artificial islands in the Spratly Islands, and subsequent militarisation of them. Through a mix of economic incentives and coercive diplomacy, China was accused of pursuing a divide-and-rule policy

towards ASEAN over the South China Sea issue, with Cambodia and the Philippines (after Duterte's election as president) taking China's side. China delayed concluding a binding Code of Conduct on the South China Sea with ASEAN, arguing that the timing was not right and citing lack of unity within ASEAN. The United States began freedom of navigation operations off the islands from October 2015, with regular sailings of its warships through waters now claimed by China, but not recognised by the United States. In July 2016, the UN Convention on the Law of the Sea tribunal ruled on a case brought by the Philippines against Chinese claims in the South China Sea, but China dismissed this judgment, and smoothed the Philippines government into quiescence on the issue.

- Air Exclusion Zone 2013. In November, China imposed an unusually strict Air Defense Identification Zone (ADIZ) over much of the East China Sea, including the islands (Senkaku/Diaoyu) disputed with Japan. The United States did not recognise the ADIZ, and flew two B-52s through the zone in November, though commercial airlines largely adapted to the new situation.

Despite these frictions, there has been some US–China cooperation, perhaps most notably in the six-party talks on the North Korean nuclear problem between 2003 and 2009. But increasingly the Chinese are going their own way. They have teamed up with Russia in the UN Security Council (UNSC) to defend themselves against Western pressure generally, to cover Russia's interventions in Ukraine and Syria, and to obstruct Western usage of the UNSC's authority to legitimise interventions. They have started to found their own, more China-centred IGOs to challenge Western dominance in GIS, most notably the Shanghai Cooperation Organisation (SCO), founded in 2001, the BRICS, founded in 2009–10, and the Asian Infrastructure Investment Bank (AIIB), founded in 2014 (Stuenkel, 2016: locs. 2974–3202). The SCO involves China, Russia and four Central Asian states, with India and Pakistan joining in 2017. The BRICS involves China, Russia, India, Brazil and South Africa as a kind of counter-Western grouping. China is by far the dominant economy in this group, which set up both the New Development Bank in 2014, and the BRICS Contingent Reserve Arrangement in 2015. The AIIB picked up many European and Asian members, though Japan and the United States did not join, and neither did North Korea.

Under Xi Jinping, China has clearly moved to distance itself further from the United States. After the economic crisis of 2008, it was clear that a heavily indebted United States could no longer support China's export-led growth, and that China would have to generate more growth in its domestic markets. China is also taking good advantage of the dysfunctional and dyspeptic Trump administration in the United States, as well as the division and paralysis in post-Brexit Britain, both to promote its own model of authoritarian development, and to claim a greater leadership role in GIS to fill the vacuum left by Donald Trump, and the implosion of the Anglosphere. Both lines were on clear display in Xi's speech to the nineteenth Party Congress in October 2017, where he both disparaged other forms of government and claimed that: 'It is time for us to take centre stage in the world and to make a greater contribution to humankind'.[1] The trade tensions between China and the Trump administration exacerbate the Sino-US strategic rivalry and may push China further in developing its own initiatives and influence over global governance.

China is not seeking war with the United States, or even open strategic rivalry. But it is increasingly asserting itself in Asia, and challenging the United States and Japan there for regional primacy. Xi's ambitious Belt and Road Initiative (BRI) scheme to use giant infrastructure projects to link Eurasia to China can be seen as a kind of continental grand strategy aimed at countering the maritime grand strategy of the United States (Gao, 2013; Pieke, 2016: 164–5; Stuenkel, 2016: locs. 3985–4041). Although the Chinese would not appreciate the comparison, it is possible to see some parallels between BRI and the continental strategy of Japan during the 1930s and 1940s, the Greater East Asia Co-Prosperity Sphere. Both aimed to establish their sponsor as the core of a continental economy in Asia able to stand against the United States.

Europe and Japan

The stories of Europe and Japan in relation to the United States can be told more briefly because they are mainly about the continuation of the relationships formed by the Cold War. Both NATO and the US–Japan alliance survived the end of the Cold War.

As noted above, NATO expanded not only into the former Soviet sphere in Eastern Europe, but also into parts of the former Soviet Union itself. The alliance successfully repurposed itself as a vehicle for North Atlantic, and liberal-democratic capitalist, solidarity, and remained active in a variety of ways. NATO was not involved in the US-led 'coalition of the willing' that responded to Iraq's invasion of Kuwait in 1990–1. But Britain and France were key members of the coalition, and several

---

[1] BBC World News, www.bbc.co.uk/news/world-asia-china-41647872 (Accessed 18 October 2017).

other NATO members also took part. The United States, in turn, gave military support through NATO in the interventions in Bosnia in 1992–4, and in 1999 into Kosovo, where the messy breakup of Yugoslavia exposed Europe's continued military dependence on the United States. NATO invoked article 5 (mutual support for an attacked member) in response to the 9/11 terrorist attack on the United States in 2001, and supported the United States in the subsequent invasion of Afghanistan. It also took command of the International Security Assistance Force from 2003 to 2014. The second US invasion of Iraq in 2003, however, caused deep splits in NATO, with Britain and Poland strongly supporting the United States, and France and Germany, along with Russia, strongly opposing it. NATO nonetheless provided a training mission in Iraq from 2004–11. From 2009, it also supported counter-piracy operations in the Gulf of Aden and the Indian Ocean. NATO was again active in the intervention into Libya in 2011, enforcing the no-fly zone, with the United States taking something of a back seat and the Europeans taking the lead. NATO has been entangled in Ukraine, and the complexities of Ukraine–Russia relations, since the beginning of the century, when possible Ukrainian membership of the alliance became a political issue. As noted above, this question became more urgent after Russia's assault on Ukraine in 2014, and remains an acute point of sensitivity between NATO and Russia.

The future of the alliance was thrown into some confusion by the highly inconsistent rhetoric of President Trump, and his 'America first' policy. Trump sometimes denounced NATO and sometimes praised it, raising doubts about ongoing US commitment to article 5. In 2017–18, the Europeans firmly opposed Trump's withdrawal from the nuclear treaty with Iran, which Germany, France and Britain, and the EU, and also Russia, had played a major role in negotiating. Trump's 2018 exit from the deal reopened a rift across the Atlantic at a time when the old enemy of NATO, Russia, was once again becoming a security concern for both Europeans and the United States.

The story of the US–Japan alliance is similar, but simpler. Unlike NATO, which was originally about the threat from the Soviet Union, the US–Japan alliance had, since the communist victory in 1949, also been aimed at China. And after the Cold War, China was both rising fast, and cultivating a historical dislike of Japan. Japan had had a fairly comfortable Cold War, insulated in a kind of Lagrange point between the Soviet Union and China on the one side, and the United States on the other. The United States had to protect it, and Japan gained economically, both from America's wars in Korea and Vietnam, and from keeping its defence expenditure relatively low at 1 per cent of GDP. But post-Cold War, this insulated position broke down, leaving Japan more exposed and having to worry about whether the United States would seek to accommodate China at Japan's expense.

Japan has therefore focused on maintaining the bilateral alliance with the United States. It has steadily, but incrementally, strengthened its commitment to the alliance by building a capable navy and coast guard, putting significant resources into US-led ballistic missile defence technologies, and inching away from the constraints imposed by a strict interpretation of article 9 of its constitution (Pempel, 2011: 266–73; Hagström, 2015: 130–2). Japan has slowly extended the ways in which its armed forces can be used, and increased its interoperability with US forces in the western Pacific. For its part, the United States has affirmed that the treaty covers the Senkaku/Diaoyu islands, which are controlled by Japan but claimed by China. Japan had a hard time during the 1990s, when some in the United States saw Japan as more of a challenger than an ally, but once China's rise took off Japan's relations with the United States became easier as China increasingly occupied the challenging power role in US eyes. The rise of concern about North Korea's nuclear programme since the early 1990s has also provided a shared interest between Japan and the United States. This has been strengthening recently as North Korea closed in on obtaining the capability to back up its loud and frequent threats to hit the United States itself with nuclear strikes. But in common with many other Asian states, Japan faces the dilemma of diverging economic and security interests, with the former more dependent on China, and the latter more on the United States. The cancellation of the Trans-Pacific Partnership (TPP) by President Trump has heightened this dilemma by destroying the main economic pillar of the US pivot to Asia. Along with other signatories, Japan is trying to revive the TPP without the United States, hoping to keep it open for US membership should America's post-Trump leadership take a different view. The threats from North Korea and China, and the ambivalence of Trump about US commitments, also raise the question for Japan about whether or not it should follow Britain and France in acquiring its own nuclear weapons.

India

During the Cold War, India was pretty clearly both a regional power, and a part of the Third World. But with its economic reforms in the early 1990s, its nuclear weapon tests in 1998, and its membership in the BRICS, India moved quickly into the ranks of the great powers. In doing so it maintained something of its Cold War tradition of neutralism.

It kept Russia as its principal arms supplier, and took a wary view of the rising China to the north, with which it had both active border disputes, and a more general power rivalry in South and East Asia (Ladwig, 2009; Rehman, 2009; Buzan, 2012). Since the late 1990s, the United States has continued to strengthen its ties with India (Paul, 2010: 17–18), and this has meant that India's desire to be accepted as a great power at the global level has made substantial advances. India's status as an NWS has been resolved substantially by its civil nuclear deal with the United States in 2005, and this is a key reinforcement for its claim to recognition as a great power (Pant, 2009: 276). By 2017 the United States was quite openly cultivating relations with India both as a fellow democracy (shared values – ironically, a factor for which India got little credit from the United States during the Cold War) and as a balance against the growing weight of China in Asia. India, though, has more interest in hedging against China than in openly balancing against it. Unless China becomes more openly aggressive against it, India seems likely to continue playing a middle-ground game. Like many other Asian states, it does not want to be drawn into a US–China Cold War. Yet neither does it want to face Chinese pressure alone. Part of its strategy was to cultivate strategic partnerships with Japan, Vietnam, Australia, and others in the region looking to hedge against China.

In sum, within the structure of one superpower and several great powers, the great powers were increasingly divided in whether they supported or opposed the United States. China and Russia had moved clearly into opposition, and consolidated this in a strategic partnership. Some in China were calling for the abandonment of its 'no alliances' policy to deepen this relationship (Zhang, F., 2012b; Yan, 2014). At the time of writing it was not yet clear how much damage the Trump administration would do in weakening US alliances with Japan and Europe. Neither Japan nor Europe wanted such a break, but both were having to contemplate the possibility of it. India preferred to maintain its independence in the middle ground so long as circumstances allowed it to. With the United States under Trump rapidly burning the remains of the international social capital it had accumulated since 1945, the core seemed to be drifting towards a system of no superpowers and several great powers. The United States was still the strongest power, but seemed to be losing not only the relative material strength, but also the will, to continue for much longer as a superpower. China was getting stronger, but had little political capital, and as so many substantial states were also rising (Zakaria, 2009; Stuenkel, 2016), power was becoming too diffuse to allow any state to be a superpower (Buzan, 2011; Kupchan, 2012; Buzan and Lawson, 2015a: 273–304). Unlike during the Cold War, the leading powers were now all capitalist, which considerably narrowed the ideological bandwidth of GIS. But this economic convergence did not produce political convergence around liberal democracy. Instead, several varieties of capitalism emerged within political arrangements ranging across the board from liberal democracy to deep authoritarianism (Jackson and Deeg, 2006; Witt, 2010; McNally, 2013; Buzan and Lawson, 2014b). More on all this in Chapter 9.

Alongside this decentring of power, and intertwined with it, was the blurring, or even breakdown, of the previously fairly clear boundary between core and periphery. As set out in Chapter 1, that boundary had emerged during the nineteenth century when a small group of states (Western Europe, North America, Russia and Japan) had successfully acquired the revolutions of modernity, and opened up a big power gap between themselves and everyone else. Between the First World War and the end of the Cold War, only a handful of fairly small states – the Asian Tigers: South Korea, Taiwan, Hong Kong and Singapore – had made this leap and joined the core, though China was clearly gathering steam to join them. But from the 1990s, countries that were still officially classified by the UN as developing countries began to move into the ranks of the great powers, most obviously China and India. More broadly, rising powers started to play on the global stage not as Third World countries, playing against the core from the periphery, but more like core states. One early marker of the more general blurring between core and periphery was the admission of Mexico and South Korea into the OECD club of developed states during the mid-1990s. Another was the formation of the Group of 20 (G20) in 1999, following the financial crisis of 1997–8 in East Asia. As well as the usual Western states and Japan, the G20 included Argentina, Brazil, China, India, Indonesia, Mexico, Russia, Saudi Arabia, South Africa, South Korea and Turkey, expanding the club to include rising middle-income states. But perhaps the key turning point of this development came early after the onset of a global economic crisis in 2008 (on which more below). In 2009, the G20 took over from the G8 as the main forum for global economic management. In 2010, Brazil and Turkey attempted to broker a nuclear deal with Iran. And in 2009–10 the BRICS set themselves up as an active diplomatic group.

These changes can be understood in a short-term perspective in part as consequences of globalisation and Neoliberalism integrating the planetary economy ever more tightly. Within that, they can also be understood as responses to the systemic financial crises that are a periodic feature of capitalist systems, and which required wider participation if they were to be successfully handled. They can also be understood in a longer perspective as an important stage in the unfolding of modernity that took off during the nineteenth century. The initial sharp division between core and periphery generated at that time, and lasting through most of the twentieth century, was finally breaking down as more and more states and societies were finding pathways to modernity that were sustainable within their cultures. This meant that the early modernisers, the West, Russia and Japan, were beginning to lose the dominant position in the world that they had held since the nineteenth century. Within that, they also pointed towards the erosion of US unipolarity, a process accelerated by the unilateralism of presidents Bush and Trump.

If the core was expanding, this meant that the main dynamics of international relations were moving away from the global political economy of core–periphery, and becoming increasingly about the dynamics of an enlarging core that was decreasingly dominated by the West (Buzan and Lawson, 2015a: 270). And if the core and its dynamics were expanding, that necessarily also meant that the periphery was shrinking in both size and significance.

The Periphery

The end of the Cold War had a mixed impact on security in the Third World. On the one hand, it seemed to create more favourable conditions for stability and development. A particularly transformational event was the peaceful end of the apartheid regime in South Africa, with negotiations starting from 1990 and followed by the election of Nelson Mandela as president of the country in 1994. Other developments included the settlement of Cold War regional conflicts in Southern Africa, South Asia, Central America and Southeast Asia that involved direct or indirect superpower intervention. These included the Geneva Accords (1988) resulting in the Soviet withdrawal from Afghanistan (completed in 1989), the New York Accords (1988) providing for the independence of Namibia and the Chapultepec Agreement (1992) to end the conflict in El Salvador. In Southeast Asia, the 1991 Paris Peace Agreement to end Cambodia's civil war led to the largest ever UN peacebuilding mission to date during 1992–3 to manage the country's peaceful transition to democracy.

On the negative side, the ending of the Cold War was a blow to the Third World in the sense that it took away its principal source of political cohesion (non-alignment), and reduced the room for political manoeuvre that the superpower rivalry had created. The blurring of the boundary with the core consequent on the rise of the rest also decreased the shared interest of the Third World in development. While some Third

World countries remained poor and badly governed, others were finding
the path to wealth and power, and knocking on the door of the economic
and great power clubs of the core. With the rise of China and India, the
demographic weight of the world was shifting away from underdeveloped
states and into middle- and high-income countries. The rhetoric of anti-
colonialism and development remained strong, but decolonisation was
now a fact of an earlier era, and something not personally experienced
by a rapidly growing proportion of Third World people. As others in
the Third World found viable paths to development, it became increasingly difficult for those left behind to continue to blame colonialism for
their poverty and inept government – though that did not stop many
Third World leaders from continuing to do so. Globalisation was putting everyone into the same boat, and as a political movement, the Third
World thus became a shadow of its former self. Nonetheless, ideation-
ally, sentiments against the West remained strong within the academic
and activist community, with a new wave of Postcolonial IR literature
(discussed in Chapter 8) expanding its focus to issues of racism, economic marginalisation, gender discrimination and so on.

Wars shifted to being more within states than between them, and under
the influence of both Neoliberalism and corruption, so too did inequality.
The ending of the Cold War did not bring an end to interventions from
the core, but took away the element of ideological and military competition: now interventions were mainly Western (more on this below).
Perhaps the key problem for the rump of the Third World was the number
of weak and failed states within it. During the Cold War and decolonisation era, the general expectation had been that the new states would,
with assistance from the core, somehow solve the problem of finding
a stable relationship with modernity. This assumption was bolstered by
the competition between the superpowers to peddle their ideologies and
development models to the Third World (Westad, 2007). As the era of
unipolarity, globalisation and the rise of the rest unfolded, it became
ever clearer that while some postcolonial states had, with varying degrees
of success, managed this transition, many others had not. A portfolio
emerged of weak and failed states that did not seem capable of either
governing, or developing, themselves successfully under the demanding
and highly penetrative conditions of global capitalism. Weak states in
the Third World included Chad, post-Saddam Iraq, Liberia, Mali and
Sierra Leone, with Bosnia and Ukraine in Europe as additional cases.
Failed states included Afghanistan, Democratic Republic of Congo,
Haiti, Somalia, South Sudan and Yemen. The Arab Spring of 2011–13
exposed a widespread fragility in the Middle East, with the overthrow

of governments in Egypt, Libya, Yemen and Tunisia, and the pushing of Libya and Syria into brutal civil wars and failed-state status.

Conflicts in the post-Cold War era exposed the vulnerability of women in the periphery as victims of rape, torture and sexual slavery in conflict areas and expanded the agenda of global security governance. For example, between 250,000 and 500,000 women were raped during the 1994 genocide in Rwanda (Rehn and Sirleaf, 2002: 9). Conflict zones are known for a sharp increase in domestic violence against women as well as trafficking in women. Women and children constitute a disproportionate number of refugees fleeing conflict zones. They are also drafted as combatants. In the Ethiopian conflict that led to the independence of Eritrea in 1993, women made up more than a quarter of the combatants. The Tamil Tigers, now vanquished, also deployed a large number of women as fighters, commandants and suicide squads. Women become targets of rape and sexual violence not only because they serve as a social and cultural symbol, but violence against them may also be undertaken as a deliberate strategy by parties to a conflict with a view to undermine the social fabric of their opponents. One outcome of such atrocities is the growing attention to the role of women in peace and security (Rehn and Sirleaf, 2002: 63). A UN body identified five areas that link women with the peace and security agenda: (1) violence against women and girls; (2) gender inequalities in control over resources; (3) gender inequalities in power and decision-making; (4) women's human rights; and (5) recognition of women (and men) as actors, not victims (Inter-Agency Network on Women and Gender Equality, 1999: 1). A milestone in advancing measures to address these issues was the adoption by the UNSC of resolution 1325 on Women, Peace and Security in 2000. These developments have influenced the Feminist IR and Security Studies agenda, which will be discussed in Chapter 8.

Despite the persistence of violence, the outlook for security and stability in the periphery has not been only bleak. The overall decline of armed conflicts in the periphery was a principal reason why the initial post-Cold War period saw a significant drop in the incidence of armed conflicts around the world (University of British Columbia, 2005). But this trend has not been linear. The number of armed conflicts (conflicts with at least 25 battle-related deaths where one of the parties was a state) fell from 51 in 1991 (the peak year for armed conflicts in post-Cold war era) to 31 in 2010; the year 2014 saw an upsurge, with a total of 40 armed conflicts. Conflicts claiming more than 1,000 lives, defined as wars, have declined from 16 in 1988 to 7 in 2013, but increased to 11 in 2014 (Pettersson and Wallensteen, 2015: 536, 539). Yet armed conflicts claimed relatively fewer lives since the end of the Cold War than anytime during the twentieth century (Pettersson and Wallensteen, 2015: 536).

The periphery was also affected by the expansion and decline of democracy in the post-Cold War period. Among the most notable cases of democratic transition are Indonesia, the world's fourth most populous country and the largest Muslim-majority state, after the fall of Suharto in 1998, and Myanmar (since 2011). But the so-called fourth wave of democratisation that saw the number of democracies nearly double after the end of the Cold War peaked by 2000 (Micklethwait and Wooldridge, 2014), and it faced further setbacks with the unfulfilled promise of the Arab Spring and reversals and backslidings in Egypt, Thailand and Myanmar.

Another major trend in the periphery was the proliferation of regional institutions and the expansion of their functions, which might have offset to some degree the decline of Third World solidarity. The highly sovereignty-bound OAU was replaced by the African Union (AU) (2000) with a mission for humanitarian intervention. The Southern African Development Community was created in 1992 with the membership of post-apartheid South Africa. The emergence of region-wide organisations in the Asia-Pacific began with the creation of the Asia-Pacific Economic Cooperation in 1989 and continued with the ASEAN Regional Forum (1994), the East Asia Summit (2005) and the SCO (2001). Regionalism in the periphery has expanded its scope beyond trade and security to addressing transnational challenges such as financial crises and climate change, although with mixed results.

Despite its mixed fortunes in terms of stability and cooperation, and facing the uneven impact of globalisation, the periphery remained central to the politics of GIS because of the ways in which globalisation entangled core and periphery in a variety of increasingly important shared fates. The Third World declined as a collective actor, but that was because many of its members were transitioning into the core as part of the rise of the rest. Globalisation remained strong, but also deepened and widened as a key structural feature of GIS. After the 1990s, unipolarity weakened, and GIS increasingly looked less like one superpower and several great powers, and more like several great powers, albeit with some much stronger than others. In this context, it was the interactions and interdependencies between periphery and core, and the blurring of the boundary between them, that increasingly set the agenda of GIS in the twenty-first century. Although, as noted above, some quite deep geopolitical rivalries still existed between the great powers, these were increasingly accompanied by a set of shared-fate threats that required collective action.

Core–Periphery Relations as Shared Fates

The set of shared-fate issues between core and periphery that increasingly comprised the political agenda of GIS are: the renewed proliferation of nuclear weapons, terrorism, migration, intervention, global economic management, environmental stewardship and cybersecurity. These issues are often entangled with each other in complex ways, and in what follows we review each briefly.

Resurgence of Nuclear Proliferation

During the Cold War, the proliferation of nuclear weapons was one of the few areas of agreement between the United States and the Soviet Union. The superpowers had their own interest in keeping the club of NWSs as small as possible, but inasmuch as more fingers on more triggers raised the probability of nuclear war, there was also a powerful and recognised systemic interest in non-proliferation for GIS as a whole. Around the end of the Cold War it seemed that nuclear proliferation had been more or less contained. South Africa had dismantled its small, secret stock; Russia had taken control over the former Soviet arsenal left behind in the Ukraine and elsewhere; and Brazil and Argentina had shelved their rival nuclear programmes. But during the 1990s, this issue once again became prominent.

One cause was would-be great powers adding nuclear adornments to their claims for recognition. But this applied only to India, which was thus a special case that did not threaten to open up proliferation to all and sundry. During the 1990s, India's claims for great power status were increasingly being recognised, and since each of the five permanent members of the UNSC are NWSs, that made India's move acceptable (Buzan, 2018). India's nuclear weapons tests in 1998 led fairly quickly to the United States brokering a workaround with India to bypass its legal exclusion from the group of NWSs in the Non-Proliferation Treaty. As noted above, this deal was agreed in 2005, and implemented in 2008–9. It cemented India's status as an NWS, and was a further reinforcement for its claim to recognition as a great power (Pant, 2009: 276).

The more worrying concern, at least to the United States, was attempts by some states to acquire nuclear weapons as a deterrent against US intervention against them (D. Smith, 2006). During the Clinton administration, the term 'rogue states' was applied to Cuba, Iran, Iraq, Libya and North Korea, and the subsequent Bush administration used the term 'axis of evil' in a similar vein. These states rightly felt threatened by the United States during its unipolar and unilateralist heyday. Cuba did not seek nuclear weapons, but the others did. By 2003, Libya had given up its attempt to develop a nuclear weapons programme, but North Korea, Iran and Iraq had not, and Pakistan used its fear of neighbouring India as a reason to conduct nuclear weapons tests in 1998. A grim twist to the Pakistan story was how the father of Pakistan's nuclear weapons programme, Abdul Qadeer Khan, had operated a black-market network in nuclear technology during the 1980s and 1990s. He is thought to have passed significant nuclear plans and technologies to Iran, North Korea and Libya, and possibly also to South Africa and Iraq. Khan's network was linked to middlemen and businesses in over 20 countries. He was arrested, and his network shut down in 2004 (MacCalman, 2016). Saddam's nuclear bluffing was part of the lead-in to the US-led invasion and overthrow of his regime in 2003, though no evidence was found to suggest a substantial programme.

The two key ongoing cases of 'rogue' states aspiring to NWS status are thus Iran and North Korea. Iran's nuclear programme was exposed in 2002, and in 2005–6 it was found to be in violation of safeguards and subjected to sanctions by the UNSC. Iran had succeeded in acquiring technology and expertise sufficient to shorten its lead time to being able to build nuclear weapons. Years of complex negotiations ensued and, in 2015, a nuclear deal was struck between Iran on the one hand, and the United States, China, Russia, Britain, France, Germany and the EU on the other, exchanging Iran's suspension of its weapons programme for lifting of sanctions imposed because of its earlier repeated violations. At the time of writing President Trump had rejected this deal, but it was still holding.

North Korea's case has gone much further. North Korea came under suspicion in 1992–3 as a result of International Atomic Energy Agency inspections. Bush included North Korea in his 2002 'axis of evil' speech, and in 2003 Pyongyang announced its withdrawal from the Non-Proliferation Treaty. In October 2006, North Korea conducted its first nuclear test. It did so after a long period of six-party talks and bargaining among it, China, Japan, Russia, the United States and South Korea failed to prevent it. Pyongyang made its second nuclear test in 2009, and was at the same time conducting regular missile tests. China seemed curiously indifferent to this development, or at least unwilling to take serious measures against its North Korean ally, even though Pyongyang's provocations and inflammatory rhetoric risked both a major military crisis with the United States, and the possibility that Japan and South Korea would eventually feel forced to acquire their own nuclear deterrents. Japan has long had a policy of 'recessed' deterrence: the threat to go nuclear very quickly should it feel seriously threatened militarily.

It has all of the capabilities to enable it to put together deliverable nuclear weapons, probably within a few months (Buzan and Herring, 1998: 50–1, 172–3). China's insouciance continued right up to the time of writing, by which point North Korea was on the brink of having nuclear weapons that it could deliver onto US territory. As noted above, Japan and South Korea were also under rising pressure from North Korea's nuclear threats and capabilities, enhanced by doubts about the US guarantee to defend them arising from both the vulnerability of the United States to North Korea, and the contradictory positions within the Trump administration about alliance guarantees. It was unclear at the time of writing whether anything of substance would emerge from the ongoing talks between Trump and Kim Jong-un, although the prospects for a complete denuclearisation of North Korea resulting from these talks warrants considerable scepticism.

Terrorism

Terrorism was certainly on the international security agenda both during the Cold War and during the 1990s, mainly linked to conflicts in and around the Islamic world. But until the events of 2001, it was a relatively peripheral concern on the agenda of international security (Buzan and Hansen, 2009: 227–55). From the 2001 attacks on New York and Washington by Al Qaeda, the so-called 'global war on terrorism' (GWoT) became arguably the principal focus of global security (Buzan, 2006). Ironically, Al Qaeda had its roots in the US proxy war against the Soviet Union in Afghanistan during the 1980s when the United States armed and backed radical Islamist militias against the Soviet occupation (Westad, 2007: 353–7). Early signals of its activity and intent were the bombing of the World Trade Center in New York in 1993, bombings of US embassies in Tanzania and Uganda in 1998, and the attack on USS *Cole* in Aden in 2000. The 2001 attacks precipitated the US-led invasions of Afghanistan in 2001 and Iraq in 2003, on which more below. It also linked to nuclear proliferation, migration, cybersecurity and global economic management. The United States finally killed Osama bin Laden in May 2011 in his hideout in Pakistan, a supposed ally of the United States. But Al Qaeda had by then already spawned a successor, Islamic State. Islamic State started as an offshoot of Al Qaeda in 1999, participating in the civil war in Iraq following the political chaos in that country left by the 2003 US invasion and subsequent American occupation. It came to prominence in its own right in 2014 when, exploiting the chaos of weak states and civil wars, it was successful in recruiting soldiers and supporters from many countries in the West and in the Islamic world.

It took over large swathes of Iraq and Syria, linking together the civil wars in those countries. NATO began bombing Islamic State in 2014, and Islamic State extended its attacks to Europe, and became active in the civil wars in Libya, taking significant territory in 2014–15, and also in Nigeria, where Boko Haram affiliated to it in 2015.

The key events of international terrorism post-2001 were as follows:

2002	Moscow theatre attack
2002	Bombing of tourists in Bali (Indonesia)
2004	Moscow Metro attack and Beslan School hostages
2004	Madrid train bombings
2005	Bombings of trains and buses in London
2006	Train bombing in Mumbai, India
2008	Attacks in Mumbai
2010	Moscow Metro again
2013	Boston Marathon bombing
2015	Ankara bombings
2015	Paris shootings
2016	Orlando nightclub shooting
2016	Istanbul airport
2016	Nice (France) attack
2016	Berlin Christmas market attack
2017	Westminster Bridge, London Bridge and Borough Market, and Manchester Arena attacks
2017	Barcelona attack
2017	New York attack

There were many other attacks in Indonesia, Iraq, Israel, India, Pakistan, Russia, Turkey and elsewhere, including in China in 2011 (Kashgar) and 2014 (Kunming). Between a few hundred and a few thousand people have been killed each year since the 1970s, with more than double that number of casualties. Terrorism was a threat to all countries, and the priority it was given was as much to do with the potential for much greater harm if nihilistic and ruthless terrorists got their hands on weapons of mass destruction. Concerns about proliferation and terrorism thus to some extent danced in tandem. Terrorism was probably more of a threat to democratic societies than authoritarian ones, because it confronted them with the awful dilemma of how to protect their populations without compromising the openness that they stood for by becoming police states. Authoritarian societies that were already police states did not share this dilemma, though they did have to worry that terrorism would undermine the credibility of their sense of control, and thus their legitimacy.

Migration

Migration had not been a major issue for the core states during the Cold War, but from the 1990s onwards it became an increasing political concern, though mainly for Europe and the United States. Post-Cold War migration was driven by various factors, ranging from the traditional economic migrants looking to better their prospects by moving from poor countries to rich ones, to asylum-seekers fleeing from war, famine or repression. In core–periphery terms, there were elements of the empires striking back, as people from former colonies made their way to their former metropolitan powers as economic migrants: South Asians and Caribbeans to the United Kingdom, Africans and Arabs to France. Informal empire links worked in the same way, with Turks heading for Germany and Latin Americans for the United States. The EU created its own particular migration issue by combining the openness of its single market with expansion into the relatively poor countries of East and Southeast Europe. Although migration from periphery to core attracted the most attention, there was also a lot of South–South migration. Refugees from conflicts, for example, mainly flee either within their own countries (internally displaced) or to neighbouring countries which are often culturally similar to them. As the UN (2016: 16) notes: 'The majority of the international migrants originating from Asia (60 per cent, or 62 million persons), Europe (66 per cent, or 40 million), Oceania (59 per cent, or 1 million) and Africa (52 per cent, or 18 million) live in another country of their major area of origin'.

Migration got onto the security agenda in Europe immediately after the end of the Cold War when the breakup of former Yugoslavia triggered small but brutal wars (Wæver et al., 1993). The early 1990s saw perhaps 300,000 refugees heading for northern Europe. The Kosovo crisis of the late 1990s meant that by 2000 there were perhaps two million people of Balkan origin in the EU, though many Kosovars subsequently returned.

Migration was kept on the European agenda by the cascade of wars and interventions that followed on from the GWoT. A pulse pattern of refugees and returnees from Afghanistan had started with the Soviet invasion and war during the 1980s, and continued with the repressive Taliban regime during the 1990s. Iran and Pakistan took the bulk of them. As of 2014 there were still some 2.5 million Afghans in Iran and Pakistan. But other countries with over 50,000 Afghans were Germany, Tajikistan, the United Kingdom and the United States, plus Canada with 48,000 (IOM, 2014). The number of Afghan asylum-seekers reaching Europe began to accelerate in 2014, rising sharply to nearly three-quarters of a million in 2015–16, creating a particular crisis in Greece where the bulk of the 2014–15 arrivals were concentrated (EU, 2016). Invasion and internal violence also drove a wave of migration from Iraq in 2006. As of 2015, nearly 1.5 million Iraqis lived abroad, approaching 4 per cent of the population. They were widely distributed both in Iraq's neighbours (over half a million), and in Europe (nearly half a million, mostly in northern European countries) and North America (nearly a quarter of a million) (IOM, 2015). Since the outbreak of the civil war in Syria in 2011, the United Nations High Commissioner for Refugees (UNHCR) estimates that 4.8 million Syrians have fled to Turkey, Lebanon, Jordan, Egypt and Iraq, and 6.6 million are internally displaced within Syria. About one million requested asylum to Europe, of which Germany took more than 300,000 applications and Sweden 100,000 (EU, 2016). Syrians, Afghans and Iraqis made up over 88 per cent of the surge of nearly one million arrivals to Greece in 2015 (IOM, 2017: 12).

Looking at the migration issue more in aggregate, although the number of people residing in a country other than their country of birth reached 244 million in 2015, up by 41 per cent since 2000, migrants as a proportion of the global population were fairly constant at around 3 per cent over the last two decades (IOM, 2017: 5). South–South migration is slightly higher than South–North migration, with North–North migration being about two-thirds the size, and North–South migration being one-seventh of South–North (IOM, 2017: 7). Developing regions hosted 86 per cent of the world's refugees (12.4 million persons), the highest value in more than two decades. The least developed countries provided asylum to 3.6 million refugees, or 25 per cent of the global total. In 2014, Turkey became the country hosting the largest number of refugees worldwide, with 1.6 million refugees. Turkey was followed by Pakistan (1.5 million), Lebanon (1.2 million), the Islamic Republic of Iran (1 million), Ethiopia and Jordan (0.7 million each). More than half (53 per cent) of refugees under UNHCR's mandate come from just three countries: Syria (3.9 million), Afghanistan (2.6 million) and Somalia (1.1 million) (UN, 2016: 9).

Migration had definite upsides: 'remittances sent by international migrants back to their families in origin countries amounted to USD 581 billion in 2015', most of this going to low- and middle-income economies for which remittance inflows measured three times more than foreign aid received by such countries in the same year (IOM, 2017: 15). But when flows were large, and either sudden or sustained, it created huge stresses on the receiving societies. By 2015, the EU was cracking under the strain of migrant flows across the Mediterranean. In 2016, fear of migration was a significant issue in both the vote for Brexit in the United Kingdom, and the election of Trump in the United States. Migration had strong links to war and intervention in both core and periphery. Fears over the identity implications of mass flows of people of different cultures raised identity issues that empowered right-wing populists in many Western countries. Migration also linked powerfully to terrorism, and the fear that hidden among the flows of asylum seekers and economic migrants were terrorists bent on attacking the host countries from the inside.

Interventions

As should by now be apparent, interventions were another key issue entangling core and periphery, with ramifications for nuclear proliferation, terrorism and migration. Initially, there was a shift from the competitive interventions of the Cold War, to Western-driven ones in the 1990s and noughties. But increasingly the pattern returned to competitive intervention, most obviously in Syria after 2011. These interventions were sometimes on national security grounds into 'rogue' states that were thought to threaten the West (initially Afghanistan and Iraq), and sometimes on human security grounds into other people's civil wars (former Yugoslavia, Libya, Syria and, after the initial interventions, also Afghanistan and Iraq).

The breakup of Yugoslavia into several states in 1991 resulted in war in Croatia between Serbs and Croats in 1991–2. When Bosnia-Herzegovina seceded in 1992, the Bosnian war with Serbia began. In 1992–3, NATO got drawn into the war, initially with monitoring operations, and then enforcing UNSC-mandated sanctions and no-fly zone resolutions (UNSC resolutions 713, 757, 781). In 1993–4, NATO provided air support for the UN Protection Force; and in 1995 it conducted heavy bombing attacks on Serbia. After the Drayton Accords of 1995, NATO provided peacekeeping forces which were eventually incorporated into the Stabilization Force. This was followed by a secessionist war between the Republic of Yugoslavia and Kosovo rebels, which emerged in the mid-1990s and intensified in 1998–9. NATO intervened on humanitarian grounds in March–June 1999 with a bombing campaign against Serbia, done without UNSC authorisation because Russia and China would have blocked it. Kosovo seceded from Serbia in 2008 with Western support, but it was not recognised by Russia or China.

The 2001 intervention into Afghanistan had been brewing since the mid-1990s, when the Taliban, backed by Pakistan and Saudi Arabia, defeated the warlords who had taken over after the Soviet withdrawal, and seized Kabul. Having been driven out of Sudan, Osama bin Laden moved his Al Qaeda operation to Afghanistan, helping the Taliban in their ongoing civil war against the Tajik and Uzbek warlords of the Northern

Alliance. Bin Laden was already wanted by the United States because of his involvement in the 1998 bombings of US embassies in Tanzania and Uganda. Taliban-ruled Afghanistan become the first target of George W. Bush's GWoT, because it hosted bin Laden and Al Qaeda. At first bin Laden denied responsibility for the 9/11 attacks on New York and Washington, but claimed it later in 2004. Initially, the US intervention was successful, quickly defeating the Taliban in 2001–2 and disrupting the bases and operations of Al Qaeda in Afghanistan. The United States installed a government in Kabul, and NATO took an increasing role in the whole operation. But then, in something of a replay of the Soviet experience in Afghanistan during the 1980s, the United States found itself in an expensive and fruitless quagmire defined by weak, corrupt and ineffective governments in Kabul, and ruthless tribal and Islamic insurgencies that were well-motivated and well-armed, and had outside support. Like the Soviet Union, the United States was able to win battles, but not create either a government capable of legitimately ruling the whole country, or an Afghan army capable of either winning the war or holding territory. The Taliban and other, mainly Islamist, groups have waged a durable and effective guerrilla war against both NATO forces and the Afghan government in Kabul. They can mount attacks almost anywhere, and have succeeded in occupying substantial parts of the country. Despite the formal ending of the NATO intervention in 2014, this war still drags on painfully and expensively, with no obvious exit for US forces that will not hand the country back to the Taliban.

Having defeated, but not overthrown, Saddam in 1990–1, the United States returned to the job in 2003. The rationale for this intervention linked both to the GWoT and alleged Iraqi nuclear weapons, though neither charge was ever substantiated. Saddam's army was quickly defeated by a US- and UK-led coalition, and subsequently disbanded. Weak Iraqi governments exacerbated divisions between Shi'as and Sunnis, and created doubt about whether the Iraqi state could be held together, or would split into Sunni, Shi'a and Kurdish territories. The Coalition Provisional Authority which governed the country in 2003–4 was largely incompetent, and its banning of Baath Party members from government provided the insurgents with a useful supply of trained and alienated recruits. A gruelling insurgency against US and allied forces started to grow almost immediately. A US troop surge in 2007 held the line, followed by winding down in 2011, then a re-engagement with the Islamic State offensive from 2014. The war deepened US hostility to Iran, which supported the Shi'a side in both Iraq and Syria, adding into the picture another dimension to the overall US engagement in the Middle East on the side of Israel and Saudi Arabia. Saddam's Iraq had been supported and armed by the West and by the Soviet Union against Iran during the 1980s, following Khomeini's Islamic revolution in Iran in 1979. Naive American optimism about the ease of democratisation was reflected both in their name for the military operation against Saddam: 'Operation Iraqi Freedom'; and in the relatively small occupation force that Defense Secretary Donald Rumsfeld thought would suffice after the overthrow of Saddam. Hope for this quickly evaporated in the face of multiple armed insurgents, fractious and often authoritarian national politics, and the widespread influence of armed and authoritarian Islamists. Although the Iraq war was justified in the name of counter-terrorism and non-proliferation, a good case could be made that it greatly exacerbated both problems. It served as an excellent recruiting sergeant and training ground for terrorist groups, and helped to convince the North Korean leadership that they had better accelerate their nuclear weapon programme if they wanted to avoid the fate of Saddam.

NATO also led an intervention into the Libyan civil war in 2011. This was mainly an air campaign, and included non-NATO countries such as Qatar, the United Arab Emirates and Sweden. The Arab League backed a no-fly zone on humanitarian grounds. The original UN-mandated purpose in UNSC resolution 1973 was humanitarian, but NATO ended up pursuing regime change and the toppling of Muammar Gaddafi. Russia and China abstained on resolution 1973, and were subsequently critical of the intervention for violating the idea of Responsibility to Protect (R2P) and using it for regime change.

The return to competitive intervention foreshadowed by this split turned up during the Syrian civil war triggered by the Arab Spring of 2011. Harsh government repression of protesters quickly evolved into a brutal, multi-sided conflict. Iran, and the Hezbollah militia supported by it, both backed the Assad government, as did Russia. Saudi Arabia and the United States supported some of the anti-Assad groups, as did Turkey. A variety of ethnic and religious militias fought both the government and each other, some looking to replace the government, others, such as the Kurds, looking for autonomy and their own territory. The breakdown of a UN-brokered ceasefire in 2012 led to full-scale civil war by 2013, with more moderate rebel forces and Islamic State fighting both each other and the government. Islamic State mounted a major offensive in Syria in 2013, and by 2014 controlled perhaps a third of Syrian territory and much of its oil. In 2014, Turkey got involved against both Islamic State and the Kurds, and the United States started air strikes against Islamic State. Islamic State was nonetheless successful in holding and expanding its territory in 2015. Russia intervened with air strikes in September 2015 against both Islamic State and other anti-Assad militias. France made air strikes against Islamic State in response to terrorist attacks in Paris, and Britain also made air strikes. This extraordinarily messy conflict contained elements of a proxy war between the United States and Russia despite their cooperation on a largely failed truce in 2016. Turkey invaded Syria in August 2016 to take on both Islamic State and the Kurds. In 2017 the United States made direct air attacks on Syrian government forces in response to the use of chemical weapons. The Syrian civil war linked into the Iraq one via the territorial gains of Islamic State. Islamic State captured Mosul and much else in Iraq, taking advantage of the political split between Sunnis and Shi'as in post-Saddam Iraq. By 2015 Islamic State controlled substantial areas of western Iraq and eastern Syria, constituting a coherent territory with the capital of its so-called caliphate in Raqqa. Major counter-attacks eroded most of this by late 2017, including the loss of Mosul in July 2017.

Global Economic Management

Core and periphery have been entangled in a single global economy since the nineteenth century, and their increased merging in terms of global economic management was already apparent in the story of the G20 told above. There are also clear spillovers between the economic sector and other of the shared fates linking core and periphery, for example: economic inequality was one of the drivers of migration; and the imposition of sanctions relating to nuclear proliferation and terrorism were derogations from the normal rules of trade and finance. The shared fate of core and periphery in the global economy during this period was manifested by two developments: economic crises and the reshaping of economic inequality.

Periodic economic crises have been a feature of industrial capitalism since the nineteenth century, so in one sense fit a known pattern rather than being something new. In recent times, these crises have mainly originated from financial liberalisation, and the consequent propensity of the global economy to generate debt crises through excessive and unwise lending. An earlier crisis of this kind had hit Latin America during the 1980s, and in 1997 something similar happened in East Asia where a combination of high indebtedness from excess borrowing, plus hot money fluidity, led to a collapse in economic confidence and currencies in East Asia, a sharp recession, and fears of global spread. China gained some standing in this crisis by not devaluing the RMB. Indonesia, South Korea and Thailand were particularly hard hit, and the crisis was contained in part by a USD 120 billion IMF bailout.

A much bigger, longer and more consequential financial crisis hit in 2008. It spread from a US subprime mortgage crisis of 2007 that left many banks holding large enough amounts of devalued or worthless financial instruments to make them insolvent. The consequence was a sharp shrinkage of liquidity in the banking system overall, and a sharp reduction of lending. The collapse of Lehman Brothers in 2008 was followed by many state-funded bank rescues and huge stimulus packages. In 2008, China launched a stimulus package of USD 586 billion, followed shortly after in 2009 by a US one of USD 787 billion (Skidelsky, 2009: 18). A general shrinkage of economic activity led to the great recession of 2008–12 and to the related 2009–14 European debt crisis within the Eurozone, mainly affecting Greece, Portugal, Ireland, Spain and Cyprus. This caused severe unemployment and financial constraint, and required governments to resort to massive quantitative easing and sustained low interest rates.

In many ways, this was a classic crisis of financial liberalisation. The lure of deregulating finance is constantly present in the system because it allows an expansion of the amount of credit that can be leveraged off any given stock of capital. More credit increases the possibilities for investment, consumption and growth fuelled by those extra resources. So long as people believe that the credit system is stable, then the extra resources generated by expanding credit are real and useable. The danger is that nobody knows how far such leverage can be pushed, and nobody wants to be the first to exit from what is an extremely profitable activity. But when the ratio between actual capital and the amount of credit extended from it becomes too high, then confidence breaks, causing a massive, rapid and painful implosion of liquidity and credit. Complex financial innovations, risky loans and predatory profit-taking erode the credibility of the system, and some trigger (in the 2008 case, the US subprime mortgage fiasco) reveals the bubble, and causes a rapid collapse of confidence. Robert Skidelsky (2009: 1–28) and Martin Wolf (2014), both set out how this crisis unfolded along these lines, and both argue that such crises are caused by basic weaknesses in economic theory, especially the under-appreciation of financial risk – i.e. such crises are *internal* to the capitalist system, not caused by exogenous shocks. Just as the expansion of credit fuels the real economy, so its contraction shrinks it, causing pain across core and periphery from resource exporters to manufacturing heartlands.

In the case of the 2008 crisis, one of the key political effects was to expose the growing inequality between rich and poor that was being generated by the global capitalist system. While the wealth differentials *between* countries were in significant ways becoming less as a result of the spreading of development and modernity, *within* countries the differentials between rich and poor were rising. According to the World Bank (2016: 9–12), the Gini coefficient for inequality *among* countries fell steadily from 0.80 in 1988 to 0.65 in 2013, while for inequality *within* countries it rose sharply during the 1990s, tending to level off in the noughties. As the OECD (2011: 22) reports: 'The Gini coefficient ... stood at an average of 0.29 in OECD countries in the mid-1980s. By the late 2000s, however, it had increased by almost 10% to 0.316'. The *Financial Times* (Waldau and Mitchell, 2016) reported that the Gini coefficient for China was 0.49, up from around 0.3 in the 1980s, and significantly higher than the comparable figure for the United States (0.41). The Gini coefficient for Russia in 2013 was 0.40, and for India 0.34 (UNDP, 2016). For the 27 EU countries, the Gini coefficient for 2016 was 3.1 (Eurostat, 2017). The rise of the rest was beginning to close the inequality gap between the developed few and the underdeveloped many that had opened up during the nineteenth century. But within many countries, most notably the United States, China and Russia, the gap between the very rich and the rest had opened up sharply.

In combination, the great recession starting in 2008 and the seeming breakdown in the social contract of capitalism reflected in rising inequality opened up a crisis of legitimacy. The opening shots in this crisis came with the vote for Brexit and the election of Trump in 2016. Rapid advances in the development of artificial intelligence (AI), and their application to production, looked set to extend this crisis further by eroding the legitimacy of capitalism both within countries (adding fear of permanent unemployment to resentments about inequality), and between them (threatening the established pattern of periphery development through cheap labour and export-led growth).

Environmental Stewardship

Environmental stewardship is perhaps the ultimate shared-fate issue linking core and periphery. Regardless of differences in wealth, power and culture, all human beings share one planet, and if that physical environment is changed in certain ways, or damaged, we all suffer the consequences. Threats to the planetary environment come in many forms, some natural (earthquakes, volcanoes, space rocks, climate cycles, plagues) and some generated by humans (nuclear winter, engineered diseases, pollution of land, sea and air). Some issues are a mix, such as when human farming practices, for example creating large concentrations of animals, both accelerate the evolution of bacteria and viruses, and increase the possibility of crossover from animals to humans (e.g. bird flu, camel flu). Humans have acquired capabilities to deal with some of the natural threats, but at the same time their activities are beginning to geo-engineer the planet in unintended and often harmful ways. Human effects include: acidifying and warming the oceans; changing the chemical composition of the atmosphere in ways that amplify its greenhouse effect; accelerating the evolution of bacteria and viruses by challenging them with drugs; and narrowing the diversity of the biosphere by pushing many species to extinction. There is a strong link between environmental stewardship and development, because it is often economic activities that generate environmental damage. This link raises the political dilemma of putting development and environmental stewardship at odds with each other unless ways can be found to make development sustainable. We look briefly at two specific issues – climate change and global disease control – to get the flavour of this shared fate.

Climate change is both a natural cycle of warm and cold periods whose operation is clearly observable in the historical record, but whose causes are imperfectly understood; and a human-generated threat driven by the pumping of both greenhouse gases and particulates into the atmosphere. As Robert Falkner and Barry Buzan (2017) argue, the norm of environmental stewardship had a long gestation stretching back to the nineteenth century. But it was only in the post-Cold War decades that this norm made the breakthrough to becoming an institution of GIS. The Stockholm Conference in 1972 generated global political awareness of the issues, and the norm, activating both civil society and domestic political action in some leading states. The 1992 Rio Conference began the process of reconciling what was still mainly a Western norm of environmental stewardship with concerns of the Third World about development. But while Rio successfully globalised the norm, it did not solve the problem of allocating responsibility to act on it, particularly with the problem of atmospheric pollution driving climate change.

The principle of 'common but differentiated responsibilities' for dealing with greenhouse gases was established at Rio, and effectively meant that the developed states carried nearly all of the burden of doing something, while the developing countries could pursue development without environmental responsibility. That impasse crippled the Copenhagen Conference in 2009, with China siding with the developing countries. But it was solved at the Paris Conference in 2015, where it was agreed that voluntary emissions targets would apply to all. This solution traded a looser, more voluntary set of commitments for a more universal acceptance of responsibility to act. Similar to the response to the depletion of the ozone layer in the late 1980s, when the Montreal Protocol banned the production of ozone-depleting chemicals (Benedick, 1991), the rise of environmental stewardship to the status of a new primary institution of GIS signalled that when faced with pressing shared-fate issues, international society could find significant collective responses despite the political, economic and cultural differences among its members.

Global disease control has a long history, but a particular landmark was in 2000, when for the first time the UNSC acknowledged the link between health and security by declaring the HIV/AIDS pandemic as 'a risk to security and stability' in resolution 1308 (Poku, 2013: 529; Deloffre, 2014). Since the end of the Cold War, increasing interaction capacity, and the integration of China and the successor states to the former Soviet Union into the global economy, has, for better and for worse, put people everywhere into more intimate contact with each other through trade, travel and migration. This has raised global concerns about disease control. Since the 1990s, the possibility that Avian flu would give rise to strains capable of infecting people on a large scale has been active, especially in East Asia. Human cases have turned up occasionally, and large numbers of infected birds have been periodically culled. Given the ease with which flu can spread, and the high death rates associated with some strains, this remains a concern. The flu pandemic that followed the First World War almost certainly killed more people than did the war itself.

Although there has as yet been no pandemic outbreak on the scale of 1918–20, there have been several events sufficient to maintain the level of collective concern. In 2002–3 there was an outbreak of severe acute respiratory syndrome, mainly in China, with several thousand cases and hundreds of deaths. In Saudi Arabia (2014) and South Korea (2015) there were small outbreaks of Middle East respiratory syndrome, also known as camel flu. In 2013–16 there was a quite substantial outbreak of the Ebola virus disease in West Africa. The first alert regarding the outbreak was from the World Health Organization (WHO) in March 2014, though no decisive actions were taken by GIS at that time. It turned out to be the largest, longest and most severe and complex outbreak of the virus since it was discovered in 1976. When the crisis was at its peak in September 2014, weekly cases reached almost 1,000 (WHO, 2014; Santos et al., 2015). When WHO officially declared it over on 14 January 2016, the crisis had lasted about two years, during which time more than 28,600 people were infected with the virus and more than 11,300 lives were lost, mostly in Guinea, Liberia and Sierra Leone (WHO, 2016). There was a considerable international response to contain the disease, with the United States and China sending military personnel to work alongside non-state actors such as Médecins Sans Frontières. The UNSC adopted resolution 2177 on 18 September 2014, declaring that the outbreak of Ebola in Africa constituted 'a threat to international peace and security', pushing the scale and depth of securitisation of health to an unprecedented level (Snyder, 2014). Although humankind has not yet been put to a severe twenty-first century test on this shared fate, its existence is acknowledged in the Global Outbreak Alert and Response Network established in 2000 to link together many public and private organisations that work to observe and respond to threatening epidemics.

Cybersecurity

A somewhat more complicated shared-fate issue increasingly goes under the label of cybersecurity (Hansen and Nissenbaum, 2009). Cybersecurity is complicated because it is both a shared fate or common security issue (to the extent that the global economy and global social networks depend on the efficient functioning of the internet as a global system), and a divisible fate or national security issue (to the extent that both states and non-state actors have the means and the incentives to attack each other through the internet, creating targeted disruptions). The national security aspect makes cyberwar a crucial concern (Singer and Friedman, 2014). Estonia, Georgia, Iran, the United States and China are among the many states that have suffered such attacks. Attacks are often difficult to source, and may come from other states or from non-state actors.

Cybersecurity arises as a shared-fate issue because of the way in which the rise of the internet has followed on from the telegraph, telephone and radio as the next phase of globally integrated communication. The internet has brought high volume, high speed, low-cost communications, and access to information, to vast numbers of people around the world. Starting from military communication facilities in the 1960s, the internet became a network of networks during the 1980s, and took off into mass communications with the introduction of the worldwide web format in 1993. Perhaps 150 million people were online by the late 1990s (Christensen, 1998). Estimates suggest that well over two billion people were online by 2013, and that internet traffic was growing at a rate of 50 per cent per year (Mulgan, 2013: 46). The internet does not increase the range or the speed of communication over earlier electronic means. But by lowering costs the internet has heightened both access to and the volume of communication, and in myriad and sometimes important ways changed the content and purpose of communication. In doing so, the internet has increased the reach, depth and impact of the communications revolution in ways that could be seen as transformative of the human condition. It is now a global resource whose loss would have a huge impact. But it is also a divisible good whose use links not only to the functioning of the global economy and world society, but also to terrorism, migration and nuclear proliferation.

Conclusion: From Version 1.1 towards Version 1.2 Global International Society

As suggested in the introduction to this chapter, the story of the world since 1989 marks both the high point of the version 1.1 (Western-global) GIS that emerged after 1945, and the opening stages of a clear transition to a version 1.2 (post-Western) GIS. In a longer perspective, this transition marks a move away from both version 1.0 GIS (nineteenth century to 1945) and version 1.1 GIS, both of which were, in different ways centred on the dominance of the West. The transition now underway still keeps the state-centrism of the earlier versions, but moves away from Western dominance towards a post-Western era. As we have shown in this chapter, there is now an increasing diffusion of wealth, power and cultural authority towards deep pluralism in a context of continuing intensification of globalisation and interdependence.

Towards the end of the period covered in this chapter there were clear signs of the overall economic transformation of the periphery. Most dramatic has been the growth of several countries in Asia, led by China and India. The EU Institute for Security Studies (EUISS, 2012) estimates that by 2030, China and India could account for over 34 per cent of the global economy. A report by PricewaterhouseCoopers (2015) predicts that China and India would emerge as the top two economies of the world by 2050, followed by the United States, Indonesia, Brazil, Mexico, Japan, Russia, Nigeria and Germany. If this prediction bears out, seven of the top ten economies of the world will be Non-Western, and out of 32 leading economies in the world by purchasing power parity terms, 20 (not including Japan and Russia) will be from the Non-Western world by 2050.

To be sure, economic development across the periphery is markedly uneven and will remain so. Yet the world is witnessing a more general economic 'rise of the rest' (Zakaria, 2009; Acharya, 2014b: 27–31). According to the UN Development Programme (UNDP, 2013: 2) the Global South's share of the global GDP rose from 33 per cent in 1980 to 45 per cent in 2010. During the same period, their share of world merchandise trade rose from 25 per cent to 47 per cent. The OECD estimates that the Global South could account for 57 per cent of the global GDP by 2060 (Guardian Datablog, 2012). The rise of the rest is also reflected in the growing density of South–South interactions.

According to UNDP (2013: 2), South–South trade has jumped from less than 8 per cent of world merchandise trade in 1980 to over 26 per cent in 2011. And UNCTAD (2015: 5, 8–9) estimates that South–South flows in foreign direct investment now constitute over a third of global flows. It also finds that, in 2015, multinational enterprises (MNEs) from developing Asia (excluding Japan) became the world's largest investing group for the first time, accounting for almost one-third of the world total. Outward investment by Chinese MNEs grew faster than inflows into the country, reaching a new high of USD 116 billion.

The 2008 economic crisis might perhaps serve as the benchmark date for the turning point between version 1.1 and 1.2 GIS, with both the United States and the EU descending into deep crisis, and China, Russia, Turkey and others feeling palpably more confident. The economic crisis has weakened the West materially, and in addition the liberal ideology that underpinned its authority has also eroded. Rising inequality is questioning the compatibility of capitalism and democracy, and US practices in the GWoT have undermined its ability to speak for human rights. Arguably, Trump's United States is beginning to resemble the Cold War Soviet Union in its declining years: militarily strong, though unable to use that strength to much good effect; and increasingly less impressive economically, socially and politically/ideologically.

What we have is a GIS with an expanding core, eroding West-centrism and a shrinking periphery. The liberal teleology is losing credibility, and the votes for Trump and Brexit suggest a looming crisis of capitalism and democracy in the core. The liberal assumption that democracy is the natural and inevitable accompaniment of capitalism is no longer credible, and the CCP is openly challenging it. The opening out into varieties of capitalism naturally opens debate, and provides new concrete examples, of how best to manage the trade-offs between liberty and control, individual and collective interests and rights, prosperity and inequality, and openness and flexibility versus stability. It is not obvious that there will be convergence on a single 'best' model of political economy, or that if such convergence occurred, it would be along classical liberal-democratic lines. If there is to be convergence, it looks like being more towards the middle of the spectrum. While China and India and others have opened up their economies and societies to some extent, the traditionally liberal powers have been forced by economic crisis and migration politics to reassert more state control. Into this mix, the set of transnational, shared-fate issues outlined above is gaining importance over traditional inter-state ones.

Chapter 9 picks up these threads and examines how they might unfold in the decades ahead into a GIS defined by *deep pluralism*.

8   International Relations after 1989

Introduction

In Chapter 6, we argued that IR underwent a second founding. Its institutionalisation widened and deepened; the United States became the core of the discipline (though failing to achieve intellectual hegemony); much from before 1945 was forgotten; and the discipline became more academic, with more subdivision into specialised subjects and approaches. It remained mainly core-centred in its concerns, and much less impacted by decolonisation than by superpower nuclear rivalry. But that said, there were some signs of integration between IR thinking in core and periphery as decolonisation legitimised the anti-colonial and anti-racist perspectives that were previously isolated in the periphery. We looked at the dominance of Neorealism and Neoliberalism (and the Neo-Neo synthesis), and we discussed a variety of challengers to them, some more critical (Marxism, Peace Research, Postcolonialism, Dependency Theory) and some more orthodox (the ES, Liberal IPE).

In this chapter, we follow these stories through, and add to them some new approaches and subdivisions within the discipline such as Critical Theory, Feminism and Constructivism. In elaborating the evolution of the discipline, we take into account Chapter 7's discussion of the growing globalisation of world politics triggered by the end of bipolarity and the so-called 'unipolar moment' of the United States as the sole superpower. This period is ideologically simpler because capitalism (though not democracy) won the Cold War, but it is also marked by complex global power shifts. The United States is briefly dominant, and its alliances remain robust, but then it is increasingly challenged both by other great powers and its own domestic politics. The Third World gets collectively weaker, but some of its members, notably China and India, move into the great power club, and China and Russia align against the United States. The previously clear boundary between core and periphery begins to blur. Mixed in with all this is the rise of complex transnational challenges such as terrorism, crime, human rights and migration, and an array of pressing shared fates including instabilities in the world economy and a variety of environmental threats.

Although 1989 did not mark a transformation of GIS to the same extent as 1945 (Buzan and Lawson, 2014a), we nevertheless argue that during the first decade of the twenty-first century, a shift from version 1.1 to version 1.2 GIS gets underway. The dominance of GIS by the West since the nineteenth century begins visibly to be displaced by a more diffuse distribution of wealth, power and cultural authority, a structure we labelled *deep pluralism* (on which more in Chapter 9). While one cannot always establish a direct or tight correlation between global transformations and the prominence of dissenting theories, we can certainly trace the impact of these ir developments on IR thinking, partly in terms of what kind of issues hold centre stage, partly in how the real-world developments challenge various theoretical approaches and partly in who is doing IR and where. Perhaps most significant from our point of view is how the rise of Non-Western countries and the increasing globalisation of GIS combine to erode the boundary between core and periphery in both ir and IR. That in turn has opened space for voices calling for a greater pluralisation of the field, and fuelling the demand for a Global IR that goes beyond the earlier Critical Theories and draws more than them from the hitherto neglected Postcolonial voices. Although we argue that the core–periphery structure is breaking down, for the sake of continuity we keep the same structure as for previous chapters: institutionalisation and IR thinking in the core and in the periphery.

Institutionalisation

In Chapter 6 we argued that the great expansion of institutionalisation of IR after 1945 was a key element in the case for a second founding for the discipline. The main pattern of academic associations, journals, think tanks and university teaching of IR was set up during the Cold War period, and continues today. But up until 1989, these institutional developments were largely in the core, with only a smattering in the periphery. What has happened in terms of institutionalisation since 1989 is basically a widening and deepening of that pattern, its extension beyond the core into the periphery, and to a significant extent the erosion of the institutional boundaries between core and periphery.

Where institutionalisation had already been established, it continued to widen and deepen, both within the core and beyond it. While the

Table 8.1 *New Academic Associations*

#	Association	Year	Place
1	Nordic International Studies Association	1991	Odense, Denmark
2	European International Studies Association (EISA)	1992	–
3	Finnish International Studies Association	1993	–
4	World International Studies Committee (WISC)	1993	–
5	Central and East European International Studies Association (CEEISA)	1996	Prague
6	Portuguese Political Science Association	1998	Lisbon
7	Russian International Studies Association	1999	Moscow
8	Asian Political and International Studies Associatio	2001	Manila
9	South African Association of Political Studies	2001	Pretoria
10	International Relations Council of Turkey	2004	Istanbul
11	Taiwan International Studies Association	2004	Taipei
12	Brazilian International Relations Association	2005	Belo Horizonte, Brazil
13	Taiwan Association of International Relations	2007	Taipei
14	Turkish International Studies Association	2007	–
15	Korea International Studies Association	2009	Seoul
16	Colombian Network of International Relations	2009	Bogota
17	Polish International Studies Association	2009	Warsaw
18	Association of Internationalists	2009	Paris
19	Chilean Association of International Specialists	2015	Santiago de Chile
20	Philippine International Studies Organization	2015	Manila
21	Kazakhstan International Relations Association	–	–
22	Turkish Political Science Association	–	Istanbul
23	Israeli Association of International Studies	–	–
24	Argentine Federal Council for International Studies	–	Buenos Aires
25	Italian Association of Political Science	–	Trento, Italy
26	Croatian International Studies Association	–	–

United States was fully equipped with academic associations, several new ones were set up in Eastern and Western Europe, and at least 15 more outside the West, mainly in Asia and Latin America (see Table 8.1).

The (North American) ISA still remained by far the biggest and wealthiest of these, as it had been up to 1989. The number of ISA 'sections', representing interests of subject or approach, grew to 30 by 1917, showing the ever-expanding range of interests embodied in IR.[1] ISA's membership had grown to 7,000 by 2017.[2]

---

[1] www.isanet.org/ISA/Sections (Accessed 18 September 2017).
[2] www.isanet.org/ISA/About-ISA/Data/Membership (Accessed 18 September 2017).

Table 8.2 *New IR Journals*

#	Journal	Year	Published by
1	*Security Studies*	1991	
2	*Review of International Political Economy*	1994	
3	*Journal of International and Area Studies*	1994	Seoul National University
4	*Zeitschrift für Internationale Beziehungen*	1994	German Association for Political Science – International Relations section
5	*Global Governance*	1995	Academic Council of the UN System
6	*European Journal of International Relations*	1995	Standing Group on International Relations, European Consortium for Political Research and EISA
7	*International Studies Review*	1999	ISA – taken over from Mershon Center
8	*International Relations of the Asia-Pacific*	2001	JAIR
9	*Yale Journal for International Affairs*	2005	Yale
10	*Asian Security*	2005	
11	*Alternatives*	2005	Centre for the Study of Developing Societies
12	*Foreign Policy Analysis*	2005	ISA
13	*Chinese Journal of International Politics*	2006	Institute of International Relations, Tsinghua University
14	*International Political Sociology*	2007	ISA
15	*International Theory*	2009	ISA
16	*European Journal of International Security*	2016	BISA

At least 16 new journals were launched, enabling Europe and Asia to begin challenging America's near monopoly on the top IR journals commanding the intellectual heights of the discipline (see Table 8.2).

In addition, a wave of new think tanks spread across both core and periphery: 39 in the West (including Japan, South Korea, Israel, Australia and New Zealand), 25 in the Global South, 18 in the former Soviet Union and Eastern Europe, and one in China (see McGann, 2018). The presence of IR courses and research in universities also increased in both core and periphery.[3]

---

[3] It would be difficult to track this development in any reliable way, and it is beyond the scope of this book to do so. The existence of academic associations (see Table 8.1) is a useful proxy for countries where IR is taught, because most of the members of such associations will be university teachers and researchers.

In addition to this very substantial widening and deepening of the institutionalisation of IR, there was a significant breakdown of the division between core and periphery. Many academic associations and think tanks were networked with each other across this divide, and journals increasingly catered to a global IR market. It was important where journals were based and edited, but, for most IR journals, readerships, editorial teams and authors were increasingly global. The bigger IR conferences generally attracted participants from many regions. So, IR was not just putting down roots in more places, but also linking up into an increasingly globalised framework. Perhaps the lead symbols of this development were ISA itself, and WISC, which originated in 1993, adopted a charter in 2002, and began holding regular conferences in 2005. During the late 1980s, ISA made a significant effort to become the global ISA not just by recruiting more foreign members, but by integrating them into its governance structure. This provoked some resistance on the grounds that American IR was already too dominant, and that globalising ISA would strengthen that hegemony. As a consequence, moves got underway to establish the more confederative global body that eventually became WISC. At the same time, however, the sheer size and weight of ISA meant that it became in some senses a *de facto* global body. Its annual conferences were the most convenient place to do global networking, and ISA went out of its way to cooperate with other ISAs and to hold some of its many conferences in other regions, including in Asia and Latin America. As of 2018, ISA had some 75 partner organisations with around a third of those being in Asia, Latin America, the Middle East and Africa.[4] WISC has 24 member organisations, including ISA, and with a similar distribution across the continents.[5] Together, and in their different ways, ISA and WISC are the public face of just how far IR has come in making itself a global discipline. In some ways, these two organisations have carried through the linking up of core and periphery that began with the ISC during the interwar period.

IR Thinking in the Core

As with IR between 1945 and 1989, the story of IR since 1989 will be familiar to most readers, and a lived experience for many. We therefore

---

[4] www.isanet.org/ISA/Partners (Accessed 14 March 2018).
[5] www.wiscnetwork.org/about-wisc/members (Accessed 14 March 2018).

take the same approach as in Chapter 6, linking this familiar story to two themes:

- To what extent and in what ways did the development of IR reflect the main developments in the real world of ir?
- What was the evolving balance within IR between the interests and perspectives of the core, and those of the periphery, and to what extent did this distinction remain significant?

In Chapter 6 we established the theme of diversity and differentiation in IR thinking in the core. That process continues during this period, increasingly merging with the breakdown of the barriers between IR in the core and in the periphery. An important element in this is the development of the internet, which, from the 1990s, made world-wide communication cheaper, faster, easier and more widely available. Although initially concentrated in the core, the internet soon went global, facilitating academic communication and cooperation across the core–periphery boundary. Although the United States remained the biggest centre for IR, and still very influential, the peak of US power in the unipolarity and globalisation of the 1990s was not accompanied by strengthened American intellectual hegemony in IR. Instead, the diversity of the challenges to the Neo-Neo synthesis and positivist interpretations of 'science' both widened and deepened, not just from elsewhere in the core but also increasingly from the periphery, and indeed from within the United States itself. In what follows, we start by looking at how the Neo-Neo synthesis and Security Studies adapted to the post-Cold War world, and then at the challengers to it both old (ES, Peace Research) and new (Constructivism, Feminism, Critical Theory). We end with a look at the third round of IR's 'great debates'.

Realism

Having failed to predict the end of the Cold War, Neorealists entered the 1990s somewhat on the back foot. With the demise of the Soviet Union, what was in front of them was a shift from a bipolar to a unipolar system. But their theory had no place for a unipolar structure, which, according to Realist logic, should be prevented by the balance of power. Perforce, they had to see this unipolarity as a brief transitional moment to be followed by an inevitable return to a multipolar system (Layne, 1993, 2006; Waltz, 1993). Neorealist polarity theory also made no distinction between great powers and superpowers, and found itself poorly placed to conceptualise a world in which the United States was still a super-power, but operating alongside several great powers. Many Neorealists saw multipolarity as less stable and more risky than bipolarity, and so predicted a more turbulent world, especially for Europe and the Global South (Gaddis, 1986: 103–4; Cintra, 1989: 96–7; Mearsheimer, 1990; Hoffmann, 1991: 6) – in Carpenter's (1991) much reused phrase, a 'new world disorder'. But as the US unipolar 'moment' grew ever longer, many Neorealists somehow became comfortable with the idea of a uni-polar power structure despite the fact that it gutted the balance of power as the driving logic of their theory (Huntington, 1999; Kapstein and Mastanduno, 1999; Wohlforth, 1999).

Realism also sprouted some internal differentiations. Led by John Mearsheimer (2001: 402), 'Offensive Realists', seeing states as power maximisers, took on 'Defensive Realists', such as Kenneth Waltz, Robert Jervis (1994, 1999) and Jack Snyder, who maintain that states are security maximisers. This position was fuelled by the rise of China, which Offensive Realists saw as inevitably pointing towards conflict between China and the United States, and therefore the dangers of American engagement with China to bring it into the global economy. Offensive Realists were sceptical about international institutions, arguing that they are

basically a reflection of the distribution of power in the world. They are based on the self-interested calculations of the great powers, and they have no independent effect on state behavior. Realists therefore believe that institutions are not an important cause of peace. They matter only on the margins. (Mearsheimer, 1994/95: 5)

Another variation was so-called 'Neoclassical Realism', which sought to roll back the excessive simplification of Neorealist structural theory by bringing domestic and cognitive factors back into Realist analysis (Lobell, Ripsman and Taliaferro, 2009).

Ironically, the rise of China rescued Neorealists from some of their theoretical contradictions because it enabled them to back away from unipolarity and talk more about 'power transitions' and the possibility of a return to bipolar or multipolar global power structures. During the first and second decades of the twenty-first century, the evidence mounted that America's unipolar moment was drawing to an end. Not only was China rising but also India. Russia, while not a rising power, recovered some of its military capability and most of its antagonism to the West. Thus something like the 'multipolarity' predicted by Neorealists imme-diately after the implosion of the Soviet Union was finally beginning to emerge. Some Realists challenged the idea that multipolar systems were necessarily unstable (Copeland, 2010). While being rescued from the theoretical impossibility of unipolarity, however, Neorealism failed to address the distinction between superpowers and great powers. It was therefore poorly placed to make sense of the emerging world of deep pluralism noted in Chapter 7 and which will be elaborated in Chapter 9. Was this world going to be one of great powers, with the United States declining into that status, and China failing to become a superpower? Or was it going to be a mix of superpowers (United States and China) and great powers (Russia, India, EU, Japan) (Buzan, 2004a)? Because it depended on state-centric assumptions about the international system, Realism was also not well placed to deal with the GWoT, which elevated non-state actors to a main role in war.

International Security Studies

Since the 1980s, but more rapidly after 1989, Strategic Studies and Peace Research had been drifting towards the common ground of security, and the overarching label of International Security Studies (ISS).[6] Neither element entirely surrendered either its identity or its institutions, but the sense of opposition between them lessened, and their research agendas increasingly occupied common ground in the areas of human security and other non-traditional security sectors. At the same time, a diversity of other approaches emerged to complicate what had been a simple binary division: the Copenhagen School, Critical Security Studies, Feminist Security Studies, Postcolonial Security Studies, and Poststructuralist Security Studies.

That the ending of the Cold War had a dramatic effect on ISS is not surprising given its close linkage to day-to-day policy issues. Once the superpower rivalry had become history, the obsessive focus on nuclear deterrence and war quickly evaporated, as did much, but not all, of the concern with the relentless evolution of military technology. Two things filled the void. One was the longstanding concern about nuclear proliferation which had been subordinate to deterrence. The other was a general widening and deepening of the agenda of international security away from the traditional high politics and military issues approach and towards non-military or 'non-traditional' security issues with an

---

[6] For the full story and references supporting this section see Buzan and Hansen (2009: chs. 6–8).

international security perspective. This involved questioning the centrality of the state as the commanding referent object of security. The ending of the Cold War did not reduce the concern about security so much as transform its foundations.

As noted in Chapter 6, the issue of nuclear proliferation goes back in the literature to the 1950s. The countries of concern changed over time, but the arguments for keeping the nuclear club as small as possible and for controlling the links between civilian ('peaceful') and military nuclear technology remained largely the same. Post-Cold War, concern largely focused on what the United States labelled 'rogue states', particularly North Korea, Iran and Iraq (under Saddam), and also, up to a point, Pakistan. As noted, India was close to being accepted as a great power, and was therefore a more legitimate aspirant to NWS status. After the attacks on the United States by Al Qaeda in 2001, worries about proliferation expanded to include terrorist groups, again bringing to the fore ongoing discussions about terrorism that had previously been in the background of the security literature.

The widening and deepening of ISS involved both different ways of thinking about security (deepening) and a wider range of threats and referent objects being treated as security issues. One key approach to deepening was the Copenhagen School, which applied Constructivist approaches to understanding security (Buzan, Wæver and de Wilde, 1998). Rather than taking threats in given material terms, the Copenhagen School looked at the process of *securitisation*, asking how, by whom and why some things were constructed as threats in speech acts, and accepted as such by relevant audiences. Another deepening approach was through Poststructuralism, which questioned whether states mainly pursued security, or also needed an element of external threat in order to maintain their own composition (Campbell, 1998). Constructivists revived the old idea of security communities to look at the positive side of security and not just threats (Adler and Barnett, 1998).

Alongside this deepening was a very substantial widening of the issues defined in security terms. In addition to the traditional concerns about political and military security, debates emerged around environmental security, economic security, human security, identity security, cybersecurity, health security and suchlike. To military and ideological threats were added threats and securitisations from migration, economic instability and inequality, climate change, pollution, disease transmission, attacks on the internet and suchlike. Some of this agenda can be tracked back to environmental and economic security debates already active during the 1970s. But only during the 1990s did these and the other non-traditional issues become mainstream within ISS. Human security gave prominence to people as the key referent object against the state. Postcolonialism and Critical Security Studies questioned national security in the Third World and other contexts in which the state was often the main threat to its citizens. Feminist Security Studies questioned masculinist assumptions within mainstream ISS, and sought to bring women back in as both subjects and objects of security. Many of the non-military threats came in the form of shared-fate issues, thus generating a logic of common security (security with …) alongside the traditional logic of national security (mainly security against …). This new and revamped ISS emerged and consolidated mainly during the 1990s. Two big events then impacted on this new structure: the terrorist attacks on the United States in 2001; and the emergence of China and the recovery of Russia as great power challengers to the United States.

The 9/11 attacks predictably triggered a huge and durable spike in what had up until the late 1990s been the somewhat marginal field of Terrorism Studies. The GWoT more subtly put non-state actors into the heart of traditional thinking about military security. Being mainly non-territorial, non-state actors fell largely outside traditional ways of thinking about deterrence and national security. Up to a point they could be associated with sponsoring states, and this logic underpinned major US-led interventions into Afghanistan and Iraq. The GWoT, like many of the issues on the non-traditional security agenda, tended to dissolve the boundary between domestic and international security.

As it did for Realism, the rise of China and the recovery of Russia as great powers since the beginning of the twenty-first century created increasing pressure to return to the traditional Strategic Studies agenda of the Cold War. The old Cold War-style interest in military security and deterrence never disappeared entirely. But post-Cold War interest in deterrence was largely confined to tense regions such as South Asia and the Middle East. Interest in the ever-unfolding progress of military technology continued throughout, especially in relation to stealth missiles, aircraft and ships; information processing and communications; and defences against ballistic missiles. But this interest was mainly framed in terms of the threat from relatively minor rogue states, and was therefore much less intense than during the Cold War. The rise of China and the recovery of Russia steadily put great power military competition back onto the ISS agenda. Russia is not much more than a significant nuisance. Although somewhat recovered from its nadir in the 1990s, it is a declining power, albeit one still possessing the legacy of advanced military technology from its superpower days. The development of China is much more significant. It is a rising power with increasing technological skills, and the wealth and will to construct itself as a wide-spectrum and formidable military player. India is increasingly also a player in this new great power nuclear game. These developments increasingly put great power deterrence, and concerns about the competition in advanced military technologies, back onto the agenda of ISS, albeit now alongside the wider and deeper agenda that emerged during the 1990s, with migration, health, environment, the world economy and cybersecurity remaining as central security concerns.

In many ways, therefore, the ISS that emerged after the Cold War was much less East–West focused, and considerably more North–South. Up to a point it was also South–South oriented in terms of studying nuclear deterrence at the regional level in South Asia and the Middle East, and regional wars and interventions, particularly in the Middle East. Regional security began to differentiate itself as a distinct topic not solely driven by superpower rivalries (Buzan and Wæver, 2003). Concerns about nuclear proliferation post-Cold War had a mainly North–South orientation, as did the GWoT and its associated wars of intervention led by the United States. Neither of these was now associated with the risk of escalation to great power nuclear war, and the concern with guerrilla war morphed into a wider North–South issue of 'asymmetric war'. Much of the wider security agenda was also now mainly North–South and South–South: migration from Africa and the Middle East into Europe, from Latin America into the United States, and from many countries in the South to their neighbours; global warming now being driven as much by pollution from China as from the United States; the stability of the global economy now depending on a wide range of players in all regions; and global health depending on transmission belts linking all parts of the planet. Even the rise of China can in part be seen in North–South terms, though as China and India achieve great power status, the North–South framing becomes less useful, giving way to a more global perspective on both traditional and non-traditional security. In a more globalised and interdependent world, where developing countries are also great powers, even the return of traditional great power security dynamics will not return ISS to its traditionally narrow focus on the world of white great powers.

Liberalism, Neoliberalism and International Political Economy

While the ending of the Cold War was quite traumatic for Realists of all stripes and those in ISS, the opposite was true for Liberals of all stripes and those studying IPE. The combination of unipolarity and globalisation that we noted in Chapter 7 as the key features of the immediate post-Cold War period opened up major prospects for them. A liberal sole superpower was in a powerful position to project and protect key liberal values such as democracy, the market and human rights. Globalisation under a liberal superpower brought ideas of democratic peace and multi-lateral international relations to the fore. It offered a way to bring a rising China into the Western system of rules and institutions, and raised hopes that human rights might be pursued more effectively than was possible during the Cold War. This liberal moment had a powerful effect on IR during the 1990s, but increasingly soured thereafter.

The Neo-Neo synthesis noted in Chapter 6 strengthened during the 1990s. Neoliberals and Neorealists broadly agreed about power polarity, Rationalist method and a mainly materialist approach to the study of international relations. Yet there were significant disagreements between them. Realists tended to marginalise the impact of institutions, whereas Liberals gave institutions a major role (Keohane and Martin, 1995: 47). In general, Neorealists and Neoliberals disagreed over the relative importance of anarchy, with the former viewing 'anarchy as placing more severe constraints on state behaviour than do neoliberals' (D. Baldwin, 1993: 5). Neorealists saw cooperation as 'harder to achieve, more difficult to maintain, and more dependent on state power' (Grieco, 1993: 302). Whereas Neorealists stressed relative gains, which encourage competition, Neoliberals emphasised absolute gains, which facilitate cooperation. Unlike Neorealists, Liberals had no problem with unipolarity, which fits nicely with their ideas about hegemonic stability discussed in Chapter 6. Unlike for Realists, whose balance-of-power theory either forbade unipolarity or made it a short and highly unstable phenomenon, hegemonic stability looked to a dominant power to provide the public goods for global order. The failure of balancing behaviour to occur during the 1990s reinforced the Liberal view. The two sides also tended to disagree about China, with Realists seeing it as an inevitable threat to the United States, and Liberals seeing globalisation as a great opportunity to facilitate China's peaceful rise to the benefit of all. Globalisation was broadly compatible with both perspectives, albeit in different ways: as a feature of open liberal economic orders, and as a consequence of American power and primacy. It was a bonus for both that their theories were flattering to the United States, putting the sole superpower at the centre of analysis.

Several distinctive literatures flourished during the Liberal period following 1989. Globalisation emerged as almost a separate field of study, partly within IR and partly outside it because it transcended the state-centric framework (Hirst and Thompson, 1996; Sassen, 1996; Clark, 1999; Held et al., 1999; Keohane and Nye, 2000; Scholte, 2000; Woods, 2000; Ripsman and Paul, 2010). IPE expanded from its beginnings in the 1980s, increasingly acquiring its own journals (e.g. *Review of*

International Political Economy) and textbooks (Spero, 1990; Stubbs and Underhill, 1994), and becoming a major subfield within IR. In the United States, IPE converged around a dominant Rationalist approach, the Open Economy Politics (OEP) school, which was heavily influenced by neoclassical economics and international trade theory (Lake, 2008; Oatley, 2011). The end of the Cold War brought a further loss of diversity, especially with the decline of Marxist IPE. Gilpin (2001) published a new text, under the title *Global Political Economy*. Despite the suggestive shift in the main title from his 1987 book, and although his intent was to give an account of the profound changes that had happened since its publication, Gilpin would confirm his theoretical position as that of a state-centric Realist.

But the OEP school came to be criticised for creating an American IPE 'monoculture', marked by a methodological reductionism that focused on state interests as the main explanatory variable without saying much about how interests are constructed (Farrell, 2009). Other approaches to IPE emerged in the United States, especially those that stressed the 'interaction between societal interests and political institutions' (Oatley, 2012: 12). In addition to the more general theoretical work of British and Canadian scholars mentioned in Chapter 6, in Australia Richard Higgott (Higgott and Stubbs, 1995) and John Ravenhill (2001) made contributions to IPE from a regional vantage point, focusing on regionalisation and regionalism in the Asia-Pacific. Although they (Higgott and Watson, 2007; Ravenhill, 2007) rejected Benjamin Cohen's (2007, 2008) attempt to distinguish 'American' and 'British' schools of IPE as an oversimplification, the debate served to highlight some of the key differences between mainstream IPE scholarship in the United States and that in other parts of the West, especially in Britain, Canada and Australia. One major difference, not surprisingly, lay in the non-positivist methodology of the latter, which shunned its US counterpart's penchant for hypothesis testing and quantitative research. The non-US approaches were also more interdisciplinary and more normative than their American counterpart (Cohen, 2014: 50–1), having more in common with the non-mainstream American IPE.

Aside from IPE, human rights generated an extensive Liberal literature parallel in some ways to the human security one discussed above, and with a distinctly promotional purpose (Barkin, 1998; Dunne and Wheeler, 1999; Reus-Smit, 2001; Sikkink, 2016). A big literature on Democratic Peace Theory (DPT) developed, arguably triggered by Michael Doyle's (1986) revival of the classical Liberal association of democracy and peace (Ray, 1995; Brown, Lynn-Jones and Miller, 1996; Weart, 1998). DPT was also picked up and cultivated by Peace Researchers (Gleditsch,

1992). The basic idea was an empirical claim that democracies do not go to war with each other, and this line of thinking was influential in both the Clinton and George W. Bush administrations in the United States, which sought to expand the zone of democracy. DPT generated a lot of controversy about what counted as being a democracy, what counted as going to war and what the causal mechanisms might be (Maoz and Russett, 1993). It was also accused of being Eurocentric in not being applicable in many other regions (Friedman, 2000: 228), and not accounting adequately for colonial wars and the propensity for democracies to intervene in the periphery (M. Haas, 1995; Mann, 2001; Barkawi and Laffey, 2001; Ravlo, Gleditsch and Dorussen, 2003: 522; Acharya, 2014a).

Perhaps the main Liberal literature, however, was that which focused generally on the liberal order (or liberal hegemonic order) that was seen to have emerged as a consequence of unipolarity and globalisation. The principal exponent of this was John Ikenberry (Deudney and Ikenberry, 1999; Ikenberry, 2001, 2009, 2011), who in a series of books and articles made the case that the liberal international order created and led by the United States was not only beneficial, but also potentially durable. The institutionalised liberal order not only bound the power of the United States, but also served the interests of many by providing rules and institutions to stabilise the global capitalist economy (Ikenberry, 2001: 29). Ikenberry (2011: 9, 15; 2009) thought that the liberal order created legitimacy and supporting constituencies beyond the United States and the West, and would therefore endure even if the United States declined. He argued that the liberal order was 'easy to join and hard to overturn' (Ikenberry, 2011: 9). Yet despite being dressed up in consensual terms, the story of the liberal international order is essentially a story about the emergence, consequences and legitimation of American hegemony. The claim that 'The British and American-led liberal orders have been built in critical respects around consent' (Ikenberry, 2011: 15) had distinct echoes of the Gramscian notion of hegemony, so internalised that its presumed benefits do not have to be seen to be believed, and one does have to be asked to offer allegiance. But it overlooks the significant coercive and contested aspects of the history of that order (Acharya, 2014d).

But after the liberal golden decade of the 1990s, much of this began to go sour. Human rights came increasingly to be seen as the new standard of 'civilisation' (Donnelly, 1998; Buzan, 2014: 107). The democratic peace morphed into arrogance of power and liberal hubris in the 'concert of democracies' idea to sideline the UN and turn the management of GIS over to a group of like-minded democratic states (Ikenberry and Slaughter, 2006). Particularly in the United States there was a weakening of liberal values and perspectives, partly driven by the exigencies of the GWoT, and partly by the increasing inequality and instability generated by the Neoliberal global economy. Thus the liberal heyday during the 1990s under Clinton turned into betrayal on human rights during the GWoT by Bush, and outright opposition to much of the American legacy of institutionalism and open economies by Trump. By 2018, the United States no longer owned the future, and liberal values were no longer understood as the inevitable teleology of GIS.

In terms of sustaining or reducing the barriers between core and periphery in IR, Liberalism comes out with a mixed record. HST, human rights, the 'concert of democracies' and DPT all emphasised the core, with what might be called 'Offensive Liberalism' replaying the role of the standard of 'civilisation'. But the emphasis on institutions opened legitimate political space for the periphery, and globalisation and IPE directly promoted a holistic view of the international system/society. With the gradual decline of the liberal order even before the advent of the Trump administration, there was not only room for the periphery in understanding and managing the global economy and security (Acharya, 2018: 199–206), but also increasing space for both periphery and critical perspectives. With the rise of China and others to the middle ranks of development, the whole structure and significance of core–periphery was changing fast.

Constructivism

Realism, ISS and Liberalism were all traditional, mainly materialist, approaches to IR that adapted themselves to the new circumstances of the post-Cold War world with varying degrees of success. Constructivism, by contrast, was a new arrival to IR as a mainstream theory. It was not new in itself, but rather an existing approach to social theory that was newly adapted to the study of international relations, by, among others, John Ruggie, Friedrich Kratochwil, Alexander Wendt, Nicholas Onuf, Emanuel Adler and Peter Katzenstein. Unlike Realism, Security Studies and Liberalism, Constructivism was not specifically a theory of international relations. To its critics as well as some of its proponents, Constructivism was more of 'a philosophical category, a meta-theory or a method of empirical research' (Zehfuss, 2002: 8) that was not specific to IR, but could be applied to it.

For Constructivists, international politics is not just about material forces such as power and wealth, but is also shaped by subjective and intersubjective factors, including ideas, norms, culture and identity. They see international relations as being governed by a logic of appropriateness, or considerations of right or wrong, rather than a logic of consequences, or cost and benefit calculations. Constructivists reject the Rationalist (utilitarian) and materialist biases in Realism and Neoliberal Institutionalism. They see the interests and identities of states not as pre-ordained, or given, but emerging and changing through a process of mutual interactions and socialisation. Conditions such as anarchy and power politics are not permanent features of international relations, but are socially constructed and can have different outcomes: in Wendt's (1992) famous formulation, 'anarchy is what states makes of it'. Norms have a life of their own, not only creating and redefining state interests and approaches but also regulating state behaviour, and constituting state identities. Through interaction and socialisation, states may develop a collective identity that would enable them to overcome power politics and the security dilemma.

Like all other approaches to IR, Constructivism quickly splintered into many strands, some, such as Wendt (1999), more state-centric, and others more focused on non-state actors (Keck and Sikkink, 1998). Some strands were, in Ted Hopf's (1998; see also: Reus-Smit, 2005) and Maja Zehfuss's (2001) terms, more conventional (using identity as a causal variable) and others more critical (investigating how identity comes about in the first place). Conventional Constructivists adopted a 'scientific' approach, rather than an interpretative one, thereby blurring their divide with Rationalism. The debate between Rationalism (both Neoliberalism and Neorealism) and Constructivism became the major point of contestation in international relations theory in the 1990s (Katzenstein, Keohane and Krasner, 1999: 6). But like the earlier 'debate' between Neorealism and Neoliberalism, the Rationalist–Constructivist divide ended in a partial synthesis, either trying to link Instrumental Rationality and Social Construction (Finnemore and Sikkink, 1999: 270, 272; Barkin, 2010: 7–8) or to locate Constructivism as a middle way between Rationalism and Reflectivism (Adler, 1997; Fearon and Wendt, 2002: 68; Checkel, 2013: 222–3).

Constructivism rapidly gained popularity during the 1990s, and again, this development can be linked to developments in the real world of ir. Mainstream IR had failed to see the end of the Cold War coming, and that failure, combined with the non-appearance of frenzied balancing against the United States, discredited materialist theories in the eyes of many. The implosion of the Soviet Union was as much or more about the collapse of a political idea as it was about a change in material circumstances. When it died, the Soviet Union was still in possession of massive military power. Much the same could be said of the surrender of the apartheid regime in South Africa, also during the early 1990s, and in reverse, the progress of the EU. The 1990s also saw the rise of intense identity politics in the former Soviet Union and the successor states to Yugoslavia. These events not only exposed the huge role of ideas and identities in ir, but also suggested that major peaceful change in GIS was possible.

At first, Constructivism showed a clear potential to secure greater recognition for the agency of Non-Western actors. Lacking in material power, weak states often resort to normative action and agency to realise a measure of autonomy and reshape power politics. Donald Puchala (1995: 151) notes that for 'third world countries, ideas and ideologies are far more important' than power or wealth, because 'powerlessness' and 'unequal distribution of the world's wealth' are 'constants' that 'drive world affairs'. Constructivism also allows the possibility of cooperation in the absence of strong formalistic, legalistic institutions. Its main causal mechanisms for change, especially ideas and norms, could be diffused without formal organisations with large, permanent bureaucracies, such as the EU (Acharya, 2001a, 2009). This meant Constructivism could capture many types of international and regional cooperation found in the Third World. Indeed, the fashion for it quickly spread into periphery IR, with influential exponents emerging in China (Qin, 2009, 2011a, 2016) and elsewhere.

But its challenge to the Rationalism of Neorealism and Neoliberalism notwithstanding, Constructivism could not completely rise above the penchant for ignoring the agency of Non-Western actors. Amitav Acharya (2004, 2009) stressed the theory's tendency to privilege the moral cosmopolitanism of Western transnational actors in explaining norm diffusion in world politics. It is as if all the big ideas come from the West, transmitted mainly by Western transnational movements, and the Non-Western actors are passive recipients. This echoes ES insights by Clark (2007) and Andrew Hurrell (2007: 111–14; see also Armstrong, 1998) that the non-state actors increasingly populating global civil society are mainly Western, and serve to enhance Western dominance by projecting Western values. In response, Acharya (2004, 2009) shifted the focus of Constructivist norm scholarship from whether ideas matter to the question: *whose ideas matter.*

The English School

Unlike for Realism, ISS and Liberalism, the ending of the Cold War did not have any immediate implications for the ES. Yet the 1990s and onwards was nonetheless a time when the School moved beyond its home base in the Anglo-core and became more globally established as a mainstream approach to IR. In part, this happened because the ES got itself more organised, and developed a more visible presence at the main IR conferences. But it was also helped by two other developments. First, the coming into fashion of Constructivism in the United States opened the door there to the ES (Dunne, 1995). Constructivism somewhat loosened the grip of positivist epistemology, easing the way to those interested in more historical and social structural ways of thinking about IR. From 2003 there has been an ES section of ISA, and the ES has become more accepted in the United States as a mainstream approach to IR, albeit as a minority taste. The second development was the opening up, and rapid expansion, of IR in China. The newly developing academic IR community in China took an interest in the ES (Zhang, Y., 2003; Zhang, X., 2010), albeit again as a minority taste, for three reasons. One was that the ES encouraged historical and cultural approaches, and many Chinese IR scholars were keen to get their own history and political theory into the IR game. Another was that the label 'English School' seemed to justify the creation of national schools of IR theory. Although the ES can hardly be described as a national school, that did not stop it being used to support the development of a so-called 'Chinese School' (Wang and Buzan, 2014; Zhang and Chang, 2016). The third reason was simply that the ES was not American: while the new Chinese IR community was keen to be at the cutting edge of IR theory, it did not wish to become an intellectual colony of the United States. In this sense, the ES became part of the growing challenge to the global dominance of American IR. From an outside perspective, American IR was a kind of 'national school', even though few Americans saw their own activities in that perspective.

As interest in the ES became more global, a new generation of scholars took over from the founding fathers, maintaining some of the tradition and opening up some new avenues. Its holistic, normative approach through the order/justice (pluralism/solidarism) debate remained a robust and influential way of viewing the world order, and the ES remained an active side of the wider 1990s debates about human rights (e.g. Dunne and Wheeler, 1999; Wheeler, 2000; Hurrell, 2007). A new departure was that the structural approach to international society, clearly implicit in Bull (1977), was made explicit, and set up alongside the School's normative approach (Buzan, 2004b; Holsti, 2004). And at least in part in response to working within the American IR environment, the School became more methodologically self-conscious (Navari, 2009). There was more interest in exploring primary institutions, world society and international society at the regional level; and more concern to contest the rather Eurocentric account of the expansion of international society to global scale given in the classical literature.[7] In response to the supposedly unipolar world order that arose during the 1990s, the ES took more interest in hegemony and hierarchy (Dunne, 2003; Clark, 2011; Buzan and Schouenborg, 2018), an aspect of international society that had intrigued Adam Watson and Martin Wight, but had been sidelined within the School in favour of a sovereign-equality approach to international society (Watson, 2001).

In various ways the ES began to accommodate the Third World more than it had done before. The idea of international society at the regional level was picked up, especially so in Latin America (Merke, 2011). Questions were raised about the suitability of the 'like units' approach to international society given the very significant differences of both history and culture, and economic and political development, within the membership (Buzan and Schouenborg, 2018). The critique of Eurocentrism in the expansion story pushed towards a more even-handed and global account of how international society was made (Keene, 2002; Buzan and Little, 2014; Dunne and Reus-Smit, 2017). The first generation's concern about the 'revolt against the West' was not carried forward. To the contrary, more effort was made to understand the social structures of the world onto which the Europeans imposed themselves during the nineteenth century (Suzuki, 2009; Suzuki, Zhang and Quirk, 2014). That said, however, the ES's focus still remained predominantly on the core rather than the periphery, and that was true for both international and world society. Working against this ongoing neglect, however, was its privileging of great powers as the main makers and managers of international order. As developing countries such as India and particularly China made their way into the ranks of the great powers, they naturally came more into focus within ES accounts (Zhang, Y., 1998; Zhang, X., 2011a, b).

Critical Theories

Like Constructivism, Critical Theory[8] was both an import to IR from outside, and in many ways more of a method, or way of thinking about IR, than an IR theory in itself. Critical Theory was not unique to the 1990s. It had roots in earlier Marxist thinking about IR, especially Gramsci's; in various branches of Political Philosophy and Sociology, particularly in Paris and Frankfurt; and also in the radical side of Peace

---

[7] For summaries and sources on all this, see Buzan (2014).

[8] Critical Theory, in upper case, usually refers to the Frankfurt School, but here we use the term to include a variety of theories which are usually placed in lower case in the literature.

Research. Critical Theories came into prominence in IR during the 1980s, and by the 1990s were in a position to stand as a radical alternative to mainstream IR in IR's 'third debate' (on which more below). It is beyond the scope of this section to unfold the myriad diversities and complexities of Critical Theory, which range across Postmodernism, Poststructuralism and the more radical sides of Constructivism, Security Studies and Feminism (see Devetak, 1996a). Postcolonialism maintains a distance from these Critical Theories, for reasons to be discussed later in this chapter.

Critical Theory was driven by the urge to change the world by thinking differently about it. Its challenge to the mainstream was both normative and epistemological, with the two overlapping in complex ways. The tension and alienation between critical and mainstream IR theorists was generally stronger than that between the mainstream IR theorists and Constructivists, with accusations that Critical Theories 'substitute ideology for explanation and engage in wishful thinking unconstrained by reality' (Viotti and Kauppi, 2011: 336). The normative challenge from Critical Theory is perhaps best captured by Robert Cox's (1981: 128–30) distinction between *problem-solving* and *critical* theory, with the former working within existing orthodoxies to improve them, and the latter questioning them and looking to alternatives.[9] International Relations theory, as Cox (1986: 207) famously put it, 'is always for someone and for some purpose'. Critical theorists questioned the exclusion and domination of any social groups based on gender, race, ethnicity, class, etc., and made the idea of emancipation, rooted in the Enlightenment, a central concern (Devetak, 1996a: 166). Linklater (1996: 280–1) argues that 'knowledge about society is incomplete if it lacks the emancipatory purpose'; hence Critical Theory 'envisages new forms of political community which break with unjustified exclusion'. Unlike traditional Marxism, which focused on economic forces shaping history and the marginality of the working class in the mode of production, Critical Theory pays attention to other excluded groups by 'analyzing the variety of forces, including production, which shape the contours of human history' (Linklater, 1996: 280).

The epistemological challenge was more wide-ranging. Critical theorists questioned the appropriateness of positivist approaches as a basis for understanding the social world. They denied the idea of there being an objective reality out there, and therefore of the possibility of a 'politically neutral analysis of an external reality' (Linklater, 1996: 295). They saw knowledge as always coloured by certain inherent and inescapable

---

[9] Ashley's (1980: 175–6) distinction between 'technical rationality' and 'rationality proper' was doing the same work.

values and 'pre-existing social purposes and interests' (Linklater, 1996: 279). They wanted more holistic, more historical and more human (as opposed to state-centric) approaches, stressing dissent and interpretation. Drawing from Michel Foucault's work, Poststructuralists cultivated 'genealogy', which is 'a style of historical thought which exposes and registers the significance of power–knowledge relations', and brings to surface 'those things or thoughts which have been buried, covered over, or excluded from view in the writing and making of history' (Devetak, 1996b: 184). Richard Ashley (1996: 246) argued for 'the innovation and elaboration of deconstructive, genealogical, interpretive–analytic and other "methods" that, though problematizing the very notion of methodology, nevertheless enable an engaged, rigorous, criticism-conscious exploration of events and activities at once imposing and transgressing limits of social possibility'.

Critical Theory, like Constructivism, was perhaps mainly a response to dissatisfaction with the normative and epistemological qualities of mainstream IR theory, particularly Realism. As attested by the work of Ashley and Cox, such dissatisfaction existed during the Cold War. Because of the failures and incoherence of Realism, it gained more scope after 1989. As David Campbell (2013: 226) argues:

Critical scholars were dissatisfied with the way realism – and its revivification at that time through neorealism – remained powerful in the face of global transformations. These scholars felt that realism marginalized the importance of new transnational actors, issues, and relationships and failed to hear (let alone appreciate) the voices of excluded peoples and perspectives. As such, poststructuralism began with an ethical concern to include those who had been overlooked and excluded by the mainstream of IR.

But it was also a response to events in the real world. Cox's Critical Theory grew partly in response to

the crisis of multilateralism [that] emerged in the 1980s in a tendency on the part of the United States and some other powerful countries to reject the United Nations as a vehicle for international action and a movement on the part of these countries towards either unilateralism or collective dominance in world economic and political matters. (R.W. Cox, 1981: 137)

Cox's contribution to Critical Theory was distinctive in highlighting (relative to other Critical Theories except Postcolonialism) the marginalisation of the Third World. Cox highlights the impact of the reduced aid from the rich to the poor nations arising from the economic crisis of the mid-1970s; the growing reliance on aid conditionality, free-market deregulation and privatisation as pursued by 'the principal agencies of the western dominated world economy', i.e. the IMF and the World

Bank; the North–South conflict arising from resistance to Western economic dominance from the Third World states acting through the UN General Assembly; and the loss of Soviet support for the Third World due to its domestic problems in the 1980s (R. W. Cox, 1981: 137). These concerns continued into the 1990s, when the unfolding of unipolarity and globalisation provided the same kind of boost for Critical Theory as it did for Liberalism, by making the world look more like their theories. Yet apart from Cox (1993; see also Cox and Sinclair, 1996), Critical Theory more generally had little focus on the Non-Western world and the ills of imperialism and colonialism. The Postcolonial critique of Critical Theories is that they remain focused on the European Enlightenment, and are universalist as opposed to being relativist (Krishna, 1993). Marxism also comes in for Postcolonial critique on similar grounds (Kennedy, 1996: 348; Chibber, 2013). In the words of Linklater (1996: 296), 'Critical theory maintains its faith in the enlightenment project and defends universalism in its ideal of open dialogue not only between fellow-citizens but, more radically, between all members of the human race'.

As noted above, Critical Theory successfully established a branch in Security Studies, focusing on emancipation as necessary to security in any deep sense, and on human as opposed to national security. The other area in which it was influential was Feminism.

Feminism

Like Critical Theory, Feminism was gaining momentum during the 1980s, a period that witnessed the rise of Feminist movements throughout the world, and the rise of Feminist theory in the social sciences more generally. It shared Critical Theory's concerns about emancipation, the sources of knowledge, the relationship between knowledge and power, and the dominance of state-centrism in IR thinking. Also like Critical Theory, Feminism was a reaction against the perceived shortcomings, distortions, hierarchies and biases of mainstream IR theory (Sylvester, 1994). But Feminism was not wholly part of Critical Theory. Feminist strands exist in Liberal and Constructivist IR theories as well as Poststructuralist and Postcolonial ones (Tickner and Sjoberg, 2013). Feminism's focus was on gender as a separate category of analysis, different from other categories such as race and class because it pervades all other categories. For Feminist IR scholars, gender is the 'primary way to signify relationships of power not only in the home, but also in the world of foreign policy and international relations' (Viotti and Kauppi, 2011: 363). Most knowledge is created by men (Tickner and

Sjoberg, 2013: 207) and Feminist IR theory is concerned with how this relationship affects the theory and practice of international relations. In a seminal essay, J. Ann Tickner (1997: 612) refuted those who wondered if 'gender [has] anything to do with explaining the behavior of states in the international system' and rejected the claim that Feminism is not concerned with 'solving "real-world" problems such as Bosnia, Northern Ireland or nuclear proliferation'. Ann Towns (2009: 683; see also Towns, 2010) shows how during the nineteenth century the 'full-scale exclusion of women from politics' and the linkage of female roles in politics to 'savagery', and female exclusion from politics with 'civilisation' became an informal standard of 'civilisation'.

Like Liberalism, Feminism gathered strength from the opening up of the 1990s. Globalisation and the removal of the Cold War obsessions with national security and deterrence made more room for consideration of a wider range of issues and actors. For example, it afforded greater opportunity for Feminist voices, especially in shaping the agenda of international institutions in recognising the importance of gender in world politics. Feminist coalitions were able to push for recognition of women's rights as human rights and challenge rape and violence against women as an instrument of war adopted by regimes and groups in conflict zones (True, 2017). Like Critical Theory, and echoing some strands of Peace Research, Feminism opened up a significant strand in Security Studies (see Buzan and Hansen, 2009: 208–12). Feminists took a wider view of conflict and violence, including 'economic dimensions and issues of structural violence', and put greater 'focus on consequences, than causes of war' (J. A. Tickner, 1997: 625–6). Laura Sjoberg (2012) makes the ambitious argument that gender hierarchy is a structural feature of world politics, and a better explanation for war than Waltz's anarchic structure.

Overall, Feminist perspectives have made important contributions in not only exposing the exclusionary nature of IR theorising, but also in offering pathways in respect of how this can be overcome. In that sense, Feminism operates powerfully across the barriers between core and periphery. There is an interesting contrast between the way in which gender and race have played into international relations. Especially before the mass migrations of modern times, race differences were generally much stronger *between* societies than within them. Racism was thus an extremely strong factor of differentiation between core and periphery during colonial times, and the bitter memory of that still plays powerfully in world politics. By contrast, as Sjoberg (2012: 7) observes, masculine and feminine behavioural traits, and the hierarchies associated with them, show 'surprising similarities across recorded history' especially in the major civilisations. Because gender privilege was so widely practised *within* the major powers in the international system, it did not so obviously create the status differentiations *between* states and societies that gave racism its big impact on GIS.

But a challenge facing Feminist scholarship lies in bridging the divide between its Western-dominated scholarship and Postcolonialism, including Postcolonial Feminists. While some Feminists had argued that Feminism can be used as a term for all kinds of oppressed actors and their upliftment (True, 1996), the gap between race and gender remains. J. Ann Tickner and Jacqui True (2018: 11) lament that 'While there are thriving fields of scholarship on race and gender in the discipline, we infrequently bring these approaches together with analysis of socioeconomic class to reveal a different taxonomy of global power from the dominant, state-centric one.' Indeed, as will be seen in our discussion of Postcolonialism in this chapter, Postcolonial scholars have accused Western Feminist scholarship of marginalising the role and agency of women in the periphery.

Great Debates Part 3

IR's rather complicated 'third debate'[10] embodied the rift between critical and mainstream IR theory described above. It began in the 1980s with the growing disenchantment with Neorealism, Neoliberalism and the 'Neo-Neo' synthesis, but spilled over to the 1990s, when it had its broadest impact by encouraging greater diversity in IR theory. A key catalyst of the third debate between Rationalists and Reflectivists was Yosef Lapid's (1989) article in *International Studies Quarterly*, which 'became a touchstone for a variety of theoretical and methodological debates in the field'. Although not 'the only call for questioning the foundations and direction of the field in the post-Cold War era, [it] managed to knit together the "Great Debates" narrative of the field's origins and development with a call for diversity and pluralism that struck a responsive chord with many' (Jackson, 2014).

The third debate questioned 'the singularity of the positivist vision, exposing the limits of empiricist epistemology or, at the least, the narrow range of ontological claims it permits'. As part of the debate, Critical theorists 'emphasis[ed] the non-neutrality of knowledge' and 'have

---

[10] Wæver (1996) prefers to see two debates from the 1980s. Aside from the third debate between positivists and post-positivists, he calls for recognising a fourth debate pitting 'Reflectivist' approaches, such as Critical Theory, Postmodernism, Poststructuralism and some variants of Feminism and Constructivism, against the 'Rationalist' combination of Neorealism and Neoliberalism.

sought to expose positivism's underpinning political interests to present alternative, emancipatory possibilities' (Butler, 2010). Yale Ferguson and Richard Mansbach (2014) argue that the impact of the third debate was limited in the United States (compared to Europe).[11] It 'did not alter the views of the field's positivists who continue to dominate many leading departments and journals especially in the United States'. But in general, 'it did dramatically sensitize scholars, especially younger scholars, to the role of such factors as norms, identities, ideas, and principles'. It spawned a turn to ideas and away from materialism. 'As a consequence, IR scholars other than those still wedded to narrow positivism no longer believe that "facts" speak for themselves and insist that we give greater emphasis to meaning and interpretation of events filtered through subjective lenses.' The third debate provided the framing for diversification of IR theory described above. It rendered 'agency' more salient and 'highlighted the limits of "structural" perspectives like neorealism'. It gave voice to a variety of approaches including 'different strains of constructivism, English School, normative theory, critical theory, feminist theory, postmodernism, or post-colonial theory'.

Yet the great debates of IR, whether one counts three or four, did little to bring the Global South 'in', in the sense of paying attention to the history, ideas and agency of Non-Western societies. Wæver's (1996) depiction of the fourth debate, for example, does not include Postcolonialism under the 'Reflectivist' category, even though Postcolonial scholarship's critique of exclusion, call for emancipation and advocacy of epistemological and methodological openness are no less powerful than those of Critical Theory, Poststructuralism and Feminism. This 'exclusion by the excluded' would produce a Postcolonial disillusionment with and challenge to Critical Theories (Krishna, 1993).

IR thinking in Japan stood somewhat apart from these theoretical debates in the Western core. It experienced no particular shock after 1989, and remained largely empirical in focus (Inoguchi, 2007, 2009). Japanese IR remained focused on policy ideas, especially related to Asia-Pacific regionalism. The importance of pacifism was challenged, even as the concept of human security replaced the earlier notion of comprehensive security, reflecting shifts in Japanese foreign policy. But these ideas have not coalesced to produce a distinctive Japanese approach to the study of IR. Japan lacked a usable 'deep past' for IR theory, though interestingly there was some revival of interest in the Kyoto School (D. Williams, 2004; Goto-Jones, 2005; Shimizu, 2015). As with Karl

---

[11] All subsequent quotes in this paragraph are from Ferguson and Mansbach's unpaginated essay.

Schmitt in the West, associations with Fascism that had precluded engagement with some interwar thinkers were beginning to drop away, especially where some of their ideas still seemed relevant.

IR Thinking in the Periphery

In this section we start by looking at the unfolding of Postcolonialism after 1989, and then review other developments in the periphery on a region-by-region basis.

Postcolonialism

As argued in Chapter 6, academic Postcolonial IR emerged during the 1980s, around the same time as Critical Theories started gaining prominence in IR. Importantly, Postcolonialism, like Feminism, shares many aspects of Critical Theory (e.g. challenging the Rationalist theories of Neorealism and Neoliberalism, questioning and highlighting the relationship between knowledge and power, and seeking to advance values of justice, peace and pluralism in the world) while at the same time being differentiated from it. Some Postcolonial scholars have been critical of some of the leading sources of Critical Theory. Spivak challenged Foucault for treating 'Europe as a self-enclosed and self-generating entity, by neglecting the central role of imperialism in the very making of Europe' (Ahmad, 1997: 374). Said (1994: 278) accused Foucault not only of 'ignoring the imperial context of his own theories', but also of offering a perspective that 'fortifies the prestige of the colonial system' and renders it as 'irresistible'. Sankaran Krishna (1993) criticises Critical Theory for remaining Eurocentric or Western-centric, and not acknowledging the Non-Western world. In this sense, Postcolonialism goes beyond Critical Theory in its emancipative aspect. Yet both in its elements of kinship with Critical Theory and in the personnel who adopt the approach, Postcolonialism represents a very significant breakdown of the old barriers in IR between core and periphery.

Another shared theme between Postcolonial scholarship and Critical Theory is critiquing Western universalism, and instead emphasising cultural relativism. Universalism in the social sciences, and specifically in IR, is most often the projection of Western ideas, values and culture to the rest of the world. In IR, this is evident in how the ideas of the early thinkers such as Thucydides, Machiavelli, Hobbes, Kant, Locke and Smith are seen as being applicable to *all* states and societies. Western concepts such as international law, the nation state and the market are, in reality, constructed (Seth, 2013). Cultural relativism, in contrast to universalism, recognises differences in cultures. The cultures of Africa, Asia and Latin America are different, both among each other and as compared to the West. While Postcolonialism focuses on identity and culture, it eschews 'essentializing' a particular culture (Grovogui, 2013: 253). Using anthropological approaches, it seeks to recover the voices of the colonised, and set them up in opposition to the dominant Eurocentric narratives of imperialism and colonialism. Postcolonialism highlights not only the after-effects of Western colonial domination in the past, but also the continued domination of the West in contemporary discourse and practice. In this vein, modern-day globalisation, the war on terror and democratisation are examples of the dominance of Western ideas (Darby, 2004). But it also cultivates 'hybridity', the idea that the colonial encounter was also a two-way street, with each culture reshaping the other in significant ways.

Like Critical Theory and Feminism, Postcolonialism has occupied the fringes of IR compared to the mainstream, yet has also been successful in establishing bridgeheads into other approaches. Postcolonialism has, for example, inspired a powerful critique of Western dominance in Feminist theory (Mogwe, 1994). Postcolonial Feminist scholars such as Chandra Mohanty (1984), Aihwa Ong (2001), Swati Parashar (2013), and Anna Agathangelou and L. H. M. Ling (2004) have exposed and rejected the dominance of Western Feminists and their mis(representation) of women in the Third World as 'passive, backward and needing to be rescued by their liberated white sisters' (Persaud and Sajed, 2018a: 8), and accused them of ignoring differences in their position, experience and response to oppression. This strand of Feminism addresses problems and issues of the marginalised (women from the developing world) *within* the marginalised (women in general). While this divide between Western and Postcolonial Feminists remains, the 'intersectionality' approach, a major contribution of Black Feminist scholarship, offers a helpful way of bringing together studies of 'race, gender, class, nationality, and sexuality' and thereby 'identifying the reality of diverse standpoints and the need to generate unified coalitions to bring about social and global change' (Tickner and True, 2018: 11).

Postcolonialism has also inspired and has been inspired by Subaltern Studies, an Indian contribution, which rejects the elitist historiography of India's experience with colonialism in *both* Western (Cambridge University-based) and Indian writings. It affirms the agency of the 'subalterns' as makers of their own destiny against both the legal and institutional framework as well as the ideological-symbolic means and physical force employed by the colonial regime (Guha, 1982). This revises a perception associated with Spivak's (1985) position on the implausibility of the subaltern voice ('Can the Subaltern Speak?'). Spivak's position, which might be a misreading, was criticised for ignoring Third World agency; or, as Benita Parry (cited in Persaud and Sajed, 2018a: 8) put it, for its 'deliberate deafness to the native voice where it can be heard'. In an important recent synthesis, Randolph Persaud and Alina Sajed (2018a: 2) argue that, for Postcolonialism, the 'Third World has been a maker of the international system as much as it has been made by it'. Postcolonial thinkers Dipesh Chakrabarty (2000) and Ashis Nandy (1995) have argued that 'history' and the 'past' are much hinged upon our understanding of the 'present', as well as our conception of the 'future' (and on this note, of 'modernity'). Recent scholarship (Persaud and Sajed, 2018b) has not only acknowledged this diversity in Postcolonial thought, but also highlighted common elements.

At first, Postcolonialism was not explicitly interested in Security Studies (Persaud, 2018). But as the Cold War drew to a close, Postcolonialism began to make a significant contribution to addressing the ethnocentrism of ISS, especially in the sense of the neglect of the Non-West and developing conceptual tools for security analysis from the experience of the Non-West, instead of simply using standard Western categories. The work of Mohammed Ayoob (1984, 1991, 1995), Edward Azar and Chung-in Moon (1988) and Yezid Sayigh (1990) critiques the concept of security for its inability to capture the security problems facing Third World countries. Acharya (1996) argues that the contribution of such scholarship on security in the periphery could become central to redefining the concept of national security and become the basis of reinventing the field of ISS. Such work is not grounded on assertions about the cultural uniqueness of the Third World. Rather, it identifies a specific Third World 'predicament', in which the security concerns of states and regimes focus not so much on protection of sovereignty and territorial integrity from external threats, but on the preservation of regime security and political stability from internal threats (Job, 1991; Ayoob, 1995). Another aspect of this category of work has been the attempt to build models of foreign policy and security that fit the conditions of the Third World, especially in terms of comprehensive security, non-traditional security and human security (Sen, 2000; Acharya, 2001b; Caballero-Anthony, Emmers and Acharya, 2006; Tadjbakhsh and Chenoy, 2007; Caballero-Anthony, 2015).

Race is a more distinctively central issue in Postcolonial scholarship, often linked to colonialism (Persaud and Walker, 2001; J. M. Hobson, 2012; Bell, 2013; Henderson, 2013; Persaud, 2014). Race determined not only the origin and trajectory of the Western colonial project, but also the global economic structure, through racialised labour supply. Colonialism and racialism combined to significantly affect the spatial and demographic make-up of the world (Persaud and Walker, 2001). As we have shown, in spite of its prominence before 1945, race got little attention in post-1945 mainstream IR theory despite its role as a 'fundamental force in the very making of the modern world system' (Persaud and Walker, 2001: 374). Even some Critical theorists from Postmodern and Poststructuralist schools stayed away from exploring issues of race. Marxism-influenced Postcolonial thought (with exceptions such as Fanon) focused on the economic dimension, but the later work of this genre such as that of Andre Gunder Frank and Barry Gills (1992) has included the place of race. The gendered nature of race relations has also become a significant theme of Postcolonial Feminism with a key development being the 'intersectionality' between race, gender and class (Persaud and Sajed, 2018a: 8–9).

Postcolonialism provided both a critique of core IR and, in various ways, a bridge across the IR divide between core and periphery. Alongside it were a variety of IR developments within the different regions of the periphery that were doing much the same thing: both differentiating from and integrating with a more global IR. But as the distance from the colonial era grew longer, and differentiations in development larger, the periphery itself became more fragmented, both politically and in relation to the development of IR. The binding legacies of anti-colonialism and anti-racism, although still strongly in play, were a diminishing resource. The longstanding periphery interest in regionalism began to do as much to differentiate Asia, Africa, Latin America and the Middle East from each other as from the West. As IR followed ir in becoming more globalised, the focus shifted to being less about alienation from the core and more about how to find distinctive positions with a globalising IR. In Asia, and especially in Northeast Asia, IR became big and well resourced, and displayed an interesting mix of integrating itself with the IR of the core, working hard to establish distinctive modes of IR thinking reflecting local history and culture. Elsewhere in the periphery, IR was generally less well resourced, and tended to be drawn into the core, while retaining a focus on local foreign policy issues.

Asia

In the post-Cold War period, the 'master narratives' (Alagappa, 2011: 204) of IR in Asia shifted. In India, the shift was from non-alignment to India's economic opening and then to its role as an emerging power. China's master narrative shifted from that of a low-profile, almost status quo state to one of a reformist and rising global power. While these shifts provided a certain policy context, IR thinking in most of Asia was, as it had earlier been in the core, becoming less the province of political leaders, and more that of academics. As part of that shift, IR in the periphery became both more distinctive and better connected to the debates and approaches in the core. While there is growing interest in theoretical work throughout the region, there is no emergent regional school. Obstacles to that include the distinctive local conditions and intellectual predispositions, often shaped by national ideologies and foreign policy frameworks, of scholars in the various parts of the region, especially China and India (Alagappa, 2011). Another constraint on the development of an Asian school of IR is the rather limited nature of exchange and interaction among scholars from the different subregions of Asia. We therefore look at IR developments in Asia mainly country by country.

The dual process of differentiation and integration was most clearly visible in China, where IR had had, from the 1980s, to rebuild itself almost from scratch after the suppression and chaos of the Mao years. As Qin Yaqing (2010, 2011a) tells it, this was done by a quite systematic process of importing and translating the IR 'classics', mastering them and then trying to develop distinctive Chinese forms of IR theory. Chinese IR first absorbed and discussed Realism, Liberalism, Constructivism and the ES, and generated influential exponents of each.[12] It then went on to develop IR thinking based on Chinese history and political theory (e.g. Yan, 2011, 2014) and on Confucian cultural characteristics and behaviour (e.g. Qin, 2009, 2011b, 2016). There was even some metatheoretical work taking on the 'great debates' frontally, such as Tang Shiping's (2013) 'Social Evolution Paradigm', which argues that no single theory is valid across all time, and that IR theories, especially Realism and Liberalism, 'are appropriate to different phases of history' (Buzan, 2013: 1304; see also the discussion of 'theoretical pluralism' by Eun, 2016). The idea of developing a 'Chinese School' of IR caused much debate (Wang and Buzan, 2014). It was opposed by some on the grounds that IR theory should strive to be universal, not particular. National schools also raise the danger of becoming too closely identified with the centres of national power and security. This seemed a particular danger in China, where an authoritarian government with few inhibitions about suppressing criticism was increasingly adopting Confucian rhetoric of *Tianxia* and harmonious relations to frame its foreign policy. Qin (Relationalism), and Yan and Tang (Realism) were all assiduous in presenting their theoretical work as of universal relevance, publishing it in the West to underline

[12] Yan Xuetong for Realism, Wang Yizhou for Liberalism, Qin Yaqing for Constructivism, Zhang Xiaoming for the ES.

this point. Empirically, there was a great deal of IR work in China that analysed China's relationship with the United States specifically, and its position as a rising power within GIS more generally. There was also a lot of work around key Chinese foreign policy initiatives and concepts, such as 'peaceful rise', 'Belt and Road' and 'new type of major power initiative'.

Indian IR did not experience the disruption that affected China, and did not have much of a language barrier separating it from the largely Anglosphere core of IR thinking. But neither did Indian IR experience either the resources boom that benefitted IR in China, or the stimulation of being exposed to a world long denied. Postcolonialism remained prominent in India, and as in China, but to a lesser extent, India showed a growing attempt by scholars to draw on classical traditions and civilisations to challenge Western IR theory and propose alternative or indigenous concepts and theories (Shahi and Ascione, 2016). Like in China, there is a growing interest among Indian scholars to draw upon classical Indian texts such as the epic *Mahabharata* (Narlikar and Narlikar, 2014; Datta-Ray, 2015) and the secular treatise *Arthasastra* (Gautam, 2015) traditions to explain Indian foreign policy and strategic choices. But such talk is yet to grow into a self-conscious attempt to develop an Indian School of IR (Acharya, 2013a). As in China, 'indigenous historical knowledge' has its supporters and opponents in India (Mishra, 2014: 119, 123). Empirically, Indian IR scholars, often with an eye towards Indian government policy, wrote about the relevance of non-alignment; nuclear non-proliferation; India's relations with its South Asian neighbours, especially Pakistan; India's role as a globally emerging power; Sino-Indian rivalry; and, more recently, on the 'Indo-Pacific' region (which is becoming more prominent relative to 'Asia-Pacific').

Constructivism gained popularity in Southeast Asia, where there was also some interest in looking to the local historical resources as a basis for IR theorising (Chong, 2012; Milner, 2016). IR in Korea and Taiwan expanded and flourished after 1989, but both were closely linked to American IR thinking, and both were mainly concerned with their big local problems, respectively reunification and cross-strait relations (Inoguchi, 2009). One notable exception was Shih's (1990; Shih and Yin, 2013) Relational Theory, which like Qin's aimed for universal applicability. Korean-American scholars such as David Kang (2003, 2005) and Victor Cha (1997, 1999, 2000, 2010) also made an impact in thinking globally about Northeast Asian international relations.

Alastair Iain Johnston's (2012) scepticism about the value of theoretical work from Asia does not now seem justified, if it ever was, being based on US-centric standards of what counts as theory. Asian developments in thinking about IR have already been significant, both in themselves and in exposing the limitations of Western IR theories, especially their applicability to Asia. Realist predictions of a post-Cold War breakdown of order in Asia proved as wrong there as elsewhere, and Asia has evolved forms of regionalism quite different from the EU model. Asian IR thinking is beginning now to explore the reasons that differentiate its international relations from those of the West.

Elsewhere in the periphery there was nothing like the Chinese effort to found a distinctive school, though various cultural foundations existed that could be used for that purpose. The main theme was integration into core IR, while trying to maintain both a distinctive position and a focus on local foreign policy issues.

Latin America

Academic IR expanded significantly in Latin America, but was drawn increasingly into the core in terms of thinking about the subject. Latin American states variously adjusted their foreign policy perspective to the changing, post-1989 GIS. For example, Brazilian Foreign Minister Lampreia moved past the Cold War notion of 'autonomy through distance', and formulated the term 'autonomy through integration' to characterise the policy of the Cardoso government (Bernal-Meza, 2016: 8–9). A more rejectionist approach to the prevailing international order came, not surprisingly, from Hugo Chávez's Venezuela. The idea of 'founding insubordination', contained in a foreign ministry document of 2012, highlighted the hegemonic power structure that consisted of subordinating and subordinated states, and the possibility of ceasing to be a subordinated state and becoming a subordinating one by reaching a 'threshold power', a concept coined by Marcelo Gullo earlier (Bernal-Meza, 2016: 12–13). Other concepts in Latin American IR sought to redefine their foreign policy in the context of the ongoing global power shift, especially the rise of new powers from the periphery at the international and regional levels. This is indicated in the idea of 'big peripheral states' developed by Samuel Pinheiro Guimarães (2005), which included China, India and Brazil. Despite their rise, these states continued to operate within the existing 'hegemonic power structures' with a view to secure their own status and role. There was a growing interest in the region in the idea of regional power (also popular in other regions of the periphery), which used domestic economic liberalisation and multilateral action to shape their foreign policy and operate in the globalised world. Finally, the Chilean notion of 'double asymmetry' implied the simultaneous relationship which Chile has with both the major economies of the world and those whose relative power is clearly lesser (especially neighbouring northern countries, such as Peru and Bolivia) (Bernal-Meza, 2016: 24).

In contrast to the state-centric notions above, the idea of 'Peripheral Realism', developed by Argentinian Political Scientist Carlos Escudé, held that the call for autonomy, hitherto stressed by Latin American countries, must be assessed against its costs. Escudé was mindful that the uncritical adoption in the periphery of theoretical frameworks produced primarily in the United States served the ideological purposes of the elites in these countries. While Realist theory has been used to justify aggressive foreign policies on the part of the periphery, interdependence has led to an overestimation of the periphery's scope for action. In a 1995 work, Escudé questioned classical Realism's 'anthropomorphic fallacy', meaning its tendency to regard the state as a person, which led to a stress on national interest and power, and privileged some group interests over others, while ignoring the interests of the people. Instead, he argued for a 'citizen-centric realist approach' (cited in A. B. Tickner, 2003a: 332).

Florent Frasson-Quenoz summarises the different worldview of Latin Americans from Europeans and Americans based on their opposition to Eurocentrism and their attempt to redefine concepts befitting and con-stitutive of national and regional perspectives. Despite the core ideas of dependency and autonomy, and the tendency to adopt inductive theorising, Frasson-Quenoz finds that there is no Latin American school of thought because of the close affinity of these concepts with Marxism and because 'the ontological/methodological options chosen in Latin America are not different from Western ones' (Frasson-Quenoz, 2015: 72).

Africa

In Africa, the development of academic IR remained relatively weak and poorly resourced. There was no serious effort to create an 'African School of International Relations'. Instead, the main effort was to estab-lish African perspectives, agency and voice in the emerging Global IR, based on the belief that 'African voices and contributions should have a global resonance and can be brought to the core of the discipline of IR' (Bischoff, Aning and Acharya, 2016: 2). The narrative of marginalisa-tion, a key theme in African IR, persisted into the post-Cold War period. In this view, traditional IR theory marginalises Africa based on the 'arro-gant assumption that it lacks meaningful politics', and uses Africa as the 'Other for the construction of the mythical Western Self' (Dunn, 2001: 3). Relatedly, African scholars, like those in Asia and elsewhere, continued to challenge the relevance of Western IR concepts and theories for their region. The usefulness of the concept of state as a unit of analysis and national borders were especially challenged for not reflecting the true 'structures of authority, sovereignty and governance' in Africa, which belong to 'warlords, non-governmental organizations or ethnic groups' (K. Smith, 2012: 28).

Instead of focusing on the artificial nation state, African IR scholars, as noted in Chapter 6, have called for more attention to internal and transnational social, economic and governance challenges facing the continent. Yet, Karen Smith, a South African scholar, cautions against rejecting Western concepts outright. Citing recent works by African scholars on 'middle power', 'isolated states' and the collectivist notion of *Ubuntu*, she argues that

theoretical contributions from the global South – and in this case, from Africa – do not need to be radically different from existing theories to constitute an advancement in terms of engendering a better understanding of international relations. Reinterpretations or modifications of existing frameworks and the introduction of new concepts for understanding are equally important. (K. Smith, 2017: 1)

The question of African agency (Bischoff, Aning and Acharya, 2016: 11–17) assumed greater significance in the post-Cold War era, and might be regarded as the African answer to the growing interest in Latin American and Asian IR in the role of emerging powers and regional powers. William Brown (2012: 1891) defines African agency in multiple dimensions: 'as a collective international actor; as a collection of states with (in the "broadest of sweeps") a shared history; and as a discursive presence, used by both Africans and outsiders, in international politics and policy'. Brown (2012: 1902) argues that 'a proper account of agency needs to identify how the accumulations of past practice are present in the everyday realities facing contemporary agents'. In the literature on its possibility, African agency is defined broadly to include both material and ideational elements, in regional and international relations, covering areas where Africa's contributions are especially visible and relevant, such as regionalism, security management and Africa's relations with the outside world. African scholars (van Wyk, 2016: 113–17) point to such examples of African agency as the international campaign against apartheid (which succeeded in having apartheid declared a crime against humanity), declaring the whole continent a nuclear-free zone, creating the New Partnership for African Development, providing leadership in the creation of international regimes such as the Kimberley process on blood diamonds, and more generally through African participation in Non-Western or South–South groupings such as BRICS and IBSA (India, Brazil, South Africa). Unlike in the past, the new discourse on African agency is not exclusively about 'African solutions to African problems'. Rather it covers a range of 'contributions in which Africans define the terms for understanding the issues and set the terms for the nature and scope of outside involvement' (Bischoff, Aning and Acharya, 2016: 1–2). Neither is the new conception of African agency based exclusively on claims about African distinctiveness or African exceptionalism.

Regionalism has been a major facet of African agency. The establishment of the AU, displacing the OAU, rekindled scholarly interest in African regionalism, intersecting with the emerging global debates about humanitarian intervention and later R2P. African scholars highlight the normative and practical agency of African countries through contributions by African leaders and diplomats, such as Nelson Mandela, Thabo Mbeki, Olusegun Obasanjo, Boutros Boutros-Ghali, Kofi Annan, Salim Ahmed Salim, Mohamed Sahnoun and Francis Deng, in producing a global shift of attitude from the old doctrine of non-intervention to humanitarian intervention (Adebajo and Landsberg, 2001; Swart, 2016) and R2P (Acharya, 2013b). These ideas echoed earlier proposals, discussed in Chapter 6, such as Nkrumah's proposal for an African High Command and Ali Mazrui's call for intra-African intervention to secure Africa's peace and security. Algeria's Sahnoun, who co-chaired the International Commission on Intervention and State Sovereignty (ICISS), which shaped the R2P idea, claims that along with the norm of non-indifference to mass atrocities in the AU's Constitutive Act as well as the 'sovereignty as responsibility' concept developed by Deng, a Sudanese scholar and diplomat, who became a South Sudanese citizen after the formation of that country, the R2P was 'in many ways an African contribution to human rights' (Sahnoun, 2009). Unlike regional groups in Asia and Latin America, the AU and ECOWAS have undertaken collective intervention, making a break with the past attachment to non-intervention. In this, they were not passive recipients of this emergent global norm, but active champions. Kwesi Aning and Fiifi Edu-Afful (2016: 120) argue that, despite limited resources and political will among some of the countries in the region, the AU and ECOWAS have demonstrated African agency in regional and international security and have been 'global leaders in embracing and operationalising Responsibility to Protect (R2P)'.

Finally, Africa has been posited as the source of new or alternative thinking in IR, 'to create a new language, a new way of thinking about IR' (Dunn, 2001: 6). Some African scholars go as far as to argue for the possibility of more than one international system (Claassen, 2011: 182). As such, there has been discussion of an African IR theory based on the African intellectuals' return to pre-colonial and primordial political reality in sub-Saharan Africa. But some have cautioned that this might lead to a 'further marginalization' of Africa (Claassen, 2011: 181). Others see the challenge of IR scholarship as being to recognise that there are multiple Africas, which entails the proliferation of multiple IRs based on the 'manifold ways in which IR play out and to recognize those dimensions not typically considered part of the analytical corpus' (Cornelissen, Cheru and Shaw, 2012: 16).

Middle East

In most of the Arab world, academic IR remained weakly developed because of either political chaos or authoritarian control. Outside the Arab world, academic IR developed significantly in Israel and Turkey, and up to a point in Iran, but in the former two it was largely integrated with core IR.

The post-Cold War era nevertheless saw Islam as a potentially rich source of IR thinking in the region. Scholars have remained divided over how to 'bring Islam in'. Some scholars dismiss the notion of an Islamic IR theory as distinctive because of its ambiguous position on the place of the nation state. 'The classical model of Islamic IR theory', Shahrbanou Tadjbakhsh argues, 'does not fit the inherited nation states that have been formed in the region as a result of colonization and modernization'. Hence, Islam has 'constructed its own vision of International Relations ... Islam as a worldview, as a cultural, religious and ideational variant, has sought a different foundation of truth and the "good life" which could present alternatives to Western IRT' (Tadjbakhsh, 2010: 174). Moreover, Islamic IR theory should be seen as a 'systemic theory, not of how states interact with each other or how the system affects the state, but ... rather a concept of world order that focuses on the relations between the Muslim/Arab and the non-Muslim/Arab sphere and how that realm should be ordered'. The Islamic worldview is so different from contemporary concepts in IR that it cannot be fitted into existing theories. Hence Islam has to be treated 'as a paradigm of international theory in its own right' (Turner, 2009).

But despite this scepticism, it is possible to relate Islam to IR concepts and employ the Islamic worldview for the construction of Islamic IR theory – one that is built upon the 'power of ideas such as faith, justice, and striving towards the "good life" of religious morality, as opposed to the pursuit of material interests and power per se' (Tadjbakhsh, 2010: 191). Tadjbakhsh, an Iranian scholar in France, argues that an Islamic IR theory can be based on classical sources such as the Qur'an, Hadith, Sunnah and the *ijtihad*; on fundamentalism and modernism which are both reactionary and defensive; and on Islamisation of knowledge as the 'third way' between fundamentalism and modernism (Tadjbakhsh, 2010: 176–7). While Islamic philosophy is usually portrayed in the West as non-Rationalist, the idea of *ijtihad* is represented as part of 'rational Islamic theology', which holds that 'God could only be comprehended through unaided and individualistic human reason' (Tadjbakhsh, 2010: 178). In the past, Islamic philosophers al-Kindi (800–73), al-Razi (865–925), al-Farabi (873–950), Ibn Sina (980–1037), Ibn Rushd (1126–98) and al-Zahrawi (936–1013) were counter to the prevailing 'Catholic belief in the authority of the divine' and stressed 'the centrality of the individual' (J. M. Hobson, 2004: 178–80).

Islam is not the only potential source of developing indigenous IR concepts and theories in the Middle East. The region might follow China and India, not to mention the West, in looking at its classical civilisations, including Egyptian, Sumerian and Persian, as the basis for drawing IR theories. This potential remains to be exploited, but the study of Amarna diplomacy with the use of IR theory (Cohen and Westbrook, 2000; Scoville, 2015) is a promising example of such efforts.

Academic IR developed strongly in Turkey. Where earlier it had focused on training policy-makers and diplomats at the expense of the development of theory and theorising (Aydinli and Mathews, 2009: 209; Turan, 2017: 2), Seçkin Köstem (2015: 59) found that the study of IR in Turkey was moving away from the dominance of Diplomatic History approaches 'towards embracing grand theoretical debates in the wider field of IR'. The growth of IR has been influenced by the impact of the country seeking EU membership and hosting conferences by international associations, such as WISC. There is a growing interest in regionalism and the global power shift, within which to examine the role of emerging powers such as Turkey itself. Yet much of Turkish IR 'is still mostly focused on various regional and thematic aspects of Turkey's foreign relations, with little original theoretical insights' (Köstem, 2015: 62), and has made little inroads into the 'grand theories of IR' (Turan, 2017: 3). That said, as with China, a number of Turkish scholars working inside and outside the country have made significant international impacts and reputations, and been an important part of the integration of IR between core and periphery. These include: Bahar Rumelili (2004) on identity; Ayşe Zarakol (2011, 2014) (who now teaches at Cambridge) on stigmatisation; Turan Kayaoğlu (2010a) on the critique of 'Westphalian Eurocentrism' and extraterritoriality (Kayaoğlu, 2010b); Nuri Yurdusev (2003, 2009) on the ES; and Pinar Bilgin (2004a, b, 2008) on Postcolonialism, Feminism and Security Studies.

Russia and East and Central Europe

As noted in Chapter 6, the development of IR in the former Soviet Union and the communist bloc countries of Eastern Europe during the Cold War had features similar to that in both the core and periphery, but especially important were the political constraints imposed by the communist regimes, which were akin to those which prevailed in the authoritarian countries of the periphery. With the fall of communism, the IR community in the region found more space to engage with a wider range of themes and theories. In Russia, this broadening was evident in interest in 'globalisation ... the legal and economic aspects of the international activity of Russia's regions; new challenges and threats; European integration and so on' (Lebedeva, 2004: 278). In terms of theory, Liberalism and Constructivism found footholds, Realism remained very influential and morphed into a strong interest in Geopolitics. As an example of this, Huntington's 'clash of civilizations' thesis found greater resonance in Russia than Fukuyama's 'end of history' thesis (Lebedeva, 2004: 275). The emerging multipolarity, in which Russia can recover its identity as a longstanding member of the European great power system, presented a way for projecting a distinctive Russian identity vis-à-vis the West. While some Russian scholars accepted the relevance of Western IR theory, others believed that it needed to be interpreted according to Russian traditions, conditions and identity. Some Russian IR scholars sought to use multipolarity and civilisation as the basis for developing a 'Non-Western' Russian approach to IR, or even a school of IR (Makarychev and Morozov, 2013: 329, 335). This is somewhat similar to the emergence of a 'Chinese School of IR' discussed earlier, but less successful. The emerging civilisational and geopolitical discourse in Russian IR cuts both ways, simultaneously creating the basis for a distinctive Russian approach but also preventing the development of a broader global agenda in IR scholarship (Makarychev and Morozov, 2013: 339). The major tension within the Russian IR community has been aptly summed up by Andrey Makarychev and Viatcheslav Morozov (2013: 345):

the disciplinary field of IR in Russia is characterized by a wide chasm between scholars who treat Russia as a case governed by the general laws of modernization and transition to democracy, and their colleagues who insist that Russia's standing is unique to the extent that it requires an elaboration of a qualitatively different theoretical platform. In the final analysis, this split is caused by politicization of academic discourse, which happens around the notion of identity.

Compared to its relatively inward turn in Russia, IR in East and Central European states in the post-communist phase was more outward looking, especially towards the liberal West, helped by the entry of several countries to NATO and the EU. While the newly established CEEISA, and its flagship publication, the *Journal of International Relations and Development*, created a focal point of IR scholarship within the region, the scholarship was heavily influenced by Western theories and scholarship and financial support (Drulák, Karlas and Königová, 2009: 243). Despite this external support, or perhaps because of it, the state of IR in the region remained underdeveloped in terms of theory and method. And the external dependence might have played a part in ensuring that, unlike in Russia, IR scholarship in Central and East European countries did not develop 'any appropriate general concepts and perspectives that would refer to the local context' (Drulák, Karlas and Königová, 2009: 258).

Conclusions

Based on the discussion in Chapters 2, 4, 6 and 8, three concluding observations about the development of IR thinking in the periphery can be made: about regional diversity, about the relative thinness of theoretical development and about scholar-activism.

First, there is a great deal of diversity both between and within regions. Variation between regions is to be expected, given their different geographic, cultural and political histories. Indeed, it can be argued that IR thinking in the periphery primarily reflects a regional or local context. Different regions have stressed different core narratives: for example, dependency, hegemony and autonomy for Latin America; marginalisation and agency for Africa; and civilisational pasts and colonial humiliation for Asia. For the Middle East (excluding Israel), Islam has been an additional focus, albeit linked to both past civilisational and present political conditions in the region. While IR in Asia is now increasingly looking at the return to status and power, this is not true of the Arab Middle East, reflecting its lesser state of economic development and strategic power. Intra-regional diversity is along national and sub-regional lines. IR seems to be most advanced in China and India, as well as South Korea, Taiwan, Hong Kong and Turkey. Southeast Asia shows greater national differences; Singapore is unquestionably ahead of its neighbours, but Malaysia, Thailand, Indonesia and Philippines are also witnessing a surge of interest. In the Middle East, somewhat distinctive national approaches seem to be emerging in Iran and Turkey, and around the theme of Islam.

Second, with a few exceptions most notably from China and Turkey, theoretical work still remains scarce. Latin America has not really followed through with its early, distinctive theoretical contribution of Dependency Theory, and thinking about IR in most of the Non-Western world was atheoretical at birth. In many cases, IR studies began with the purpose of training diplomats. Where there were theoretical ideas, especially when one takes a broad definition of theory, these went unnoticed in the West because they did not relate to the concepts and vocabulary of Western IR (including terms such as Realism, Idealism and Liberalism, balance of power or security dilemma). Furthermore, many of the scholars from the Global South who have contributed to IR are based in the West. Postcolonialism, which some view as a successor to Dependency, and whose major writers are scholars from the Global South (though many are based in the West), has yet to count as mainstream within core IR, though it does now register increasingly strongly in Western theoretical debates, and its presence is noticeable in major IR texts in recent times. But predominantly, IR studies in the Global South have been driven by current events, policy concerns and applied theoretical knowledge. All regions of the periphery show a close nexus with policy and praxis. While some in the West lament the academia–policy divide in IR, the reverse may be true in many Third World regions, especially Asia (Acharya, 2014d). Notwithstanding a few notable exceptions, to a large extent, the periphery remains a consumer of Western IR theories.

One familiar criticism of Non-Western IR theory is that it does not go far beyond existing Western IR theories and methods, but simply puts indigenous culture and local agency into the familiar, modern Western-derived IR concepts and categories. But the diffusion of Western IR theory in the Non-Western world is rarely a matter of wholesale adoption. Rather, IR in general, and theory in particular, proceeds through 'local-isation' (Acharya, 2004, 2009),[13] whereby local scholars select, modify or adapt foreign ideas and concepts to suit the local (national and regional) context and need. Another relevant process is captured in notion of *norm subsidiarity*, whereby Global South scholars marry indigenous cultural and political concepts with imported ones to give them a more universal framing (Acharya, 2011b). This not only accounts for the variations in 'theoretical turns' that undoubtedly exist among different regions, but also offers an important contribution or 'agency' of the periphery in the spread of IR around the world: a crucial pathway to building Global IR. As Tickner and Wæver (2009c: 338) conclude, 'International Relations the world over is clearly shaped by Western IR. And yet, the situation

---

[13] We prefer it to 'translation' which does not convey who the translator is, that is the local agency, and 'vernacularisation', which stresses language, rather than substance. See Acharya (2018).

is certainly not one of "uniformity" and the "same", precisely because Western IR translates into something different when it travels to the periphery.'

This means theoretical work in the periphery is neither the wholesale adoption of Western theories on the one hand, nor an outright rejection or call for a completely new beginning on the other. Localisation, subsidiarity and hybridity in IR theory in the Non-Western world occur as Global South scholars, to whom Western concepts may initially seem relevant and even attractive, soon grow disillusioned with their Eurocentrism. This accounts for why so much Non-Western IR thinking and doing appear as hybrids (A. B. Tickner, 2009: 33) or, in Bilgin's (2008: 19–20) words, to be 'almost the same but not quite' as Western IR. While insufficient to counter the perception that the Global South is mainly the consumer of IR theories produced in the West, especially the United States, these localisations have contributed to a growing theoretical turn in the Global South and justify the urgings of some Global South scholars (Bilgin, 2008; K. Smith, 2012: 28–9) not to ignore or dismiss their importance.

We have discussed the advantages (mobilisation) and disadvantages (parochialism, state capture) of 'national schools' of IR elsewhere (Acharya and Buzan, 2007a). The key concern about any national school is whether it can 'deprovincialise' (Acharya, 2014c), that is, travel beyond the national or regional context from which it is derived in the first place, as the ES and the Copenhagen School (securitisation theory and regional security complexes) have done. If 'schools' are only useful for explaining developments with regard to a specific country or region, then their proliferation carries a greater risk of the fragmentation of the discipline. This is indeed a major challenge for developing a Global IR from local thinking and sources. As we have shown, some leading Chinese scholars are taking up this challenge, which should be of great interest to their counterparts in Asia and the wider IR community. Western and Non-Western, traditional and Global IR are not meant to be mutually exclusive but convergent and mutually reinforcing. This is consistent with a core element of Global IR in that it does not displace existing IR theories but seeks to enrich them with the infusion of ideas and practices from the Non-Western world.

Third, IR thinkers from the periphery were often scholar-activists. They not only contributed to a critique of imperialism or colonialism, such as Naoroji's drain theory or C. L. R. James's case for decolonisation of British West Indies, or organised anti-colonial movements on a national or regional basis (Garvey's Pan-Africanism being a major example of the latter). They also contributed to the critique of Western thought, including Marxist ideology which was a powerful current in both the colonial world and in the former colonies of Latin America. Examples of those who challenged and modified Marxism at an intellectual level include the Peruvian thinkers Haya and Mariátegui, James of Trinidad and M. N. Roy of India. Some rejected communism; Garvey believed communism was more beneficial to the white race who would use blacks to gain power. James did not think the black nationalist movement needed the vanguard role of a Troskyite party and was better organised independently from it. Mazrui also did not see communism as an ally of nationalism and progress.

Many of them directly combined political activism and leadership with intellectual explorations and analysis. Garvey, James and Rodney belong to the activist-scholar category, similar to Gandhi, Rizal, al-Afghani, Qichao, Sun and many others in an earlier era. In the scholar-leader category, one could place Eric Williams of Trinidad, Chedi Jagan of Guyana (who espoused the notion of a Global Human Order) and Michael Manley of Jamaica (who argued for democratic Socialism). These scholar-leaders evoked the likes of Nehru and other earlier thinker-leaders. There were also many instances of thinkers influencing leaders, James with Nkrumah, Mazrui with Nyerere, recalling Tagore's relationship with Gandhi.

Another aspect of this group was the transnational nature and impact of their thinking and the movements that they led. They interacted with and learned from each other, and also engaged in passionate debates and disagreements. C. L. R. James and George Padmore were childhood friends and partners in anti-colonial struggle and were influenced by Garvey's writings. In the 1930s and 1940s, Gandhi and Bose differed on the utility of non-violence as an anti-colonial approach. In the 1920s, Haya and Mariátegui differed on the 'united front' approach (combining the efforts of revolutionary and sympathetic bourgeois forces) and whether capitalism would be the final or the first stage of colonialism in the non-European world. In the 1930s, Du Bois rejected Garvey's black nationalism for being too extreme, amounting to a concession that blacks cannot be equal to whites, while Garvey was suspicious of Du Bois's closeness to the white race and judged him to be biased against him due to his Caribbean upbringing. In 1970, Mazrui debated with Rodney on the benefits of colonialism, especially the English language, for native peoples.

In terms of movements, a few key examples can be considered. Gandhi launched his anti-colonial ideas and campaign in South Africa, before moving to India. The First International Congress against Imperialism and Colonialism, held in Brussels in 1927, brought together many anti-colonial leaders, among them India's Nehru, Mohammad Hatta of Indonesia (future vice-president of the country), representatives of the African National Congress and Algeria's North African Star revolutionary movement. A founder of India's Congress Party, Naoroji, attended the first Pan-African Conference in London in 1900. India's M. N. Roy was a founder of the Mexican Communist Party. Many Caribbean and African thinkers interacted with each other not only in those regions, but also in Europe and/or the United States, where they studied and sometimes worked.

While many of these intellectuals were educated in the West, some in elite universities such as Oxford, London School of Economics and Harvard, their thinking and writings always focused on the circumstances of place and circumstances of origin. Their ideas were influenced by Western thinking, but they often rejected that thinking or adapted it to the context and needs of the societies they came from. In reconstructing the history of IR we thus need not only to look further back in time, but also more widely in space. Because of the institutional weakness and late development of academia in most of the Third World, IR thinking there was done much more by public intellectuals and political leaders than by academics. Much the same was true of IR thinking in the core during the nineteenth and early twentieth centuries, where, as we have shown, IR only became predominantly academic after 1945. That there is a disjuncture in the developmental timing of IR thinking in core and periphery is hardly surprising, and is no reason to exclude IR thinking in the periphery from the history of the discipline.

9   The Post-Western World Order:
Deep Pluralism

Introduction: Global International Society
in Transition/Crisis

In Chapter 7 we argued that, since around 2008, GIS had quite visibly begun to move into a transition between the Western-dominated, core–periphery structured versions 1.0 and 1.1, and a post-Western, version 1.2 GIS. We charted how the core was expanding in relation to the periphery as big developing countries such as China and India began to take up roles as great powers. Wealth, power and cultural authority were all diffusing away from the old Western core and Japan. This was paralleled by a steady decline in the standing of the United States as the sole superpower both in terms of material capacity and ideational status and authority. The liberal project that had long lent a teleological myth to the dominance of the West in general and the United States (and the Anglosphere) in particular was in deep crisis as a result of the great recession beginning in 2008 and the votes for Trump and Brexit in 2016. Yet while the dynamics of the core were becoming larger and more dominant in GIS, and those of the periphery smaller and weaker, both core and periphery were being increasingly entangled in a set of threatening shared fates. All of these changes stemmed from the ongoing working out of deep processes unleashed by the revolutions of modernity discussed in Chapter 1. Basically, the great unevenness of development created at that time was now beginning to even out with the rise of the rest, and the great shrinkage of the planet was accelerating into unprecedented levels of global interdependence. There seemed to be no doubt that changes to GIS of this kind, and on this scale, would not only create a much more pluralist GIS (pluralist in the sense of a wider diffusion of not only wealth and power, but also cultural authority), but also both challenge and change the nature of global governance and great power management.

In this section, we elaborate on the transition/crisis, and then review the terms and concepts with which one might capture the nature of the emerging post-Western GIS. The following section sets out assumptions about seven key structural features of the emerging GIS and the rationales supporting the argument. The third section provides both some specific predictions looking forward, and an analysis of some of the main structural features and dynamics of a post-Western GIS. The conclusions point out the scope for agency.

Even before the upheavals of Brexit and Trump in 2016, there was a widespread sense that GIS was in a significant period of transition, or even crisis, with the longstanding Western order being under siege from several different directions (Zakaria, 2009; Kupchan, 2012; Acharya, 2014d; Buzan and Lawson, 2015a, b; Stuenkel, 2016). The rise of China, India and 'the rest' is steadily eroding the relative dominance of the West, both material and ideational. This is a deep and ongoing process of redefining the structure and distribution of power and authority in GIS that began with the rise of Japan in the late nineteenth century, and reflects the successful adaptation to the revolutions of modernity of more and more states and societies. While decolonisation undid the political side of the Western colonial order, the rise of the rest is steadily undoing its more durable economic and cultural core–periphery structure. At the same time, transnational terrorism, mass migrations and mass communications have become seemingly permanent assaults on the territorial and political order of the postcolonial settlement. In parts of the periphery they threaten the postcolonial state (most obviously in the Middle East and Africa), and in the core they threaten the longstanding package of primary institutions – sovereignty, territoriality and nationalism – that constitutes states as the members of GIS.

That package was also threatened by the globalised Neoliberal capitalism that was the big winner of the Cold War, but that now seems to be entering a substantial crisis. Inequality is undermining its political legitimacy, and automation and globalisation are undoing its model of wealth distribution through mass employment. This dual crisis threatens the political stability of the basic engine of wealth and power that has driven the world along for the past two centuries. Capitalism's addiction to growth as the necessary condition for making inequality acceptable also links to environmental crises that seem to loom over the near horizon, threatening the basic operating conditions of all human societies. And capitalism's relentless innovation links to the multiple and complex ways in which the internet is changing the relationships between state, society and economy on which the existing order rests. Cumulatively, an increasingly interdependent human species on an ever more densely occupied planet is facing a variety of intensifying shared-fate issues ranging from climate change and global diseases, through terrorism and threats to the internet, to instabilities in the global economy and the biosphere. Although GIS is less threatened by interstate war than it has been for a long time, and has a deeper economic order than ever before, it nevertheless looks unstable. By dropping the Anglosphere out of its longstanding leadership role at the core of GIS, Brexit and Trump heighten the sense that a big transition to a post-Western GIS is underway.

This composite threat to the existing GIS from both the diffusion of wealth, power and authority and the intensification of shared-fate issues is no small matter. When modernity remade the world during the nineteenth century, it created an intensely combined, interdependent order on a global scale for the first time. Because the leading edge of the revolutions of modernity was concentrated in the West, and Japan, this version 1.0 GIS was deeply dominated by European/Western institutions, practices and ideas. Early Non-Western modernisers, most notably Japan, were forced to adapt to the Western model in order to get recognition. Since then, GIS has experienced many crises, including world wars, economic recessions and depressions, and decolonisation and the replacement of an imperial order by one of equality of both states and peoples. But through all of this turbulence, the West in general, and the Anglosphere in particular, won all the big wars and remained firmly as the core of GIS. This dominance meant that Western-style states based on popular sovereignty, territoriality and nationalism defined the membership of GIS. It also meant, at least in the West after 1945, that GIS had an almost teleological liberal agenda, most successfully in the economic sector, but also in expectations about the eventual triumph of democracy and human rights. This liberal teleology was periodically challenged, as in the interwar years by Fascism, and in the Cold War by communism. But somehow the Anglosphere always won out, keeping alive its claim to own the future. By the early 1990s, it looked as if the Western liberal model had no serious challengers left.

This Western-dominated GIS is the only international order on a planetary scale that we have ever known, and it is the Western-domination part that is now weakening fast. The West is losing not only the material predominance of power and wealth, but also the ideational legitimacy and the domestic will necessary to play the leading role. The crisis of capitalism plays into this, and it is a toss-up as to whether the onset of the economic crisis in 2008 or the 'Brexit plus Trump' rejection of global capitalism in 2016 will become the accepted benchmark date for the turning point. There are no precedents either for the transition process or for what another kind of global order might look like. So far we can only talk about it in terms of what it is not. It is more than *postcolonial* because the former periphery not only has its political independence, but increasingly the wealth and power to express and pursue its many cultures, and to pursue its many historical grievances. It is probably not *post-Westphalian*, because the core package of sovereignty, territoriality and nationalism looks well placed to survive and prosper. What it will unquestionably be is *post-Western*, not in the sense that the West will disappear as Rome did, but that it will become just one among several centres of wealth, power and cultural authority.

Much of the discussion about the present situation occurs in narrow bands. Will China surpass the United States and trigger a power transition crisis? Will the global economy get stuck in the doldrums created by an overstretched financial structure and/or by increasing nativist reactions against the social impacts of globalisation? Will some environmental crisis, whether global warming, sea-level rise or a global plague, change the basic geopolitical and geoeconomic assumptions? This chapter aims to identify a set of plausible assumptions about all of the major structural features that will shape GIS during the coming few decades, and by so doing build a holistic picture of the post-Western landscape that lies in front of us. By structural features we mean both material and ideational arrangements, and the directions in which they seem to be unfolding. These are drawn from across the spectrum of theoretical perspectives in IR, but for reasons of space, we do not make this theoretical substrate explicit. Those who are interested in IR theory will see it easily enough. Those who are not can still assess the arguments on their empirical merits. By identifying such structures, we hope both to expose their basic assumptions to scrutiny and to create a relatively simple foundation on which one can build post-Westphalian scenarios that take into account the likely synergies and contradictions between and among these structures. Only when we can see what these look like can we begin to think about what room for agency we might find within them.

This exercise assumes that no game-changing wild cards will emerge from the deck of international relations during the next two or three decades: no big and sudden climate change, no large-scale nuclear war, no global plague, no massive collapse of the global economy or infrastructure, no challenge to human dominance by super-intelligent AIs and suchlike. As we argue below, concern about these things might well be in play. To exclude them is not to say that they absolutely cannot or will not happen. Rather, it is to simplify the conditions of the analysis and to suggest that while some of these actualities are quite likely to occur at some point, if they happen they are likely to be somewhat further down the line. Thinking about the nature of GIS after the onset of one or more wild cards is a different exercise from this more extrapolative one, although some of the ideas here might be applied to it.

We are, of course, not the first people to attempt both to look beyond the transition we are now in and to find ways of labelling the emergent new structure of GIS. There is some consensus, at least outside of Realist circles, that the classical idea of *multipolarity* is inadequate to the task. Certainly, there will be several centres of wealth, power and cultural authority, and thus in a sense GIS will be multipolar. But there will be many non-state actors in play in this GIS, some of which will wield significant amounts of wealth, power and authority. States will probably remain the dominant form of actor, but much more entangled in webs of global governance than is implied either in the term multipolarity or in the ES's institution of *great power management* (Cui and Buzan, 2016). Even just thinking about states, the emerging GIS will still not be multipolar as classically understood because, lacking any superpowers or any aspiring superpowers, it will not feature a Realist-type struggle for domination of the whole system. This will be a global system, but one without superpowers, and containing several great powers and many regional ones. Various labels have already been put forward to capture the novelty and complexity of this construction: *plurilateralism* (Cerny, 1993), *heteropolarity* (Der Derian, 2003), *no one's world* (Kupchan, 2012), *multinodal* (Womack, 2014), *multiplex world* (Acharya, 2014a), *decentred globalism* (Buzan, 2011; Buzan and Lawson, 2014b, 2015a), *polymorphic globalism* (Katzenstein, 2012) and *multi-order world* (Flockhart, 2016).[1]

Building on, and extending, our own and others' conceptual work, we have decided to float a small, integrated set of conventional concepts that we think capture what is now unfolding: *deep pluralism* and *contested* versus *embedded pluralism*. By *deep pluralism* we mean a diffuse distribution of power, wealth and cultural authority, set within a strongly integrated and interdependent system, in which there is a significant move towards a GIS in which both states and non-state actors play substantial roles. While power asymmetries remain, it describes a world not only without a global hegemon, but in which the very idea of such a role is no longer legitimate. Such a world might feature different economic and political ideologies and systems, including the remnants of the liberal order (Buzan, 2011; Acharya, 2014a, 2017, 2018; Buzan and Lawson, 2014b, 2015a). Deep pluralism describes where the current momentum of GIS is taking us whether we like it or not. But we also need terms to indicate whether that condition is understood and acted upon in a positive or negative light, and where the scope for agency and policy lie. *Contested pluralism* means that there is substantial resistance to the material and ideational reality of

---

[1] For detailed discussion and critique of the oversimplification of polarity theory see Buzan (2004b, 2011) and Acharya (2014b: locs. 343–492).

deep pluralism. This might take various forms: states resisting the roles and standing of non-state actors; former superpowers (most obviously the United States) refusing to give up their special rights and privileges; great powers refusing to recognise each other's standing, and playing against each other as rivals or enemies. *Embedded pluralism* we adapt from Ruggie's (1982) idea of 'embedded liberalism'.[2] Embedded pluralism means that the main players in GIS not only tolerate the material, cultural, ideological and actor-type differences of deep pluralism, but also respect and even value them as the foundation for coexistence.[3] Another way of seeing this is that embedded pluralism is about the preservation and/or cultivation of the political and cultural diversity and distinctness that are the legacy of human history (Jackson, 2000: 23). The normative stance of embedded pluralism is thus grounded in a practical ethics conception of the responsible management and maintenance of a culturally and politically diverse GIS (Jackson, 1990; Cochran, 2008). Embedded pluralism might also be supported by a degree of intersubjective realisation of common interest in dealing with the set of inescapable shared-fate issues discussed in Chapter 7.

Plausible Assumptions about the Future of Seven Key Structural Features of Global International Society

Drawing on the narratives in Chapters 1, 3, 5 and 7, this section sets out assumptions about seven key structural features of the emerging GIS, and the rationales supporting them. The intention is to make explicit the foundations for thinking ahead into the nature and operation of deep pluralism. The seven structural features are: the global economy, the distribution of power, the nature of great powers, scientific knowledge and technology, shared fates, normative structures, and conflict and violence. Some of these require only one assumption, others several.

---

[2] Additional support for embedded pluralism can also be found in John Williams' (2015) arguments about the need for genuine acceptance of both difference and coexistence: 'intolerance of intolerance', and in Phillips and Sharman's (2015) demonstration that units of different types can successfully and durably generate order so long as they have some non-conflicting and/or compatible aims. Even Bull's (1977: 286–7) classical defence of pluralism against more ambitious schemes that try to override or ignore the deep divisions in the human community might be read as pointing towards embedded pluralism as the desired attitude. We are here building on a first attempt to work out the *deep* and *embedded* pluralism ideas in Buzan and Schouenborg (2018).

[3] There are similarities between this dynamic and the idea of a 'consociational security order' proposed by Acharya (2014b) to analyse Asian security.

The Global Economy

Assumption   The global market capitalist system initiated by the United States after the Second World War, and greatly strengthened by China's reform and opening up from the late 1970s and the implosion of the Soviet Union in the early 1990s, will, despite its current troubles, continue as the basic economic structure. This means that world trade and global finance will remain as key features of the global economy though perhaps with more restrictions than before 2016. There will be no collapse back to autarky, on either national or regional scale. Since the global market economy cannot function without a significant amount of regulation and management, this creates a powerful imperative to maintain a substantial degree of global governance and great power management at the global level. But changing technological and political conditions mean that its institutional structures and practices will be forced to adapt and evolve in significant ways.

Rationale   Given the quite serious crisis of capitalism suggested above, and the increasing political weight of anti-globalisation populism indicated by Brexit plus Trump, this assumption might seem rather heroic. There are two rationales behind it. First, global capitalism stands as the fastest and most effective means of acquiring wealth and power, and there is no alternative to it. Deng recognised this and committed China to it. Both known alternatives – imperial preference capitalism and totalitarian command economies – have been tried and failed, a process that occupied much of the twentieth century. The main lesson of the Second World War was that an imperial preference capitalism that divided the world into exclusionary and competitive capitalist spheres produced too much conflict. Even China, despite its defensive political and cultural exceptionalism, has not looked in that direction. The main lesson of the Cold War, driven home by the rise of Japan to number two, was that command economies, even on the scale of the Soviet Union, could not compete with capitalist ones. If wealth and power are the main goals of most states and peoples (and we assume that this is true in most places and will remain so) there are currently no serious alternatives to global market capitalism. A collapse back to some form of neo-mercantilism, even at the regional level, would generate significant economic contraction, and a consequent invidious politics of redistribution, for almost everyone.

Second, capitalism is by nature not only prone to periodic crises, but also flexible and adaptive. It has survived many predictions of being in decline or terminal crisis, and is continuously learning and evolving in response to the technological and social changes that its operation generates. Capitalism is a form of permanent revolution that outperforms even Mao's dreams. This process is certainly not smooth, and adaptation to relentless changes may not come without crises, sometimes severe. The current challenges of inequality, migration, financial instability, environmental overload and (un)employment are serious, and the solutions are not obvious. The temptation to liberalise finance, and to extend credit beyond sustainable levels, is a structural problem of the capitalist system (M. Wolf, 2014). But the bet for this rationale is that adaptation will continue to outpace both anti-globalisation reaction and terminal disaster.

The Distribution of Power

Assumption a Power in the international system/society is becoming more diffuse. In terms of states, there will be no more superpowers (powers for whom the world is their region), but a state system dominated by great powers (influential in more than one region) and regional powers (mainly influential within their home region) (Buzan and Wæver, 2003). The world order will thus remain globalised (economically and environmentally) but become politically decentred in terms of power and authority. Given a structure of several great powers, with no superpowers attempting to enforce a global order, it is reasonable to expect that a decentred global political order will be significantly regional in form, with great powers dominating their own local spheres. That said, one should not underestimate the degree to which there are disagreements within most regions, and strong resistance to the hegemony of local powers (Acharya, 2014b: locs. 1705–804). Regions without a local great power (Africa and the Middle East) will not have the problem of local hegemony, but will have the problem of whether they can provide sufficient local order without either a local hegemon or an intervening superpower. Probably the change in the distribution of power will have little impact on them, with both remaining as chaotic as they have been since decolonisation. Regions with more than one great power (Asia) will have to choose between a local contested pluralism based on internal rivalry between them, or constructing a consensual regional international society based on embedded pluralism.

Rationale a There has been a long period during which power has been concentrated in the hands of a relatively small number of mainly Western societies and states and Japan. This concentration was based on the massive unevenness of development that resulted from the way the revolutions of modernity unfolded during the nineteenth and twentieth centuries. From the late nineteenth century, the rise of Japan anticipated the rise of the rest, but for a century it had no followers. As the recent rise of China, India and others indicates, those revolutions are now becoming available to more and more states and peoples, who, as a consequence, are acquiring the elements of wealth and power that used to be confined to a few. As this process unfolds, the power of states and peoples in the international system/society is becoming more widespread and less concentrated. Because many are rising, the new great powers will not be able to achieve the concentrations of relative wealth and power that enabled Britain and the United States to operate as global superpowers in the days before modernity became so widespread. The old centres of power are not going away, only losing relative strength. The US position as the last superpower will continue to erode, perhaps quite quickly if Trump succeeds in unravelling the trust, alliances and institutions that support US leadership in GIS.

Assumption b   In a more diffuse distribution of power, there is scope for regional competition between the great powers over the boundaries of their spheres.

Rationale b   There is already such competition between China and the United States in East Asia, between India and China in South and Southeast Asia, and between Russia and Europe in Ukraine and the Baltic states. There is scope for competition between China and India in the Gulf, on whose oil both (and Japan) depend. Such competition is about spheres, not about domination of GIS as a whole.

Assumption c   The diffusion of power will also play between states and societies, albeit in complicated ways. Some non-state actors will acquire the power to challenge or ally not just with other non-state actors, but also with states, both their own, and/or others more distant. States at the weak/failed end of the spectrum will be more susceptible to challenges from non-state actors. From the middle of the spectrum up to the strong state end, the diffusion of power to non-state actors and their ability to challenge the state will depend on how open or closed the particular state is. Strong states may well ally with non-state actors for a range of purposes from aid and development through to subversion and destabilisation of other states, regimes and non-state actors. This layered view of power is captured by some of the terms noted above: *heteropolarity*, *multiplex*, *multi-order world* and *plurilateralism*.

Rationale c   In some ways the diffusion of power is empowering states against their populations, as most obviously in China. But in other ways it is empowering non-state actors against both their local state and, transnationally, against other states, other non-state actors and GIS. There is already a long record of non-state actors attacking their local state (e.g. in Afghanistan, Nigeria, Turkey, Sri Lanka, India, Congo and many Arab states) and also distant targets (Al Qaeda and Islamic State). Non-state actors are also more influential in non-violent political ways, as in campaigns on environmental issues and human rights, and in delivering aid, development assistance and disaster relief.

The Nature of Great Powers

Assumption   The group of great powers that will dominate GIS in the decades ahead will be inward-looking to the point of being *autistic*. In people, autism is about being overwhelmed by input from the surrounding society, making their behaviour much more internally referenced than shaped by interactions with others. In states it can be understood as where reaction to external inputs is based much more on the internal processes of the state – its domestic political bargains, party rivalries, pandering to public opinion (whether it be nationalist or isolationist) and suchlike – than on rational, fact-based assessment of and engagement with the other states and societies that constitute international society (Senghaas, 1974; Buzan, [1991] 2007: 277–81; Luttwak, 2012: 13–22). To some extent autism in this sense is a normal feature of states. It is built into their political structure that domestic factors generally take first priority, whether because that is necessary for regime survival, or because the government is designed in such a way as to represent its citizens' interests. But great powers are in part defined by their wider responsibilities to what Watson (1992: 14) labelled *raison de système*, defined as 'the belief that it pays to make the system work'. This stands as a counterpoint to the idea of *raison d'état*, which is explicitly central to Realism, and implicitly to much Western IR theory and practice. To the extent that states, and especially great powers, have autistic foreign policies, they not only fail to uphold *raison de système*, but also lose touch with their social environment, and are blind to how their policies and behaviours affect the way that others see and react to them. In such conditions a cycle of prickly action–overreaction is likely to prevail, and building trust becomes difficult or impossible. Everyone sees only their own interests, concerns and 'rightness', and is blind to the interests, concerns and 'rightness' of others. If this diagnosis of autism turns out to be correct, then we are unlikely to see responsible great powers. The absence of responsible great powers in conditions of deep pluralism points to a contested pluralist GIS, weak and possibly quite fractious.

Rationale Autism will be strong in the current and near future set of great powers for two reasons. First, the old, advanced industrial great powers (the United States, the EU, Japan) are not going to go away, but they are exhausted, weakened both materially and in terms of legitimacy, and are increasingly unable or unwilling to take the lead. No clearer illustration of this could be desired than the surprising 2016 successes in attracting voter support of both the Brexit campaign in the United Kingdom and Trump's 'America first' campaign in the United States. The EU has weak foreign and security policy institutions anyway, and is too mired in its own local problems of the Euro, Brexit, migration, Turkey and Russia to have much diplomatic energy or legitimacy left for *raison de système*. It is barely maintaining *raison de région*. Japan is pre-occupied with recovering its status as a 'normal country' and trying to deal with the rapid rise of a China that seems committed to maintaining historical hostility against it. The rising great powers (China and India, possibly Brazil) are very keen to claim great power status, and might provide new blood to the great power camp. But they are equally keen not to let go of their status as developing countries. They want to assert their own cultures against the long dominance of the West, and some, notably China, are cultivating a nationalism based on historical grievance. But while they know what they are against, the rising powers have as yet shown little clear idea about what kind of alternative GIS they want. That combination leads them to give priority to their own development. They argue, not unreasonably, that their own development is a big and difficult job for them, and that developing their own big populations is a sufficient contribution to GIS in itself. On that basis, they resist being given wider, global managerial responsibilities. Russia is not a rising power, and is too weak, too unpopular, too self-centred and too stuck in an imperial mind-set to take a consensual global leadership role. The cycle of prickly action–overreaction relations typical of autism is already visible in US–China, Russia–EU, US–Russia and China–Japan relations.

Scientific Knowledge and Technology

Assumption The rapid accumulation, advancement and distribution of scientific knowledge and technology that took off during the nineteenth century will continue across a broad spectrum. This will not only add more and more new capabilities to the toolkit of humankind, but also, as it has been doing since the nineteenth century, put continuous and massive pressure on economic, social, political, legal, military and moral structures. Humankind will thus remain locked into the knowledge explosion that started during the nineteenth century, and the seemingly permanent social revolution that it has been driving ever since. The exact shape and character of the social changes precipitated by new technologies is difficult to predict. Hardly anyone understood the consequences of the internet when it began to take off in the 1990s. Those currently thinking about the so-called *singularity* (the point at which a form of intelligence appears, whether machine or biological, that equals or outpaces the mark-one human being) have no consensus about whether such a development, which they expect in the next few decades, will be benign or disastrous for humankind (Mills, 2013; Bostrum, 2014; Brynjolfsson and McAfee, 2014).

Rationale This is a well-established pattern now deeply embedded in most states and societies, and reinforced by the globalisation of capitalism. Seeking advance in this way was not controversial even during major ideological confrontations such as the Cold War. To disrupt it would require either a very massive ideational transformation away from rationalism and the wealth and power it generates, or a very major and durable breakdown of the social order necessary to support it. Either development would move from the extrapolation model to the 'wild card' one. In theory, the possibilities of knowledge and technology might be finite and so self-limiting, but if this is the case there are no signs that we are close to that point. In almost every sector from materials science, through physics and astronomy, to biotechnology and computing, new knowledge and technology continue to be developed at a rapid pace. The speed and scale of advances in information technology, material sciences and genetics over recent decades illustrate the point. There is certainly strong, and politically exploitable, sentiment against experts. But it is very far from obvious that policy on complex issues of technology, governance and economy is better made from a perspective of ignorance, than in the light of the best knowledge available.

Shared Fates

Assumption As reviewed in detail in Chapter 7, humankind will become increasingly vulnerable to shared fates, some of them natural and others human-generated (Rees, 2003; Bostrum and Ćirković, 2008; N. Wolf, 2011; Mills, 2013; Homer-Dixon et al., 2015). The rise of these non-traditional shared-fate threats will increasingly compete for dominance of the security agenda with the more traditional military/political threats posed by states and societies to each other. As these wider logics of 'common security' (security *with*) become more intense, they will compete with logics of 'national security' (security *against*) (Buzan and Hansen, 2009: 187–225; Cui and Buzan, 2016). Some of these shared fates will create sustained pressure for global management, most obviously the global market, climate change, disease control and planetary protection against space rocks. But some will create both pressures for global cooperation and opportunities for weaponisation in great power competitions, most obviously in cybersecurity, migration and the rise of AI. Which tendency dominates will interplay strongly with whether GIS trends towards contested or embedded pluralism.

Rationale   As humankind occupies its planet ever more densely, with interdependence and development both rising and becoming more complex on the back of increasing interaction capacity, this condition makes humankind structurally more vulnerable to the range of shared fates noted above. The rising density of human occupation of the planet as a function of increasing human numbers will lessen in most parts of the world excepting Africa and the Middle East, where it looks set to increase. But as the diffusion of the revolutions of modernity progresses, density resulting from development and rising living standards will increase almost everywhere. The ambitions of Elon Musk to colonise Mars notwithstanding, there will be no 'off planet' solution to this problem for many decades, if ever.

Normative Structures

This structural feature is about society, and, since society is a contested concept, requires some explanation. All societies, including international and world ones, require some sort of normative or moral foundation that underpins the identities with which peoples define themselves and 'Others'. Such normative structures identify who counts as a legitimate member of the society, and what counts as legitimate behaviour within that society. Whether any kind of society exists at the global level is contested. The ES makes a good case for the existence of an *international* (i.e. interstate) *society* that defines itself and its membership by a shared set of primary institutions ranging from sovereignty and diplomacy to nationalism and human equality (Bull, 1977; Buzan and Schouenborg, 2018). This is a society of states that might also be thought of as a society of societies. It has a relatively small number of members (circa 200) and a relatively clear set of defining norms and institutions commonly held by its state members. Sociologists have taken relatively little interest in interstate society, and many of them would not accept that it counts as a form of society. A *world society* comprising all of humankind is a better fit with the mainstream sociological understanding of society, but in practice is much more a philosophical construct than a discernible reality. Where human beings are the members of society, there is little more cohesion at the global level than the widespread recognition that all humans are equal (replacing the longstanding assumption on grounds of race, class, gender or status that they were not, which underpinned racism, slavery, empire and the inferior status of women). Looked at in global perspective, the normative structure of humankind as individuals is powerfully fragmented into many subglobal civilisational, national and religious identities (J. Williams, 2015; Buzan, 2017; Buzan and Schouenborg, 2018). Mediating between the interstate dynamics of GIS and the identity dynamics of interhuman society is an increasingly dense and complex array of non-state transnational actors, both civil and uncivil.

This division between an international society of states and a world society of people(s) produces strongly contrasting assumptions about the normative structure of the emerging GIS.

Assumption a   The global normative structure of the *society of states* is stronger than it has ever been and, despite some fault lines, shows clear signs of deepening and widening its range of primary institutions.

Rationale a   Since the end of the Cold War, there has been a considerable and widespread consensus on a broad set of primary institutions that define GIS. These include: sovereignty, territoriality, diplomacy, international law, the market, development, nationalism, human equality, great power management and, up to a point, war. The consensus around global market capitalism is notable, with all of the great powers and many of the regional ones now being in some significant sense capitalist. This marks a considerable narrowing of the ideological bandwidth of GIS since the Cold War, during which the core issue was 'capitalism or not'. This is not to say that there are no disputes or disagreements about these things, for example, about non-intervention, how to run the global market and how great power management should work. There are disagreements in principle about human rights and democracy, and these therefore do not count as global institutions of international society (Buzan, 2014: 158–61; Buzan and Schouenborg, 2018). But despite these disagreements, there is a broad, robust and in some aspects (e.g. sovereignty, territoriality, nationalism, diplomacy, human equality) quite deep normative structure underpinning contemporary interstate society. Some aspects of this, such as nationalism and human equality, play strongly in world society as well. Environmental stewardship, the idea that humankind has a collective responsibility and self-interest to look after the planet, has recently emerged as a new primary institution during the twenty-first century, as nationalism did during the nineteenth, and the market during the twentieth (Falkner, 2016; Falkner and Buzan, 2017). Shared fates have the potential to generate elements of shared morality and culture that push upward from world society to interstate society (Clark, 2007). The core of this normative structure (sovereignty, territoriality, nationalism) looks stable, but normative political polarisation between authoritarians and democracies, and great power rivalry over spheres of influence, could put significant brakes on an otherwise strengthening interstate society (Buzan and Schouenborg, 2018).

Assumption b The global normative structure of *world society* will become more openly fragmented and diverse than it has appeared to be over the previous few decades.

Rationale b The long dominance of the West, and its liberal 'standard of civilisation' provided a veneer of global culture and morality. Driven by the Anglosphere core, this gave the appearance of a global ascendency of liberal ideas, defined mainly in terms of economic interests. This thin veneer was reinforced by the power of the teleological liberal claim to own the future, which was in turn reinforced by the material ascendency of the Anglosphere, and hid much cultural diversity beneath it. The relative decline of the West means that both material power and moral authority are becoming more diffuse across a wider range of actors. The reality of a truly postcolonial world society is now becoming visible as modernity spreads beyond its original small core. Liberal values will remain strong within the West, though even there they are under serious challenge from nativist, populist and neo-Fascist anti-globalisation views. Liberal values are spread more thinly elsewhere, and will remain globally influential as one of the main political views in play. But the rise of the rest, and the internet-fuelled influence of a host of transnationally operating non-state actors, will re-empower a variety of cultural moral alternatives, most obviously from Islam and Confucianism, but also from native traditions of authoritarianism. Collectively, that will lead to a more pluralist moral/cultural order. This is already evident in the assertion of 'Chinese characteristics' by Beijing, the cultivation of *Hindutva* in India, Russia's swing back to a Slavophile identity and the promotion of Islam as an alternative moral order. Enthusiasm for globalisation is weakening, and both nationalism and what might be called *civilisationalism* are resurgent. The dominance of identity politics over economics plays not only in

China, Russia, Japan and much of Asia, but also in the liberal heartlands of Europe and the United States. In a sense, world society is returning to its historical condition of cultural diversity as the aberration of a brief but powerful Western ascendency gives way to the global spread of the revolutions of modernity.

Conflict and Violence

Assumption a All-out great power war will remain highly constrained. It could happen through accident or carelessness, but it is highly unlikely to be a rational policy choice in the way that it was for the powers that initiated the First and Second World Wars. Hegemony-seeking on a global scale by great powers will continue to weaken as a motive for great power conflict and war. If there is to be global order on the basis of embedded pluralism, it will have to be negotiated and consensual. That said, in a decentred GIS, hegemony-seeking on a regional scale, and spheres of influence rivalries between great powers, might well remain quite strong.

Rationale a Great power global war no longer offers good, or perhaps any, option of gains outweighing losses. The means of destruction have become too great; the costs too high, the legitimacy of territorial gain by conquest too low; and the prospect of resistance in occupied territories too high. In addition, in a world of great powers (i.e. no superpowers), none will have the capability, and perhaps none will have the ambition, to bid for global hegemony. As the US experience over the last couple of decades shows, that job involves increasingly expensive and impossible burdens, and both the job itself and the US incumbency in it have declining legitimacy. As noted above, the rhetoric of rising great powers such as India and China makes clear that they are hesitant to carry even great power responsibilities, let alone superpower ones, preferring to give priority to their own development. In this priority, they do not differ much from the United States in its isolationist period up to 1941. The current rivalry between the United States and China, though often understood as being about global supremacy, is more about which power dominates Asia. That said, great powers might well seek regional primacy, though where there is more than one great power in a region, fear of war will constrain the use of all-out war to achieve such goals.

Assumption b Interstate wars generally will remain infrequent, the exception rather than the rule. This does not by any means rule out quite a lot of military swaggering, shoving and pushing, and arms racing.

Rationale b The same arguments as for rationale (a) apply here. The South China Sea looks like becoming a test case for both assumptions (a) and (b).

Assumption c Wars between states and non-state actors, and between rival non-state actors, will become the main form of 'international' violence.

Rationale c It has been clear since 2001 and the onset of the GWoT that non-state actors have the capability to recruit, train, motivate and equip significant fighting forces. There is a growing record of them both fighting each other (mainly in the Middle East) and attacking more distant targets in Europe and the United States. The breakdown of the postcolonial political order in parts of the Middle East, Africa and Asia, and the emergence of several failed states and many weak ones in those places, provide good opportunities for violent non-state actors to establish bases. The resurfacing of moral/cultural diversity in a context of ongoing historical resentment of colonialism, and still significant vestiges of Western hegemony, provides powerful legitimacy to jihadists. The globalised economy makes it easy for them to buy equipment and find sponsors, both in (un)civil society and from some states.

Assumption d Interstate dynamics will remain a significant, but relatively declining, driver of conflict and violence. Racism will continue to decline as a driver of conflict, but cultural differences look set to remain strong, especially when linked to migration issues. Given the widespread adoption of global market capitalism, ideological drivers are also in decline. But given the crisis of capitalism discussed above, economic inequality might well become a rising driver of conflict, as much, and possibly more, within states than between them. As shown in Chapter 7, global capitalism is closing the gaps between states, while opening up inequalities within them. This pattern of motives suggests the violence and conflict will be located more within states, and/or transnationally, than between them.

Rationale d Many states continue to be ready to fight over territorial issues, especially where these have been sacralised by nationalism. States will also compete and perhaps use force over local/regional status issues. But global capitalism acts as a hedge against the use of force for economic reasons, and the steam has gone out of the competition for global hegemony. Deep ideological differences like those of the twentieth century are no longer in play, though the divide between authoritarians and democracies could remain significant. Racist motives have been subdued by the widespread postcolonial commitment to the idea that all humans are equal, but reactions to mass migration in many places suggest that cultural and, perhaps especially, religious differences matter a lot. Identity politics now seems to rest more on culture than on race. Capitalism has not yet found an answer to the extremes of inequality, which continue to grow and become politically more sensitive. The traditional solution of maintaining steady economic growth to legit-imise inequality is looking ever weaker and more difficult since the eco-nomic crisis of 2008. As Brexit and Trump show, the nineteenth-century response of promoting nationalism to counter class differences might still have some mileage in it, but risks disrupting the global economy on which all depend for wealth and power. The demise of capitalism because of its internal contradictions has been predicted, wrongly, many times, suggesting that one should never underestimate the learning cap-acity and adaptability of capitalism as a system. But if wealthy elites try to entrench their position, whether by capturing the state, or using tech-nologies of control, or retreating into protected enclaves, then conflict can be expected.

If one takes this set of assumptions and rationales as reasonable, then both synergies and contradictions between them are evident. These syn-ergies and contradictions do not yield a simple picture. The main message is that while powerful structural forces are in play for both continuity and change, these forces are frequently pulling in opposite directions. What does this tension tell us about the outlook for GIS and the possibilities for agency in the choices between contested and embedded pluralism in the decades ahead?

The Outlook: A Post-Western Global International Society

The analysis supports three predictions about GIS in the coming decades. The first is that it is entering a period of quite deep and sustained tran-sition. The second is that what is emerging will not be any form of 'back to the future', but something quite novel that stands substantially outside mainstream IR theories. The third is that the emerging GIS will display a deeply pluralist structure layered between regional and global levels.

Transition

GIS is now clearly moving away from its longstanding form of being a Western-dominated core–periphery structure, US-led, and with a relatively small core and a large periphery. It is moving towards reflecting a culturally and politically diverse group of great and regional powers, with an expanding core and a shrinking periphery. At the same time, the overall state-centrism of GIS is being reshaped by the increasing role and power of a diverse range of non-state actors, both civil and uncivil, and by the relentless increase in interaction capacity and shared fates. The material and normative structures of this emerging, version 1.2 post-Western GIS will be strikingly different from the Western-global model. Material power will be more diffuse, and normative legitimacy will be more diffuse and stemming from multiple cultures, including Liberalism but no longer dominated by it. This cultural pluralism will be the case not only among states, but also between states and a wide variety of non-state actors. All of this is accompanied by a political shift away from the left–centre–right ideological dispositions that drove much of twentieth-century international politics, and towards a tension defined by those who favour inward-looking, protectionist nationalism and nativist identity politics on the one hand, and those who favour open societies and globalisation on the other. Most societies are torn by this question, and their domestic politics are likely to oscillate around it in potentially unstable ways. Russia and India are exemplars of the inward-looking stance. China has done well from globalisation but is generally inward looking. Japan likewise has done well from globalisation but is also strong on identity politics. The former bastions of Liberalism – the United States, Britain and the EU – are deeply split on the question.

Not 'Back to the Future'

This movement towards cultural and material pluralism is not, how-ever, simply a return to the *status quo ante* of premodern times in which civilisations were semi-autonomous developments, and the world had sev-eral centres of wealth and power, mostly thinly connected to each other. In the emerging GIS, the diffusion of power and normative legitimacy will take place in a context of sustained, deep and unavoidable interconnectedness. Thus, even though cultures subordinated by Western power and Liberalism during the nineteenth and twentieth centuries are now re-emerging, they are far from doing so in an autonomous way. While the rising powers may be re-discovering and re-authenticating their cultural roots, they are also inescapably fusions, with the ideas and institutions of modernity. Modernity is now woven into their social, economic and political fabric, and, just as for the West, is essential to their pursuit of wealth and power. Rising powers thus represent cultural fusions quite different from their premodern forms. Just as Western culture was transformed by modernity, so too are all other cultures that encounter it (Katzenstein, 2010: 14–38). Outside the West, Japan led the way in developing a stable fusion of its own culture with modern ideas and practices, and China and others are now well advanced down the same path. Modernisation and the logic of uneven and combined development has not resulted in Japan or China or India becoming clones of the West; far from it (Rosenberg, 2013, 2016). It has resulted in unique fusions, different from the West and different from each other, in which each society finds its own way of integrating the ideas and institutions of modernity into its own culture. Thus although the GIS that is emerging may be more culturally pluralist than that of the period of Western domination, it will also share a significant substrate of the ideas and institutions of modernity as a legacy of its formative process.

A Layered, Deeply Pluralist, Post-Western Global International Society

The fact that structural pressures are often pushing in opposite directions will produce a more deeply pluralist, layered form of GIS. The desire among states and peoples for more political, cultural and, up to a point, economic differentiation is strong, and increasingly linked to a more diffuse distribution of power and cultural legitimacy. That combination, along with the autistic tendencies of the likely great powers, suggests a powerful trend towards more regionalised and culturally and politically differentiated international societies. Yet at the same time, the normative structure of GIS is relatively robust, and the imperatives of shared fates, including the maintenance of the global economy, make a substantial amount of global-level cooperation unavoidable unless states and peoples are prepared to accept big reductions in their wealth, power and security. The fact that there are strong forces pulling in opposite directions suggests not only that the scope for agency for both state and non-state actors is substantial, but also that the victory of either direction – a weaker, more fragmented and regionalised GIS; or a stronger, more coherent and more globalised one – may not be the most likely outcome. Regional and global levels of order can be zero-sum, as they were during the 1930s. They can also be compatible, as suggested by economic regionalisms such as the EU, which provide not just an alternative to, or fall-back from, global economic order, but also a way of constructing a stronger negotiating position within a global game. The world we are facing offers a somewhat different dialectic between the regional and global levels than either the 1930s or the EU. The strength of the forces currently pushing both options suggests that, in the coming decades, having some version of both is the most likely outcome. The puzzle for the coming decades will be how to reconcile the localising imperatives of revived cultural diversity with the globalising ones of shared fates, and how to do so in a deeply pluralist world with no dominant superpower, core group or culture, or ideology.

What these seemingly contradictory structural pressures point to is a more layered GIS in which regional and/or subglobal differentiation driven by civilisationalism will play alongside a pluralist global level sustained by the need to deal with shared fates. Happily, a pluralist interpretation of the institutions of GIS is in many ways quite accommodating to cultural diversity. Sovereignty, non-intervention, territoriality and nationalism all support the preservation and/or cultivation of the political and cultural difference and distinctness that are the legacy of human history. In practical terms, this dual movement will involve a shift of purpose between the regional and global levels. On the regional level, governance will become more general in order to support political and cultural differentiation. This might be done by local hegemonic leadership, as seems to be the drift in the neo-imperial projects of Russia and China. Or it might be done more consensually, as in the EU, or as hinted at by talk of African defections from the International Criminal Court. In this specific sense, the EU might become the model it has always wanted to be inasmuch as it shows how to do culturally based regional differentiation. On the global level, governance will become less general, and more focused on the specific functional issues raised by shared fates. The Western project to promote liberal values as the universal underpinning, or 'standard of civilisation', for global order will weaken globally even if it remains strong within the West (which Trump and Brexit suggest it may not) and to some extent elsewhere. And nothing 'universal', in the sense of a broad view of what is politically and morally right, will replace it. Modernity will unfold along several political and social lines rather than just one.

Those in China, Russia, Iran, France, India and elsewhere who have long opposed US/Western hegemony and called for a more 'multipolar' international order will get their wish. But in the tricky tradition of 'wish' stories, they will not get what they expected. Regions will increasingly, and for better or for worse, be left to fend for themselves. In the absence of both superpowers and globally dominant ideologies, the global level will not be about the world political and social order in general, as it has been over the past several decades. Rather, it will be about a series of specific functional agreements and institutions to deal with shared-fate issues that are recognised and accepted by all as such, and are not treated as areas of political contestation. The retreat of GIS to a limited set of functional specifics was perhaps foreshadowed by the ability of the United States and the Soviet Union to agree on non-proliferation of nuclear weapons even during the depths of their otherwise zero-sum rivalry. More recently, the shift from disagreement to consensus on climate change between Copenhagen in 2009 and Paris in 2015 suggests the emergence of specific functional cooperation against a shared threat (Falkner and Buzan, 2017). This agreement is beginning to look robust enough to survive Trump's opposition, and thus add to the signals of US retreat from superpower status.

A dual-track development along these lines would amount to a very substantial reconceptualisation of GIS from what we have been used to over the past decades. In one sense, it would break with the liberal solidarist assumption that there was a defining set of universal political and social values to which all must eventually adhere. It would be an explicitly deep, embedded, pluralist GIS in cultural and political terms, but one resting on a strong substrate of shared primary institutions, and pressured by an array of shared-fate problems. It might well therefore contain substantial solidarist elements in terms of functional arrangements to deal with shared threats. The alternative to it would be a contested deep pluralism in which autistic great powers neglect the fact that they are locked into a highly globalised context of interdependence and shared fates, and pursue only their own narrow interests. In that case, we could expect serious under-management of the shared fates at the global level, and a lot of jostling over regional spheres of influence.

The question is how to balance the emergent deep pluralist GIS so that it can both deal with shared-fate problems at the global level and meet the demand for cultural pluralism within world society. Autistic great powers both old and new will need to shift their focus away from clashing ideas about democracy versus authoritarianism, or the general principles of world order. They will need to pursue tolerance and coexistence in relation to their broader political and cultural projects, and focus on the specific functional areas of cooperation at the global level necessary to deal with shared fates. If regionalising imperatives tend towards turbulence and competition among the great powers, that would make more controversial the distinction between what might be considered a shared-fate global issue and one that might be used in competition among the great powers. A killer asteroid on a collision course with Earth would clearly count as a shared-fate issue, overriding all differences. So might maintaining the stability of global trade, and the need to defend against a global plague. But issues like migration and nuclear proliferation, and cybersecurity, might be seen in more sectional terms, where specific developments would harm some and favour others. The recent suspicion that Russia was quite happy to foment a refugee crisis for the EU, whether true or not, is a good example of how this sectional logic might work. Cybersecurity might have the same logic of being partially a global shared fate, and partly a conflict resource among rival powers. How well or how badly GIS functions will thus depend on whether the game is played mainly as coexistence at the global level, or mainly as rivalry at the regional one.

A key factor in the scope for agency between coexistence and rivalry outcomes is how problems of historical memory are handled. One possible benefit from the fading away of Western and US hegemony, and liberal universalism, could be the easing of some of the problems of reaction, resentment and opposition to such hegemony that have bedevilled GIS since the end of the Cold War. As US and Western leadership have declined in legitimacy, this has weakened the leadership of GIS without putting anything in its place. The easing of reaction, resentment and opposition would, however, depend on the fading of the historical memories of bullying and indignity that still feed postcolonial resentments, and that might take a long time. Such memories have political utility to ruling regimes in many places, and the CCP's creation of a Chinese nationalism that is strongly anti-Japanese and anti-Western is only the leading example of governments assiduously cultivating (and distorting) such memories for their own ends. Imperial Japan did this in its heyday, Russia and Iran are playing the same game, and India could tip in that direction though so far has not. Historical resentment against the West could long outlast the period of Western dominance, and if it does, that will weaken the chances for adequate management of shared-fate problems at the global level, and exacerbate regional rivalries.

Either way, one firm, specific prediction is that the general diffusion of power and authority, and the increasing role of non-state actors alongside states, will put a lot of pressure on the existing structure of IGOs. As indicated by the inability to bring Germany and Japan into the UNSC, the current array of IGOs is already quite out of date even within the assumption of a Western-dominated GIS. In a post-Western GIS marked by deep pluralism and an expanding core, the IGOs formed after the Second World War will face a mounting crisis of legitimacy if they do not adapt to the more diffuse distribution of wealth and power, and the more morally and culturally plural ideational landscape. Responding to the slowness of adjustment within these core institutions, China's promotion of the AIIB is perhaps the harbinger of what will be a decades-long game to remake IGOs and regimes so that they fit better with the duality of the emerging post-Western world order, and the changing division of purpose between the regional and global levels.[4] The upside to this,

---

[4] For a detailed review of the emerging game around reform and remaking of IGOs, see Stuenkel (2016, chs. 4 and 5).

as argued by Oliver Stuenkel (2016: locs. 434–532), is that the Non-Western states mainly support the existing order, but want to improve their position within it. The problem will be whether the West in general and the United States in particular can make the adjustment from thinking of themselves as the indispensable providers of global leadership and universalist liberal vision to understanding themselves as being just one part of a deeply pluralist GIS composed of culturally and politically differentiated peers. The US opposition to AIIB even under Barack Obama suggests that this process will be long and difficult.

The growth of so-called 'global governance' in which lesser powers and non-state actors play significant roles in global norm- and institution-building is a likely additional factor in this process. Great power management and global governance have so far been seen more as in opposition than as working together, with global governance advocates somewhat seeing great power (mis)management as the problem. In a deeply pluralist GIS, neither great power management nor global governance will be sufficient in themselves to support the degree of order and management necessary to deal with shared fates. Either they must work together or GIS will be weak and under-managed (Cui and Buzan, 2016).

Conclusions

This exercise in looking ahead hardly offers a crystal ball showing a detailed picture of post-Western GIS. But it does offer a plausible overview of the landscape into which we are moving, and the major dynamics in play. It provides a sketch of the future that is solidly enough grounded to serve as a basis for both theory and policy discussion. We show what is strongly determined and what is still open, and thus identify a considerable scope for agency. We are not trying to be either optimistic or pessimistic. We are confident that some version of deep pluralism is what lies ahead, but within that, readers can come to their own conclusions about the positives and negatives of pursuing either contested or embedded pluralism. Neither are we trying to take sides in the many impassioned debates about the rights and wrongs of world history. We are trying to show that, whether one likes it or not, humankind is moving into a global political and cultural landscape quite different from, though still strongly shaped by, the one we have been in since the nineteenth century. The post-Western world is now standing in front of us. We can identify many of its key features, and we have choices about how we might try to navigate within this new global landscape.

10   Towards Global International Relations

Introduction

In this concluding chapter, we first make brief observations about the findings of the book as they relate to the evolution of ir and IR. We then discuss some of the recent directions in IR theory and discipline, highlighting the broadening of the field but also the persisting Western-centrism that continues to mark the literature. Next, we examine the emergence of Global IR (and related concepts such as Non-Western or post-Western IR). We look at the key elements of Global IR, sketch out some of these debates around it, and the ways in which it can be pursued and advanced, and the challenges these efforts face. We call for a third founding or refounding of the discipline, not just on normative grounds, but as a necessity to retain IR's relevance in a globalised, deeply pluralist, post-Western world.

In Chapter 9, we introduced the ideas of *contested* and *embedded* pluralism to conceptualise the post-Western world order. To the extent that IR thinking follows ir reality, and this book is closely premised on our view that this is often the case, we anticipate greater pluralisation of IR, both the discipline itself and its theory. By pluralisation, we mean diversification rather than fragmentation in a negative sense, although some degree of the latter will be unavoidable. But the transition to a post-Western world order has only been obvious for a couple of decades, and will take several more to work itself through. This is not a quick transition like those that accompanied the defeat of the Axis powers in 1945 and the implosion of the Soviet Union after 1989. The accompanying global 'idea-shift' (Acharya, 2016) in the IR discipline will also work itself out on this timescale, hopefully not lagging too far behind the unfolding of deep pluralism, and perhaps even anticipating it in some respects. Progress towards Global IR is already happening and will intensify. But it faces serious obstacles, not least the stickiness of Western dominance of the discipline, and the persistence of conditions in the Global South that obstruct a quick realisation of the Global IR project.

A key finding of this book is that despite efforts to introduce greater diversity into the field, most IR theories, with the important exception of Postcolonialism, remain Western-centric, and that IR continues to be a predominantly Western, though certainly not an exclusively American, social science. Our findings resonate with those of Postcolonialists (Nandy, [1983] 2009; Dirlik, 1999; Chowdhry and Nair, 2004; J. M. Hobson, 2012) and others (Acharya, 2014b: 25–6; Kuru, 2016) about the several persisting and overlapping dimensions of Western dominance of IRT:

- Eurocentrism. The tendency to theorise key principles and mechanisms of international order from Western (mainly West European, but with the subsequent imprint of the United States) ideas, culture, politics, historical experiences and contemporary praxis. Conversely, it is reflected in the disregard, exclusion and marginalisation of Non-Western ideas, culture, politics, historical experiences and contemporary praxis. Part of this Eurocentrism can be attributed to a still potent sense of superiority of the Western pattern over the Non-Western one (Acharya, 2000). Its effectiveness is amplified by the West's power to control the representation of things so as to normalise existing hierarchies.
- False Universalism. The tendency to view or present Western ideas and practices as the universal standard, while Non-Western principles and practices are viewed as particularisms, aberrations or inferiorities. As we have shown, this practice stretches from Realist and Liberal assumptions about the state, to Feminist ones about the position of women.
- Racism. The persistent forgetting in the West of the major role played by race hierarchies in colonialism, and the ongoing legacies of this in both Western practices and periphery resentments and anger.
- Disjuncture. The lack of fit between what passes for IR theory and the experience of the Non-Western world, although Western scholars seldom see this as an obstacle to theory-building. There are serious problems about applying theories of conflict, cooperation, institution-building, norm diffusion dynamics, empire, Feminism, etc. that dominate the literature of IR to the Non-West.
- Agency denial. The lack of acknowledgement of the agency of Non-Western states, regional institutions and civil society actors in contributing to world order, including serious additions and extensions to the principles and mechanisms which were devised by the West. As argued in Chapter 8, the Non-West are seen as consumers, rather than producers, passive recipients rather than active borrowers, of theoretical knowledge claims.

Taken together, these practices tend to override the significance of cultural differences, which is one reason why culture and culturalism become the main arena for both defence and counterattack against Western hegemony in both ir and IR. How can Global IR address these issues so as to keep the discipline aligned with the emerging post-Western world order?

Hegemony and 'Diversity' in IR

Looking back at how IR theory has developed in the past decade, several trends stand out. First, the field's mainstream, centred on the West, especially the United States, appears to have moved past the 'great debates' about paradigms and 'isms' (Jackson and Nexon, 2013: 545–8). The most recent debate, between Rationalism (Realism and Liberalism) on the one hand and Constructivism on the other, has given way to attempts at paradigm bridging, theoretical pluralism and analytical eclecticism (Dunne, Hansen and Wight, 2013). Kahler (1997) questions the utility of the great debates, while Jonas Hagmann and Thomas Biersteker (2014: 294–5) provide a revisionist account of their locations and sequences. They point to variations between Europe and the United States: for example, the presence of strong Realist thinking in Europe during the interwar period when American IR was in the 'Idealist' mode; and the Idealist turn in German IR after the Second World War when American IR was turning Realist. The French remained unaffected by the great debates; there were different debates in different places.

Second, the fading interest in the 'big' or meta-theoretical debates has been accompanied by the growing popularity of 'middle-range theories'. Such work identifies research questions or 'issue-oriented puzzles' (Walt, 2005: 33) in international affairs and explains them with the help of IR literature's 'widely accepted causal mechanisms' (Jackson and Nexon, 2013: 548) that specify the relationship between variables. The vast majority of work in major IR journals in the United States falls into this category (Jackson and Nexon 2013: 548), though that is much less true of European IR journals, most of which maintain a broad spectrum of epistemological approaches. The rising IR journals in Asia (*Chinese Journal of International Politics, International Relations of the Asia-Pacific*) also contain a broad spectrum of theoretical approaches. The narrow positivist approach has been criticised for being constrained by prevailing epistemological and ontological assumptions (Dunne, Hansen and Wight, 2013: 418), for producing mostly conditional or contingent generalisations (Walt, 2005: 33) and for focusing too much on 'practically relevant knowledge' (Reus-Smit, 2013: 601–3), at the expense of theoretical innovation. Hence, the talk of 'the end of international theory' (Dunne, Hansen and Wight, 2013).[1]

The rise of middle-range theory has mixed implications for those seeking to open IR theory up to the Non-Western world. On the one hand, these theories have expanded the use of IR theory in general. They have stoked the curiosity of Western scholars about the wider world of regions and helped to engage the interest of Non-Western scholars in IR theory. On the other hand, to the extent that writings using hypothesis testing and mid-range theories speak to an overwhelming positivist bias in American IR (Colgan, 2016: 495), it is not helpful to Global South scholars in getting published in major Western journals, since such scholars usually prefer non-positivist approaches. The concepts and causal mechanisms employed for formulating hypotheses are derived mainly from Western history and experience. This entrenches the tradition of Western dominance in IR theory.

A third development in IR theory is the ongoing rise of Constructivism. In the 2014 Teaching, Research and International Policy (TRIP) survey, Wendt came first as 'the scholar whose work has had the greatest influence on the field of IR in the past 20 years'.[2] Constructivism came out as the top choice of an IR paradigm at 22.5 per cent, followed by Realism and Liberalism, but the numbers of those who opted for 'I do not use paradigm' exceeded Constructivism.[3] This attests to the aforementioned point about the declining interest in paradigm debates.

The rise of Constructivism has some positive implications for those committed to the project of a more universal discipline of IR or Global IR. Lacking material power, developing countries often resort to ideational forces (Puchala, 1995: 151), and this is where Constructivism

---

[1] Not everyone agrees with the 'end of theory' in IR. Colgan (2016) argues that while looking solely at journals might show the growing popularity of mid-range theories and hypothesis testing, this contrasts with what is being taught at universities in the United States at the PhD level (especially the 'field seminars'), which remains dominated by big theoretical issues and framing. Kristensen (2018: 12) argues that while a citation analysis of journal articles confirms a widening gulf between theory-driven work and quantitative modelling, the latter is not 'overtaking the discipline'.

[2] TRIP survey (2014), https://trip.wm.edu/charts/#/bargraph/38/5045 (Accessed 27 June 2018). Keohane occupied the top IR scholar spot in the 2009 TRIP survey (www.wm.edu/offices/itpir/_documents/trip/final_trip_report_2009.pdf, accessed 27 June 2018), while Wendt came first in the 2012 TRIP survey (www.wm.edu/offices/itpir/_documents/trip/trip_around_the_world_2011.pdf, accessed 27 June 2018).

[3] The survey question asked: 'Which of the following best describes your approach to the study of IR? If you do not think of your work as falling within one of these paradigms or schools of thought, please select the category into which most other scholars would place your work. TRIP survey (2014), https://trip.wm.edu/charts/#/bargraph/38/5052 (Accessed 27 June 2018).

is especially useful. It offers greater scope for capturing their normative role in world politics, such as in contesting and localising Western norms and creating new ones to reform and strengthen world order.[4] Second, Constructivism has made inroads into the study of regional dynamics by both Western and Non-Western scholars (see, e.g. Barnett, 1995, 1998 on the Middle East; Kacowicz, 2005 and Sikkink, 2014 on Latin America; Johnston, 1998 and Hemmer and Katzenstein, 2002 on East Asia; and Acharya, 2001a, 2004, 2009, 2011b on Southeast Asia and Asian regionalism in general). The influential Constructivist book *Security Communities* (Adler and Barnett, 1998) largely focused on regions, both Europe and outside. All this literature has been invaluable in stimulating theory-guided debates and analysis and communication among both Western and Non-Western scholars.

With its emphasis on culture and identity, Constructivism has offered a valuable bridge between the Area Studies tradition that is popular in the IR literature in the Non-Western world and the centres of IR in the West. As a Malaysian IR scholar (Karim, 2007) writes, 'Thinking in the constructivist vein has been about the best gift made available to scholars and leaders in the region.' Yet, Constructivism remains largely a Western-centric enterprise. While Constructivism has moved beyond its initial privileging of Western norms and norm protagonists, it continues to neglect issues of race and pre-Westphalian civilisations in Asia, the Middle East and elsewhere that might bring new insights into IR theory from outside the core sourcing areas of the West. A recent study analysing an extensive journal-based data set (Bertucci, Hayes and James, 2018: 23) finds that 'despite constructivism's place as the leading theoretical alternative to rationalist approaches to the study of international relations, in terms of its substantive and empirical scope, constructivism does not look much different than rationalist alternatives like realism and liberalism. In all cases, scholarship primarily focuses on security processes and outcomes taking place in the North Atlantic region and Europe'. From the other side, most Relationalist work in Northeast Asia seems to make only tenuous connections with work going on under the same label in the United States (Qin, 2009, 2016, 2018; Shih and Yin, 2013), although this is now changing (Qin, 2018).

---

[4] On the normative agency of the Global South, see *Global Governance* (2014) with contributions by Eric Helleiner (international development), Kathryn Sikkink (human rights), Martha Finnemore and Michelle Jurovitch (universal participation) and Amitav Acharya (normative impact of the 1955 Asia–Africa Conference in Bandung on human rights, sovereignty, disarmament and the UN). See also the essays in Weiss and Roy (2016).

This leads to a fourth trend of the past decade: the persistence of American and Western dominance, both institutionally and in terms of setting the theoretical agenda of IR. There is some dispute about the existence or extent of American dominance. Norman Palmer (1980: 347) asserts that 'international relations is an international area of inquiry, not even confined to the social sciences, and has many roots and antecedents, not all of them, by any means, rooted in the American soil ... International relations, like Topsy, was not invented, least of all by Americans; it would be more accurate to say that, like Topsy, it "just growed"'. Yet this view does not accord with the fact that many scholars, American or not, take the British and American origins of the discipline for granted and ignore its more diverse origins. Tony Porter (2001: 131) argues against the existence of any singular *American* dominance because there is no common thing among American scholars other than their nationality. 'What do Kenneth Waltz, Richard Ashley, Cynthia Enloe, and Craig Murphy have in common?', he asks. Moreover, because American IR has strong European roots, given the influence of scholars such as Morgenthau or Deutsch, the analytical utility of nationality in Hoffmann's 'American social science' formulation can be questioned (Porter, 2001: 137). Yet this ignores the fact that the diversity of thought and approach within the United States is still a limited one. One has to ask whether the Europeans on American soil would have made their impact had they stayed on in their home countries and whether it is enough to make IR less ethnocentric?

Lately, there have emerged revisionist and more complex and nuanced accounts of the origins of IR that challenge Hoffmann's formulation. Some argue that diversity already exists (Maliniak et al., 2018). A revisionist sociology of IR literature offers different accounts of the origins of IR as a discipline in different locations. Hagmann and Biersteker claim that 'the discipline is today understood to have evolved from a series of sources and institutions ranging from political theory, colonialism, and anthropology to the *Kolonialinstitut* in Hamburg or the League of Nations in Geneva' (2014: 294–5). But here again, the question can be raised: understood by whom? Perhaps only by a small number of scholars such as Hagmann and Biersteker themselves, who actually focus on the sociology of the discipline. One has to be sceptical whether the vast majority of trainers and trainees are aware of these diverse origins of their subject or take them seriously. While Hagmann and Biersteker are right that the sociology of IR is becoming sceptical of 'the very idea of homogeneous national or continental IR communities', the accompanying claim that the literature has 'significantly expanded the focus beyond the West, systematically assessing

IR practices in other regions of the world' (Hagmann and Biersteker, 2014: 296) is an exaggeration, as is evident from recent surveys (on which more below).

Even those who agree about US or Western dominance of IR don't agree whether this is good or bad. After bemoaning the 'limited worldview' of 'many American scholars … when it comes to teaching undergraduates or writing textbooks', Friedrichs (2004: 17) credits American dominance with helping to maintain the field's coherence. To him, the 'fit between the intellectual hegemony of American IR and the realities of power politics' need not be bad, since it is 'natural for American IR to set the intellectual agenda about international power as well'. Moreover, 'the strength of American IR is an important source of legitimacy for weak university departments in the peripheries … There is a broad consensus that American IR is the place where the action is, and in a certain sense IR scholars in the peripheries are simply serving their real or perceived interests when paying tribute to American social science'. Some see existing IR theories as adequate to explain developments in the Non-Western world, such as Asia, because, despite its distinctive features, the latter has been progressively integrated into the modern Europe-derived international system and adopted its behavioural norms and attributes (Ikenberry and Mastanduno, 2003: 412–23). And then there is John Mearsheimer (2016: 147–9), who, with his characteristic penchant for provocation, finds nothing wrong with the American dominance of the field because it is 'benign'.

Mearsheimer's complacent insider view does not reflect the gatekeeping experience of many periphery scholars trying to access Western journals and publishers, where language, culture, style and topic form subtler, more indirect forms of exclusion. It will be interesting to see how the spread of IR journals and publishers based outside the West will impact on this element of ongoing Western dominance. Whether one sees American hegemony within IR as good or bad, it is important to note that, as we argued in Chapter 8, in some ways it stands on fragile foundations. American IR is hegemonic mainly on material grounds because it is big (as the relative size of ISA indicates, American IR scholars and institutions are perhaps still a majority of IR scholars and institutions globally), rich and located in the sole superpower. Its ideational position is much less hegemonic, with many inside and outside the West rejecting its link to Political Science and positivist epistemology. As the relative size and wealth of American IR declines with the rise of IR in Europe, Japan, China, India, Turkey, etc., we might expect US hegemony to decline proportionately. The size and wealth of IR in Asia and elsewhere will begin to challenge the material basis of US hegemony, and to generate its own lines of IR theorising, just as Europe has done. In this perspective, US hegemony is a removable obstacle on the road to Global IR.

To sum up, some degree of diversity has already been achieved in existing thinking about IR, but it is still thin and shallow. Diversity is not just a matter of theoretical or methodological orientation. It is also about the identity of the group: who is included and excluded. For example, based on his review of the state of IPE, Cohen (2014: 132–3) argues that IPE is no longer insular or hegemonic (dominated by the 'American School'): 'across the globe, lines of communication [among scholars] are mostly open … [but] links vary in intensity and are uneven at best'. But what exists now is not diversity in the sense of a mutual give and take of knowledge and ideas between different IPE communities, which would be the ideal type of diversity based on 'reasonably symmetrical flows of information, with "exporters" of knowledge also being "importers" from other sources' (Holsti, 1985: 13). This can apply to the field of IR as a whole. This deeper diversity continues to elude IR, and addressing that weakness is a major goal of Global IR.

It is revealing that a review of both older and more recent surveys of the field suggests that much of the diversity claimed by Western scholars often refers to diversity *within the core*, and among the three mainstream theories: Realism, Liberalism and Constructivism. Nearly twenty years ago, Kalevi Holsti, the author of the well-known work on diversity *The Dividing Discipline*, noted that 'the theoretical aspects of international politics are no longer predominantly an American enterprise' (Holsti, 2001: 90). But his reference to the 'vibrant theoretical work' being undertaken outside of the United States was 'primarily' to scholarship in the United Kingdom and Western Europe, including Scandinavia, as well as Australia and Canada. Similarly, Wæver's (1998: 688) notion of a 'more pluralistic or balanced' field of IR was mainly about a hopeful prognosis of 'academic communities forming around their own independent cores in Europe'. It was only in China that he foresaw the possibility of the development of an independent IR tradition (Wæver, 1998: 696). Although we now see vibrant national IR communities also emerging in Japan, South Korea, Brazil, Taiwan, Turkey and India, these are yet to render the field truly 'pluralistic and balanced' globally. American and European dominance remains a fact of life. The same applies to the diversity uncovered by Robert Crawford (2001). This diversity was linked 'more explicitly to intellectual constructs than the "national identity" or "location" of particular individuals', whereas 'most of those who "do IR" in the restrictive sense of the word, tend to have been acculturated to its ways, methods, and theories in one of the hegemonic (teaching) centers of global power (i.e., North America, Western Europe, and, to a lesser degree, Australia and New Zealand) each of which has demonstrated a marked dependency on, or propensity to follow, American constructs' (Crawford, 2001: 20). There was scant indication in any of these studies of anything but the marginal place of the periphery in the field.

A decade later, a study of 12 leading IR journals plus an analysis of 3 IR faculty surveys explored 'the extent of theoretical, methodological, and epistemological diversity in the American study of IR', and found increasing theoretical diversity (Maliniak et al., 2011: 444). Yet diversity here meant the declining importance of paradigm-driven articles, the fading of Realism relative to Liberalism, and the rise of Constructivism in the early 1990s. Moreover, the increasing mainstream theoretical diversity has to be viewed against a decline of methodological diversity (quantitative approaches being 'the most frequently used method in journal articles' (Maliniak et al., 2011: 454)) as well as a lack of epistemological diversity evident in the scarcity of non-positivist approaches among journal articles (Maliniak et al., 2011: 456).[5]

Peter Marcus Kristensen's (2015) study, using bibliometric methodology and data to analyse the 'geography of the International Relations (IR) discipline, particularly the notion of IR as an "American social science"', found IR to be 'less "American" than other social sciences', as well as 'less "American" than in its past', at least compared to 45 years ago, judging by the share of US scholars in journal articles (Kristensen, 2015: 265). Despite this, the study concluded that 'a less "American" discipline is not necessarily a truly international discipline that better represents nations, peoples, and cultures around the world' (Kristensen, 2015: 259). While more scholars from more countries were publishing in the IR journals surveyed, the share of the top five producers (usually the United States, the United Kingdom, Germany, Canada and Australia) still accounted for 60 per cent of all journal articles in 2010 (compared to 84 per cent in 1970, 75 per cent in 1980, 77 per cent in 1990 and 72 per cent in 2000). Kristensen's study indicates that between 1966 and 2010, the participation of Global South scholars in the ten leading IR journals increased little, by about 3 per cent. He found that 'Hoffmann's argument is still widely accepted', and observes that the 'problem of American dominance' is mainly about ethnocentric bias, which is manifested in the belief in superiority and claim to universality (Kristensen, 2015: 248–50). Kristensen also found that IR is not

---

[5] These conclusions themselves reflect Eurocentrism. Of the 12 journals used in the survey more than half were American and nearly all of the rest European.

'all-American'; with the northeastern United States dominating the production of journal articles (Kristensen, 2015: 265).

The US dominance of IR, it should be noted, is found not only in higher-
level theoretical literature but also introductory textbooks. Nossal (2001:
168) finds the 'same "American" characteristics that Stanley Hoffmann
attributed to the discipline of IR as a whole are reflected in the IR textbooks
that are used to introduce students to the field'. American IR has also been
parochial in terms of the kind of PhD education that US universities have
produced, which has become 'overwhelmingly rationalist and positivist in
[its] theoretical orientation'. Given the nature of American parochialism as
'rationalistic, positivistic, US centric, monolingual, recently published, and
written by men', there emerged no 'theoretical cosmopolitanism' as evident in the 'decreased tendency to engage theoretical traditions developed
outside America' (Biersteker, 2009: 320). All these point to only limited
progress of IR towards deeper global diversity.

Against this backdrop, it is hardly surprising that calls for making IR
less US-centric are growing. In marked contrast to the 'benign hegemony'
perspective, scholars from the Global South, and their collaborators and
like-minded scholars from the West, have become increasingly vocal in
highlighting the persisting parochialism of the mainstream IR scholarship (some examples, far from exhaustive, would include: Neuman, 1998;
Ling, 2002, 2010; A. B. Tickner, 2003a, b; Chowdhry and Nair, 2004;
Thomas and Wilkin, 2004; K. Smith, 2006; Acharya and Buzan, 2007a, b,
2010; Bilgin, 2008, 2013; Agathangelou and Ling, 2009; Tickner and
Wæver, 2009a; Behera, 2010; Shilliam, 2010; Acharya, 2011a, 2014a;
Tickner and Blaney, 2012). The theme of ISA's 2015 convention in New
Orleans, 'Global International Relations and Regional Worlds', served
as a focal point for highlighting the American and Western dominance
of IR. The incumbent ISA President Amitav Acharya's use of 'Global
IR' rather than Non-Western IR theory was deliberate, and intended
to address some of the concerns raised against the latter including
from scholars working on Global South issues. Almost a quarter of
the total number of panels and roundtables at the New Orleans convention were devoted to the convention theme, which set a historic
record and demonstrated the level of interest that the idea of Global
IR generated among the ISA members. Just before the convention, the
2014 TRIP survey released its report. Among its findings was that a clear
majority of its respondents believe that IR is both American *dominated*
and Western *dominated*.[6] When asked if IR is an American-dominated

---

[6] The 2014 TRIP survey split the sample so that respondents either received the question
with American dominance (and later countering this dominance) or Western dominance.

discipline, 49 per cent agreed and 11 per cent strongly agreed, for a total of 60 per cent. When asked if IR is a Western-dominated discipline, the result was that 53 per cent agreed, and 22 per cent strongly agreed. Thus, an overwhelming 75 per cent of the total number of respondents agreed or strongly agreed that IR is a Western-dominated discipline (for details, see Wemheuer-Vogelaar et al., 2016). And for the first time, at the same New Orleans convention, a scholar from outside the West (China), Tang, won the ISA's best book prize (on a shared basis), for his theoretical work, *The Social Evolution of International Politics* (Tang, 2013).

Whether this is a turning point or a passing phase remains to be seen. At the very least, there seems to be a growing awareness cutting across the West–Rest divide that IR theory needs to be more reflective of the Global South and take the direction of Global IR (Eun, 2016; Dunne and Reus-Smit, 2017). Perhaps the best that can be said is that whether it is recognised in the United States or not, the global challenge to the epistemologically narrow and self-referential American way in IR is getting stronger. As in the real world, the legitimacy of American hegemony is in sharp decline even while its material power remains dominant. Interestingly, Asia's rising IR theory is, like Europe's, often standing outside the American mainstream, and keeping open a wider range of theoretical approaches. Rising powers may bring diversity into thinking about IR, but they may also reinforce some of the universalist claims of Western IR theory. There is no doubt, for example, that Realism will always have a strong appeal in rising great powers because it offers a way, as it does for the existing great powers, of privileging their position over the rest (Simpson, 2004). The strength of Realism in China is notable, and perhaps ominous, in this regard (Shambaugh, 2013: 26–44).

Origins of Global IR

The idea of 'Global IR' responds to the growing dissatisfaction among scholars of international relations around the world about the existing state of their discipline. Despite its growing popularity worldwide, IR privileges Western history, ideas, practices and leadership, while marginalising those of the Rest. Global IR aspires to level the playing field, and to develop a genuinely inclusive and universal discipline that truly reflects the growing diversity of its IR scholars and their intellectual concerns. Both of us have been committed to developing global and world historical perspectives on IR, and both have acquired a deepened

---

The term 'Western' triggered significantly more agreement in terms of dominance than the term 'American'.

awareness and understanding of the problem of West-centrism in IR (Buzan and Little, 2000; Buzan, 2011; Acharya, 2014a, b; Buzan and Lawson, 2014a, b, 2015a).

In 2007 we published a forum in *International Relations of the Asia-Pacific*, 'Why Is There No Non-Western IR Theory?'. There, and in a subsequent book (Acharya and Buzan, 2010), we posed it as a challenge to Asian IR scholars to get their voices and their histories into the global debates on how to think about IR, both for their sakes and as a necessity for the balanced development of the discipline. These projects discussed the reasons for the absence of a Non-Western IR or Global IR. Briefly, these range from the first-mover advantage of Western scholars, through the extensive training of Asian (and more generally Non-Western) scholars in the United States and the hegemonic status of Western scholars, publications and institutions in IR, to a widespread belief that Western IR has discovered the right path to understanding IR or the right answers to the puzzles and problems of the day, a serious lack of institutional resources and the problem of English as IR's hegemonic language. There is also the issue of an uncritical acceptance of Western theory, a lack of confidence to take on Western theorists, blind deference to scholars from prestigious Western institutions, and too much political and policy engagement for IR scholars in universities in the developing world. A follow-up piece showed that this work had resonance and impact well beyond the region (Acharya and Buzan, 2017). Our aim in this book is to renew, and refocus, the challenge to IR scholars more broadly, and our hope is that this will contribute to the building of Global IR.

The idea of a Non-Western IR theory sparked controversy. Some would rather call the new project 'post-Western' (Shani, 2008: 723), with a more radical agenda to disavow and displace the existing 'Western' IR. To us, the idea of post-Western assumes the end of Western dominance as an objective fact or a normative aspiration, neither of which is accurate or helpful for the purpose of making IR theory more inclusive. At the same time, as Bilgin notes, the idea of Non-Western in IR scholarship does not imply passive submission to IR knowledge generated by the West. What may be regarded as Non-Western does not necessarily originate within 'teleological Westernisation', and those that do not appear to be radically different but seem to be framed within the categories and concepts of Western IR theory cannot be dismissed as 'the robotic "Stepford Wife" to "Western IR"'. Such a stance, Bilgin concludes, 'denies agency to "non-Western" scholars and represents them as unthinking emulators' (Bilgin, 2008: 13).

In this context, both of us have come to appreciate some of the key insights of Postcolonialism. We are on side with its campaign to restore the perceptual balance against Eurocentrism, to bring the Non-West fully back into world history and to highlight the ongoing impact on international relations of both cultural hybridity and ongoing resentments of colonialism and racism. That said, we do not necessarily accept all of Postcolonialism's political, philosophical and linguistic baggage, and we are aware of its problematic dependence on both European languages and (Postmodern) Western philosophers. If, as Dane Kennedy (1996: 347) puts it, Said's key thesis was that 'the dismantlement of Western modes of domination requires the deconstruction of Western structures of knowledge', then it is far from clear that Postcolonialism has achieved this goal.

The label 'Non-Western IR theory' served a crucial purpose in generating debate that drew a good deal of attention to the parochialism of IR. One of the criticisms, which we had taken into consideration in the 2007 *International Relations of the Asia-Pacific* special issue, but has since become even more salient, is that globalisation and income convergence make the categories West and Non-West, and the distinction between core and periphery, less and less meaningful, especially in an era of rising powers such as China and India. As the earlier chapters in this book have shown, there has been real progress from the almost total differentiation and separation of core and periphery in ir and IR in the nineteenth century, to the substantial cross-overs and mergers between them in the twenty-first. Many of the components of Global IR have been in the making since the nineteenth century. Yet even though the core is expanding, and the barriers to the periphery eroding, these distinctions still have some utility. The term 'West' remains politically and culturally useful to both the rising powers in defining their identity, and to the Western nations (in dealing not only with non-Europeans, but also, as seen in the Ukraine crisis, with Russia and Eastern European societies).

But while the idea of Global IR is an extension of our notion of Non-Western IR, it goes beyond it for both normative and instrumental reasons. The project of making IR inclusive cannot be a conversation among the like-minded, whether from IR's mainstream, or from its Critical and Postcolonial alternatives. We reject the idea of a zero-sum choice between mainstream IR and its critical and cultural challengers. All sides have a lot to offer, and none has a monopoly on truth or insight. A real world structured by deep pluralism needs a Global IR that reflects and understands that structure, both in terms of the history that created it, and in terms of the political legacies from that history that continue to shape world politics. Exposing the interplay between ir and IR, and how things have moved from extreme differentiation of core and periphery towards increasing integration between them, was our aim in structuring this book as we did. As of the time of writing, the component parts of a Global IR are coming more clearly into view, and the task is to bring them together.

Global IR is likely to fail if it does not draw in the broadest group of scholars, including both critics and those in the Western mainstream. The problem is how to both invent a Global IR and still engage with those schooled in the existing IR traditions in a meaningful two-way dialogue (Acharya, 2011a). Labels matter. Global IR does not reject the terms 'Non-Western' or 'post-Western', but views them 'as part of a broader challenge of reimagining IR as a global discipline' (Acharya, 2014a: 649). Global IR transcends the distinction between West and Non-West – or any similar binary and mutually exclusive categories. While these categories might persist as terms of convenience, they lose analytical significance in the world of Global IR. Global IR resonates with and complements attempts at making the field more inclusive by bringing about the field's 'worlding beyond the West' (Tickner and Wæver, 2009a).

At this point, some clarifications about the idea of Global IR need to be made. First, Global IR is not a theory or method. It is more a framework of enquiry and analysis of international relations in all its diversity, especially with due recognition of the experiences, voices and agency of the Non-Western peoples, societies and states that have so far been marginalised in the discipline. The idea of Global IR urges the IR community to look past the American and Western origins and dominance of the field, and embrace greater diversity, especially by recognising the places, roles and contributions of Non-Western peoples and societies (Acharya, 2014a). Global IR draws from a broad canvas of human interactions, with their multiple origins, patterns and distinctions, to challenge IR's existing boundary markers set by dominant American and Western scholarship. It seeks to encourage new understandings and approaches to the study of world politics. It serves as a framework for advancing IR towards a truly inclusive and universal discipline. Hence, the Global IR research agenda calls scholars to discover new patterns, theories and methods from world histories; analyse changes in the distribution of power and ideas after more than two hundred years of Western dominance; explore regional worlds in their full diversity and interconnectedness; engage with subjects and methods that require deep and substantive integration of disciplinary and Area Studies knowledge; examine how ideas and norms circulate between global and local levels; and investigate the mutual learning among civilisations, of which there is more historical evidence than there is for the 'clash of civilizations' (Acharya, 2014a).

Second, Global IR cannot resolve, nor is it primarily concerned with, inter-paradigmatic and 'isms' debates in IR, which, as noted earlier, have run their course. Global IR is not a paradigm to be juxtaposed against other theoretical approaches. Global IR calls more for synthesis than for choosing one approach over others.

Third, the term Global IR does not expect that the IR community should engage in a single global conversation about theory or method. Global conversations across national and regional borders should and do happen, as with the conventions organised by ISA, WISC and EISA. We certainly encourage more such dialogues. But Global IR is not limited to a single global dialogue, as some mistakenly interpret our position (see Maliniak et al., 2018: 34). Global IR is comfortable with multiple parallel conversations undertaken by groups whose members share a particular theoretical, methodological or epistemological position (Lake, 2011). Yet, what matters for Global IR is not how many conversations are going on, but who is excluded from each of these. If multiple conversations are carried out within mutually exclusionary groups, whether from the West or the Rest, that is business as usual: traditional IR, not Global IR. Theoretical and methodological diversity is always welcome in Global IR, but not mutual exclusion.

In advancing the idea of Global IR, we agree that the existing IR 'does not do justice to the development of International Relations theory in other parts of the world' (Friedrichs, 2004: 14). But the rationale for Global IR not only has a normative basis, i.e. promoting inclusion and avoiding ethnocentrism, but also extends to overcoming the divide between the West and Non-Western world. As we have shown in the chapters of this book, there are also powerful pragmatic reasons for embracing Global IR. The ir chapters show the global power shift associated with countries such as China and India, which are major civilisations and once and future world powers. This trend towards deep pluralism is itself deep and unstoppable. The IR chapters showed the steady globalisation of the study of international relations around the world. In this vein, Steve Smith (2008: 727–8) aspires for a less American-dominated discipline: 'If international relations remains a narrow American social science, then the dangers are that it will be irrelevant to the concerns of large parts of the world's population, and more problematically it may become increasingly part of the process of US hegemony.' In the years since he wrote that sentence, US hegemony has become a diminishing issue compared with how to handle the emerging deep pluralism, which has no hegemony. But his point about the danger of IR becoming irrelevant if it fails to develop a broader and more global perspective remains powerful. If IR remains predominantly Western, it will become increasingly parochial and out of tune with the emerging post-Western world order.

Dimensions of Global IR

The 'global' in Global IR is not merely or even mainly a geographic or substantive (issue areas) expression. Of course, the term 'global' in its dictionary meaning has the connotation of 'relating to the whole world' and 'relating to or encompassing the whole of something, or of a group of things'.[7] Global can also mean universal, inclusive (both actors and issue areas) or worldwide. But we are concerned with more than that here. Global is also an intersubjective notion conveying interdependence and linkages between actors, such as states and societies, and areas, such as regions and the world order. It also means looking at the origins and meanings of concepts and practices by paying attention to their autonomous, comparative and connected histories and manifestations, and especially bridging the divide between the dominant and neglected understandings of IR concepts and theories.

In our view, 'doing' and writing Global IR revolves around seven main dimensions:[8]

(1) It is founded upon a pluralistic universalism: not 'applying to all', but recognising and respecting the diversity of humankind.
(2) It is grounded in world history, not just Greco-Roman, European or US history, and it respects historical time and context.
(3) It subsumes rather than supplants existing IR theories and methods, and pays attention to both material and ideational/normative causes and consequences.
(4) It integrates into IR the study of regions, regionalisms and Area Studies.
(5) It eschews concepts and theories that are solely based on national or cultural exceptionalism.
(6) It recognises multiple forms of agency beyond the state and material power, including resistance, normative action and local constructions of global order.
(7) It responds to the increasing globalisation of the world not only in terms of the diffusion of wealth, power and cultural authority, but also in terms of rising interdependence and shared fates.

---

[7] https://en.oxforddictionaries.com/definition/global (Accessed 6 October 2018).
[8] This section draws heavily from Acharya (2014a).

Following are brief elaborations on each of these dimensions.

First and foremost, Global IR calls for a new understanding of universalism or universality. The dominant meaning of universalism in IR today is homogenising, carrying the sense of 'applying to all'. It corresponds closely to Enlightenment universalism. As Robert Cox (2002: 53) put it: 'In the Enlightenment meaning universal meant true for all time and space – the perspective of a homogenous reality.' And this universalism also had a dark side: the suppression of diversity, and the justification of Western imperialism based on the universalisation of a European 'standard of civilisation'. In IR theory and method, Western IR has set the universal standard, and been used as a way of standard setting, gatekeeping and marginalising of alternative narratives, ideas and methodologies.

Cox (2002: 53) offers an alternative conception of universalism, which rests on 'comprehending and respecting diversity in an ever changing world'. This universalism rejects the false and politically inspired dichotomy between universalism and relativism. The opposite of homogenising universalism is not relativism, but pluralism. Pluralistic universalism views IR as a global discipline with multiple foundations. But this is not pluralism as understood in recent writings on IR theory (for a survey of the literature on pluralism, see Dunne, Hansen and Wight, 2013; Eun, 2016). Pluralism in Global IR does not mean relativism, or accepting a variety of theories to co-exist, or seeking unity or synthesis among theories, or pursuing 'analytic eclecticism'. Nor is it only what Tim Dunne, Lene Hansen and Colin Wight (2013: 416) call 'integrative pluralism' that 'accepts and preserves the validity of a wide range of theoretical perspectives and embraces theoretical diversity as a means of providing more comprehensive and multi-dimensional accounts of complex phenomena'. Pluralism in Global IR does not accept and preserve existing theories *as is*, but expects them to give due recognition to the places, roles and contributions of Non-Western peoples and societies. In this sense, Global IR is really more about pluralisation *within* theories, rather than just *between* them.

Although IR has pretensions to be about all times and all places, in fact it is a rather parochial expression of the short period in world history when the West was dominant. As argued in the Introduction, the discipline would look very different if it had been invented in China, India or the Islamic world. As the period of Western dominance begins to ebb, IR needs now to break away from this parochial bias by incorporating perspectives from other histories and political theories. Global IR contextualises the concepts and theories of IR, and identifies their contested and contingent meanings, rather than assuming them to be universal categories. For example, IR textbooks present the ideas of sovereignty and non-intervention as European inventions that were simply inherited by postcolonial societies. Yet this standardised account overlooks the different interpretations of sovereignty in different regions of the world, not only between Europe and the rest of the world, but also between different non-European regions (see Acharya, 2011a). Similarly, regionalism is often presented as being of European origin, even though it had emerged in Latin America a hundred years before the EEC, often viewed as the mother of all regionalisms. While globalisation is said to originate with the expansion of Europe and the promotion of free trade by the British and then the United States, the true origins of globalisation lie in the multi-cultural trading systems that have linked Eurasia and Africa for more than two millennia. These 'silk roads' involved sophisticated regimes on both land and in the Indian Ocean, and it was not until the nineteenth century that Europeans came to dominate them. A good part of this history involves the rise of Islam from the eighth century onwards, when the West was a medieval backwater while the Islamic world linked trade routes from Spain to Asia. This system involved sophisticated arrangements for the protection of foreign trade diaspora communities. Human rights texts routinely ignore such examples of the protection of the safety and dignity of the individual from cruel and unjust punishment by the ruler in other societies through history. Broadening the genealogy of the key concepts of IR across multiple sources in different times is thus a crucial element of Global IR, and one that stretches much further back in time than the two centuries covered by this book.

Second, and following on from pluralistic universalism, Global IR calls for IR to be more authentically grounded in world history, rather than Western history, and in the ideas, institutions, intellectual perspectives and practices of both Western and Non-Western societies. World history means not only finding a holistic perspective on the scale of the planet and humankind, but also bringing in the local histories, including the Western one, in their own right. Global IR recognises the voices, experiences and values of all people in all parts of the world. But 'bringing the Rest in' does not mean simply using the Non-Western world as a testing ground to revalidate existing IR theories after a few adjustments and extensions. Neither does it mean trying to replace the parochial 'universalism' of Western history with some equally parochial 'universalism' based on the history of some other civilisation. Global IR must be a two-way process. A key challenge for theories and theorists of Global IR is to develop concepts and approaches from Non-Western contexts on their own terms, and apply them not only locally, but also to other contexts, including the larger global canvas. In this context, it is important to study world politics stretching over the 5,000 years during which many civilisations, empires and societies have made and left their mark, and many other forms of international relations have come and gone. It is not just Eurocentric, but absurdly limiting for IR/World Politics to ignore its global heritage and confine itself to the events and ideas from the last few hundred years (Buzan and Little, 2000). This is especially so when the move towards deep pluralism is re-empowering many of the civilisations briefly overridden by the West.

In bringing history in, it is important to avoid two common problems. The first is historicism, or the belief in the continuity of history, or that history repeats itself. The other is 'tempocentrism' ('taking a reified present and extrapolating it back in time') (Lawson and Hobson, 2008: 430), or projecting modern concepts such as sovereignty, power, norms, human rights, democracy and balance of power backwards to establish uniformity, continuity and universality of modern concepts and theories. It is important to recognise that some of these concepts may not apply in the past in the same form, and across cultures. Careful consideration of history serves two main purposes. The first is searching for parallels, approximations, similarities, differences and variations in relation to the core concepts used to study IR. This allows us to critically examine whether certain concepts and theories are truly universal or not. Concepts thus discovered may not be exactly the same as terms in current use, but may help us to ascertain the extent of the universality of modern categories, such as power, anarchy, order, institutions, security, hegemony, empire, suzerainty or welfare, and add variations to them. A second purpose is to identify or discover entirely new concepts and approaches to theory and practice which have been neglected or hidden from view because of Eurocentrism. Current work on Chinese history and political philosophy offers perhaps the most promising prospect for such discovery.

Third, Global IR subsumes, rather than supplants, existing IR knowledge, including the theories, methods and scientific claims that we are already familiar with. It seeks not to displace existing Western-dominated IR knowledge in itself, but only to displace its hegemony by placing it into a broader global context. Global IR thus takes a pluralistic approach to theory and method. Global IR embraces both mainstream (Realism, Liberalism, ES and some versions of Constructivism) and Critical approaches, and is agnostic about the theoretical and methodological instincts and preferences of the scholars. Unlike some Critical Theories and Postcolonial scholarship, Global IR does not reject mainstream theories but only challenges their parochialism and urges them to accept the ideas, experiences and insights from the Non-Western world. All paradigms and *isms* have their place in Global IR, which sees theories as a natural scientist would see lenses: each lens (e.g. natural light, infrared, X-ray), just like each IR theory, makes some aspects of the subject sharper and more visible, while hiding other aspects. The analyst needs many lenses, each of which exposes part of the truth. Some developments along these lines are already visible. IR theories are hardly monolithic or unchanging when it comes to dealing with the Non-Western world. Some theories, especially Postcolonialism and Feminism, have been in the forefront of efforts to recognise events, issues, agents and interactions outside the West and to draw theoretical insights from them to enrich the study of IR. The ES has likewise started to take more account of the role and experience of the periphery in the expansion and evolution of international society generally, and the construction and evolution of primary institutions in particular. Even Realism, always ahead of Liberalism in drawing insights from the Non-Western world, has added new variants – Subaltern Realism, Neoclassical Realism and Defensive Realism – that have rendered Realism more relevant to the Non-Western world. As noted in Chapter 8, Constructivism has been especially important in opening space for scholarship on the Non-Western world because of its stress on culture and identity. Economic interdependence, multilateral institutions and democratisation, pathways to order that Liberalism identifies and prescribes, make that theory potentially more applicable to the Non-Western world.

Karen Smith (2017: 1), in a recent article, argues that Global IR cannot be completely divorced from Western IR. Indeed, she contends that 'theoretical contributions from the global South ... do not need to be radically different from existing theories'. Thus, 'Reinterpretations or modifications of existing frameworks ... can assist us in not only better understanding international relations in a particular part of the world, but can in fact provide greater insights into the field as a whole'. Global IR is not against mimicking as long as it also refines, refutes and advances existing theories. At the same time, Global IR does not leave the mainstream theories *as is*. Instead, it urges theorists to rethink their assumptions and broaden the scope of their investigation. For Realism, the challenge is to look beyond conflicts induced by national interest and distribution of power, and acknowledge other sources of agency, including culture, ideas and norms that make states and civilisations not clash but embrace and learn from each other. For Liberals, there is a similar challenge to look beyond *American hegemony* as the starting point of investigating multilateralism and regionalism and their institutional forms. Liberalism also needs to acknowledge the significant variations in cooperative behaviour that exist in different local contexts, such that no single model of integration or interactions can account for all or most of them. For Constructivism, taking stock of different forms of agency in the creation and diffusion of ideas and norms remains a major challenge. The ES needs to strengthen its conceptualisation and understanding of world society and its interplay with the society of states.

We have argued that Global IR should embrace theoretical and methodological pluralism, and engage both critical and mainstream theories. But we also think some theories, such as Postcolonialism, Feminism and especially Postcolonial Feminism and Black Feminism with its powerful contribution of the idea of intersectionality (Persaud and Sajed, 2018b), can be regarded as 'vanguard' theories, because they have already contributed to the effort to expand IR beyond the West. In the light of the story of IR that we have told in this book, these vanguard theories can be seen as bringing into IR the anti-colonial, anti-racist and regionalist/culturalist perspectives that developed first in the periphery, but were for a long time shut out of IR in the core. More work is needed to chart a closer nexus between Feminist scholarship, Postcolonialism and Global IR. But what is clear is that Global IR draws inspiration and ideas from Feminist and Postcolonial scholarships' shared struggle against their historical and deep-rooted exclusions and marginalisations by IR scholarship. Postcolonialism and Global IR can adapt the powerful prose of Feminist scholars Tickner and True (2018: 1) and justifiably claim that the periphery, like women, 'did not come late to international relations. Rather, international relations came late to the periphery'.

Global IR has a place for all theories and is open to scholars from the South and the North. But not all scholars outside the mainstream see the need for a Global IR out of fear that it might compromise their distinctiveness. Some Critical theorists, including Postmodern and Poststructuralist scholars, may already be sympathetic to Global IR, but still prefer to maintain a separate, or distinctive, identity, or at least do not engage sufficiently with the 'global'. There are important similarities between Postcolonialism and Global IR. Both highlight and reject Eurocentric theories of IR. Both affirm the agency of the Third World. Both emphasise the multiple origins of the modern international system, rejecting the dominance of perspectives that privilege its European/Westphalian origin. But the fact that Global IR does not reject existing mainstream theories but challenges them to be more sensitive to Non-Western ideas and agency claims is a major point of difference between Global IR and Postcolonialism. Unlike the latter, Global IR does not present itself as an alternative to any particular theory, but calls upon all theories to shed their Eurocentrism. Many Feminist scholars share with Global IR a concern for marginalised groups. The tension between Western and Postcolonial Feminists, with the latter seeing Western Feminist scholarship as domineering and exclusionary of Global South identities, is also in line with Global IR's aim of challenging false universalisms and deparochialising existing lines of IR theory.

Fourth, to have Global IR as the designation of the field does not mean diminishing the importance of regions and regionalisms, and the contribution of Area Studies. Instead, Global IR gives centre stage to regions. While the world is not being fragmented into regions, it is also not moving inexorably towards a seamless globality. Regions are no longer viewed as fixed physical, cartographic or cultural entities, but as dynamic, purposeful and socially constructed spaces. Regionalism today is less territorially based and state-centric, and encompasses an ever-widening range of actors and issues. The traditional divide between regionalism and universalism may be breaking down. The study of regions is not just about the how regions self-organise their economic, political and cultural space, but also about how they relate to each other and shape global order. In addition, focusing on regions is central to forging a close integration between disciplinary approaches and Area Studies.[9]

Fifth, although pluralistic universalism inevitably involves a degree of cultural differentiation and relativism, a truly global IR cannot be based on cultural exceptionalism and parochialism. Exceptionalism is the tendency to present the characteristics of a social group as homogeneous, collectively unique and superior to those of others. Claims to exceptionalism often underpin false claims to universalism such as the Western 'standard of civilisation' imposed on the rest of the world during the colonial era of the nineteenth and twentieth centuries. An earlier example of exceptionalism was classical China's tribute system, and a more recent one is the idea of a league or concert of democracies to supplant the UN. Such claims are also frequently associated with the domestic political agendas and purposes of the ruling elite, as is evident in concepts such as 'Asian values' and 'Chinese characteristics', which are often associated with authoritarianism. Exceptionalism in IR also often justifies the dominance of the big powers over the weak. American exceptionalism, seemingly benign and popular at home, can

---

[9] On the logic of regionalism in GIS, see Buzan and Schouenborg (2018: ch. 4).

be associated with the Monroe Doctrine and its self-serving global interventionism. One strand of Japan's pre-war Pan-Asian discourse, which was founded upon the slogan of 'Asia for Asians', also illustrates this tendency. Efforts to invoke the unique Chinese tributary system as the basis of a new Chinese School of IR are pregnant with similar possibilities. While the development of national schools of IR can broaden and enrich IR, if based mainly on exceptionalism they will challenge the possibility of Global IR. Kahler (1993: 412) is right to argue that 'Growing national parochialism does not augur well for the future development of the field'.

Global IR thus allows us to uncover the biases, parochialisms (sometimes hidden) and ethnocentrism in existing IR theories. While IR textbooks do present criticisms of the main theories, they seldom highlight their ethnocentric assumptions. For example, undergraduate students studying Realism and Liberalism as universal theories of IR are seldom told about their link with and justification for cultural racism and imperialism. Some of the biggest founding philosophers of Liberalism, such as Locke, backed European imperialism, directly or indirectly, in the name of efficiency and free trade. Others, such as Adam Smith and, notably, Kant, rejected Western imperialism but posited a normative universalism that expected indigenous peoples to evolve into European standards. Kant would not accord unqualified sovereignty to non-Europeans unless they renounced their 'lawless savagery' and accepted these standards. Realism's foundations include the Geopolitical theories of Mackinder and Mahan, which called for a Western Anglo-Saxon alliance and its offensive to prevent the yellow barbaric threat (or 'yellow peril') from moving onto the West's doorstep. In more recent times, the Liberal theory of Democratic Peace refused to consider colonial wars, while structural Realism viewed bipolarity as a 'long peace', because of the absence of war in Europe, while disregarding the numerous conflicts and casualties in the developing world during the Cold War. Constructivism gave little recognition to norm creation by the developing countries, and the contestation among different normative systems. A related point is the lack of fit between existing theories, derived from a predominantly Western context, and the realities of the Non-Western world. There are plenty of examples of this, including the limited applicability of regional integration theories outside of Western Europe, which are often glossed over in the best-selling IR texts. Other examples include the limitations of the concept of national security (developed mainly in the United States) to capture the security predicament of the Third World, and the focus in international development theory (developed in United States and Europe) on economic growth at the expense of human development needs.

Sixth, Global IR takes a broad conception of agency. Various IR theories have denied the agency claims of the Non-Western societies. Not so long ago, agency in international relations was viewed primarily in terms of a 'standard of civilisation' in which the decisive element was the capacity of states to defend their sovereignty, wage war, negotiate treaties, enforce compliance, manage the balance of power and construct empires over peoples deemed 'uncivilised'. This self-serving, ahistorical and brazenly racist formulation by the European colonial powers ignored the fact that sophisticated forms of statecraft were present in many early Non-Western civilisations. While the mainstream IR theories viewed the so-called Third World or Global South as marginal to the games that states play, some of the Critical Theories actually thrived on this presumed marginality. They rightly criticised mainstream theories for excluding the South, but did little exploration, at least initially, of alternative forms of agency in the South, since recognising that agency might risk undermining the central part of their narrative.

While global disparities in material power are not going to disappear, we need to adopt a broader view of agency in international relations that goes beyond military power and wealth. Agency is both material and ideational. It is not the prerogative of the strong, but can manifest as the weapon of the weak. Agency can be exercised in global transnational space as well as at regional and local levels. It can take multiple forms (Acharya, 2018: 12–23). It can describe acts of resistance to and localisation of global norms and institutions. Agency also means constructing new rules and institutions at the local level to support and strengthen global order against great power hypocrisy and dominance. Agency means conceptualising and implementing new pathways to development, security and ecological justice.

Examples of such agency abound, though ignored by mainstream IR scholarship. Sovereignty was redefined and broadened at the Asia–Africa Conference in Bandung. Africa created a form of regionalism to maintain postcolonial boundaries. India's first prime minister, Nehru, was the first to propose a nuclear test ban. Some of these acts of agency are not just for specific regions or for the South itself, but are important to global governance as a whole. Recent research shows that Latin American, Asian (China and India) and East European countries played a major role in crafting the Bretton Woods institutions (Helleiner, 2014). The origins and strengthening of modern human rights and disarmament norms can be traced to efforts made by Latin American, Asian and African nations in championing these norms (Sikkink, 2014, 2016; Acharya, 2016: 1160–1). The ideas of human development and human security were pioneered by South Asian development economists Mahbub ul-Haq and Amartya Sen (Acharya, 2016: 1162–3; 2018: 137–41), while the idea of 'Responsibility to Protect', usually attributed to the Canadian-sponsored ICISS, as shown in Chapter 8, owes much to African leaders and diplomats. From climate change negotiations, we see the developing countries offering the idea of the 'common but differentiated responsibility' norm (Acharya, 2018: 195–7). Using this broader framework of agency, we can find that the South has had a voice, that the 'subaltern could indeed speak' and act, even if IR theories ignore them. Building these into the IR texts' accounts of global political economy, global security and global ecology is critical to reducing the Western bias and developing a Global IR narrative.[10]

Seventh, and finally, Global IR responds to the increasing globalisation of the world in a comprehensive sense. Globalisation in the sense of rising interconnectedness and interdependence is a long-term trend that shows no sign of weakening. But there are two significant lines of change that increasingly apply to this narrower process. First is that it is decreasingly organised on a core–periphery basis, and more and more on the basis of deep pluralism. So while the era of Western dominance is ending, both the motor driving globalisation, and the responsibility for its consequences, have become much more planetary in scale. Second is that the rising density and intensity of interconnectedness and interdependence is now conspicuously giving rise to a set of shared fates, discussed in Chapter 7, in which all of humankind is ensnared and for which responsibility is collective. How this shared-fate aspect of globalisation plays into the more diffuse political structure of deep pluralism is a major question for Global IR.

A Global IR Research Agenda

Acharya (2014a) has identified and discussed certain elements of a Global IR research agenda. Without going into details, these may be summarised as:

- Discovering new patterns, theories and methods from world histories.
- Analysing changes in the distribution of power and ideas after more than two hundred years of Western dominance.
- Exploring regional worlds in their full diversity and interconnectedness.
- Engaging with subjects and methods that require deep and substantive integration of disciplinary and Area Studies knowledge.

---

[10] For further discussion of Southern agency, see special section of *Global Governance* (2014).

- Examining how ideas and norms circulate between global and local levels.
- Investigating the mutual learning between civilisations, of which there is more historical evidence than there is for the 'clash of civilizations'.

While these six themes may be a good starting point for discussions and debates necessary for the broadening of our discipline, they are by no means exhaustive. Rather, 'The idea of Global IR should remain a broad umbrella, open to contestation, interpretation, elaboration, and extension' (Acharya, 2014a: 652).

Another way of advancing the Global IR project is to look at the possible sources of theorising across regions. Building on our earlier work (Acharya and Buzan, 2007a, b; 2010), there are five useful sources for developing more global IR theory: classical religious and philosophical traditions; the IR thinking of historical religious, political and military figures; the IR thinking of contemporary postcolonial leaders; the work of contemporary Critical IR scholars with a global perspective; and insights drawn from the *praxis* of global politics.

First, classical traditions including religious philosophy such as that of Buddhism, Hinduism, Confucianism, Islam, Judaism, Christianity and different sections within these, as well as later religions such as the Khalsa Panth, might provide insights relevant to IR theory. This, however, raises epistemological questions. Global IR embraces pluralism in method and epistemology. But we want to make a special case for further broadening what is meant by the science of IR by incorporating insights from the world's religions. Global IR accepts positivist approaches, but firmly rejects that they are the only valid path to knowledge of IR. It is noteworthy that our review of regional IRs shows a preference for the classical, rather than the positivist approach that characterises much of American IR. Patrick Thaddeus Jackson contends that 'to be genuinely non-Western, we need ways of generating theory that is not prone to King, Keohane, and Verba type of generating theory'.[11] What is then important is not just the content of IR, but the ways of doing IR. Part of the answer lies in broadening our conception of what the philosophy of science behind IR actually means. Jackson (2010) makes a powerful case for pluralism in IR, particularly in so far as our understanding of what constitutes 'science' is concerned. In so doing, he strikes a powerful blow to the claims of those who have found it convenient to dismiss

---

[11] Comments at the launch of *Non-Western International Relations Theory*, by Amitav Acharya and Barry Buzan, American University, Washington, DC, 3 May 2010. The reference was to Gary King, Robert O. Keohane and Sidney Verba (1994).

Non-Western experiences and voices as 'the stuff of Area Studies' or 'unscientific'.

But Jackson (2010: 196) also insists that 'putting the "science question" to rest certainly does not mean that we enter a realm where anything goes'. Scientific knowledge for him has three indispensable 'constituent components': it must be systematic, it must be capable of taking (and one presumes tackling successfully) public criticism, and 'it must be intended to produce worldly knowledge' (Jackson, 2010: 193). But one has to be careful here. A good deal of what one might bring into IR theory from the Non-Western world may indeed be 'worldly knowledge'. But other sources could be from religion, cultural and spiritual knowledge that might not strictly qualify as 'this-worldly'. They may lie at some vague intersection between science and spirituality or combine the material with the spiritual. Thus, Giorgio Shani (2008: 722) suggests the Sikh Khalsa Panth or Islamic Ummah as sources of post-Western IR theory, because these concepts offer 'an alternative conception of universality – and a potentially more "solidarist" conception of international society – than that offered by western Westphalian IR'. The same could be said for the Chinese concept of *Tianxia* (all under heaven). Hinduism presents another example. The Hindu epic *Mahabharata* is a meta-narrative of just and unjust war, alliances and betrayals, self-interest and morality, and good and bad governance.[12] Within it, the *Bhagavad Gita* contains thoughts on the practice of war in the form of Lord Krishna's pleadings with the warrior Arjuna: 'If you refuse to fight this righteous war, then, [you would be] shirking your duty and losing your reputation' (ch. 2, passage 33); 'the warrior chiefs who thought highly of you, will now despise you, thinking that it was fear which drove you from battle' (ch. 2, passage 35); 'Die, and you will win heaven; conquer, and you will enjoy sovereignty of the earth; therefore stand up, Arjuna, determined to fight' (ch. 2, passage 37) (Kaushik, 2007: 55–7). In other words, not to abstain from war resonates with the logic of righteous action which is both 'this-worldly' (honour, shame, power) and 'other-worldly' (the indestructibility of the soul or the *atman*).

Buddhist philosophy, which has received practically no attention from scholars of international relations,[13] offers another example. The present Dalai Lama explores the relationship between science and Buddhist philosophy. Buddhist philosophy accepts and employs the empiricism of science, especially 'direct observation' and 'reasoned inference' (i.e. knowledge 'can be phenomenally given or it can be inferred'), but parts

---

[12] One might also look at Cohen and Westbrook (2008).
[13] With the admirable exception of Chan, Mandaville and Bleiker (2001).

company with science when it comes to a third way, 'reliable authority'. Buddhist philosophy believes in a 'further level of reality, which may remain obscure to the unenlightened mind'. These include 'law of karma', 'scripture cited as a particularly correct source of authority', or the teachings of Buddha, which for Buddhists 'has proven to be reliable in the examination of the nature of existence and path to liberation' (Dalai Lama, 2005: 28–9). Although Karl Popper's falsification thesis would render the gap between scientific method and Buddhism wider by excluding 'many questions that pertain to our human existence', including ethics and spirituality, falsification 'resonates with' Tibetan Buddhism's 'principle of the scope of negation', which underscores the difference between that 'which is "not found" and that which is "found not to exist"' (Dalai Lama, 2005: 35). It is not difficult to see that the 'further level of reality' may well apply to most other religious doctrines, such as the Islamic Sunnah and Hadith, or the Hindu *Bhagavad Gita*. While the Dalai Lama argues that science excludes questions of metaphysics and ethics, all IR theory (although some versions more so than others) does not.

Can we bring these insights into IR knowledge if we restrict ourselves to a conduct of enquiry that insists on a strict separation between this- and other-worldliness, and between the material and the spiritual? We could of course self-consciously include elements such as scriptural knowledge, which may not easily pass the test of this-worldliness, and call them the non-scientific elements of IR theory. But that might mean consigning them to second-class status, since, as Jackson points out, the labelling of 'scientific' carries much prestige and disciplining impact in IR theory. Insistence on science thus risks further marginalising a good deal of the sources of IR knowledge which are wholly or partially unscientific or whose affinity with science cannot be clearly established.

Second, in addition to religions, the Non-West has plentiful examples of historical religious, political and military figures who have thought about IR. These include Sun Tzu, Han Feizi and Confucius from China; and Ashoka, Kautilya and Nagarjuna (a Buddhist philosopher in India during the first–second century) from India. What is especially interesting is that these included a diversity of thinking and approach within the same societies, cultures and even time periods. The fact that one can find within a relatively short period of the north Indian classical age both the *realpolitik* of Kautilya's *Arthasastra* and the righteousness of Ashoka's *Dharma*, and in China during the pre-Qin dynasty period the contemporaneous doctrines of arch-Realist Han Feizi and moral philosopher Confucius suggests that it is wrong to stereotype Eastern civilisations as a philosophical straightjacket. The reality is that they accommodated a plurality of ideas and approaches to politics and international relations. In the Islamic world of the Middle East, notable examples of thinkers include Ibn Sina (a Persian polymath known to the West as Avicenna) and the Arab *Falsafa* (philosophy) thinkers between the ninth and twelfth centuries, such as al-Kindi (who worked in the House of Wisdom in ninth-century Baghdad, where many crucial Greek philosophical and scientific texts were translated into Arabic), al-Farabi and Ibn Rushd (Averroës to the West). Through translations into Arabic and interpretations, these and other Muslim scholars not only preserved but also advanced a good deal of Greek philosophical knowledge otherwise forgotten or lost in their original Greek versions after the fall of Alexandria and the conversion of the Roman emperors. Later, before and at the onset of the European Renaissance, these Arabic texts and knowledge would be translated in Islamic Spain into Latin and medieval French and influence the thinking of not only Christian theologians such as Thomas Aquinas, but also early modern European rationalism in Paris and Oxford universities. There already exists a secondary political theory type literature on these thinkers, which can be brought into the domain of IR. Equally important among Islamic thinkers was Ibn Khaldun (1332–1406 AD) of Morocco, whose dynamic theory of interaction between sedentary and nomadic societies as the motor of history influenced the work of seventeenth-century Ottoman historians like Kâtip Çelebi, Ahmed Cevdet Pasha and Mustafa Naima, and was invoked by the contemporary IR scholar Robert Cox (1992b).

Third is the thinking and approach of political thinkers and leaders in the colonised world. As we have detailed in earlier chapters, anti-colonial, nationalist and pan-regionalist ideas and movements, whether from political activists or scholars (with many being both), was a prime source of thinking about international relations found in every region. The fact that some of these formed partnerships in ideas (such as that between Tagore and Okakura) or movements, or both, makes their thinking all more important as foundations of Global IR. It is important to note that, like in the classical past, international thinking in the modern period in the Non-Western world was hardly uniform. For example, in Japan one might find ideas, sometimes divergent and sometimes complementary, about international relations from the late nineteenth century through to the post-Second World War period, in Shigejiro Tabata, Yoshikazu Sakamoto, Masataka Kosaka, Masamichi Royama, Akira Osawa, Nishida Kitaro, Kisaburo Yokota, Hikomatsu Kamikawa, Kotaro Tanaka, Kaoru Yasui and Shigejiro Tabata (Shimizu et al., 2008). Similarly, scholars looking for important but divergent sources of IR thinking in India should study the writings of K. M. Panikkar, Sisir

Gupta, A. Appadorai, A. P. Rana, Jayantanuja Bandyopadhyaya and Ashis Nandy (Mallavarapu, 2018).

A fourth source from which Global IR thinking and theorising might draw is the work of those contemporary scholars who have engaged with and in most cases challenged Western IR theory, from different locations around the world. The list, to give but a few leading examples, might include Mohammed Ayoob (United States), Arlene Tickner (Colombia), Pinar Bilgin (Turkey), Bahgat Korany (Egypt), Navnita Chadha Behera (India), Kanti Bajpai (India), Takashi Inoguchi (Japan), Qin Yaqing (China), Yan Xuetong (China), Tang Shiping (China), Siba Grovogui (United States), L. H. M. Ling (United States), Randolph Persaud (United States), Sankaran Krishna (United States), Robbie Shilliam (United States), Diana Tussie (Argentina), Evelyn Goh (Australia), Oliver Stuenkel (Brazil), Swati Parashar (Sweden), Chandra Mohanty (United States), Yongjin Zhang (United Kingdom), Shogo Suzuki (United Kingdom) and W. Andy Knight (Canada). We would like also to include J. Ann Tickner (United States), Jacqui True (Australia), Andrew Hurrell (United Kingdom), Louise Fawcett (United Kingdom), Peter Katzenstein (United States), David Kang (United States), Eric Helleiner (Canada), T.V. Paul (Canada) and Andrew Phillips (Australia). The list is far from exhaustive and does not do justice to the differences between these scholars and the complexity of their thought, but it does suggest that Global IR is already an emergent enterprise with contributions from scholars from East and West, North and South. The fact that some of these, such as Ayoob, Grovogui, Knight, Krishna and Persaud, were originally from the Global South but have moved to the United States makes them no less contributors to Non-Western thought; in fact one can argue that their contribution benefits from the insights that come with being a part of both worlds.[14] What is also interesting is that some scholars, such as Tickner and Stuenkel, have moved from the West to their present positions in the Global South. Many of these scholars have retained close links with their countries of origin, or their work at least partly focuses on their countries/regions of origin and they have maintained close links with the ideas and institutions of those regions. The work of many of these scholars reflects the historical and current conditions of the Global South, especially their own country/region of origin.

---

[14] We might add that one of the present authors, Amitav Acharya, now also based in the United States, grew up in India, has spent a significant amount of his academic life in Asia (Singapore and China), while holding substantial visiting faculty positions in South Africa, Thailand and Japan, and is a citizen of Canada.

While the common thread of their work is a call for greater understanding and inclusion of Non-Western ideas and approaches, these scholars pursue a diversity of theoretical interests and approaches. Bearing in mind that classifying their writings into the prevailing theoretical 'camps' can be grossly oversimplifying and misleading, one may still make some plausible generalisations. Persaud, Shilliam, Ling, Bilgin, Krishna and Grovogui clearly identify themselves as belonging to the Postcolonial school. Tickner and Behera are also broadly in the Postcolonial school. Qin's thinking is mainly Constructivist (albeit heavily influenced by Chinese culture in his leadership of the Chinese School of IR), while his compatriot Yan, who draws equally from Chinese culture, rejects the idea of a Chinese School and calls his theory 'Moral Realism'. Tang has developed an eclectic 'social evolutionary' approach, which fits a Constructivist understanding of IR. Bajpai, Inoguchi, Stuenkel and Knight are closer to Liberalism, while Ayoob has developed an approach that he calls 'Subaltern Realism'. Hurrell, Suzuki and Zhang are associated with the ES. Such divergence is the hallmark of the Global IR project, which embraces theoretical pluralism, including existing IR theories and challengers. Those interested in the Global IR project should draw on and engage thinkers, leaders and contributions from different theoretical and methodological traditions.

A fifth source for Global IR thinking might also draw on *praxis*, especially broad and long-term patterns of relationships, interactions and institution building in different parts of the world. Drawing upon practice to build theory is commonplace in Western IR scholarship. Hence the Concert of Europe has been the basis for the literature on 'security regimes', the EU is the main springboard of Neoliberal Institutionalism, and the classical European balance-of-power system informs a good deal of theorising about power transitions (now being applied to China's rise), alliance dynamics and 'causes of war' literature. Hence the question: 'if European and North Atlantic regional politics could be turned into international relations theory, why not Asian regional politics?' (Acharya, 2015).

As we have shown in previous chapters, regionalism is a key, and long-established, area of international relations thinking and practice in many parts of the Global South. It is now well understood that the different regions of the world pursue different pathways to regional cooperation (Acharya and Johnston, 2007). Regional cooperation approaches in Asia, Latin America, Africa and the Middle East are all important avenues of broadening IR studies and its theory development. Here, as with the ideas and approaches of classical, nationalist and pan-regionalist traditions and thinkers, comparative work is especially helpful. While each region considers itself as having unique or distinctive trajectories and approaches, in reality there are also some similarities between them. For example, consensus decision-making is a worldwide practice of regional multilateral institutions, even though they do acquire a certain myth of distinctiveness in local contexts and are recognised and accepted as such.

Caveats and Risks

There are, of course, caveats and risks associated with Global IR that require further attention and debate. To invoke Robert Cox (1981: 128) again, 'Theory is always for someone and for some purpose.' Who is Global IR for, and for what purpose? Among the other concerns about Global IR, the following are especially noteworthy:

- The risk of focusing exclusively or mainly on the stronger and more resource-rich Non-Western countries: India, China, Brazil, South Africa, Turkey, etc., where IR scholarship is progressing more rapidly, while neglecting the weaker countries of the developing world. The emergence of a Chinese School of IR attests to this possibility.
- The possibility of repeating or reproducing Western ideas with minor modifications. Global IR might end up globalising traditional IR theories and concepts, albeit filling in new content by collecting concepts around the world. This might also call into question the emancipatory claims of Global IR.
- The difficulty of studying all nations, civilisations and issue areas under one framework, especially with the significant cultural, political and economic variations among societies and regions.
- The risk of making IR too broad, lessening its analytic value and making theory-building difficult.
- By aspiring to build a common narrative and seeking to end the exclusion of the Rest, Global IR may divert attention from other and more specific forms of exclusion, such as gender, race, etc.

These risks are not trivial, but keeping them in focus would help Global IR scholars to avert them.

In keeping with our idea of embedded pluralism, we do not see Global IR as a big bang project. It is more likely to come alive during the next decades in a thousand small steps around the world. One aspect of its emergence is the growing sensitivity to the Global South in the textbooks, research agendas and teaching and training programmes in the core countries of the West. More important, however, are the efforts to decolonise IR in different places that have been hitherto deprived of recognition and voice. Here local institutions, collaborations and publications matter. Western International Studies organisations remain dominated by traditional perspectives and are still managed by a mainly Western leadership, only some of which are sensitive, let alone empathetic, to a post-Western world. This situation is unlikely to change quickly. At the same time, as the study of IR continues to advance around the world, the Western mainstream will witness growing resistance to its foundational myths and rejection of its dominant narratives. This diversification and pluralisation does not portend the 'end of IR' as a discipline or theory, but rather a new founding based on the principle of 'pluralistic universalism' discussed above. The Global IR approach represents an important way forward for a discipline that has traditionally been viewed as an 'American social science' that marginalised the developing world. We hope this volume powerfully illustrates the transformative potential of local efforts on the larger landscape of Global IR.

Conclusions

To become global, IR therefore has to make a substantial effort to refound itself once again. As we have shown, the modern discipline's first and second foundings took place during the era of peak Western dominance. Both of those foundings happened within the core, and involved institutional developments centred mainly in the Anglosphere countries. Both the institutions of IR and its subject matter and theory reflected the interests and perspectives of the dominant core powers. IR was thus strongly shaped both by the issues and practices of ir, which were largely defined by Western great powers, and by a view of world history that was mainly an extension of European history. To answer the Coxian question raised in the previous section, IR was designed institutionally, theoretically and in terms of its view of history by and for the core countries. From its founding, the discipline reflected, and still reflects, the context made by those countries of an extreme core–periphery colonial and quasi-colonial GIS. The perspectives and concerns of the core are thus structured deep into the very DNA of the discipline. To say this is not so much to make a normative critique, as a historical and structural observation. Under the circumstances of its founding, it would have been astonishing if IR had from its origins taken a truly global form in the sense advocated here. It is neither surprising nor unique to IR that an academic discipline should reflect the social conditions around it, especially during its formative stages. So the point is not so much to critique IR's past, as to point out where it needs to go from here in order to grow out of the peculiarities of its founding.

Our key themes in this book have been institutionalisation, theory (aka 'thinking about IR') and history, and we can sum up and look ahead in those terms.

As we have shown in the preceding chapters, the institutionalisation of IR has for several decades now been not only spreading beyond the core, but also building genuinely global networks and structures. These developments have successfully eroded the earlier separation of IR in the periphery from that in the core. There is a lot more to do before anything like equality of opportunity reigns across the planet, but the IR developments in China, Turkey, Latin America and elsewhere are moving in the right direction. Those institutional developments are generally welcomed, and up to a point supported, by the IR communities in the core. They have been integrated into global institutions, and are generally seen more as an opportunity to expand the discipline than as any kind of threat. Institutionally, the path to Global IR, while long, looks relatively smooth. Perhaps the main obstacle will be how to bring together IR communities in authoritarian states, where academic organisations are heavily penetrated by the government, with those in democratic states, where they have much greater autonomy as independent membership organisations. China is the obvious current exemplar of this problem.

The story with IR theory is in some ways similar to that for institutions. The periphery has opened itself up to some of the theorising of the core, while at the same time the core has made some room for Postcolonial thinking. Again, the situation is hardly one of balance, and there is a lot more to do. Postcolonialism, alongside other Critical Theories, has found a marginal niche within core IR. This marginalisation is a source of complaint, but it is also a sign of progress that even niche recognition has been established. The efforts in China and elsewhere to bring their own histories and political theories into the discipline are still at an early stage, and are generally welcomed. Whether such developments are seen, or will come to be seen, as threatening is an interesting question, and more difficult to answer than in the case of institutionalisation. Postcolonialism might well be seen by some in the IR mainstream as threatening, both on grounds of 'science' and because of the political baggage carried by many of its exponents. But that does not differentiate it strongly from other lines of Critical Theory where the tensions and disputes are largely within the core. Like Postcolonialism, many of these also come with both political baggage, and a thick coating of self-ghettoising jargon and verbiage that are difficult for outsiders to penetrate. Again, the trends are in the right direction towards a more global IR, but the path ahead is both long and steep, and could well be rocky in places. IR in the core has already become theoretically diverse, so this door is also relatively open.

The question of history poses perhaps the deepest and most difficult obstacle to Global IR. IR needs to break out not just from the 'prison of Political Science' (Rosenberg, 2016), but also from the ghetto of its Eurocentric view of history. Crucial to taking this big step will be a vigorous questioning of the powerful myth that because Western history became the main driver of world history during the nineteenth and twentieth centuries, it is justified to read both the future and the deeper past through that lens. The case for reading the premodern past in Eurocentric terms is self-evidently weak, but nonetheless powerfully embedded. Given the extraordinary impact of the West in creating the first modern GIS, there is more to be said for giving Eurocentrism a significant role in thinking about the future. Yet as we argued in Chapter 9, in a world of deep pluralism, cultural multiplicity, backed by wealth and power, is rapidly reshaping GIS. The myth of a universal liberal teleology is giving way to something much more diffuse. Deep pluralism will reshape GIS in very significant ways. But deep pluralism will itself still be substantially shaped by the Western legacy. To cope with this shift, Global IR does not want to lose sight of Western history, but needs to embed that particular history in a deeper world historical perspective. As argued above, Global IR needs to embody pluralistic universalism and be grounded in a truly world history.

What is emerging as the reality of the world is a novel synthesis between, on the one hand, the multiplicity of civilisations and cultures that is the legacy of humankind's deep past and, on the other hand, the condition of modernity, interdependence and globalisation that is the legacy of modernity and Western dominance during the nineteenth and twentieth centuries. Only when IR has been able to broaden its historical perspective will it be in a position to properly comprehend and theorise this rapidly unfolding global synthesis between culture and modernity. The grounds for optimism about breaking down this deeply rooted fixation on Western history is that, as we have argued in this book, IR has always been a flexible discipline, able to adapt quickly to the changes offered up by its turbulent subject matter. As we have shown, the development of IR has in many ways followed the events and structures of ir across several periods. As the peculiar era of a narrow Western dominance of GIS draws to a close, IR needs now to perform this trick again. IR has already served and adapted to two distinct eras of ir: the version 1.0 Western-colonial GIS up to 1945, and the version 1.1 Western-global GIS between 1945 and roughly 2008. Now version 1.2 GIS is emerging quickly. It will be post-Western in the sense that the West will no longer define the leading core, and therefore it will be a very major departure from the conditions that have defined IR since its origins. And it will be deep pluralism in the sense of having several major centres of wealth, power and cultural authority, some new and some old. The world is becoming truly one again, not just in the sense normally understood by 'globalisation', but in the sense of modernity becoming both cross-cultural, and broadly based in humankind, and not only the privilege of a small minority. Global IR needs to go with this flow, and continue its already not inconsiderable progress towards bringing core and periphery thinking about IR into a single institutional, theoretical and world historical frame.

References

Abdulghani, Roeslan (1964) *The Bandung Spirit*, Jakarta: Prapantja.

Abernathy, David B. (2000) *The Dynamics of Global Dominance*, New Haven, CT: Yale University Press.

Acharya, Amitav (1996) 'The Periphery As the Core: The Third World and Security Studies', in Keith Krause and Michael Williams (eds.), *Critical Security Studies*, Minneapolis: University of Minnesota Press, 299–327.

(2000) 'Ethnocentrism and Emancipatory IR Theory', in Samantha Arnold and J. Marshall Bier (eds.), *(Dis)placing Security: Critical Re-evaluations of the Boundaries of Security Studies*, Toronto: Centre for International and Security Studies, York University, 1–18.

(2001a) *Constructing a Security Community in Southeast Asia: ASEAN and the Problem of Regional Order*, London: Routledge.

(2001b) 'Human Security: East versus West', *International Journal*, 56:3, 442–60.

(2004) 'How Ideas Spread: Whose Norms Matter? Norm Localization and Institutional Change in Asian Regionalism', *International Organization*, 58:2, 239–75.

(2009) *Whose Ideas Matter? Agency and Power in Asian Regionalism*, Ithaca, NY: Cornell University Press.

(2011a) 'Dialogue and Discovery: In Search of International Relations Theories Beyond the West', *Millennium*, 39:3, 619–37.

(2011b) 'Norm Subsidiarity and Regional Orders: Sovereignty, Regionalism, and Rule-making in the Third World', *International Studies Quarterly*, 55:1, 95–123.

(2013a) 'Imagining Global IR Out of India', Keynote speech to Annual International Studies Conference, 10–12 December, Jawaharlal Nehru University, New Delhi, India.

(2013b) 'The R2P and Norm Diffusion: Towards a Framework of Norm Circulation', *Global Responsibility to Protect*, 5:4, 466–79.

(2014a) 'Global International Relations (IR) and Regional Worlds: A New Agenda for International Studies', *International Studies Quarterly*, 58:4, 647–59.

(2014b) *The End of American World Order*, Cambridge: Polity Press.

(2014c) 'International Relations: A Dying Discipline', World Policy Blog, 2 May, www.worldpolicy.org/blog/2014/05/02/international-studies-dying-discipline (Accessed 27 May 2018).

(2014d) 'International Relations Theory and the Rise of Asia', in Saadia Pekkanen, John Ravenhill and Rosemary Foot (eds.), *The Oxford Handbook of the International Relations of Asia*, Oxford: Oxford University Press, 120–37.

(2015) 'Identity without Exceptionalism: Challenges for Asian Political and International Studies', *Asian Political and International Studies Review* 1, 1–11.

(2016) 'Idea-shift: How Ideas from the Rest Are Reshaping Global Order', *Third World Quarterly*, 37:7, 1156–70.

(2017) *East of India, South of China: Sino-Indian Encounters in Southeast Asia*, New Delhi: Oxford University Press.

(2018) *Constructing Global Order: Agency and Change in World Politics*, Cambridge: Cambridge University Press.

Acharya, Amitav and Barry Buzan (2007a) 'Why Is There No Non-Western International Relations Theory? An Introduction', *International Relations of the Asia-Pacific*, 7:3, 287–312.

(eds.) (2007b) 'Why Is There No Non-Western International Relations Theory? Reflections on and from Asia', *International Relations of the Asia-Pacific*, special issue, 7:3, 285–470.

(eds.) (2010) *Non-Western International Relations Theory: Perspectives on and beyond Asia*, London: Routledge.

(2017) 'Why Is There No Non-Western International Relations Theory? Ten Years On', *International Relations of the Asia-Pacific*, 17:3, 341–70.

Acharya, Amitav and Alastair Iain Johnston (eds.) (2007) *Crafting Cooperation: Regional International Institutions in Comparative Perspective*, Cambridge: Cambridge University Press.

Adachi, Mineichiro and Charles De Visscher (1923) 'Examen de l'organisation et des statuts de la Société des Nations', *Annuaire de l'Institut de droit international*, 30, 22–64.

Adebajo, Adekeye and Chris Landsberg (2001) 'The Heirs of Nkrumah: Africa's New Interventionists', *Pugwash Occasional Papers*, 2:1, 17 pp.

Adem, Seifudein (2017) 'Was Ali Mazrui Ahead of His Time', in Kimani Njogu and Seifudein Adem (eds.), *Perspectives on Culture and Globalization: The Intellectual Legacy of Ali A. Mazrui*, Nairobi: Twaweza Communications, 243–59.

Adler, Emanuel (1997) 'Seizing the Middle Ground: Constructivism in World Politics', *European Journal of International Relations*, 3:3, 319–63.

Adler, Emanuel and Michael Barnett (eds.) (1998) *Security Communities*, Cambridge: Cambridge University Press.

Agathangelou, Anna M. and L. H. M. Ling (2004) 'The House of IR: From Family Power Politics to the Poisies of Worldism', *International Studies Review*, 6:4, 21–49.

(2009) *Transforming World Politics: From Empire to Multiple Worlds*, London: Routledge.

Ahmad, Aijaz (1997) 'Postcolonial Theory and the "Post-" Condition', in Leo Panitch (ed.), *Ruthless Criticism of All that Exists, The Socialist Register 1997*, London: Merlin Press, 353–81.

Ahrari, M. Ehsan (2001) 'Iran, China and Russia: The Emerging Anti-US Nexus?', *Security Dialogue*, 32:4, 453 66.

Alagappa, Muthiah (2011) 'International Relations Studies in Asia: Distinctive Trajectories', *International Relations of the Asia-Pacific*, 11:2, 193–230.

Albert, Mathias and Barry Buzan (2017) 'On the Subject Matter of International Relations', *Review of International Studies*, 43:5, 898–917.

Allinson, Jamie C. and Alexander Anievas (2010) 'The Uneven and Combined Development of the Meiji Restoration: A Passive Revolutionary Road to Capitalist Modernity', *Capital & Class*, 34:3, 469–90.

Ambrosio, Thomas (2001) 'Russia's Quest for Multipolarity: A Response to US Foreign Policy', *European Security*, 10:1, 45–67.

Amin, Samir (1972) 'Underdevelopment and Dependence in Black Africa: Origins and Contemporary Forms', *Journal of Modern African Studies*, 10:4, 503–24.

Anderson, Benedict (2006) *Imagined Communities: Reflections on the Origin and Spread of Nationalism*, London: Verso.

Angell, Norman (1909) *The Great Illusion* (Original title: Europe's Optical Illusion), London: Simpkin, Marshall, Hamilton, Kent & Co.

Aning, Kwesi and Fiifi Edu-Afful (2016) 'African Agency in R2P: Interventions by African Union and ECOWAS in Mali, Cote D'ivoire, and Libya', *International Studies Review*, 18:1, 120–33.

Antonius, George ([1938] 2001) *The Arab Awakening: The Story of the Arab National Movement*, London: Routledge.

Appadorai, A. (1979) 'The Asian Relations Conference in Perspective', *International Studies*, 18:3, 275–85.

Ariga, Nagao (1896) *La guerre sino-japonaise au point de vue du droit international*, Paris: A. Pedone.

Armstrong, David (1998) 'Globalization and the Social State', *Review of International Studies*, 24:4, 461–78.

Ashley, Richard K. (1980) *The Political Economy of War and Peace*, London: Frances Pinter.

(1996) 'The Achievements of Poststructuralism', in Steve Smith, Ken Booth and Marysia Zalewski (eds.), *International Theory: Positivism and Beyond*, Cambridge: Cambridge University Press, 240–53.

Ashworth, Lucian M. (2002) 'Did the Realist–Idealist Great Debate Really Happen? A Revisionist History of International Relations', *International Relations*, 16:1, 33–51.

(2008) 'Feminism, War and the Prospects of International Government – Helena Swanwick and the Lost Feminists of Interwar International Relations', *Limerick Papers in Politics and Public Administration*, 2, 18 pp.

(2013) 'Mapping a New World: Geography and the Interwar Study of International Relations', *International Studies Quarterly*, 57:1, 138–49.

(2014) *A History of International Thought: From the Origins of the Modern State to Academic International Relations*, London: Routledge.

(2017) 'Women of the Twenty Years Crisis: The Women's International League for Peace and Freedom (WILPF) and the Problem of Collective Security', Paper for the BISA Conference, Brighton, 14–16 June.

Ashworth, William (1975) *A Short History of the International Economy since 1850*, 3rd edn., London: Longman.

Axline, W. Andrew (1977) 'Underdevelopment, Dependence, and Integration: The Politics of Regionalism in the Third World', *International Organization*, 31:1, 83–105.

Aydin, Cemil (2007) *The Politics of Anti-Westernism in Asia*, New York: Columbia University Press.

Aydinli, Ersel and Julie Mathews (2008) 'Periphery Theorising for a Truly Internationalised Discipline: Spinning IR Theory out of Anatolia', *Review of International Studies*, 34:4, 693–712.

(2009) 'Turkey: Towards Homegrown Theorizing and Building a Disciplinary Community', in Arlene B. Tickner and Ole Wæver (eds.), *International Relations Scholarship around the World*, Abingdon: Routledge, 208–22.

Ayoob, Mohammed (1984) 'Security in the Third World: The Worm about to Turn', *International Affairs*, 60:1, 41–51.

(1986) 'Regional Security and the Third World', in Mohammed Ayoob (ed.), *Regional Security in the Third World: Case Studies from Southeast Asia and the Middle East*, London: Croom Helm, 3–27.

(1991) 'The Security Problematic of the Third World', *World Politics*, 43:2, 257–83.

(1995) *The Third World Security Predicament: State Making, Regional Conflict, and the International System*, Boulder, CO: Lynne Rienner.

Azar, Edward and Chung-in Moon (eds.) (1988) *National Security in the Third World*, Aldershot: Edward Elgar.

Bailey, S. H. (1932) *The Framework of International Society*, London: Longmans, Green, and Co.

Bairoch, Paul (1981) 'The Main Trends in National Economic Disparities since the Industrial Revolution', in Paul Bairoch and Maurice Lévy-Leboyer (eds.), *Disparities in Economic Development since the Industrial Revolution*, London: Macmillan, 3–17.

(1982) 'International Industrialization Levels from 1750–1980', *Journal of European Economic History*, 11:2, 269–333.

Baldwin, David (ed.) (1993) *Neorealism and Neoliberalism: The Contemporary Debate*, New York: Columbia University Press.

Baldwin, Richard (2016) *The Great Convergence*, Cambridge, MA: Belknap Press.

Banks, Michael (1985) 'The Inter-Paradigm Debate', in Margot Light and John R. Groom (eds.), *International Relations: A Handbook of Current Theory*, London: Frances Pinter, 7–26.

Barkawi, Tarak and Mark Laffey (eds.) (2001) *Democracy, Liberalism, and War: Rethinking the Democratic Peace Debate*, Boulder, CO: Lynne Rienner.

Barkin, J. Samuel (1998) 'The Evolution of the Constitution of Sovereignty and the Emergence of Human Rights Norms', *Millennium*, 27:2, 229–52.

(2010) *Realist Constructivism: Rethinking International Relations Theory*, Cambridge: Cambridge University Press.

Barnett, Michael (1995) 'Sovereignty, Nationalism, and Regional Order in the Arab States System', *International Organization*, 49:3, 479–510.

(1998) *Dialogues in Arab Politics*, New York: Columbia University Press.

Barone, Charles A. (1985) *Marxist Thought on Imperialism: Survey and Critique*, Armonk, NY: M. E. Sharpe.

Batabyal, Rakesh (2015) *JNU: The Making of a University*, New Delhi: Harper Collins.

Bayly, Martin J. (2017a) 'Imagining New Worlds: Forging "Non-Western" International Relations in Late Colonial India', *British Academy Review*, 30, 50–3.

(2017b) 'Global at Birth: The Multiple Beginnings of International Relations', Unpublished manuscript, 28 pp.

Bayly, Susan (2004) 'Imagining "Greater India": French and Indian Visions of Colonialism in the Indic Mode', *Modern Asian Studies*, 38:3, 703–44.

Behera, Navnita Chadha (2007) 'Re-imagining IR in India', *International Relations of the Asia-Pacific*, 7:3, 341–68.

(2009) 'South Asia: A "Realist" Past and Alternative Futures', in Arlene B. Tickner and Ole Wæver (eds.), *International Relations Scholarship around the World*, Abingdon: Routledge, 134–57.

(2010) 'Re-imagining IR in India', in Amitav Acharya and Barry Buzan (eds.), *Non-Western International Relations Theory: Perspectives on and beyond Asia*, London: Routledge, 92–116.

Belich, James (2009) *Replenishing the Earth: The Settler Revolution and the Rise of the Anglo-World, 1783–1939*, New York: Oxford University Press.

Bell, Duncan (2007) *The Idea of Greater Britain: Empire and the Future of World Order, 1860–1900*, Princeton: Princeton University Press.

(2013) 'Race and International Relations: Introduction', *Cambridge Review of International Affairs*, 26:1, 1–4.

Bell, Sydney Smith (1859) *Colonial Administration of Great Britain*, London: Longman, Brown, Green, Longmans and Roberts.

Benedick, Richard E. (1991) *Ozone Diplomacy: New Directions in Safeguarding the Planet*, Cambridge, MA: Harvard University Press.

Bernal-Meza, Raúl (2016) 'Contemporary Latin American Thinking on International Relations: Theoretical, Conceptual and Methodological Contributions', *Revista Brasileira de Política Internacional*, 59:1, 1–32.

Bertucci, Mariano E., Jarrod Hayes and Patrick James (2018) 'Constructivism in International Relations: The Story So Far', in Patrick James, Mariano E. Bertucci and Jarrod Hayes (eds.), *Constructivism Reconsidered: Past, Present and Future*, Ann Arbor, MI: University of Michigan Press, 15–31.

The Bhagavad-Gita (1986) Translated by Barbara Stoler Miller, New York: Bantam Dell.

Biersteker, Thomas (2009) 'The Parochialism of Hegemony: Challenges for "American" International Relations', in Arlene B. Tickner and Ole Wæver (eds.), *International Relations Scholarship around the World*, Abingdon: Routledge, 308–27.

Bilgin, Pinar (2004a) *Regional Security in the Middle East: A Critical Perspective*, London: Routledge.

(2004b) 'International Politics of Women's (In)security: Rejoinder to Mary Caprioli', *Security Dialogue*, 35:4, 499–504.

(2008) 'Thinking Past "Western" IR?', *Third World Quarterly*, 29:1, 5–23.

(2013) 'Pinar Bilgin on Non-Western IR, Hybridity, and the One-Toothed Monster called Civilization', Theory Talks (forum), 20 December, www.files.ethz.ch/isn/175508/Theory%20Talk61_Bilgin.pdf (Accessed 23 September 2016).

Bischoff, Paul-Henri, Kwesi Aning and Amitav Acharya (2016) 'Africa in Global International Relations: Emerging Approaches to Theory and Practice, an Introduction', in Paul-Henri Bischoff, Kwesi Aning and Amitav Acharya (eds.), *Africa in Global International Relations: Emerging Approaches to Theory and Practice*, London: Routledge, 1–21.

Bloch, Ivan (1898) *La Guerre Future* (English title: Is War Now Impossible?) Paris: Guillaumin et C. Editeurs.

Booth, Ken (1975) 'The Evolution of Strategic Thinking', in John Baylis, Ken Booth, John Garnett and Phil Williams, *Contemporary Strategy: Theories and Policies*, London: Croom Helm, 22–49.

(1996) '75 Years On: Rewriting the Subject's Past – Reinventing its Future', in Steve Smith, Ken Booth and Marysia Zalewski (eds.), *International Theory: Positivism and Beyond*, Cambridge: Cambridge University Press, 328–39.

Bostrum, Nick (2014) *Superintelligence: Paths, Dangers, Strategies*, Oxford: Oxford University Press.

Bostrum, Nick and Milan M. Ćirković (eds.) (2008) *Global Catastrophic Risks*, Oxford: Oxford University Press.

Bouchet, Nicolas (2013) 'Bill Clinton', in Michael Cox, Timothy J. Lynch and Nicolas Bouchet (eds.), *US Foreign Policy and Democracy Promotion: From Theodore Roosevelt to Barack Obama*, Abingdon: Routledge, 159–77.

Bowden, Brett (2009) *The Empire of Civilization: The Evolution of an Imperial Idea*, Kindle edn, Chicago: University of Chicago Press.

Bowman, Isaiah (1921) *The New World: Problems in Political Geography*, Yonkers-on-Hudson, NY: World Book Company.

Brewin, Christopher (1995) 'Arnold Toynbee, Chatham House, and Research in a Global Context', in David Long and Peter Wilson (eds.), *Thinkers of the Twenty Years' Crisis: Inter-War Idealism Reassessed*, Oxford: Clarendon Press, 277–301.

Bridgman, Raymond L. (1905) *World Organization*, Boston: Ginn & Co.

Brodie, Bernard (1946) *The Absolute Weapon: Atomic Power and World Order*, New York: Harcourt Brace.

Brown, Michael E., Sean M. Lynn-Jones and Steven E. Miller (1996) *Debating the Democratic Peace*, Cambridge, MA: MIT Press.

Brown, Philip Marshall (1923) *International Society: Its Nature and Interests*, New York: Macmillan Company.

Brown, William (2012) 'A Question of Agency: Africa in International Politics', *Third World Quarterly*, 33:10, 1889–908.

Brownlie, Ian ([1966] 1998) *Principles of Public International Law*, New York: Oxford University Press.

Brynjolfsson, Eric and Andrew McAfee (2014) *The Second Machine Age: Work, Progress and Prosperity in a Time of Brilliant Technologies*, New York: W. W. Norton.

Buell, Raymond Leslie (1925) *International Relations*, New York: Henry Holt.

Bukharin, Nikolai (1916) *Imperialism and World Economy*, London: Martin Lawrence.

Bull, Hedley (1966) 'International Theory: The Case for a Classical Approach', *World Politics*, 18:3, 361–77.

(1977) *The Anarchical Society: A Study of Order in World Politics*, London: Macmillan.

(1984) 'The Revolt against the West', in Hedley Bull and Adam Watson (eds.), *The Expansion of International Society*, Oxford: Oxford University Press, 217–28.

Bull, Hedley and Adam Watson (1984a) 'Introduction', in Hedley Bull and Adam Watson (eds.), *The Expansion of International Society*, Oxford: Oxford University Press, 1–9.

(eds.) (1984b) *The Expansion of International Society*, Oxford: Oxford University Press.

Burchill, Scott and Andrew Linklater (2013) 'Introduction', in Scott Burchill, Andrew Linklater, Richard Devetak, Jack Donnelly, Terry Nardin, Matthew Paterson, Christian Reus-Smit and Jacqui True (eds.), *Theories of International Relations*, 5th edn., New York: Macmillan Palgrave, 1–31.

Butler, Dell Marie (2010) 'What Is at Stake in the Third Debate and Why Does It Matter for International Theory?', *E-International Relations*, 16 January, www.e-ir.info/2010/01/16/what-is-at-stake-in-the-third-debate-and-why-does-it-matter-for-international-theory/ (Accessed 27 May 2018).

Buzan, Barry (1973) 'The British Peace Movement from 1919 to 1939', London University, PhD thesis.

(1983) *People, States and Fear*, Brighton: Wheatsheaf Books.

([1991] 2007) *People, States and Fear*, Colchester: ECPR Press.

(2004a) *The United States and the Great Powers*, Cambridge: Polity Press.

(2004b) *From International to World Society? English School Theory and the Social Structure of Globalisation*, Cambridge: Cambridge University Press.

(2006) 'Will the "Global War on Terrorism" Be the New Cold War?', *International Affairs*, 82:6, 1101–18.

(2011) 'A World Order without Superpowers: Decentred Globalism', *International Relations*, 25:1, 1–23.

(2012) 'The South Asian Security Complex in a Decentering World Order: Reconsidering *Regions and Powers* Ten Years On', *International Studies*, 48:1, 1–19.

(2013) 'Review of *The Social Evolution of International Politics*,' *International Affairs*, 89:5, 1304–5.

(2014) *An Introduction to the English School of International Relations*, Cambridge: Cambridge University Press.

(2017) 'Revisiting *World Society*', *International Politics*, 55:1, 125–40.

(2018) 'Nuclear Weapons and Deterrence in the Post-Western World Order', *International Security Studies*, 1, 53–73 (in Chinese).

(forthcoming) 'The Dual Encounter: Parallels in the Rise of China (1978–) and Japan (1868–1945)', in Takashi Inoguchi (ed.), *Sage Handbook of Asian Foreign Policy*.

Buzan, Barry and Lene Hansen (2009) *The Evolution of International Security Studies*, Cambridge: Cambridge University Press.

Buzan, Barry and Eric Herring (1998) *The Arms Dynamic in World Politics*, Boulder, CO: Lynne Rienner.

Buzan, Barry and George Lawson (2014a) 'Rethinking Benchmark Dates in International Relations', *European Journal of International Relations*, 20:2, 437–62.

(2014b) 'Capitalism and the Emergent World Order', *International Affairs*, 90:1, 71–91.

(2015a) *The Global Transformation: History, Modernity and the Making of International Relations*, Cambridge: Cambridge University Press.

(2015b) 'Twentieth Century Benchmark Dates in International Relations: The Three World Wars in Historical Perspective', *International Security Studies* (Beijing), 1:1, 39–58.

(2018) 'The English School: History and Primary Institutions as Empirical IR Theory?', in William R. Thompson (ed.), *The Oxford Encyclopedia of Empirical International Relations Theories*, New York: Oxford University Press, 783–99.

Buzan, Barry and Richard Little (2000) *International Systems in World History: Remaking the Study of International Relations*, Oxford: Oxford University Press.

(2010) 'The Historical Expansion of International Society', in Robert Allen Denemark (ed.), *The International Studies Encyclopedia*, Chichester: Wiley-Blackwell.

(2014) 'The Historical Expansion of International Society' in Cornelia Navari and Daniel M. Green (eds.), *Guide to the English School in International Studies*, Chichester: Wiley-Blackwell, 59–75.

Buzan, Barry and Laust Schouenborg (2018) *Global International Society: A New Framework for Analysis*, Cambridge: Cambridge University Press.

Buzan, Barry and Ole Wæver (2003) *Regions and Powers: The Structure of International Security*, Cambridge: Cambridge University Press.

Buzan, Barry, Ole Wæver and Jaap de Wilde (1998) *Security: A New Framework for Analysis*, Boulder, CO: Lynne Rienner.

Caballero-Anthony, Mely (ed.) (2015) *An Introduction to Non-Traditional Security Studies*, London: Sage.

Caballero-Anthony, Mely, Ralf Emmers and Amitav Acharya (eds.) (2006), *Non-Traditional Security in Asia: Dynamics of Securitisation*, London: Ashgate.

Calhoun, Craig (2017) 'Nation and Imagination: How Benedict Anderson Revolutionized Political Theory', ABC, 9 May, www.abc.net.au/religion/articles/2017/05/09/4665722.htm (Accessed 27 May 2018).

Campbell, David (1998) *Writing Security: United States Foreign Policy and Politics of Identity*, 2nd and revised edn., Manchester: Manchester University Press.

(2013) 'Poststructuralism', in Tim Dunne, Milja Kurki and Steve Smith (eds.), *International Relations Theories: Discipline and Diversity*, 3rd edn., Oxford: Oxford University Press, 223–46.

Cardoso, Fernando and Enzo Faletto (1972) *Dependency and Development in Latin America*, Berkeley and Los Angeles: University of California Press.

Carozza, Paolo G. (2003) 'From Conquest to Constitutions: Retrieving a Latin American Tradition of the Idea of Human Rights', *Human Rights Quarterly*, 25:2, 281–313.

Carpenter, Ted Galen (1991) 'The New World Disorder', *Foreign Policy*, 84, 24–39.

Carr, E. H. ([1939] 2016) *The Twenty Years' Crisis, 1919–1939*, London: Palgrave Macmillan.

(1946) *The Twenty Years' Crisis, 1919–1939: An Introduction to the Study of International Relations*, 2nd edn., London: Macmillan.

(1964) *The Twenty Years' Crisis, 1919–1939: An Introduction to the Study of International Relations*, 2nd edn., New York: Harper & Row.

Carvalho, Benjamin de, Halvard Leira and John Hobson (2011) 'The Big Bangs of IR: The Myths That Your Teachers Still Tell You about 1648 and 1919', *Millennium*, 39:3, 735–58.

Castle, David Barton (2000) 'Leo Stanton Rowe and the Meaning of Pan-Americanism', in David Sheinin (ed.), *Beyond the Ideal: Pan Americanism in International Affairs*, Westport, CT: Praeger, 33–44.

Cerny, Phil (1993) '"Plurilateralism": Structural Differentiation and Functional Conflict in the Post-Cold War World Order', *Millennium*, 22:1, 27–51.

Césaire, Aimé (1955) *Discourse on Colonialism*, translated by J. Pinkham, New York: Monthly Review Press.

Cha, Victor D. (1997) 'Realism, Liberalism, and the Durability of the US–South Korean Alliance', *Asian Survey*, 37:7, 609–22.

(1999) 'Engaging China: Seoul–Beijing Detente and Korean Security', *Survival*, 41:1, 73–98.

(2000) 'Abandonment, Entrapment, and Neoclassical Realism in Asia: The United States, Japan and Korea', *International Studies Quarterly*, 44:2, 261–91.

(2010) 'Powerplay: Origins of the US Alliance System in Asia', *International Security*, 34:3, 158–96.

Chakrabarty, Dipesh (2000) *Provincializing Europe: Postcolonial Thought and Historical Difference*, Princeton: Princeton University Press.

Chan, Stephen, Peter G. Mandaville and Roland Bleiker (eds.) (2001) *The Zen of International Relations: IR Theory from East to West*, New York: Palgrave.

Chatterjee, M. N. (1916) 'The World and the Next War: An Eastern Viewpoint', *Journal of Race Development*, 6:4, 388–407.

Chatterjee, Partha (1993) *The Nation and Its Fragments: Colonial and Postcolonial Histories*, Princeton: Princeton University Press.

Checkel, Jeffrey (2013) 'Theoretical Pluralism in IR: Possibilities and Limits', in Walter Carlsnaes, Thomas Risse and Beth A. Simmons (eds.), *Handbook of International Relations,* 2nd edn., London: Sage, 220–41.

Chibber, Vivek (2013) 'How Does the Subaltern Speak?', *Jacobin*, 21 April, www.jacobinmag.com/2013/04/how-does-the-subaltern-speak (Accessed 17 May 2018).

Chong, Alan (2012) 'Premodern Southeast Asia as a Guide to International Relations between Peoples: Prowess and Prestige in "Intersocietal Relations" in the Sejarah Melayu', *Alternatives*, 37:2, 87–105.

(2017) 'Empire of the Mind: José Rizal and Proto-nationalism in the Philippines', in Pinar Bilgin and L. H. M. Ling (eds.), *Asia in International Relations: Unlearning Imperial Power Relations*, London: Routledge, 160–71.

Chowdhry, Geeta and Sheila Nair (eds.) (2004) *Power, Postcolonialism, and International Relations: Reading Race, Gender, and Class*, London: Routledge.

Christensen, Jens (1998) 'Internettets Verden' [The World of the Internet], *Samvirke*, 4 (April), 106–12.

Cintra, Jose Thiago (1989) 'Regional Conflicts: Trends in a Period of Transition', *Adelphi Papers*, 29:237, 94–108.

Claassen, Casper Hendrik (2011) 'The Africanist Delusion: In Defence of the Realist Tradition and the Neo-Neo Synthesis', *Journal of Politics and Law*, 4:1, 181–7.

Clark, Ian (1997) *Globalization and Fragmentation: International Relations in the Twentieth Century*, Oxford: Oxford University Press.

(1999) *Globalization and International Relations Theory*, Oxford: Oxford University Press.

(2007) *International Legitimacy and World Society*, Oxford: Oxford University Press.

(2011) *Hegemony in International Society*, Oxford: Oxford University Press.

Clausewitz, Carl von ([1832] 1968) *On War*, Harmondsworth: Penguin.

Clodfelter, Michael (2002) *Warfare and Armed Conflicts: A Statistical Reference to Casualty and Other Figures, 1500–2000*, 2nd edn., London: McFarland & Co.

Cochran, Molly (2008) 'The Ethics of the English School', in Christian Reus-Smit and Duncan Snidal (eds.), *The Oxford Handbook of International Relations*, Oxford: Oxford University Press, 286–97.

Cohen, Benjamin J. (2007) 'The Transatlantic Divide: Why Are American and British IPE so Different?', *Review of International Political Economy*, 14:2, 197–219.

(2008) *International Political Economy: An Intellectual History*, Princeton: Princeton University Press.

Cohen, Benjamin (2014) *International Political Economy*, Cheltenham, UK: Edward Elgar.

Cohen, Raymond and Raymond Westbrook (2000) *Amarna Diplomacy: The Beginnings of International Relations*, Baltimore: Johns Hopkins University Press.

(eds.) (2008) *Isaiah's Vision of Peace in Biblical and Modern International Relations: Swords into Plowshares*, New York: Palgrave.

Colgan, Jeff D. (2016) 'Where Is International Relations Going? Evidence from Graduate Training', *International Studies Quarterly*, 60:3, 486–98.

Collins, Michael (2011) *Empire, Nationalism and the Postcolonial World*, London: Routledge.

Copeland, Dale (2010) 'Realism and Neorealism in the Study of Regional Conflict', Paper presented at conference on 'When Regions Transform', McGill University, 9 April.

Cornelissen, Scarlett, Fantu Cheru and Timothy M. Shaw (2012) 'Introduction: Africa and International Relations in the 21st Century: Still Challenging Theory?', in Scarlett Cornelissen, Fantu Cheru and Timothy M. Shaw (eds.), *Africa and International Relations in the 21st Century*, Basingstoke: Palgrave, 1–17.

Cox, Michael (2001) 'Introduction', in E. H. Carr (ed.), *The Twenty Years Crisis*, Basingstoke: Palgrave, ix–lxxxii.

Cox, Robert W. (1980) 'The Crisis of World Order and the Problem of International Organization', *International Journal*, 35:2, 370–95.

(1981) 'Social Forces, States and World Order: Beyond International Relations Theory', *Millennium*, 10:2, 126–55.

(1986) 'Social Forces, States, and World Orders: Beyond International Relations Theory', in Robert O. Keohane (ed.), *Neorealism and Its Critics*, New York: Columbia University Press, 204–54.

(1987) *Production, Power and World Order: Social Forces in the Making of History*, New York: Columbia University Press.

(1992a) 'Multilateralism and World Order', *Review of International Studies*, 18:2, 161–80.

(1992b) 'Towards a Post-Hegemonic Conceptualization of World Order: Reflections on the Relevancy of Ibn Khaldun', in James Rosenau and Ernst-Otto Czempiel (eds.), *Governance without Government: Order and Change in World Politics*, Cambridge: Cambridge University Press, 132–59.

(1993) 'Production and Security', in David Dewitt, David Haglund and John Kirton (eds.), *Building a New Global Order: Emerging Trends in International Security*, Toronto: Oxford University Press, 141–58.

(2002) 'Universality in International Studies', in Frank P. Harvey and Michael Brecher (eds.), *Critical Perspectives in International Studies*, Ann Arbor, MI: University of Michigan Press, 45–55.

Cox, Robert and Timothy J. Sinclair (1996) *Approaches to World Order*, Cambridge: Cambridge University Press.

Cox, Wayne S. and Kim Richard Nossal (2009) 'The "Crimson World": The Anglo Core, the Post-Imperial Non-Core, and the Hegemony of American IR', in Arlene B. Tickner and Ole Wæver (eds.), *International Relations Scholarship around the World*, Abingdon: Routledge, 287–307.

Crawford, Robert M. A. (2001) 'International Relations as an Academic Discipline: If It's Good for America, Is It Good for the World?', in Robert A. Crawford and Darryl S. L. Jarvis (eds.), *International Relations – Still an American Social Science? Toward Diversity in International Thought*, New York: State University of New York Press, 1–23.

Cui, Shunji and Barry Buzan (2016) 'Great Power Management in International Society', *The Chinese Journal of International Politics*, 9:2, 181–210.

Cumings, Bruce (1984) 'The Origins and Development of the North East Asian Political Economy: Industrial Sectors, Product Cycles, and Political Consequences', *International Organization*, 38:1, 1–40.

Curtin, Philip D. (2000) *The World and the West: The European Challenge and the Overseas Response in the Age of Empire*, Cambridge: Cambridge University Press.

Dalai Lama (2005) *The Universe in a Single Atom: The Convergence of Science and Spirituality*, New York: Morgan Road Books.

Darby, Phillip (2004) 'Pursuing the Political: A Postcolonial Rethinking of Relations International', *Millennium*, 33:1, 1–32.

Datta-Ray, Deep K. (2015) *The Making of Indian Diplomacy: A Critique of Eurocentrism*, Oxford: Oxford University Press.

Davenport, Andrew (2011) 'Marxism in IR: Condemned to a Realist Fate?', *European Journal of International Relations*, 19:1, 27–48.

Davies, Thomas (2013) *NGOs: A New History of Transnational Civil Society*, London: Hurst.

Deloffre, Maryam Zarnegar (2014) 'Will AFRICOM's Ebola Response Be Watershed Moment for International Action on Human Security?', *The Washington Post*, 29 September.

Der Derian, James (2003) 'The Question of Information Technology', *Millennium*, 32:3, 441–56.

Deudney, Daniel H. (2007) *Bounding Power*, Princeton: Princeton University Press.

Deudney, Daniel and G. John Ikenberry (1999) 'The Nature and Sources of Liberal International Order', *Review of International Studies*, 25:2, 179–96.

Deutsch, Karl W. (1961) 'Security Communities', in James Rosenau (ed.), *International Politics and Foreign Policy: A Reader in Research and Theory*, New York: Free Press, 98–105.

Deutsch, Karl W. and J. David Singer (1969) 'Multipolar Power Systems and International Stability', in James N. Rosenau (ed.), *International Politics and Foreign Policy: A Reader in Research and Theory*, New York: Free Press, 315–24.

Devetak, Richard (1996a) 'Critical Theory', in Scott Burchill and Andrew Linklater (eds.), *Theories of International Relations*, New York: St Martin's Press, 145–78.

(1996b) 'Postmodernism', in Scott Burchill and Andrew Linklater (eds.), *Theories of International Relations*, New York: St Martin's Press, 179–209.

de Wilde, Jaap (1991) *Saved from Oblivion: Interdependence Theory in the First Half of the 20th Century – A Study on the Causality between War and Complex Interdependence*, Aldershot, Hampshire: Dartmouth Publishing.

Dibb, Paul (1986) *The Soviet Union: The Incomplete Superpower*, Basingstoke: Palgrave.

Dickinson, G. Lowes (1916) *The European Anarchy*, London: G. Allen & Unwin.

Dikötter, Frank (2011) *Mao's Great Famine*, Kindle edn., London: Bloomsbury.

(2016) *The Cultural Revolution: A People's History, 1962–1976*, New York: Bloomsbury Press.

Dirlik, Arif (1999) 'Is There History after Eurocentrism? Globalism, Post-colonialism, and the Disavowal of History', *Cultural Critique*, 42, 1–34.

Dominguez, Jorge I. (2007) 'International Cooperation in Latin America: The Design of Regional Institutions by Slow Accretion', in Amitav Acharya and Alastair Iain Johnston (eds.), *Crafting Cooperation: Regional International Institutions in Comparative Perspective*, Cambridge: Cambridge University Press, 83–128.

Donnelly, Jack (1998) 'Human Rights: A New Standard of Civilization?', *International Affairs*, 74:1, 1–23.

(2000) *Realism and International Relations*, Cambridge: Cambridge University Press.

Dougherty, James E. and Robert L. Pfalzgraff, Jr. (1997) *Contending Theories of International Relations: A Comprehensive Survey*, New York: Longman.

Douhet, Giulio ([1921] 1998) *The Command of the Air*, Tuscaloosa, AL: University of Alabama Press.

Doyle, Michael (1986) 'Liberalism and World Politics', *American Political Science Review*, 80:4, 1151–69.

Dreyer, June Teufel (2016) *Middle Kingdom and Empire of the Rising Sun: Sino-Japanese Relations, Past and Present*, New York: Oxford University Press.

Drulák, Petr, Jan Karlas and Lucie Königová (2009) 'Central and Eastern Europe: Between Continuity and Change', in Arlene B. Tickner and Ole Wæver (eds.), *International Relations Scholarship around the World*, Abingdon: Routledge, 242–60.

Duara, Prasenjit (2003) *Sovereignty and Authenticity: Manchukuo and the East Asian Modern*, Kindle edn., Lanham, MD: Rowman and Littlefield.

Du Bois, W. E. B. ([1940] 1992) *The Dusk of Dawn: An Essay toward an Autobiography*, New Brunswick, NJ: Transaction Publishers.

Duffy, Charles A. and Werner J. Feld (1980) 'Whither Regional Integration Theory', in Gavin Boyd and Werner J. Feld (eds.), *Comparative Regional Systems: West and East Europe, North America, the Middle East, and Developing Countries*, New York: Pergamon Press, 497–521.

Dunn, Kevin (2001) 'Introduction: Africa and International Relations Theory', in Kevin Dunn and Timothy Shaw (eds.), *Africa's Challenge to International Relations Theory*, New York: Palgrave, 1–8.

Dunne, Tim (1995) 'The Social Construction of International Society', *European Journal of International Relations*, 1:3, 367–89.

(1998) *Inventing International Society: A History of the English School*, London: Macmillan.

(2003) 'Society and Hierarchy in International Relations', *International Relations*, 17:3, 303–20.

Dunne, Tim and Christian Reus-Smit (eds.) (2017) *The Globalization of International Society*, Oxford: Oxford University Press.

Dunne, Tim and Nicholas J. Wheeler (1999) *Human Rights in Global Politics*, Cambridge: Cambridge University Press.

Dunne, Tim, Lene Hansen and Colin Wight (2013) 'The End of International Relations Theory?', *European Journal of International Relations*, 19:3, 405–25.

Eagleton, Clyde (1932) *International Government*, New York: Ronald Press Company.

The Economist (2009) 'Raúl Prebisch: Latin America's Keynes', 5 March, www.economist.com/node/13226316 (Accessed 27 May 2018).

Elam, J. Daniel (2017) 'Anticolonialism', *Global South Studies: A Collective Publication with The Global South*, https://globalsouthstudies.as.virginia.edu/key-concepts/anticolonialism (Accessed 18 May 2018).

Engelbrecht, H. C. and F. C. Hanighen (1934) *Merchants of Death: A Study of the International Armaments Industry*, New York: Dodd, Mead and Company.

EU (2016) *Syrian Refugees*, http://syrianrefugees.eu (Accessed 7 October 2017).

EUISS (2012) *Global Trends 2030 – Citizens in an Interconnected and Polycentric World*, Paris: EUISS, http://espas.eu/orbis/sites/default/files/espas_files/about/espas_report_ii_01_en.pdf, (Accessed 27 May 2018).

Eun, Yong-Soo (2016) *Pluralism and Engagement in the Discipline of International Relations*, Singapore: Palgrave Macmillan.

Eurostat (2017) 'Gini Coefficient of Equivalised Disposable Income – EU-SILC Survey', http://appsso.eurostat.ec.europa.eu/nui/show.do?dataset=ilc_di12 (Accessed 4 October 2017).

Falkner, Robert (2016) 'The Paris Agreement and the New Logic of International Climate Politics', *International Affairs*, 92:5, 1107–25.

Falkner, Robert and Barry Buzan (2017) 'The Emergence of Environmental Stewardship as a Primary Institution of Global International Society', *European Journal of International Relations*, doi: 10.1177/1354066117741948.

Fanon, Frantz (1965) *The Wretched of the Earth*, New York: Grove Press.

Farrell, Henry (2009) 'What's Wrong with International Political Economy', *The Monkey Cage*, 4 March, http://themonkeycage.org/2009/03/whats_wrong_with_international/ (Accessed 27 May 2018).

Fearon, James and Alexander Wendt (2002) 'Rationalism v. Constructivism: A Skeptical View', in Walter Carlsnaes, Thomas Risse and Beth A. Simmons (eds.), *Handbook of International Relations*, London: Sage, 52–72.

Fenby, Jonathan (2013) *The Penguin History of Modern China: The Fall and Rise of a Great Power 1850 to the Present*, London: Penguin.

Ferguson, Yale H. and Richard W. Mansbach (2014) 'Reflections on the "Third Debate"', Symposium, 20 March, www.isanet.org/Publications/ISQ/Posts/ID/312/Reflections-on-the-Third-Debate, (Accessed 27 May 2018).

Fierke, Karin M. (1999) 'Dialogues of Manoeuvre and Entanglement: NATO, Russia and the CEECs', *Millennium*, 28:1, 27–52.

Finnemore, Martha and Kathryn Sikkink (1999) 'International Norm Dynamics and Political Change', in Peter J. Katzenstein, Robert O. Keohane and Stephen D. Krasner (eds.), *Exploration and Contestation in the Study of World Politics*, Cambridge, MA: MIT Press, 247–77.

Flockhart, Trine (2016) 'The Coming Multi-Order World', *Contemporary Security Policy*, 37:1, 3–30.

Foot, Rosemary and Andrew Walter (2011) *China, the United States and Global Order*, Cambridge: Cambridge University Press.

Foreman-Peck, James (1982) *A History of the World Economy: International Economic Relations since 1850*, Brighton: Wheatsheaf.

Frank, Andre Gunder (1966) 'The Development of Underdevelopment', *Monthly Review*, 18:4, 17–34.

  (1971) *Capitalism and Underdevelopment in Latin America*, London: Penguin.

Frank, Andre Gunder and Barry K. Gills (1992) 'The Five Thousand Year Old World System: An Interdisciplinary Introduction', *Humboldt Journal of Social Relations*, 18:1, 1–79.

Fraser, C. Gerald (1989) 'C. L. R. James, Historian, Critic and Pan-Africanist, Is Dead at 88', *New York Times*, 2 June, www.nytimes.com/1989/06/02/obituaries/c-l-r-james-historian-critic-and-pan-africanist-is-dead-at-88.html (Accessed 27 May 2018).

Frasson-Quenoz, Florent (2015) 'Latin American Thinking in International Relations Reloaded', *Oasis*, 23, 53–75.

Friedman, Edward (2000) 'Immanuel Kant's Relevance to an Enduring Asia-Pacific Peace', in Edward Friedman and Barrett L. McCormick (eds.), *What If China Doesn't Democratize? Implications for War and Peace*, Armonk, NY: M. E. Sharpe, 224–58.

Friedrichs, Jörg (2004) *European Approaches to International Relations Theory: A House with Many Mansions*, London and New York: Routledge.

Friedrichs, Jörg and Ole Wæver (2009) 'Western Europe: Structure and Strategy at the National and Regional Levels', in Arlene B. Tickner and Ole Wæver (eds.), *International Relations Scholarship around the World*, Abingdon: Routledge, 261–86.

Fukuyama, Francis (1992) *The End of History and the Last Man*, London: Penguin.

Fukuzawa, Yukichi ([1875] 2009) *Bunmeiron no Gairyaku (An Outline of a Theory of Civilization)*, translated by David A. Dilworth and G. Cameron Hurst III, New York: Columbia University Press.

Fuller, J. F. C. (1945) *Armament and History: The Influence of Armament on History from the Dawn of Classical Warfare to the End of the Second World War*, New York: C. Scribner's Sons.

Funtecha, Henry F. (2008) 'Rizal as a Political Scientist', 14 August, http://knightsofrizal.org/?p=354 (Accessed 27 May 2018).

Gaddis, John Lewis (1986) 'The Long Peace: Elements of Stability in the Post-War International System', *International Security*, 10:4, 99–142.

(1992/3) 'International Relations Theory and the End of the Cold War', *International Security*, 17:3, 5–58.

Galtung, Johan (1971) 'A Structural Theory of Structural Imperialism', *Journal of Peace Research*, 8:2, 81–117.

Ganguli, Birendranath (1965) *Dadabhai Naoroji and the Drain Theory*, New York: Asia Publishing House.

Gao, Bai (2013) 'From Maritime Asia to Continental Asia: China's Responses to the Challenge of the Trans-Pacific Partnership', 22 pp., https://fsi.fsi.stanford.edu/sites/default/files/evnts/media/Gao.TPP_paper.pdf (Accessed 18 October 2017).

Garver, John W. (2016) *China's Quest: The History of the Foreign Relations of the People's Republic of China*, New York: Oxford University Press.

Gautam, Pradeep Kumar (2015) 'Kautilya's Arthasastra: Contemporary Issues and Comparison', IDSA Monograph Series no. 47, New Delhi: Institute of Defence Studies and Analysis.

Geis, Anna (2013) 'The "Concert of Democracies": Why Some States Are More Equal than Others', *International Politics*, 50:2, 257–77.

Gill, Stephen (1991) *American Hegemony and the Trilateral Commission*, Cambridge: Cambridge University Press.

Gill, Stephen and David Law (eds.) (1988) *The Global Political Economy: Perspectives, Problems, and Policies*, Baltimore: Johns Hopkins University Press.

Gilpin, Robert (1975) *US Power and the Multinational Corporation: The Political Economy of Foreign Direct Investment*, New York: Basic Books.

(1981) *War and Change in World Politics*, Cambridge: Cambridge University Press.

(1987) *The Political Economy of International Relations*, Princeton: Princeton University Press.

(2001) *Global Political Economy: Understanding the International Economic Order*, Princeton: Princeton University Press.

Gleditsch, Nils Petter (1992) 'Democracy and Peace', *Journal of Peace Research*, 29:4, 369–76.

Global Governance (2014) 'Principles from the Periphery: The Neglected Southern Sources of Global Norms', *Global Governance*, special section, 20:3, 359–417.

Goebel, Michael (2015) *Anti-Imperial Metropolis: Interwar Paris and the Seeds of Third World Nationalism*, Cambridge: Cambridge University Press.

Gong, Gerrit W. (1984) *The Standard of 'Civilisation' in International Society*, Oxford: Clarendon Press.

(2002) 'Standards of Civilization Today', in Mehdi Mozaffari (ed.), *Globalization and Civilizations*, London: Routledge.

Gordon, Lincoln (1961) 'Economic Regionalism Reconsidered', *World Politics*, 13:2, 231–53.

Goto-Jones, Christopher S. (2005) *Political Philosophy in Japan: Nishida, The Kyoto School and Co-Prosperity*, Abingdon: Routledge.

Grant, A. J. (1916) 'War and Peace since 1815', in A. J. Grant, Arthur Greenwood, J. D. I. Hughes, P. H. Kerr and F. F. Urquhart (eds.), *An Introduction to International Relations*, London: Macmillan, 1–36.

Grant, A. J., Arthur Greenwood, J. D. I. Hughes, P. H. Kerr and F. F. Urquhart (1916) *An Introduction to International Relations*, London: Macmillan.

Gray, Colin S. (2012) *War, Peace and International Relations: An Introduction to Strategic History*, 2nd edn., Kindle edn., London: Routledge.

Gray, Jack (2002) *Rebellions and Revolutions: China from the 1800s to 2000*, Oxford: Oxford University Press.

Greenwood, Arthur (1916) 'International Economic Relations', in A. J. Grant, Arthur Greenwood, J. D. I. Hughes, P. H. Kerr and F. F. Urquhart (eds.), *An Introduction to International Relations*, London: Macmillan, 66–112.

Greenwood, Ted, Harold A. Feiverson and Theodore B. Taylor (1977) *Nuclear Proliferation: Motivations, Capabilities and Strategies for Control*, New York: McGraw-Hill.

Grieco, Joseph M. (1993) 'Understanding the Problem of International Cooperation: The Limits of Neoliberal Institutionalism and the Future of Realist Theory', in David Baldwin (ed.), *Neorealism and Neoliberalism: The Contemporary Debate*, New York: Columbia University Press, 301–38.

Grovogui, Siba N. (2013) 'Postcolonialism', in Tim Dunne, Milja Kurki and Steve Smith (eds.), *International Relations Theories: Discipline and Diversity*, 3rd edn., Oxford: Oxford University Press, 247–65.

Grunberg, Isabelle (1990) 'Exploring the Myth of Hegemonic Stability', *International Organization*, 44:4, 431–77.

Guardian Datablog (2012) *Developing Economies to Eclipse West by 2060, OECD Forecasts*, www.guardian.co.uk/global-development/datablog/2012/nov/09/developing-economies-overtake-west-2050-oecd-forecasts (Accessed 27 May 2018).

Guha, Ranajit (1982) *Subaltern Studies: Writings on South Asian History and Society*, vol. 1, New Delhi: Oxford University Press.

Guimarães, Samuel Pinheiro (2005) *Cinco Siglod de Periferia*, Buenos Aires: Prometeo.

Gusterson, Hugh (1999) 'Nuclear Weapons and the Other in the Western Imagination', *Cultural Anthropology*, 14:1, 111–43.

Guzzini, Stefano (ed.) (2013) *The Return of Geopolitics in Europe?*, Cambridge: Cambridge University Press.

Haas, Ernst B. (1964) *Beyond the Nation State*, Stanford: Stanford University Press.
(1973) 'The Study of Regional Integration: Reflections on the Joys and Anguish of Pretheorising', in Richard A. Falk and Saul H. Mendlovitz (eds.), *Regional Politics and World Order*, San Francisco: W. H. Freeman, 103–31.
(1975) *The Obsolescence of Regional Integration Theory*, Berkeley: Institute of International Studies, University of California.

Haas, Michael (1995) 'When Democracies Fight One Another, Just What Is the Punishment for Disobeying the Law?', Paper presented at the 91st annual meeting of the American Political Science Association, August, Chicago.

(2016) *International Relations Theory: Competing Empirical Paradigms*, Lanham, MD: Lexington Books.

Hacke, Christian and Jana Puglierin (2007) 'John H. Herz: Balancing Utopia and Reality', *International Relations*, 21:3, 367–82.

Hagmann, Jonas and Thomas J. Biersteker (2014) 'Beyond the Published Discipline: Toward a Critical Pedagogy of International Studies', *European Journal of International Relations*, 20:2, 291–315.

Hagström, Linus (2015) 'The "Abnormal" State: Identity, Norm/Exception and Japan', *European Journal of International Relations*, 21:1, 122–45.

Halliday, Fred (1999) *Revolutions and World Politics*, Basingstoke: Palgrave.

Hansen, Lene and Helen Nissenbaum (2009) 'Digital Disaster, Cyber Security, and the Copenhagen School', *International Studies Quarterly*, 53:4, 1155–75.

Hansen, Roger D. (1969) 'Regional Integration: Reflections on a Decade of Theoretical Efforts', *World Politics*, 21:2, 242–71.

Harootunian, H. D. (2002) 'Postcoloniality's Unconscious/Area Studies' Desire', in Masao Miyaoshi and H. D. Harootunian (eds.), *Learning Places: The Afterlives of Area Studies*, Durham, NC: Duke University Press, 150–74.

Hashmi, Sohail H. (2009) 'Islam, the Middle East and the Pan-Islamic Movement', in Barry Buzan and Ana Gonzalez-Pelaez (eds.), *International Society and the Middle East*, Basingstoke: Palgrave, 170–200.

Heatley, David P. (1919) *Diplomacy and the Study of International Relations*, Oxford: Clarendon Press.

Heeren, A. H. L. (1834) *A Manual of the History of the Political System of Europe and Its Colonies, From Its Formation at the Close of the Fifteenth Century, to Its Re-establishment upon the Fall of Napoleon*, Oxford: D. A. Talboys.

Held, David, Anthony McGrew, David Goldblatt and Jonathan Perraton (1999) *Global Transformations*, Cambridge: Polity Press.

Helleiner, Eric (2014) 'Southern Pioneers of International Development', *Global Governance*, 20:3, 375–88.

(2017) 'The Latin American Origins of Bretton Woods', in Matias E. Margulis (ed.), *The Global Political Economy of Raúl Prebisch*, New York: Routledge, 78–94.

Helleiner, Eric and Antulio Rosales (2017) 'Toward Global IPE: The Overlooked Significance of the Haya-Mariátegui Debate', *International Studies Review*, 19:4, 667–91.

Hemmer, Christopher and Peter J. Katzenstein (2002) 'Why Is There No NATO in Asia? Collective Identity, Regionalism, and the Origins of Multilateralism', *International Organization*, 56:3, 575–607.

Henderson, Errol (2013) 'Hidden in Plain Sight: Racism in International Relations Theory', *Cambridge Review of International Affairs*, 26:1, 71–92.

Higgott, Richard and Richard Stubbs (1995) 'Competing Conceptions of Economic Regionalism: APEC versus EAEC in the Asia Pacific', *Review of International Political Economy*, 2:3, 516–35.

Higgott, Richard and Matthew Watson (2007) 'All at Sea in a Barbed Wire Canoe: Professor Cohen's Transatlantic Voyage in IPE', *Review of International Political Economy*, 15:1, 1–17.

Hirst, Paul and Grahame Thompson (1996) *Globalisation in Question*, Cambridge: Polity Press.

Hobden, Stephen and Richard Wyn Jones (2008) 'Marxist Theories of International Relations', in John Baylis, Steve Smith and Patricia Owens (eds.), *Globalization of World Politics: An Introduction to International Relations*, 4th edn., Oxford: Oxford University Press, 142–59.

Hobson, J. A. (1902) *Imperialism: A Study*, New York: James Pott & Co.

(1915) *Towards International Government*, London: G. Allen & Unwin.

Hobson, John M. (2004) *The Eastern Origins of Western Civilization*, Cambridge: Cambridge University Press.

(2010) 'Back to the Future of Nineteenth Century Western International Thought?', in George Lawson, Chris Armbruster and Michael Cox (eds.), *The Global 1989*, Cambridge: Cambridge University Press, 23–50.

(2012) *The Eurocentric Origins of International Relations: Western International Theory, 1760–2010*, Cambridge: Cambridge University Press.

Hodges, Michael (1978) 'Integration Theory', in Trevor Taylor (ed.), *Approaches and Theory in International Relations*, London: Longman, 237–56.

Hoffmann, Stanley (1977) 'An American Social Science: International Relations', *Daedalus*, 106:3, 41–60.

(1991) 'Watch Out for a New World Disorder', *International Herald Tribune*, 26 February.

Hollis, Martin and Steve Smith (1990) *Explaining and Understanding International Relations*, Oxford: Clarendon Press.

Holsti, Kalevi J. (1985) *The Dividing Discipline: Hegemony and Diversity in International Relations Theory*, Boston: Allen and Unwin.

(2001) 'Along the Road to International Theory in the Next Millennium: Four Travelogues', in Robert A. Crawford and Darryl S. L. Jarvis (eds.), *International Relations – Still an American Social Science? Toward Diversity in International Thought*, New York: State University of New York Press, 73–99.

(2004) *Taming the Sovereigns: Institutional Change in International Politics*, Cambridge: Cambridge University Press.

Holsti, Ole R. (2014) 'Present at the Creation', Address at the annual meeting of ISA/West, Pasadena, CA, September 27, www.isanet.org/Portals/0/Documents/Institutional/Holsti_ISA_West.pdf (Accessed 27 May 2018).

Homer-Dixon, Thomas, Brian Walker, Reinette Biggs, Anne-Sophie Crépin, Carl Folke, Eric F. Lambin, Garry D. Peterson, Johan Rockström, Marten Scheffer, Will Steffen and Max Troell (2015) 'Synchronous Failure: The Emerging Causal Architecture of Global Crisis', *Ecology and Society*, 20:3, 6.

Hopf, Ted (1998) 'The Promise of Constructivism in International Relations Theory', *International Security*, 23:1, 171–200.

Howard, Michael (1981) *War and the Liberal Conscience*, Oxford: Oxford University Press.

Howland, Douglas (2016) *International Law and Japanese Sovereignty*, New York: Palgrave Macmillan.

Hosoya, Yuichi (2009) 'Kokusaiseijishi no keifugaku – sengo Nihon no Ayumi wo chushin ni' [On the Genealogy of International Political History: Postwar Japan's Path and Before), in Nihon Kokusai Seiji Gakkai [Japan Association of International Relations] ed., *Rekishi no nakano kokusaiseiji* [Historical Approaches to International Politics], Tokyo: Yuhikaku.

Hula, Erich (1942) *Pan-Americanism: Its Utopian and Realistic Elements*, Washington, DC: American Council on Public Affairs.

Huntington, Samuel P. (1991) 'America's Changing Strategic Interests', *Survival*, 33:1, 3–17.

(1999) 'The Lonely Superpower', *Foreign Affairs*, 78:2, 35–49.

Hurrell, Andrew (2007) *On Global Order: Power, Values and the Constitution of International Society*, Oxford: Oxford University Press.

Hurrell, Andrew and Ngaire Woods (1995) 'Globalization and Inequality', *Millennium*, 24:3, 447–70.

Ikenberry, G. John (2001) *After Victory: Institutions, Strategic Restraint, and the Rebuilding of Order after Major Wars*, Princeton: Princeton University Press.

(2009) 'Liberal Internationalism 3.0: America and the Dilemmas of Liberal World Order', *Perspectives on Politics*, 7:1, 71–86.

(2011) *Liberal Leviathan: The Origins, Crisis, and Transformation of the American World Order*, Princeton: Princeton University Press.

Ikenberry, G. John and Michael Mastanduno (2003) 'Conclusion: Images of Order in the Asia-Pacific and the Role of the United States', in G. John Ikenberry and Michael Mastanduno (eds.), *International Relations Theory and the Asia-Pacific*, New York: Columbia University Press, 421–39.

Ikenberry, G. John and Anne-Marie Slaughter (2006) *Forging a World of Liberty under Law: US National Security in the 21st Century*, Princeton: Princeton Project Papers, Woodrow Wilson School of Public and International Affairs.

Inoguchi, Takashi (2007) 'Are There Any Theories of International Relations in Japan?', *International Relations of the Asia-Pacific*, 7:3, 369–90.

(2009) 'Japan, Korea, and Taiwan: Are One Hundred Flowers about to Blossom?', in Arlene B. Tickner and Ole Wæver (eds.), *International Relations Scholarship around the World*, Abingdon: Routledge, 86–102.

Inter-Agency Network on Women and Gender Equality (1999) 'Final Communiqué, Women's Empowerment in the Context of Human Security', 7–8 December, ESCAP, Bangkok, Thailand, www.un.org/womenwatch/ianwge/collaboration/finalcomm1999.htm (Accessed 2 June 2018).

International Institute for Strategic Studies (1971) *The Military Balance*, vol. 71, London: International Institute for Strategic Studies.

IOM (International Organization for Migration) (2014) *Afghanistan Migration Profile*, https://publications.iom.int/system/files/pdf/mp_afghanistan_0.pdf (Accessed 7 October 2017).

(2015) *Global Migration Flows*, www.iom.int/world-migration (Accessed 7 October 2017).

(2017) *Global Migration Trends 2015 Factsheet*, http://publications.iom.int/system/files/global_migration_trends_2015_factsheet.pdf (Accessed 7 October 2017).

Ireland, Alleyne (1899) *Tropical Colonization: An Introduction to the Study of the Subject*, New York: Macmillan & Co.

Jackson, Gregory and Richard Deeg (2006) 'How Many Varieties of Capitalism? Comparing the Comparative Institutional Analyses of Capitalist Diversity',

Köln, Max Planck Institute for the Study of Societies, Discussion Paper 06/2, 48 pp.

Jackson, Patrick Thaddeus (2010) *The Conduct of Inquiry in International Relations: Philosophy of Science and Its Implications for the Study of World Politics*, Oxford: Routledge.

(2014) 'The "Third Debate" 25 Years Later', Symposium, 20 March, www.isanet.org/Publications/ISQ/Posts/ID/297/The-Third-Debate-25-Years-Later [Unpaginated essay] (Accessed 27 May 2018).

Jackson, Patrick Thaddeus and Daniel H. Nexon (2013) 'International Theory in a Post-Paradigmatic Era: From Substantive Wagers to Scientific Ontologies', *European Journal of International Relations*, 19:3, 543–65.

Jackson, Robert H. (1990) 'Martin Wight, International Theory and the Good Life', *Millennium*, 19:2, 261–72.

(2000) *The Global Covenant: Human Conduct in a World of States*, Oxford: Oxford University Press.

James, C. L. R. (1933) *The Case for West-Indian Self Government*, London: Hogarth Press.

([1937] 2017) *World Revolution, 1917–1936: The Rise and Fall of the Communist International*, Durham, NC: Duke University Press.

([1938] 1989) *The Black Jacobins: Toussaint L'Ouverture and the San Domingo Revolution*, 2nd edn., New York: Vintage Books.

Jansen, Jan C. and Jürgen Osterhammel (2017) *Decolonization: A Short History*, Princeton: Princeton University Press.

Jansen, Marius B. (2000) *The Making of Modern Japan*, Cambridge, MA: Belknap Press.

Jervis, Robert (1994) 'Hans Morgenthau, Realism, and Scientific Study of International Politics', *Social Research*, 61:4, 853–76.

(1999) 'Realism, Neoliberalism, and Cooperation: Understanding the Debate', *International Security*, 24:1, 42–63.

Joas, Hans (2003) *War and Modernity*, translated by Rodney Livingstone, Cambridge: Polity Press.

Job, Brian L. (ed.) (1991) *The (In)security Dilemma: National Security of Third World States*, Boulder, CO: Lynne Rienner.

Johnston, Alastair Iain (1998) *Cultural Realism: Strategic Culture and Grand Strategy in Chinese History*, Princeton: Princeton University Press.

(2012) 'What (If Anything) Does East Asia Tell Us about International Relations Theory?', *Annual Review of Political Science*, 15, 53–78.

Joll, James (1982) 'The Ideal and the Real: Changing Concepts of the International System, 1815–1982', *International Affairs*, 58:2, 210–24.

Jomini, Antoine-Henri ([1838] 1854) *The Art of War*, translated by Major O. F. Winship and Lieut. E. E. McLean, New York: G. P. Putnam.

Kacowicz, Arie M. (2005) *The Impact of Norms in International Society: The Latin American Experience, 1881–2001*, Notre Dame, IN: Notre Dame University Press.

(2009) 'Israel: The Development of a Discipline in a Unique Setting', in Arlene B. Tickner and Ole Wæver (eds.), *International Relations Scholarship around the World*, Abingdon: Routledge, 191–207.

Kahler, Miles (1993) 'International Relations: An American Social Science or an International One', in Linda B. Miller and Michael Joseph Smith (eds.), *Ideas and Ideals: Essays on Politics in Honor of Stanley Hoffmann*, Boulder, CO: Westview Press, 395–414.

(1997) 'Inventing International Relations: International Relations after 1945', in Michael W. Doyle and G. John Ikenberry (eds.), *New Thinking in International Relations Theory*, Boulder, CO: Westview Press, 20–53.

Kang, David C. (2003) 'Getting Asia Wrong: The Need for New Analytical Frameworks', *International Security*, 27:4, 57–85.

(2005) 'Hierarchy in Asian International Relations: 1300–1900', *Asian Security*, 11:1, 53–79.

Kang, Yuwei ([1935] 1958) *Da Tong Shu/Ta T'ung Shu* (The Great Harmony), translated by Laurence G. Thompson, London: George Allen & Unwin.

Kaplan, Morton A. (1966) 'The New Great Debate: Traditionalism vs. Science in International Relations', *World Politics*, 19:1, 1–20.

Kapoor, Ilan (2002) 'Capitalism, Culture, Agency: Dependency versus Postcolonial Theory', *Third World Quarterly*, 23:4, 647–64.

Kapstein, Ethan B. and Michael Mastanduno (eds.) (1999) *Unipolar Politics*, New York: Columbia University Press.

Karim, Azhari (2007) 'ASEAN: Association to Community: Constructed in the Image of Malaysia's Global Diplomacy', in Abdul Razak Baginda (ed.), *Malaysia's Foreign Policy: Continuity and Change*, Singapore: Marshall Cavendish, 109–32.

Karl, Rebecca (1998) 'Creating Asia: China in the World at the Beginning of Twentieth Century', *The American Historical Review*, 103:4, 1096–1118.

Katzenstein, Peter J. (2010) 'A World of Plural and Pluralist Civilizations: Multiple Actors, Traditions and Practices', in Peter J. Katzenstein (ed.), *Civilizations in World Politics*, London: Routledge, 1–40.

(2012) 'Many Wests and Polymorphic Globalism', in Peter J. Katzenstein (ed.), *Anglo-America and Its Discontents: Civilizational Identities beyond West and East*, London and New York: Routledge, 207–47.

Katzenstein, Peter J., Robert O. Keohane and Stephen D. Krasner (eds.) (1999) *Exploration and Contestation in the Study of World Politics*, Cambridge, MA: MIT Press.

Kaushik, Ashok (ed.) (2007) *Srimad Bhagavad Gita*, English translation by Janak Datta, 7th edn., New Delhi: Star Publications.

Kawata, Tadashi and Saburo Ninomiya (1964) 'The Development of the Study of International Relations in Japan', *The Developing Economies*, 2:2, 190–204.

Kayaoğlu, Turan (2010a) *Legal Imperialism: Sovereignty and Extraterritoriality in Japan, Ottoman Empire and China*, Cambridge: Cambridge University Press.

(2010b) 'Westphalian Eurocentrism in International Relations Theory', *International Studies Review*, 12:2, 193–217.

Keck, Margaret and Kathryn Sikkink (1998) *Activists beyond Borders: Advocacy Networks in International Politics*, Ithaca, NY: Cornell University Press.

Kedourie, Eli (2018) 'Jamāl al-Dīn al-Afghānī', *Encyclopaedia Britannica*, 2 March, www.britannica.com/biography/Jamal-al-Din-al-Afghani (Accessed 27 May 2018).

Keeley, James F. (1990) 'Toward a Foucauldian Analysis of Regimes', *International Organization*, 44:1, 83–105.

Keene, Edward (2002) *Beyond the Anarchical Society*, Cambridge: Cambridge University Press.

Keenleyside, T. A. (1982) 'Nationalist Indian Attitudes towards Asia: A Troublesome Legacy for Post-Independence Indian Foreign Policy', *Pacific Affairs*, 55:2, 210–30.

Keith, A. Berriedale (1924) *The Constitution, Administration and Laws of the Empire*, London: W. Collins Sons & Co.

Kennedy, Dane (1996) 'Imperial History and Post-Colonial Theory', *Journal of Imperial and Commonwealth History*, 24:3, 345–63.

Keohane, Robert O. (1984) *After Hegemony: Cooperation and Discord in the World Political Economy*, Princeton: Princeton University Press.

  (1989) *International Institutions and State Power: Essays in International Relations Theory*, Boulder, CO: Westview Press.

Keohane, Robert O. and Lisa L. Martin (1995) 'The Promise of Institutionalist Theory', *International Security*, 19:1, 39–51.

Keohane, Robert O. and Joseph S. Nye (1977) *Power and Interdependence: World Politics in Transition*, Boston: Little, Brown.

  (2000) 'Globalization: What's New? What's Not? (And So What)', *Foreign Policy*, 118, 104–19.

Kerr, P. H. (1916) 'Political Relations between Advanced and Backward Peoples', in A. J. Grant, Arthur Greenwood, J. D. I. Hughes, P. H. Kerr and F. F. Urquhart, *An Introduction to the Study of International Relations*, London: Macmillan, 141–82.

Kindleberger, Charles P. (1973) *The World in Depression, 1929–39*, London: Allen Lane.

King, Gary, Robert O. Keohane and Sidney Verba (1994) *Designing Social Inquiry: Scientific Inference in Qualitative Research*, Princeton: Princeton University Press.

Kissinger, Henry (2011) *On China*, London: Allen Lane.

Knutsen, Torbjørn (2016) *A History of International Relations Theory*, 3rd edn., Manchester: Manchester University Press.

Kohli, Atul (2004) *State-Directed Development: Political Power and Industrialization in the Global Periphery*, Cambridge: Cambridge University Press.

Kokubun, Ryosei, Yoshihide Soeya, Akio Takahara and Shin Kawashima (2017) *Japan–China Relations in the Modern Era*, London: Routledge.

Koskenniemi, Martti (2001) *The Gentle Civilizer of Nations: The Rise and Fall of International Law, 1870–1960*, Cambridge: Cambridge University Press.

Köstem, Seçkin (2015) 'International Relations Theories and Turkish International Relations: Observations Based on a Book', *All Azimuth*, 4:1, 59–66.

Koyama, Hitomi and Barry Buzan (2018) 'Rethinking Japan in Mainstream International Relations', *International Relations of the Asia-Pacific*, lcy013, doi: 10.1093/irap/lcy013, 25 May, 1–28 (Accessed 27 June 2018).

Kramer, Martin (1993) 'Arab Nationalism: Mistaken Identity', *Daedalus*, 122:3, 171–206.

Krasner, Stephen (1976) 'State Power and the Structure of International Trade', *World Politics*, 28:3, 317–43.

Krippendorff, Ekkehart (1989) 'The Dominance of American Approaches in International Relations', in Hugh C. Dyer and Leon Mangasarian (eds.), *The Study of International Relations: The State of the Art*, Basingstoke: Palgrave, 28–39.

Krishna, Sankaran (1993) 'The Importance of Being Ironic: A Postcolonial View on Critical International Relations Theory', *Alternatives*, 18:3, 385–417.

Kristensen, Peter Marcus (2015) 'Revisiting the "American Social Science" – Mapping the Geography of International Relations', *International Studies Perspectives*, 16:3, 246–69.

(2018) 'International Relations at the End: A Sociological Autopsy', *International Studies Quarterly*, sqy002, doi: 10.1093/isq/sqy002, 3 May, 1–10 (Accessed 27 June 2018).

Kuga, Katsunan ([1893] 1968) *Gensei oyobi Kokusa Ron (On the International)*, *in* Kuga Katsunan Zenshu (Collected Complete Works of Kuga Katsunan), Tokyo: Misuzu Shobo, 123–81.

Kupchan, Charles A. (2012) *No One's World: The West, the Rising Rest, and the Coming Global Turn*, New York: Oxford University Press.

Kuru, Deniz (2016) 'Historicising Eurocentrism and Anti-Eurocentrism in IR: A Revisionist Account of Disciplinary Self-Reflexivity', *Review of International Studies*, 42:2, 351–76.

(2017) 'Who F(o)unded IR: American Philanthropists and the Discipline of International Relations in Europe', *International Relations*, 31:1, 42–67.

Kuryla, Peter (2016) 'Pan-Africanism', Encyclopaedia Britannica, www .britannica.com/topic/Pan-Africanism (Accessed 30 March 2018).

Ladwig III, Walter C. (2009) 'Delhi's Pacific Ambition: Naval Power, "Look East", and India's Emerging Influence in the Asia-Pacific', *Asian Security*, 55:2, 87–113.

Lake, David A. (2008) 'International Political Economy: A Maturing Interdiscipline', in Donald A. Wittman and Barry R. Weingast (eds.), *The Oxford Handbook of Political Economy*, Oxford: Oxford University Press, 757–77.

(2011) 'Why "Isms" are Evil: Theory, Epistemology, and Academic Sects as Impediments to Understanding and Progress', *International Studies Quarterly*, 55:2, 465–80.

Lapid, Yosef (1989) 'The Third Debate: On the Prospects of International Theory in a Post-positivist Era', *International Studies Quarterly*, 33:3, 235–54.

Lawrence, T. J. (1919) *The Society of Nations: Its Past, Present, and Possible Future*, New York: Oxford University Press.

Lawson, George (2012) 'The Eternal Divide? History and International Relations', *European Journal of International Relations*, 18:2, 203–26.

Lawson, George and John M. Hobson (2008) 'What Is History in International Relations?', *Millennium*, 37:2, 415–35.

Layne, Christopher (1993) 'The Unipolar Illusion: Why Other Great Powers Will Rise', *International Security*, 17:4, 5–51.

(2006) 'The Unipolar Illusion Revisited: The Coming End of the United States' Unipolar Moment', *International Security*, 31:2, 7–41.

League of Arab States (1955) *The Report of the Arab League on the Bandung Conference*, Cairo: League of the Arab States.

Lebedeva, Marina M. (2004) 'International Relations Studies in the USSR/ Russia: Is There a Russian National School of IR Studies?', *Global Society*, 18:3, 263–78.

Lenin, Vladimir Ilyich ([1916] 1975) *Imperialism: The Highest Stage of Capitalism*, Peking: Foreign Languages Press.

Leonard, Thomas (2000) 'The New Pan Americanism in US–Central American Relations, 1933–1954', in David Sheinin (ed.), *Beyond the Ideal: Pan Americanism in International Affairs*, Westport, CT: Praeger, 95–114.

Levy, Jack S. (1989) 'The Causes of Wars: A Review of Theories and Evidence', in Philip E. Tetlock, Jo L. Husbands, Robert Jervis, Paul C. Stern and Charles Tilly (eds.), *Behavior, Society and Nuclear War*, vol. 1, New York: Oxford University Press, 209–333.

Liddell Hart, Basil (1946) *The Revolution in Warfare*, London: Faber & Faber.

Lindberg, Leon N. and Stuart A. Scheingold (1971) *Regional Integration: Theory and Research*, Cambridge, MA: Harvard University Press.

Ling, L. H. M. (2002) *Postcolonial International Relations: Conquest and Desire between Asia and the West*, London: Palgrave.

(2010) 'Journeys beyond the West: World Orders and a 7th-Century, Buddhist Monk', *Review of International Studies*, 36:S1, 225–48.

Linklater, Andrew (1996) 'The Achievements of Critical Theory', in Steve Smith, Ken Booth and Marysia Zalewski (eds.), *International Theory: Positivism and Beyond*, Cambridge: Cambridge University Press, 279–98.

(2001) 'Marxism', in Scott Burchill, Richard Devetak, Andrew Linklater, Matthew Paterson, Christian Reus-Smit and Jacqui True, *Theories of International Relations*, 2nd edn., Basingstoke: Palgrave, 129–54.

Little, Richard (2008) 'The Expansion of the International Society in Heeren's Account of the European States-System', SPAIS Working Paper no. 07–08, University of Bristol, 20 pp.

Little, Richard and Mike Smith (1980) *Perspectives on World Politics*, London: Routledge.

Lobell, Steven E., Norrin M. Ripsman and Jeffrey W. Taliaferro (eds.) (2009) *Neoclassical Realism, the State, and Foreign Policy*, New York: Cambridge University Press.

Lockey, Joseph Byrne (1920) *Pan-Americanism: Its Beginnings*, New York: Macmillan.

Long, David (1995) 'Conclusion: Inter-War Idealism, Liberal Internationalism, and Contemporary International Theory', in David Long and Peter Wilson (eds.), *Thinkers of the Twenty Years' Crisis: Inter-War Idealism Reassessed*, Oxford: Clarendon, 302–28.

(2006) 'Who Killed the International Studies Conference?', *Review of International Studies*, 32:4, 603–22.

Long, David and Brian C. Schmidt (2005) 'Introduction', in David Long and Brian C. Schmidt (eds.), *Imperialism and Internationalism in the Discipline of International Relations*, Albany: SUNY Press, 1–21.

Long, David and Peter Wilson (eds.) (1995) *Thinkers of the Twenty Years' Crisis: Inter-War Idealism Reassessed*, Oxford: Clarendon Press.

Lorimer, James (1877) 'Le problème final du droit international', *Revue de droit international et de législation comparée*, 9:2, 161–205.

(1884) *The Institutes of the Law of Nations: A Treatise on the Jural Relations of Separate Political Communities*, Edinburgh and London: William Blackwood and Sons.

Lu, Peng (2014) 'Pre-1949 Chinese IR: An Occluded History', *Australian Journal of International Affairs*, 68:2, 133–55.

Luttwak, Edward N. (2012) *The Rise of China vs. the Logic of Strategy*, Cambridge, MA: Belknap Press.

Lynch, Timothy J. (2013) 'George W. Bush', in Michael Cox, Timothy J. Lynch and Nicolas Bouchet (eds.), *US Foreign Policy and Democracy Promotion: From Theodore Roosevelt to Barack Obama*, Abingdon: Routledge, 178–95.

MacCalman, Molly (2016) 'A. Q. Khan Nuclear Smuggling Network', *Journal of Strategic Security*, 9:1, 104–18.

Mace, Gordon (1986) 'Regional Integration', *World Encyclopedia of Peace*, Oxford: Pergamon Press, 323–5.

MacFarlane, S. Neil (1993) 'Russia, the West and European Security', *Survival*, 35:3, 3–25.

McGann, James G. (2018) '2017 Global Go To Think Tank Index Report', TTCSP Global Go To Think Tank Index Reports, 13.

Mackinder, Halford ([1904] 1996) 'The Geographical Pivot of History', in Halford Mackinder, *Democratic Ideals and Reality*, Washington, DC: National Defence University, 175–94.

(1919) *Democratic Ideals and Reality: A Study in the Politics of Reconstruction*, London: Constable and Co.

McKinlay, Robert and Richard Little (1986) *Global Problems and World Order*, London: Frances Pinter.

Mackintosh-Smith, Tim (2002) *The Travels of Ibn Battutah*, London: Picador.

McNally, Christopher (2013) 'How Emerging Forms of Capitalism Are Changing the Global Economic Order', *East-West Center: Asia-Pacific Issues*, no. 107.

Maddison, Angus (2001) *The World Economy: A Millennial Perspective*, Paris: Development Centre of the Organisation for Economic Co-operation and Development.

Mahan, Alfred Thayer (1890) *The Influence of Sea Power upon History, 1660–1783*, Boston: Little, Brown.

Makarychev, Andrey and Viatcheslav Morozov (2013) 'Is "Non-Western Theory" Possible? The Idea of Multipolarity and the Trap of Epistemological Relativism in Russian IR', *International Studies Review*, 15:3, 328–50.

Makdisi, Karim (2009) 'Reflections on the State of IR in the Arab Region', in Arlene B. Tickner and Ole Wæver (eds.), *International Relations Scholarship around the World*, Abingdon: Routledge, 180–90.

Malaquias, Assis (2001) 'Reformulating International Relations Theory: African Insights and Challenges', in Kevin Dunn and Timothy Shaw (eds.), *Africa's Challenge to International Relations Theory*, New York: Palgrave, 11–28.

Maliniak, Daniel, Amy Oakes, Susan Peterson and Michael J. Tierney (2011) 'International Relations in the US Academy', *International Studies Quarterly*, 55:2, 437–64.

Maliniak, Daniel, Susan Peterson, Ryan Powers and Michael J. Tierney (2018) 'Is International Relations a Global Discipline? Hegemony,

346   References

Insularity and Diversity in the Field', *Security Studies*, doi: 10.1080/ 09636412.2017.1416824 (Accessed 27 June 2018).

Mallavarapu, Siddharth (2009) 'Development of International Relations Theory in India: Traditions, Contemporary Perspectives and Trajectories', *International Studies*, 46:1–2, 165–83.

(2018) 'The Sociology of International Relations in India: Competing Conceptions of Political Order', in Gunther Hellman (ed.), *Theorizing Global Order: The International, Culture and Governance*, Frankfurt: Campus Verlag GmbH, 142–71.

Mani, V. S. (2004) 'An Indian Perspective on the Evolution of International Law', in B. S. Chimni, Miyoshi Masahiro and Surya P. Subedi (eds.), *Asian Yearbook of International Law, 2000*, vol. 9, Leiden: Brill, 31–78.

Mann, Michael (2001) 'Democracy and Ethnic War', in Tarak Barkawi and Mark Laffey (eds.), *Democracy, Liberalism, and War: Rethinking the Democratic Peace Debate*, Boulder, CO: Lynne Rienner, 67–85.

Maoz, Zeev and Bruce Russett (1993) 'Normative and Structural Causes of the Democratic Peace, 1946–1986', *American Political Science Review*, 87:3, 624–38.

Marder, Arthur J. (1961) *From the Dreadnought to Scapa Flow: The Royal Navy in the Fisher Era, 1904–1919*, vol. 1, *The Road to War 1904–1914*, Oxford: Oxford University Press.

Marshall, Peter J. (2001) *The Cambridge Illustrated History of the British Empire*, Cambridge: Cambridge University Press.

Marx, Karl ([1852] 1963) *The Eighteenth Brumaire of Louis Bonaparte*, New York: International Publishers.

Marx, Karl and Friedrich Engels ([1848] 2010) *Manifesto of the Communist Party*, www.marxists.org/archive/marx/works/download/pdf/Manifesto.pdf (Accessed 24 May 2017).

Maull, Hanns W. (1990) 'Germany and Japan: The New Civilian Powers', *Foreign Affairs*, 69:5, 91–106.

Mayall, James (1990) *Nationalism and International Society*, Cambridge: Cambridge University Press.

Mazrui, Ali (1967) *Towards a Pax Africana: A Study of Ideology and Ambition*, Chicago: University of Chicago Press.

(1986) *The Africans: A Triple Heritage*, Boston: Little, Brown.

Mearsheimer, John J. (1990) 'Back to the Future: Instability in Europe after the Cold War', *International Security*, 15:1, 5–55.

(1994/5) 'The False Promise of International Institutions', *International Security*, 19:3, 5–49.

(2001) *The Tragedy of Great Power Politics*, New York: W. W. Norton & Co.

(2016) 'Benign Hegemony', *International Studies Review*, 18:1, 147–9.

Meinecke, Friedrich (1908) *Weltbürgertum und Nationalstaat: Studien zur Genesis des deutschen Nationalstaates* (Cosmopolitanism and the Nationstate: Studies in the Beginning of the German Nationstates), Munich: R. Oldenbourg.

Merke, Federico (2011) 'The Primary Institutions of Latin American Regional Interstate Society', Paper for IDEAS Latin America Programme, LSE, 27 January, 38 pp.

Micklethwait, John and Adrian Wooldridge (2014) *The Fourth Revolution: The Global Race to Reinvent the State*, New York: Penguin Press.

Mill, John Stuart (1848) *Principles of Political Economy*, London: John W. Parker.

(1874) *Dissertations and Discussions: Political, Philosophical, and Historical*, New York: Henry Holt & Co.

Miller, Lynn H. (1973) 'The Prospects for Order through Regional Security', in Richard A. Falk and Saul H. Mendlovitz (eds.), *Regional Politics and World Order*, San Francisco: W. H. Freeman, 50–77.

Mills, David (2013) *Our Uncertain Future: When Digital Evolution, Global Warming and Automation Converge*, San Diego: Pacific Beach Publishing.

Milner, Anthony (2016) 'Searching for Non-Western Perspectives on "International Relations": Malay/Malaysia', Unpublished paper.

Mishra, Atul (2014) 'Indigenism in Contemporary IR Discourses in India: A Critique', *Studies in Indian Politics*, 2:2, 119–35.

Mishra, Pankaj (2012) *From the Ruins of Empire: The Revolt against the West and the Remaking of Asia*, London: Farrar, Straus and Giroux.

Mogwe, Alex (1994) 'Human Rights in Botswana: Feminism, Oppression, and "Integration"', *Alternatives*, 19:2, 189–93.

Mohanty, Chandra T. (1984) 'Under Western Eyes: Feminist Scholarship and Colonial Discourses', *Boundary*, 2, 333–58.

Molyneux, Maxine and Fred Halliday (1984) 'Marxism, the Third World and the Middle East', *MERIP Reports*, no. 120, January, 18–21.

Morgan, Kenneth O. (2012) 'Alfred Zimmern's Brave New World', 12 March, www.cymmrodorion.org/alfred-zimmerns-brave-new-world/ (Accessed 27 May 2018).

Morgenthau, Hans J. (1948) *Politics among Nations: The Struggle for Power and Peace*, New York: A. A. Knopf.

(1967) *Politics among Nations: The Struggle for Power and Peace*, 4th edn., New York: Knopf.

Morley, Felix (1932) *The Society of Nations: Its Organization and Constitutional Development*, Washington, DC: The Brookings Institution.

Mulgan, Geoff (2013) *The Locust and the Bee*, Princeton: Princeton University Press.

Murphy, R. Taggart (2014) *Japan and the Shackles of the Past*, Oxford: Oxford University Press.

Nandy, Ashis ([1983] 2009) *The Intimate Enemy: Loss and Recovery of Self under Colonialism*, New Delhi: Oxford University Press.

(1995) 'History's Forgotten Doubles', *History and Theory*, 34:2, 44–66.

Naoroji, Dadabhai (1901) *Poverty and Un-British Rule in India*, London: Swan Sonnenschein.

Narlikar, Amrita and Aruna Narlikar (2014) *Bargaining with a Rising India: Lessons from the Mahabharata*, Oxford: Oxford University Press.

Nath, Sathya and Sohini Dutta (2014) 'Critiques of Benedict Anderson's Imagined Communities', Cultural Studies (blog), http://culturalstudiesblog.blogspot.nl/2014/08/critiques-of-benedict-andersons.html (Accessed 17 May 2018).

Navari, Cornelia (2009) *Theorising International Society: English School Methods*, Basingstoke: Palgrave.

Nehru, Jawaharlal ([1946] 2003) *The Discovery of India*, 23rd impression, New Delhi: Oxford University Press.

Neuman, Stephanie (ed.) (1998) *International Relations Theory and the Third World*, New York: St Martin's Press.

Nossal, Kim Richard (2001) 'Tales that Textbooks Tell: Ethnocentricity and Diversity in American Introductions to International Relations', in Robert A. Crawford and Darryl S. L. Jarvis (eds.), *International Relations – Still an American Social Science? Toward Diversity in International Thought*, New York: State University of New York Press, 167–86.

Nye, Joseph S. (1968) 'Central American Regional Integration', in Joseph S. Nye (ed.), *International Regionalism: Readings*, Boston: Little, Brown, 377–429.

(1988) 'Neorealism and Neoliberalism', *World Politics*, 40:2, 235–51.

Oatley, Thomas (2011) 'The Reductionist Gamble: Open Economy Politics in the Global Economy', *International Organization*, 65:2, 311–41.

(2012) *International Political Economy*, 5th edn., Boston: Longman.

OECD (2011) *Divided We Stand: Why Inequality Keeps Rising*, www.oecd.org/els/soc/49499779.pdf (Accessed 4 October 2017).

Ofuho, Cirino Hiteng (2009) 'Africa: Teaching IR Where It's Not Supposed to Be', in Arlene B. Tickner and Ole Wæver (eds.), *International Relations Scholarship around the World*, Abingdon: Routledge, 71–85.

Okakura, Kakuzō (1903) *The Ideals of the East with Special Reference to the Art of Japan*, London: J. Murray.

(1904) *The Awakening of Japan*, New York: Century Co.

([1906] 1912) *The Book of Tea*, New York: Duffield & Company.

Olson, William C. (1972) 'The Growth of a Discipline', in Brian Porter (ed.), *The Aberystwyth Papers: International Politics 1919–1969*, London: Oxford University Press, 3–29.

Olson, William and A. J. R. Groom (1991) *International Relations Then and Now: Origins and Trends in Interpretation*, London: Routledge.

Olson, William and Nicholas Onuf (1985) 'The Growth of the Discipline Reviewed', in Steve Smith (ed.), *International Relations: British and American Perspectives*, Oxford: Blackwell, 1–28.

Ong, Aihwa (2001) 'Colonialism and Modernity: Feminist Re-presentations of Women in Non-Western Societies', in K. K. Bhavnani (ed.), *Feminism and Race*, New York: Oxford University Press, 108–20.

Osterhammel, Jürgen (2014) *The Transformation of the World: A Global History of the Nineteenth Century*, translated by Patrick Camiller, Princeton: Princeton University Press.

Ó Tuathail, Gearóid (1996) *Critical Geopolitics: The Politics of Writing Global Space*, Minneapolis: University of Minnesota Press.

(1998) 'Introduction' and 'Imperialist Geopolitics', in Gearóid Ó Tuathail, Simon Dalby and Paul Routledge (eds.), *The Geopolitics Reader*, London: Routledge, 1–43.

Ó Tuathail, Gearóid, Simon Dalby and Paul Routledge (eds.) (1998) *The Geopolitics Reader*, London: Routledge.

Paine, S. C. M. (2012) *The Wars for Asia, 1911–1949*, New York: Cambridge University Press.

(2017) *The Japanese Empire: Grand Strategy from the Meiji Restoration to the Pacific War*, New York: Cambridge University Press.

Palmer, Norman D. (1980) 'The Study of International Relations in the United States: Perspectives of Half a Century', *International Studies Quarterly*, 24:3, 343–64.

Pant, Harsh V. (2009) 'The US–India Nuclear Pact: Policy, Process, and Great Power Politics', *Asian Security*, 5:3, 273–95.

Parashar, Swati (2013) 'Feminist (In)securities and Camp Politics', *International Studies Perspectives*, 13:4, 440–3.

Parry, Benita (1987) 'Problems in Current Theories of Colonial Discourse', *Oxford Literary Review*, 9:1–2, 27–58.

Pasha, Mustapha Kamal (2013) 'The "Bandung Impulse" and International Relations', in Sanjay Seth (ed.), *Postcolonial Theory and International Relations: A Critical Introduction*, New York: Routledge, 144–65.

Paul, T. V. (2010) 'State Capacity and South Asia's Perennial Insecurity Problems', in T. V. Paul (ed.), *South Asia's Weak States: Understanding the Regional Insecurity Predicament*, Stanford: Stanford University Press, 3–27.

Pearton, Maurice (1982) *The Knowledgeable State: Diplomacy, War and Technology since 1830*, London: Burnett Books.

Pempel, T. J. (2011) 'Japan's Search for the "Sweet Spot": International Cooperation and Regional Security in Northeast Asia', *Orbis*, 55:2, 255–73.

Persaud, Randolph B. (2014) 'Points on Race and Global IR', [Personal email], 20 August.

(2018) 'Security Studies, Postcolonialism, and the Third World', in Randolph B. Persaud and Alina Sajed (eds.), *Race, Gender and Culture in International Relations: Postcolonial Perspectives*, London: Routledge, 155–79.

Persaud, Randolph B. and Alina Sajed (2018a) 'Introduction: Race, Gender and Culture in International Relations', in Randolph B. Persaud and Alina Sajed (eds.), *Race, Gender and Culture in International Relations: Postcolonial Perspectives*, London: Routledge, 1–18.

(2018b) *Race, Gender, and Culture in International Relations: Postcolonial Perspectives*, Abingdon: Routledge.

Persaud, Randolph B. and R. B. J. Walker (2001) 'Race in International Relations', *Alternatives*, 26:4, 373–6.

Pettersson, Thérése and Peter Wallensteen (2015) 'Armed Conflicts, 1946–2014', *Journal of Peace Research*, 52:4, 536–50.

Phillips, Andrew (2011) *War, Religion and Empire*, Cambridge: Cambridge University Press.

Phillips, Andrew and J. C. Sharman (2015) *International Order in Diversity: War, Trade and Rule in the Indian Ocean*, Cambridge: Cambridge University Press.

Pieke, Frank N. (2016) *Knowing China: A Twenty-First Century Guide*, Cambridge: Cambridge University Press.

Pines, Yuri (2012) *The Everlasting Empire: The Political Culture of Ancient China and Its Imperial Legacy*, Princeton: Princeton University Press.

Poku, Nana K. (2013) 'HIV/AIDS, State Fragility, and United Nations Security Council Resolution 1308: A View from Africa', *International Peacekeeping*, 20:4, 521–35.

Porter, Tony (2001) 'Can There Be National Perspectives on Inter(national) Relations?', in Robert A. Crawford and Darryl S. L. Jarvis (eds.), *International*

Relations – Still an American Social Science? Toward Diversity in International Thought, New York: State University of New York Press, 131–47.

Potter, Pitman B. (1922) *An Introduction to the Study of International Organization*, New York: Century.

Prabhu, Jaideep (2017) 'The Roots of Indian Foreign Policy', 4 March, https://jaideepprabhu.org/2017/03/04/the-roots-of-indian-foreign-policy/ (Accessed 27 May 2018).

Prasad, Bimla (1962) *The Origins of Indian Foreign Policy: The Indian National Congress and World Affairs, 1885–1947*, Calcutta: Bookland.

Preston, Paul (2000) 'The Great Civil War: European Politics, 1914–1945', in T. C. W. Blanning (ed.), *The Oxford History of Modern Europe*, Oxford: Oxford University Press, 153–85.

PricewaterhouseCoopers (2015) 'The World in 2050: Will the Shift in Global Economic Power Continue?', www.pwc.com/gx/en/issues/the-economy/assets/world-in-2050-february-2015.pdf (Accessed 27 May 2018).

Puchala, Donald J. (1984) 'The Integration Theorists and the Study of International Relations', in Charles W. Kegley and Eugene R. Wittkopf (eds.), *The Global Agenda: Issues and Perspectives*, New York: Random House, 185–201.

(1995) 'Third World Thinking and Contemporary Relations', in Stephanie Neuman (ed.), *International Relations Theory and the Third World*, New York: St Martin's Press, 131–57.

Puntambekar, S. V. (1939) 'The Role of Myths in the Development of Political Thought', *Indian Journal of Political Science*, 1:2, 121–32.

Qin, Yaqing (2009) 'Relational and Processual Construction: Bringing Chinese Ideas into International Relations Theory', *Social Sciences in China*, 30:4, 5–20.

(2010) 'Why Is There No Chinese International Relations Theory?', in Amitav Acharya and Barry Buzan (eds.), *Non-Western International Relations Theory: Perspectives on and beyond Asia*, London: Routledge, 26–50.

(2011a) 'Development of International Relations Theory in China: Progress through Debate', *International Relations of the Asia-Pacific*, 11:2, 231–57.

(2011b) 'Rule, Rules and Relations: Towards a Synthetic Approach to Governance', *The Chinese Journal of International Politics*, 4:2, 117–45.

(2016) 'A Relational Theory of World Politics', *International Studies Review*, 18:1, 33–47.

(2018) *A Relational Theory of World Politics*, Cambridge: Cambridge University Press.

Rahe, Paul (2013) 'Progressive Racism', *National Review*, April 11, www.nationalreview.com/article/345274/progressive-racism-paul-rahe (Accessed 21 November 2017).

Rajab, Ahmed (2014) 'Ali Mazrui Obituary', *The Guardian*, 20 October, www.theguardian.com/profile/ahmed-rajab (Accessed 27 May 2018).

Ratzel, Friedrich (1901) *Der Lebensraum: Eine biogeographische Studie*, Tübigen: Verlag der H. Laupp'schen Buchhandlung.

Ravenhill, John (2001) *APEC and the Construction of Pacific Rim Regionalism*, Cambridge: Cambridge University Press.

(2007) 'In Search of the Missing Middle', *Review of International Political Economy*, 15:1, 18–29.

Ravlo, Hilde, Nils Petter Gleditsch and Han Dorussen (2003) 'Colonial War and the Democratic Peace', *Journal of Conflict Resolution*, 47:4, 520–48.

Ray, James Lee (1995) *Democracy and International Conflict: An Evaluation of the Democratic Peace Proposition*, Columbia, SC: University of South Carolina Press.

Rees, Martin (2003) *Our Final Century*, London: William Heinemann.

Rehman, Iskander (2009) 'Keeping the Dragon at Bay: India's Counter-Containment of China in Asia', *Asian Security*, 5:2, 114–43.

Rehn, Elisabeth and Ellen Johnson Sirleaf (2002) *Progress of the World's Women 2002*, vol. 1. *Women, War and Peace: The Independent Experts' Assessment on the Impact of Armed Conflict on Women and Women's Role in Peace-Building*, Technical Report. United Nations Development Fund for Women – UNIFEM: New York.

Reinsch, Paul (1900) *World Politics at the End of the Nineteenth Century As Influenced by the Oriental Situation*, New York: Macmillan.

(1902) *Colonial Government: An Introduction to the Study of Colonial Institutions*, New York: Macmillan.

(1911) *Public International Unions – Their Work and Organization: A Study in International Administrative Law*, Boston: Ginn & Co.

Reus-Smit, Christian (1999) *The Moral Purpose of the State*, Princeton: Princeton University Press.

(2001) 'Human Rights and the Social Construction of Sovereignty', *Review of International Studies*, 27:4, 519–38.

(2005) 'Constructivism', in Scott Burchill, Andrew Linklater, Richard Devetak, Jack Donnelly, Matthew Paterson, Christian Reus-Smit and Jacqui True, *Theories of International Relations*, 3rd edn., Basingstoke: Palgrave.

(2013) 'Beyond Metatheory?', *European Journal of International Relations*, 19:3, 589–608.

Ricardo, David (1817) *On the Principles of Political Economy and Taxation*, London: John Murray.

Rich, Paul (1995) 'Alfred Zimmern's Cautious Idealism: The League of Nations, International Education, and the Commonwealth', in David Long and Peter Wilson (eds.), *Thinkers of the Twenty Years' Crisis: Inter-War Idealism Reassessed*, Oxford: Clarendon, 79–99.

Richardson, Neil R. (1989) 'The Study of International Relations in the United States', in Hugh C. Dyer and Leon Mangasarian (eds.), *The Study of International Relations: The State of the Art*, London: Macmillan, 281–95.

Riemens, Michael (2011) 'International Academic Cooperation on International Relations in the Interwar Period: The International Studies Conference', *Review of International Studies*, 37:2, 911–28.

Ripsman, Norrin M. and T. V. Paul (2010) *Globalization and the National Security State*, New York: Oxford University Press.

Rosecrance, Richard N. (1969) 'Bipolarity, Multipolarity, and the Future', in James N. Rosenau (ed.), *International Politics and Foreign Policy: A Reader in Research and Theory*, New York: Free Press, 325–35.

Rosenberg, Justin (2013) 'Kenneth Waltz and Leon Trotsky: Anarchy in the Mirror of Uneven and Combined Development', *International Politics*, 50:2, 183–230.

(2016) 'International Relations in the Prison of Political Science', *International Relations*, 30:2, 127–53.

Royama, Masamichi (1928) *Kokusai Seiji to Kojusai Gyösei (International Politics and International Administration)*, Tokyo: Ganshödö Shoten.

(1938) *Sekai no Hankyoku yo Nippon no Sekai Seisaku (The Changing World and Japan's World Policy)*, Tokyo: Ganshödö Shoten.

Ruggie, John G. (1982) 'International Regimes, Transactions, and Change: Embedded Liberalism in the Postwar Economic Order', *International Organization*, 36:2, 379–415.

(1993) *Multilateralism Matters: The Theory and Praxis of an Institutional Form*, New York: Columbia University Press.

Rumelili, Bahar (2004) 'Constructing Identity and Relating to Difference: Understanding the EU's Mode of Differentiation', *Review of International Studies*, 30:1, 27–47.

Rummel, Rudolph J. (1991) *China's Bloody Century: Genocide and Mass Murder since 1900*, New Brunswick, NJ: Transaction Publishers.

Sagan, Scott and Kenneth Waltz (1995) *The Spread of Nuclear Weapons: A Debate*, New York: Norton.

Sahnoun, Mohamed (2009) 'Africa: Uphold Continent's Contribution to Human Rights, Urges Top Diplomat', allAfrica.com, 21 July, http://allafrica.com/stories/200907210549.html?viewall=1 (Accessed 16 July 2013).

Said, Edward W. (1978) *Orientalism*, New York: Pantheon.

(1994) *Culture and Imperialism*, New York: Vintage Books.

Sakai, Tetsuya (2008) 'The Political Discourse of International Order in Modern Japan: 1868–1945', *Japanese Journal of Political Science*, 9:2, 233–49.

Sandole, Dennis J. D. (1985) 'Textbooks', in Margot Light and A. J. R. Groom (eds.), *International Relations: A Handbook of Current Theory*, London: Pinter, 214–21.

Santos, Matheus F. A. et al., (2015) 'Ebola: An International Public Health Emergency', *International Archives of Medicine*, 8:34, http://imed.pub/ojs/index.php/iam/article/view/1085 (Accessed 27 June 2018).

Sariolghalam, Mahmood (2009) 'Iran: Accomplishments and Limitations in IR', in Arlene B. Tickner and Ole Wæver (eds.), *International Relations Scholarship around the World*, Abingdon: Routledge, 158–71.

Sarkar, Benoy Kumar (1916) *The Beginning of Hindu Culture As World-Power (AD 300–600)*, Shanghai: Commercial Press.

(1919) 'Hindu Theory of International Relations', *American Political Science Review*, 13:3, 400–14.

(1921) 'The Hindu Theory of the State', *Political Science Quarterly*, 36:1, 79–90.

Sassen, Saskia (1996) *Losing Control? Sovereignty in an Age of Globalization*, New York: Columbia University Press.

Sayigh, Yezid (1990) 'Confronting the 1990s: Security in Developing Countries', *The Adelphi Papers*, 30: 251, 3–76.

Schell, Orville and John Delury (2013) *Wealth and Power: China's Long March to the Twenty-First Century*, London: Little, Brown.

Schmidt, Brian C. (1998a) *The Political Discourse of Anarchy: A Disciplinary History of International Relations*, Albany: State University of New York Press.

(1998b) 'Lessons from the Past: Reassessing the Interwar Disciplinary History of International Relations', *International Studies Quarterly*, 42:3, 433–59.

(2002) 'On the History and Historiography of International Relations', in Walter Carlsnaes, Thomas Risse and Beth A. Simmons (eds.), *Handbook of International Relations*, London: Sage, 3–22.

(2005) 'Paul S. Reinsch and the Study of Imperialism and Internationalism', in David Long and Brian Schmidt (eds.), *Imperialism and Internationalism in the Discipline of International Relations*, Albany: State University of New York Press, 43–69.

Scholte, Jan Aart (2000) *Globalization: A Critical Introduction*, Basingstoke: Palgrave.

Schuman, Frederick Lewis (1933) *International Politics: An Introduction to the Western State System*, New York: McGraw Hill.

Schwarzenberger, Georg (1951) *Power Politics: A Study of International Society*, London: Stevens and Sons.

Scoville, Priscila (2015) 'Amarna Letters', *Ancient History Encyclopedia*, 6 November, www.ancient.eu/Amarna_Letters/ (Accessed 27 May 2018).

Seeley, John Robert (1883) *The Expansion of England: Two Courses of Lectures*, London: Macmillan.

Sen, Amartya (2000) 'Why Human Security?', Speech at the 'International Symposium on Human Security', Tokyo, 28 July, www.ucipfg.com/Repositorio/MCSH/MCSH-05/BLOQUE-ACADEMICO/Unidad-01/complementarias/3.pdf (Accessed 27 May 2018).

Senghaas, Dieter (1974) 'Towards an Analysis of Threat Policy in International Relations', in Klaus von Beyme (ed.), *German Political Studies*, London: Sage, 59–103.

Sergounin, Alexander (2009) 'Russia: IR at a Crossroads', in Arlene B. Tickner and Ole Wæver (eds.), *International Relations Scholarship around the World*, Abingdon: Routledge, 223–41.

Seth, Sanjay (2013) 'Postcolonial Theory and the Critique of International Relations', in Sanjay Seth (ed.), *Postcolonial Theory and International Relations: A Critical Introduction*, New York: Routledge, 15–31.

Seton-Watson, Hugh (1972) 'The Impact of Ideology', in Brian Porter (ed.), *The Aberystwyth Papers: International Politics 1919–1969*, London: Oxford University Press, 211–37.

Shahi, Deepshikha and Gennaro Ascione (2016) 'Rethinking the Absence of Post-Western International Relations Theory in India: Advaitic Monism as an Alternative Epistemological Resource', *European Journal of International Relations*, 22:2, 313–34.

Shambaugh, David (2013) *China Goes Global: The Partial Power*, Kindle edn., Oxford: Oxford University Press.

Shani, Giorgio (2008) 'Toward a Post-Western IR: The *Umma*, *Khalsa Panth*, and Critical International Relations Theory', *International Studies Review*, 10:4, 722–34.

Shepard, Ben (2012) 'From the Ruins of Empire by Pankaj Mishra – Review', *The Guardian*, 4 August, www.theguardian.com/books/2012/aug/05/ruins-empire-pankaj-mishra-review (Accessed 27 May 2018).

Shih, Chih-yu (1990) *The Spirit of Chinese Foreign Policy: A Psychocultural View*, New York: St Martin's Press.

Shih, Chih-yu and Yin Jiwu (2013) 'Between Core National Interest and a Harmonious World: Reconciling Self-Role Conceptions in Chinese Foreign Policy', *The Chinese Journal of International Politics*, 6:1, 59–84.

Shilliam, Robbie (ed.) (2010) *International Relations and Non-Western Thoughts: Imperialism, Colonialism and Investigations of Global Modernity*, London: Routledge.

(2013) 'Intervention and Colonial-Modernity: Decolonising the Italy/Ethiopia Conflict through Psalms 68:31', *Review of International Studies*, 39:5, 1131–47.

Shimazu, Naoko (1998) *Japan, Race and Equality: The Racial Equality Proposal of 1919*, London: Routledge.

Shimizu, Kosuke (2015) 'Materializing the "Non-Western": Two Stories of Japanese Philosophers on Culture and Politics in the Inter-War Period', *Cambridge Review of International Affairs*, 28:1, 3–20.

Shimizu, Kosuke, Josuke Ikeda, Tomoya Kamino and Shiro Sato (2008) 'Is There a Japanese IR? Seeking an Academic Bridge through Japan's History of International Relations', *Afrasian Centre for Peace and Development Studies*, Ryukoku University, Japan.

Shirk, Susan (2007) *China: Fragile Superpower*, Kindle edn., Oxford: Oxford University Press.

Sikkink, Kathryn (2014) 'Latin American Countries As Norm Protagonists of the Idea of International Human Rights', *Global Governance*, 20:3, 389–404.

(2016) 'Human Rights', in Amitav Acharya (ed.), *Why Govern: Rethinking Demand and Progress in Global Governance*, Cambridge: Cambridge University Press, 121–37.

Simpson, Gerry (2004) *Great Powers and Outlaw States: Unequal Sovereigns in the International Legal Order*, Cambridge: Cambridge University Press.

Sims, Richard (2001) *Japanese Political History since the Meiji Restoration, 1868–2000*, New York: Palgrave.

Singer, P. W. and Allan Friedman (2014) *Cybersecurity and Cyberwar*, Oxford: Oxford University Press.

Sjoberg, Laura (2012) 'Gender, Structure, and War: What Waltz Couldn't See', *International Theory*, 4:1, 1–38.

Skidelsky, Robert (2009) *Keynes: The Return of the Master*, London: Allen Lane.

Smith, Adam (1776) *An Inquiry into the Nature and Causes of the Wealth of Nations*, London: W. Strahan and T. Cadell.

Smith, Derek D. (2006) *Deterring America: Rogue States and the Proliferation of Weapons of Mass Destruction*, Cambridge: Cambridge University Press.

Smith, Karen (2006) 'Can It Be Home-Grown: Challenges to Developing IR Theory in the Global South', Paper presented to the 47th Annual Convention of the International Studies Association, San Diego, March 22–25.

(2012) 'African As an Agent of International Relations Knowledge', in Scarlett Cornelissen, Fantu Cheru and Timothy M. Shaw (eds.), *Africa and International Relations in the 21st Century*, Basingstoke: Palgrave, 21–35.

(2017) 'Reshaping International Relations: Theoretical Innovations from Africa', *All Azimuth*, 1–12.

Smith, Sheila A. (2015) *Intimate Rivals: Japanese Politics and a Rising China*, New York: Columbia University Press.

Smith, Steve (2000) 'The Discipline of International Relations: Still an American Social Science?', *British Journal of Politics and International Relations*, 2:3, 374–402.

(2008) 'Six Wishes for a More Relevant Discipline of International Relations', in Christian Reus-Smit and Duncan Snidal (eds.), *The Oxford Handbook of International Relations*, Oxford: Oxford University Press, 725–32.

Snidal, Duncan (1985) 'The Limits of Hegemonic Stability Theory', *International Organization*, 39:4, 579–614.

Snyder, Jack (2004) 'One World, Rival Theories', *Foreign Policy*, 145, 52–62.

Snyder, Michael R. (2014) 'Security Council Response to Ebola Paves Way for Future Action', *The Global Observatory*, https://theglobalobservatory. org/2014/12/security-council-response-ebola-action/ (Accessed 26 June 2018).

Song, Xinning (2001) 'Building International Relations Theory with Chinese Characteristics', *Journal of Contemporary China*, 10:26, 61–3.

Spero, Joan E. (1990) *The Politics of International Economic Relations*, New York: St Martin's Press.

Spivak, Gayatri C. (1985) 'Can the Subaltern Speak? Speculations on Widow-Sacrifice', *Wedge*, 7/8, 120–30.

Spruyt, Hendrik (1998) 'A New Architecture for Peace? Reconfiguring Japan among the Great Powers', *The Pacific Review*, 11:3, 364–88.

Spykman, Nicholas (1942) *America's Strategy in World Politics: The United States and the Balance of Power*, New York: Harcourt, Brace and Company.

Stockholm International Peace Research Institute (1979) *SIPRI Yearbook 1979*, London: Taylor & Francis.

Stoddard, Lothrop (1923) *The Rising Tide of Color against White World-Supremacy*, London: Chapman and Hall.

Strange, Susan (1986) *Casino Capitalism*, Oxford: Basil Blackwell.

(1988) *States and Markets*, London: Pinter.

Stubbs, Richard and Geoffrey Underhill (1994) *Political Economy and the Changing Global Order*, Toronto: McClelland and Stewart.

Stuenkel, Oliver (2016) *Post-Western World: How Emerging Powers Are Remaking Global Order*, Cambridge: Polity Press.

Subrahmanyam, K. (1993) 'Export Controls and the North-South Controversy', *Washington Quarterly*, 16:2, 135–44.

Sun, Yat-sen (1922) *The International Development of China*, New York: G.P. Putnam's Sons.

(1941) *China and Japan: Natural Friends – Unnatural Enemies; A Guide for China's Foreign Policy*, Shanghai: China United.

Suzuki, Shogo (2005) 'Japan's Socialization into Janus-Faced European International Society', *European Journal of International Relations*, 11:1, 137–64.

(2009) *Civilization and Empire: China and Japan's Encounter with European International Society*, London: Routledge.

Suzuki, Shogo, Yongjin Zhang and Joel Quirk (eds.) (2014) *International Orders in the Early Modern World: Before the Rise of the West*, London: Routledge.

Swart, Gerrie (2016) 'An Emerging, Established or Receding Normative Agent? Probing the African Union's Recent Response to and Intervention in Libya', in Paul-Henri Bischoff, Kwesi Aning and Amitav Acharya (eds.), *Africa in Global International Relations: Emerging Approaches to Theory and Practice*, London: Routledge, 121–43.

Sylvester, Christine (1994) *Feminist Theory and International Relations in a Postmodern Era*, Cambridge: Cambridge University Press.

Tadjbakhsh, Shahrbanou (2010) 'International Relations Theory and the Islamic Worldview', in Amitav Acharya and Barry Buzan (eds.), *Non-Western International Relations Theory: Perspectives on and beyond Asia*, London: Routledge, 174–96.

Tadjbakhsh, Shahrbanou and Anuradha M. Chenoy (2007) *Human Security: Concepts and Implications*, London: Routledge.

Tagore, Rabindranath ([1917] 2002) *Nationalism*, New Delhi: Rupa and Co.

Takahashi, Sakuye (1899) *Cases on International Law during the China–Japanese War*, Cambridge: Cambridge University Press.

Tang, Shiping (2013) *The Social Evolution of International Politics*, Oxford: Oxford University Press.

Tankha, Brij and Madhavi Thampi (2005) *Narratives of Asia: From India, Japan and China*, Calcutta: Sampark.

Teschke, Benno (2008) 'Marxism', in Christian Reus-Smit and Duncan Snidal (eds.), *Oxford Handbook of International Relations*, Oxford: Oxford University Press, 163–87.

Teune, Henry (1982) 'The International Studies Association', based on a paper prepared for the 1982 ISA Leadership Meeting, University of South Carolina, www.isanet.org/Portals/0/Documents/Institutional/Henry_Teune_The_ISA_1982.pdf (Accessed 27 May 2018).

Thomas, Caroline and Peter Wilkin (2004) 'Still Waiting after All These Years: "The Third World" on the Periphery of International Relations', *British Journal of Politics and International Relations*, 6:2, 241–58.

Tickner, Arlene B. (2003a) 'Hearing Latin American Voices in International Relations Studies', *International Studies Perspectives*, 4:4, 325–50.

(2003b) 'Seeing IR Differently: Notes from the Third World', *Millennium*, 32:2, 295–324.

(2009) 'Latin America: Still Policy Dependent after All These Years?', in Arlene B. Tickner and Ole Wæver (eds.), *International Relations Scholarship around the World*, Abingdon: Routledge, 32–52.

Tickner, Arlene B. and David L. Blaney (2012) *Thinking International Relations Differently*, Abingdon: Routledge.

(2013) *Claiming International*, Abingdon: Routledge.

Tickner, Arlene B. and Ole Wæver (2009a) (eds.) *International Relations Scholarship around the World*, Abingdon: Routledge.

(2009b) 'Introduction: Geocultural Epistemologies', in Arlene B. Tickner and Ole Wæver (eds.), *International Relations Scholarship around the World*, Abingdon: Routledge, 1–31.

(2009c) 'Conclusion: Worlding Where the West Once Was', in Arlene B. Tickner and Ole Wæver (eds.), *International Relations Scholarship around the World*, Abingdon: Routledge, 328–41.

Tickner, J. Ann (1997) 'You Just Don't Understand: Troubled Engagements between Feminists and IR Theorists', *International Studies Quarterly*, 41:4, 611–32.

Tickner, J. Ann and Laura Sjoberg (2013) 'Feminism', in Tim Dunne, Milja Kurki and Steve Smith (eds.), *International Relations Theories: Discipline and Diversity*, 3rd edn., Oxford: Oxford University Press, 205–22.

Tickner, J. Ann and Jacqui True (2018) 'A Century of International Relations Feminism: From World War I Women's Peace Pragmatism to the Women, Peace and Security Agenda', *International Studies Quarterly*, sqx091, doi: 10.1093/isq/sqx091, 12 April, 1–13.

Tieku, Thomas Kwasi (2013) 'Theoretical Approaches to Africa's International Relations', in Tim Murithi (ed.), *Handbook of Africa's International Relations*, London: Taylor and Francis, 11–20.

Tikly, Leon (2001) 'Postcolonialism and Comparative Education Research', in Keith Watson (ed.), *Doing Comparative Education Research: Issues and Problems*, Oxford: Symposium Books, 245–64.

Tiryakian, Edward A. (1999) 'War: The Covered Side of Modernity', *International Sociology*, 14:4, 473–89.

Tocqueville, Alexis de ([1835] 2006) *Democracy in America*, New York: Harper Perennial Modern Classics.

Topik, Steven C. and Allen Wells (2012) *Global Markets Transformed, 1870–1945*, Cambridge, MA: Belknap Press.

Totman, Conrad (2005) *A History of Japan*, 2nd edn., Malden, MA: Blackwell, Kindle edn.

Towns, Ann E. (2009) 'The Status of Women As a Standard of "Civilization"', *European Journal of International Relations*, 15:4, 681–706.

(2010) *Women and States: Norms and Hierarchies in International Society*, Cambridge: Cambridge University Press.

Toye, John F. J. and Richard Toye (2003) 'The Origins and Interpretation of the Prebisch-Singer Thesis', *History of Political Economy*, 35:3, 437–67.

Treitschke, Heinrich von (1899–1900) *Politik*, Leipzig: S. Hirzel.

True, Jacqui (1996) 'Feminism', in Scott Burchill and Andrew Linklater (eds.), *Theories of International Relations*, New York: St Martin's Press, 210–51.

(2017) 'Feminism and Gender Studies in International Relations Theory', *Oxford Research Encyclopedias*, doi: 10.1093/acrefore/9780190846626.013.46, http://internationalstudies.oxfordre.com/view/10.1093/acrefore/9780190846626.001.0001/acrefore-9780190846626-e-46 (Accessed 27 June 2018).

Trueblood, Benjamin F. (1899) *The Federation of the World*, Boston: Houghton, Mifflin and Co.

Tudor, Daniel (2012) *Korea: The Impossible Country*, Tokyo: Tuttle Publishing.

Turan, İlter (2017) 'Progress in Turkish International Relations', *All Azimuth*, 1–6, doi: 10.20991/allazimuth.328455.

Turner, John (2009) 'Islam As a Theory of International Relations?', *E-International Relations*, 3 August, www.e-ir.info/2009/08/03/islam-as-a-theory-of-international-relations/ (Accessed 27 May 2018).

Tyner, James A. (1999) 'The Geopolitics of Eugenics and the Exclusion of Philippine Immigrants from the United States', *Geographical Review*, 89:1, 54–73.

UN (2016) *International Migration Report 2015*. ST/ESA/SER.A/375 www.un.org/en/development/desa/population/migration/publications/migrationreport/docs/MigrationReport2015_Highlights.pdf (Accessed 7 October 2017).

UNCTAD (2015) *World Investment Report, 2015*, Geneva, UNCTAD http://unctad.org/en/PublicationsLibrary/wir2015_en.pdf (Accessed 27 May 2018).

UNDP (2013) *Human Development Report 2013. The Rise of the South: Human Progress in a Diverse World*, New York: UNDP.

UNDP (2016) *Human Development Report*, http://hdr.undp.org/en/content/income-gini-coefficient (Accessed 4 October 2017).

University of British Columbia (2005) *Human Security Report 2005: War and Peace in the 21st Century*, New York: Oxford University Press.

Urquhart, F. F. (1916) 'The Causes of Modern Wars', in A. J. Grant, Arthur Greenwood, J. D. I. Hughes, P. H. Kerr and F. F. Urquhart, *An Introduction to International Relations*, London: Macmillan, 37–65.

van Wyk, Jo-Annsie (2016) 'Africa in International Relations: Agent, Bystander or Victim', in Paul-Henri Bischoff, Kwesi Aning and Amitav Acharya (eds.), *Africa in Global International Relations: Emerging Approaches to Theory and Practice*, London: Routledge, 108–20.

Vasquez, John (1993) *The War Puzzle*, Cambridge: Cambridge University Press.

Vigezzi, Brunello (2005) *The British Committee on the Theory of International Politics (1954–1985): The Rediscovery of History*, Milan: Edizzioni Unicopli.

Viotti, Paul R. and Mark V. Kauppi (2011) *International Relations Theory*, 5th edn., New York: Longman.

Vitalis, Robert (2000) 'The Graceful and Generous Liberal Gesture: Making Racism Invisible in American International Relations', *Millennium*, 29:2, 331–56.

⸀(2005) 'Birth of a Discipline', in David Long and Brian Schmidt (eds.), *Imperialism and Internationalism in the Discipline of International Relations*, Albany: State University of New York Press, 159–81.

⸀(2010) 'The Noble American Science of Imperial Relations and Its Laws of Race Development', *Comparative Studies in Society and History*, 52:4, 909–38.

⸀(2015) *White World Order, Black Power Politics: The Birth of American International Relations*, Ithaca, NY: Cornell University Press.

Vogel, Ezra F. (1980) *Japan As Number 1: Lessons for America*, New York: Harper Collins.

Wæver, Ole (1996) 'The Rise and Fall of the Inter-Paradigm Debate', in Steve Smith, Ken Booth and Marysia Zalewski (eds.), *International Theory: Positivism and Beyond*, Cambridge: Cambridge University Press, 149–85.

⸀(1997) 'Figures of International Thought: Introducing Persons Instead of Paradigms?', in Iver B. Neumann and Ole Wæver (eds.), *The Future of International Relations: Masters in the Making?*, London: Routledge, 1–37.

⸀(1998), 'The Sociology of a Not So International Discipline: American and European Developments in International Relations', *International Organization*, 52:1, 687–727.

Wæver, Ole, Barry Buzan, Morten Kelstrup and Pierre Lemaitre (1993) *Identity, Migration and the New Security Agenda in Europe*, London: Pinter.

Waldau, Gabriel and Tom Mitchell (2016) 'China Income Inequality among World's Worst', *Financial Times*, 14 January, www.ft.com/content/3c521faa-baa6-11e5-a7cc-280dfe875e28 (Accessed 26 June 2018).

Wallace, Michael and J. David Singer (1970) 'Intergovernmental Organization in the Global System, 1816–1964: A Quantitative Description', *International Organization*, 24:2, 239–87.

Wallerstein, Immanuel (1974) *The Modern World-System*, vol.1: *Capitalist Agriculture and the Origins of the European World-Economy in the Sixteenth Century*, London: Academic Press.

⸀(1979) *The Capitalist World-Economy*, Cambridge: Cambridge University Press.

(1983) *Historical Capitalism with Capitalist Civilization*, London: Verso.

(1984) *The Politics of the World-Economy*, Cambridge: Cambridge University Press.

Walsh, Edmund A. (1922) *The History and Nature of International Relations*, New York: Macmillan.

Walt, Stephen M. (1998) 'International Relations: One World, Many Theories', *Foreign Policy*, 29–46.

(2005) 'The Relationship between Theory and Policy in International Relations', *Annual Review of Political Science*, 8, 23–48.

Waltz, Kenneth N. (1964) 'The Stability of a Bipolar World', *Daedalus*, 93:3, 881–909.

(1979) *Theory of International Politics*, Reading, MA: Addison-Wesley.

(1993) 'The Emerging Structure of International Politics', *International Security*, 18:2, 44–79.

Wang, Jiangli and Barry Buzan (2014) 'The English and Chinese Schools of International Relations: Comparisons and Lessons', *The Chinese Journal of International Politics*, 7:1, 1–46.

Wang, Zheng (2008) 'National Humiliation, History Education, and the Politics of Historical Memory: Patriotic Education Campaign in China', *International Studies Quarterly*, 52:4, 783–806.

(2012) *Never Forget National Humiliation: Historical Memory in Chinese Politics and Foreign Relations*, Kindle edn., New York: Columbia University Press.

Watson, Adam (1992) *The Evolution of International Society*, London: Routledge.

(2001) 'Foreword' to 'Forum on the English School', *Review of International Studies*, 27:3, 467–70.

Weart, Spencer R. (1998) *Never at War: Why Democracies Will Not Fight One Another*, New Haven, CT: Yale University Press.

Weinstein, Franklin ([1976] 2007) *Indonesian Foreign Policy and the Dilemmas of Dependence: From Sukarno to Suharto*, Singapore: Equinox Publishing.

Weiss, Thomas G. (2013) *Global Governance: Why? What? Whither?*, Cambridge: Polity Press.

Weiss, Thomas G. and Pallavi Roy (eds.) (2016) 'The UN and the Global South, 1945 and 2015: Past as Prelude?', *Third World Quarterly*, special issue, 37:7, 1147–297.

Wemheuer-Vogelaar, Wiebke, Nicholas J. Bell, Mariana Navarrete Morales and Michael J. Tierney (2016) 'The IR of the Beholder: Examining Global IR Using the 2014 TRIP Survey', *International Studies Review*, 18:1, 16–32.

Wendt, Alexander (1992) 'Anarchy Is What States Make of It: The Social Construction of Power Politics', *International Organization*, 46:2, 391–425.

(1999) *Social Theory of International Politics*, Cambridge: Cambridge University Press.

Westad, Odd Arne (2007) *The Global Cold War: Third World Interventions and the Making of Our Time*, Cambridge: Cambridge University Press.

(2012) *Restless Empire: China and the World since 1750*, Kindle edn., London: Bodley Head.

Wheaton, Henry ([1836] 1866) *Elements of International Law*, 8th edn., London: Sampson Low, Son & Co.

Wheeler, Nicholas J. (2000) *Saving Strangers: Humanitarian Intervention in International Society*, Oxford: Oxford University Press.

Wight, Martin (1977) *Systems of States*, Leicester: Leicester University Press.

Willetts, Peter (1978) *Non-Aligned Movement: Origins of a Third World Alliance*, London: Continuum.

Williams, David (2004) *Defending Japan's Pacific War: The Kyoto School Philosophers and Post-White Power*, Abingdon: Routledge

Williams, Eric ([1944] 1994) *Capitalism and Slavery*, Chapel Hill, NC: University of North Carolina Press.

Williams, John (2015) *Ethics, Diversity, and World Politics: Saving Pluralism From Itself?*, Oxford: Oxford University Press.

Williams, Michael C. (2005) *The Realist Tradition and the Limits of International Relations*, Cambridge: Cambridge University Press.

(2013) 'In the Beginning: International Relations Enlightenment and the Ends of International Relations Theory', *European Journal of International Relations*, 19:3, 647–65.

Wilson, Peter (1998) 'The Myth of the First Great Debate', in Tim Dunne, Michael Cox and Ken Booth (eds.), *The Eighty Years' Crisis: International Relations 1919–1999, Review of International Studies*, 34:Special Issue, 1–15.

Witt, Michael A. (2010) 'China: What Variety of Capitalism?', Singapore, INSEAD Working Paper 2010/88/EPS, 15 pp.

Wohlforth, William C. (1999) 'The Stability of a Unipolar World', *International Security*, 24:1, 5–41.

(2009) 'Unipolarity, Status Competition, and Great Power War', *World Politics*, 61:1, 28–57.

Wolf, Martin (2014) *The Shifts and the Shocks: What We've Learned – and Have Still to Learn – from the Financial Crisis*, London: Penguin.

Wolf, Nathan (2011) *The Viral Storm: The Dawn of a New Pandemic Age*, New York: Times Books.

Womack, Brantly (2014) 'China's Future in a Multinodal World Order', *Pacific Affairs*, 87:2, 265–84.

Wood, James (2008) 'Calvo Doctrine', in Jay Kinsbruner and Erick D. Langer (eds.), *Encyclopedia of Latin American History and Culture*, vol. 2, 2nd edn., Detroit: Charles Scribner's Sons, 46–7.

Woods, Ngaire (ed.) (2000) *The Political Economy of Globalization*, Basingstoke: Macmillan.

Woolf, Leonard (1916) *International Government*, Westminster: Fabian Society.

World Bank (2016) *Poverty and Prosperity 2016/Taking on Inequality*, Washington, DC: World Bank, https://openknowledge.worldbank.org/bitstream/handle/10986/25078/9781464809583.pdf (Accessed 4 October 2017).

WHO (2014) 'Ebola Situation Report: 31 December 2014', Ebola Situation Reports, 31 December, http://apps.who.int/ebola/en/status-outbreak/situation-reports/ebola-situation-report-31-december-2014 (Accessed 27 May 2018).

(2016) 'Latest Ebola Outbreak Over in Liberia; West Africa Is at Zero, but New Flare-ups Are Likely to Occur', WHO Media Centre, 14 January, www.who.int/mediacentre/news/releases/2016/ebola-zero-liberia/en/ (Accessed 27 May 2018).

Wright, Quincy (1955) *The Study of International Relations*, New York: Appleton-Century-Crofts.

Yahuda, Michael (2014) *Sino-Japanese Relations after the Cold War: Two Tigers Sharing a Mountain*, London: Routledge.

Yalem, Ronald J. (1979) 'Regional Security Communities', in George W. Keeton and George Schwarzenberger (eds.), *The Year Book of International Affairs 1979*, London: Stevens, 217–23.

Yan, Xuetong (2011) *Ancient Chinese Thought, Modern Chinese Power*, Princeton: Princeton University Press.

(2014) 'From Keeping a Low Profile to Striving for Achievement', *The Chinese Journal of International Politics*, 7:2, 153–84.

Yanaihara, Tadao ([1926] 1963) *Shokumin oyobi Shokuminn Seisaku (Colony and Colonial Policy)* in *Yanaihara Tadao Zenshu (Collected Complete Works of Yanaihara Tadao)*, vol. 1, Tokyo: Iwanami Shoten.

Yurdusev, A. Nuri (2003) *International Relations and the Philosophy of History: A Civilizational Approach*, Basingstoke: Palgrave.

(2009) 'The Middle East Encounter with the Expansion of European International Society', in Barry Buzan and Ana Gonzalez-Pelaez (eds.), *International Society and the Middle East: English School Theory at the Regional Level*, Basingstoke: Palgrave, 70–91.

Zakaria, Fareed (2009) *The Post-American World and the Rise of the Rest*, London: Penguin.

Zarakol, Ayşe (2011) *After Defeat: How the East Learned to Live with the West*, Cambridge: Cambridge University Press.

Zarakol, Ayşe (2014) 'What Made the Modern World Hang Together: Socialisation or Stigmatisation?', *International Theory*, 6:2, 311–32.

Zehfuss, Maja (2001) 'Constructivism and Identity: A Dangerous Liaison', *European Journal of International Relations*, 7:3, 315–48.

(2002) *Constructivism in International Relations: The Politics of Reality*, Cambridge: Cambridge University Press.

Zhang, Feng (2012a) 'Debating the "Chinese Theory of International Relations": Toward a New Stage in China's International Studies', in Fred Dallmayr and Zhao Tingyang (eds.), *Contemporary Chinese Political Thought: Debates and Perspectives*, Lexington, KY: University Press of Kentucky, 67–88.

(2012b) 'China's New Thinking on Alliances', *Survival*, 54:5, 129–48.

Zhang, Xiaoming (2010) *English School of International Relations: History, Theory and View on China*, Beijing: People's Press (in Chinese).

(2011a) 'A Rising China and the Normative Changes in International Society', *East Asia*, 28:3, 235–46.

(2011b) 'China in the Conception of International Society: The English School's Engagements with China', *Review of International Studies*, 37:2, 763–86.

Zhang, Yongjin (1998) *China in International Society since 1949*, Basingstoke: Macmillan.

(2003) 'The "English School" in China: A Travelogue of Ideas and Their Diffusion', *European Journal of International Relations*, 9:1, 87–114.

Zhang, Yongjin and Teng-chi Chang (eds.) (2016) *Constructing a Chinese School of International Relations: Ongoing Debates and Sociological Realities*, Abingdon: Routledge.

Zimmern, Alfred (1936) *The League of Nations and the Rule of Law*, London: Macmillan.

Index

Printed in Great Britain
by Amazon

49027470R00225